The Complete Guide to
SUCCESSFUL
GARDENING

 Produced for Mayflower Books by
Intercontinental Book Productions

All rights reserved under International and Pan American Copyright Convention. Published in the United States by Mayflower
Books, Inc., New York, New York 10022 and simultaneously published in Canada by
Originally published in England by Sampson Low, Berkshire House, Queen Street, Maidenhead, Berkshire, England.
ISBN 0 8317 1625 8
Printed in Italy

Acknowledgments

This book has been compiled from the following ten titles which were originally published in England in 1977: *Gardening for
Beginners* by Violet Stevenson; *Feeding, Pruning and Pest Control* by Brian Walkden; *Garden Flowers* by F. A. Boddy; *Balcony, Patio and
Window Box Gardening* by Leslie Johns; *Fruit Growing* by Roy Genders; *Vegetable Growing* by Keith Mossman; *Herb Growing* by
Violet Stevenson; *Indoor Gardening* by Leslie Johns; *Greenhouse Gardening* by Lovell Benjamin; *100 Gardening Questions and Answers* by
Ronald Menage

The photographs in this book were supplied by Floraprint Limited (copyright I.G.A.) Leslie Johns & Associates, Harry Smith,
Syndication International, DP Press Limited, Suttons Seeds, John Topham, J. E. Downward, Bernard Alfier, Kenneth Scowen,
Marshall Cavendish, W. Schacht, Unwin's, Brighton Borough Council, Humex, Halls Homes and Gardens, Harry Hebditch,
Baco Leisure Products, N.H.P.A., Spectrum Colour Library, Elizabeth Whiting, A–Z Collection, Picturepoint, Kim Sayer.
Cover photographs were supplied by Floraprint (copyright I.G.A.).

The Complete Guide to
SUCCESSFUL
GARDENING

Consultant editor
Marjorie Dietz

MAYFLOWER BOOKS, INC.
575 LEXINGTON AVENUE.
NEW YORK CITY 10022.

CONTENTS

Gardening for beginners

1 Why garden?

The present surging interest in gardening probably originated in recent economic pressures – an interest that can reap profits to the order of at least one thousand percent on the cost of a packet of seed. Such a return on outlay must be virtually unique. Furthermore, there can be few people who do not realize that cheap, home-grown food tastes infinitely better than its store-bought equivalent. But what many people may not appreciate is that growing things is both easy and, done sensibly, relaxing.

As a whole generation of new gardeners has emerged within the last few years, there must be many who find themselves turning for the first time in their lives to tasks that, were it not for the necessity of doing them, would seem to be mere chores. But in gardening, the interest of developing a barren or overgrown piece of land into a colorful and flourishing garden cannot help but eradicate any initial reluctance you may have to get started – and once you have

started, you will undoubtedly want to keep going.

In the garden you are your own master – but, nonetheless, you are a pupil too, and you never cease to learn. You will ask questions: why do it that way? what is the best way of doing this? what can I do about that? And you will learn the answers to many of these questions through experience. You will not necessarily accept what you are told, but will make up your own mind. Sometimes you'll be right, sometimes wrong, but either way you will learn.

One of the most important lessons to learn is that a great deal of gardening lore is nonsense – nonsense that can frequently involve unnecessary time and labor, and maybe expense too. Before long, you will find the easy or the quick way, and though your flowers may not always be up to flower-show standards or your vegetables

There is no better place for children to play than in the safety and convenience of their own garden.

8

The not-so-young can have gentle exercise and at the same time economize by growing their own vegetables.

top-grade, you should find that your more realistic approach (in terms of time, effort and money) can still produce a very satisfactory showing.

People have surely never been as busy as they are today. There is always so much to do. The working week and the commuting to and from work take up so much time and energy that alternative activities should whenever possible act as a restorative. Many types of sport, educational interests, books, music, social activities, trips, home improvements – all these things make one wish for a longer day and greater reserves of energy. Gardening may seem, especially to those who have seen neighbors giving up an inordinate amount of their spare time to the cultivation of their gardens, a further drain on what little spare time they have. But it need not be. A little know-how, practice and determination can make a plot of ground productive with very little labor –

Fresh air sharpens the appetite, improves the flavor of food; a patio barbecue is an easy and delightful way to entertain.

and labor of a type so much in contrast with one's normal work that it is both pleasurable and relaxing. Before long, it will dawn on the new gardeners *why* their friends and neighbors spend so much time in their gardens: they enjoy it!

Advance planning

We generally enjoy what we do well, and as a newcomer to gardening you would be wise to consider the future before beginning to plan your plot. Make up your mind what you want from your garden. Do you want it to be economically profitable, producing food crops to stretch the family budget? Do you want a pleasure garden with flowers and shrubs to delight the senses? Do you want a children's play area, an extra 'room' for outdoor living, an exercise yard for the dog, a place to practice a golf swing, or a showplace? The probability is that it will be none of these things but rather a compromise, with a little space set aside for the children, an area for fruit and vegetables and a place in which to lie in the sun or enjoy a barbecue.

But our dreams must be limited by reality. The space available may be small or steeply sloping. Pressures of work may not allow the time needed to convert the area to some special purpose. Money may be short or the land may be waterlogged and need draining. So aspirations must be tempered by practicalities; yet, equally, a little sensible planning can facilitate the task ahead. It is often possible to do two things at once, to take advantage of one activity and to lay the basis for another.

Perhaps you may decide to have an ornamental pool in the garden, stocked with water lilies and colorful fish. But because the children are young you may feel that the water could be a dangerous temptation. In that case, dig the pool and prepare for it in every way, but do not fill it with water but with sand. When the children are older take out the sand and pour in the water. Or again, perhaps the idea of a pool appeals to you. If the notion of a rock

A patio should link the house and garden.

garden is also attractive, then use the soil excavated for the pool to help build up the raised area for the rock. Do you want a paved area, a terrace or patio, to link house and garden? Then use as a foundation for the paving slabs the builders' rubble and waste that you picked up while clearing the site and the stones you threw aside as you dug the vegetable plot.

Try always to think ahead. A large area of grass is always a perfect foil for garden plants and it makes a splendid playground for the children, but can you afford the time to mow it perhaps twice a week? And if you have built sharply-angled flower beds into the grass, can you maneuver the mower around them without wasting time and temper? Are you sure you would rather have a hedge than a labor-saving fence or wall? Must you grow tall, floppy plants that require staking and tying up? Why fly in the face of nature and try to grow rhododendrons on a soil so rich in lime that they cannot possibly live for longer than a few weeks?

Gardening should be fun, and it can be if you know a little about it and can find the quick and easy way, the profitable way, to carry out the necessary work. The following pages are an attempt to help you find the shortcuts to managing your own garden, whatever its size and type.

10

2 Planning a large garden

The larger the garden the more vital the planning, for not only does the greater area demand a larger number of plants, but there is more opportunity to go wrong. Today a large garden can be defined as one more than about 2000 sq ft (200 sq m) in area, and one of this size will accommodate almost any normal feature that can be desired – lawns, a pool, a rock garden, woodland or shrubbery, flower beds, fruit and vegetable plot, play area, patio and

A flower border of annuals, such as marigolds, petunias and salvia, brightens a garden all summer.

perhaps even a small greenhouse. It can involve a considerable amount of work and in certain circumstances could justify the employment of a part-time gardener. It would certainly require one or two power tools, such as a mower, cultivator and hedge cutter.

But given careful planning and a few power tools it should be possible for one person to handle an area of this size and to keep it attractive and productive with a very few hours' work a week. The first thing, as already indicated, is to decide

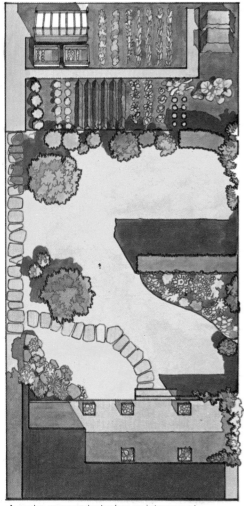

A garden area can be broken up into separate sections so there is always curiosity about what lies just around the corner.

and pleasant as possible and keep other parts relatively simple and undemanding so that they take up little time. Bear in mind always that the parts of the garden that are nearest to the house are, in effect, an additional room of the house and they must be kept as tidy and as pleasant as any of the rooms indoors. Keep this part of the garden simple, peaceful and not too strident with flowers. Green lawns with neat edges are the main requisite. If you wish for flowers, keep them in relatively small beds that can be easily reached so that planting and weeding are a simple matter. Or grow your flowers in containers on the patio, for this way they are easy to keep looking their best and are simple to replace. If you wish to grow a specimen tree or two in the lawn, make sure that its branches do not hang so low that the mower cannot conveniently travel beneath it; and make sure also that the mower can cut the grass at its foot without trouble. Remember that this tree will receive star treatment, so make it a worthy one. Grow a tree of dignity and moderate size, such as an Atlas cedar or some other evergreen that will look dominant in any season.

Although the garden near the house should be kept neat and simple, the remainder of the plot can be as varied or as complex as you can manage. No garden other than the smallest should ever reveal all its secrets at a glance. There should always be hidden corners, little surprises tucked away to be stumbled upon accidentally, unsuspected features as evidence of the gardener's taste and talent. Some gardens can be almost a series of rooms, each in some way specialized: perhaps a pool or a rock garden, or corners dominated by a particular plant, say roses in one and delphiniums in another. This way you gain the greatest impact and arouse immediate interest.

Also, this way you can justify a small area of the garden being neglected and full of natural growth. In fact, a good gardener with plenty of space available will do well

exactly what is wanted from the garden and then ask if this can be achieved with the time and labor available. Gradually a compromise will be reached and the following advice may be helpful in deciding what can and what cannot be done.

In the first place, if you have a large plot do not attempt to make a park out of it. Understand that gorgeous flower beds and rolling lawns cannot be made or maintained on a few hours' work a week. Try to make the areas nearest the house as neat

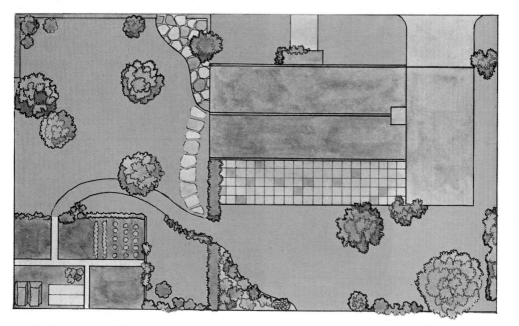

Where space permits, a large patio is always better than a small one, as it gives extra freedom of movement and greater possibilities for plant decoration.

always to leave some portion untouched, for the local 'weeds' are often the host plants and the food of butterflies and moths, the nesting places of birds and the insects they eat. An over-gardened plot, always neat and clean, will not give opportunity for the birth and nurture of some of the butterflies that are as bright and as pretty as any of the flowers that grow in regimented rows.

But it is also possible to compromise. Too much space given to lawns, for example, will demand too much time spent on mowing, but groomed lawns near the house can lead on to longer grass mown just two or three times a year. These areas can have paths curving through that will need the passage of the mower only once or twice to cut the entire width. Grasses left to flower in this way can have an interesting elegance and beauty that is all too seldom seen. Above them can grow varieties of trees and shrubs that require the minimum of attention at any time of year.

It is always wise to make a 'service area' in a large garden – a place where the tools can be kept, where supplies of peat, lime and insecticides can be stored, where the compost heap can be built and the occasional bonfire made. Choose this area with great care, making sure that it is concealed from the pleasure parts of the garden and also that it is conveniently accessible. There is much to be said for creating this area more or less in the center of the garden rather than at one end or the other, for this will save much time and energy in traveling to and fro with the mower or to fetch a trowel or sprayer. Allow plenty of room and, if possible, pave those parts that will be most frequently used to save churning up mud in bad weather.

Plants for large gardens

Trees and shrubs are the best friends of the gardener with a large area to look after, for after their first few formative years they require little or no attention. Remember, though, that when they are originally planted they are small, yet they will grow large, perhaps very large, in the course of

Welsh poppies (*Meconopsis cambrica*) grow best where summers are moist and cool. They provide ground cover and summer-long color.

time. It is possible to create a more immediate effect by close planting, but this will mean that after a few years either some of the trees or shrubs will have to be removed or they will grow into each other and become misshapen. Most nursery catalogs give the mature height and span of trees and shrubs, and it is wise to take note of these facts when planting.

Close planting can also reduce weeding, but it is better and easier in the long run to smother weeds by ground-cover plants rather than by making use of trees and shrubs. Ground-cover plants are those that creep or sprawl on the surface of the soil, growing thickly enough to inhibit the growth of weeds. Ivy makes a good ground cover and it is quick-growing yet easily controlled. Heathers make good ground cover in areas with a suitable climate and there are dwarf or prostrate conifers that look attractive, being evergreen, require no attention, yet effectively prevent weeds.

3 Adapting average-sized gardens

The average-sized garden is less than 2000 sq ft (200 sq m) in area and is probably on a suburban lot, and often part of a group of houses, all more or less similar in size and design. There is still sufficient space for several different features, such as a lawn, play area and the like, but these may have to be scaled down in size, and there is only limited opportunity to create the series of 'rooms' and the multiple features possible with the larger garden.

A compact garden like this necessitates a real discipline in planning, for to attempt to pack too much into the little space available will result only in a confused, untidy, irresolute plot without theme or purpose. Try instead to decide what is to be the one dominant feature and give this prominence, keeping the minor factors in the background.

Choose carefully which trees and shrubs you will grow in this smaller garden, for

A lavish use of paving enables one to walk to any corner of the garden without having to tread on damp grass. Stark paving slabs can be offset by bordering plants and labor-saving shrubs. A medium-sized garden lends itself well to the use of paving and to other decorative touches, such as miniature pools and bird baths.

15

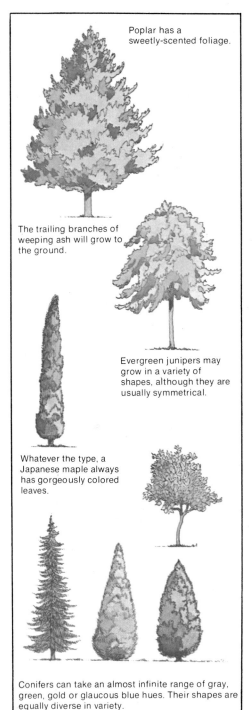

Poplar has a sweetly-scented foliage.

The trailing branches of weeping ash will grow to the ground.

Evergreen junipers may grow in a variety of shapes, although they are usually symmetrical.

Whatever the type, a Japanese maple always has gorgeously colored leaves.

Conifers can take an almost infinite range of gray, green, gold or glaucous blue hues. Their shapes are equally diverse in variety.

overambition here could mean that in a few years the area is overcrowded, dark and difficult to move through. In catalogs or at garden centers look for tall and slim ('fastigiate') trees shaped like a Lombardy poplar, for the part of the garden where there will always be space to spare is upwards into the sky.

Planning the area nearest the house

Once again, the area nearest to the house is the most important and should be kept simple, for easy and quick maintenance, and restful rather than cluttered in appearance. In the average, fairly small garden this area may well take up the greater part of the available space, so it should be both attractive in appearance and as useful as another room to the house. A paved area next to the house is almost essential here, although if space is very limited this need be no more than a pathway. It is important, however, to be able to walk around the house or from house to garden with clean shoes in any kind of weather.

If you are having a terrace or patio, this must certainly be paved, and there should be a slight slope (1 in 40 is sufficient) away from the house to avoid any damage from heavy rain. This area can be given greater importance by covering or partially covering it with a pergola or some similar structure, possibly roofed over to provide shelter, or possibly more open with climbing plants such as roses or wisteria to soften and decorate the pillars. If this pergola, or arbor structure, is covered with plants and the side of the house also has climbers on it, there may be no necessity for further plantings in or on the terrace, which can then be given up entirely to non-gardening activities.

But certainly the terrace or patio needs some plant material growing in or on it, to soften what might otherwise be a somewhat bare and arid area of paving. If trailers, creepers and climbers are not on the wall or decorating struts and props of the pergola, some plants should be grown elsewhere.

16

Colored paving loses its stridency when brilliant flowers grow nearby. Geraniums, for this reason, are splendid patio plants. They are always full of color and are able to withstand full sun and occasional dryness at the roots.

The floor area would need to be considerable to allow for the establishment of one or two beds to grow brilliant annuals, so on the whole it would be best to leave the floor space free for chairs, tables and other impedimenta of outdoor living. Grow a few plants, probably decorative annuals, in tubs or other containers, to stand on the terrace. They can be moved about according to season or function.

To emphasize that the terrace is really an outdoor extension of the house, it is helpful to construct a wall around it, linking it to the house and separating it from the garden. This wall should mainly be symbolic – certainly not high or impenetrable, anything from 1 ft (30 cm) or so high, depending on proportions – and opening onto the lawn and possibly at the sides around the house. On this low wall can be grown further plants, either in box-like containers or possibly even on the wall itself. A number of plants like aubrieta will grow quite happily in chinks in the wall, and provision can be made for them when the wall is built.

Planning the main garden area

Away from the house the area outside the terrace is best taken up by lawn, as this gives a feeling of space. Once again it is important to divide the lawn from the terrace by some means, such as a low wall or possibly some contained plants. But at the same time it is helpful to prepare an adequate and formal opening from the terrace to the lawn, perhaps in the semblance of a gateway or, if levels permit, a step or two. This gives the impression that the garden proper has been reached, passing from the house to the halfway point of the terrace and then out into the open of the garden itself.

This lawn area is important and, if space

17

make a garden look longer or wider than it really is.

Another little trick to give an impression of space is to make a pathway from the terrace down the garden to some unseen location. This pathway need be little more than symbolic, perhaps a stepping-stone path, with paving stones every 2–3 ft (60–90 cm) sunk into the grass so that the mower can pass easily and safely over them. It will draw the eye down the garden and hence appear to lengthen the actual space. If possible, conceal the destination of the path by taking it around a curve or behind a tree or hedge. If it is seen to lead directly to, say, a shed or to the vegetable garden, this destination will receive undue,

is limited, as much room as possible should be given to it, for this open space will create the strongest impression of the size of the garden. So keep beds, borders and individual plantings at the edges to allow clear and uncluttered space. If you wish to bring color to what might otherwise be an all-green background, keep flower beds either in the background or filled only with low-growing plants so that the eye can travel over them to the further distance. White, yellow and orange are advancing colors, which appear to make the bed or border come nearer, and dark colors such as blue, purple and even dark red are recessive, giving the impression that the bed is further away than it really is. You can take advantage of little tricks like these in order to

and perhaps unwanted, attention.

However, paths in a moderately small garden can be dangerous things, for they can assume greater importance than they should have in the design of the plot. To be effective a path must have a good surface, and a good surface is necessarily more or less permanent. A permanent path of concrete can sometimes look like a highway, quite alien to the garden. Paving stones of various kinds are to be preferred if they are laid well. If necessary, these can always be lifted and replaced elsewhere, while the site they occupied can be dug and seeded for lawn or planted in other ways. It is true that a properly laid path will enable you to walk from place to place in the garden with dry and clean feet in any weather; even more important, a good path will greatly ease the task of pushing a wheelbarrow about. But paths too often have a tendency to become permanent divisions or barriers in a garden, and where space is comparatively small you cannot afford for it to be further subdivided.

A grass path is usually quite effective for the greater part of the year under most conditions. But there are cases where it is just not good enough – for example, if elderly and possibly infirm people wish to stroll in the garden. Here a firm nonslip surface is essential, one that is dry and steady underfoot. Or it may be instead that the children wish to have a place to ride their tricycles, which is likely to cut up the grass, and in wet weather to bog down the tricycles.

Looking ahead

By all means always bear in mind the func-tions of the various parts of the garden and the people who use it, but also look ahead to a certain extent. The children will not always be small, so do not make the facilities you provide for them too perma-nent. Consider, too, your own position. While young you may have plenty of energy and a reasonable amount of time free for gardening. But heavier work loads and greater responsibility may reduce the amount of time you can give to the garden, and muscles will not always retain the power and elasticity of youth, so bear in mind possible limitations in the future when planning now.

To some extent all gardening is a process of thinking for the future, because unless some dreadful error is made each garden-ing act is a means to an end. Each time you dig a bed you make it a little easier to dig next time. But there are more positive, creative and permanent means of thinking of tomorrow. For example, extend your paved area near the house or by the 'service area', for this will decrease the amount of mowing or planting necessary and at the same time simplify and ease your move-ments. Consider the building of one or two

A paved path gives way to paving stones in the lawn and leads towards a raised bed of flowers that is neatly paved around and securely walled.

raised beds, so that in later years you can still indulge your pleasure in gardening but at waist height to save the strain of bending. Grow more plants in containers: doing this gives you much greater control than you have over plants growing in the open garden. Install outdoor water faucets for hoses if they are lacking, or even an irrigation system, so that watering can be carried out in any part of the garden. Install one or two electricity outlets at strategic places so that you can use cheap, efficient, silent and easy-starting electric power tools to trim your hedges or mow your lawns.

The installation of labor-saving facilities like this may be expensive and may involve some upheaval. Beds must have trenches dug through them, for example, when special insulated power lines are laid. But comfort yourself with the knowledge that you will be making life easier and more pleasant for yourself in later years, and that you are appreciably increasing the capital value of your property.

Convenience and aesthetic appeal

Try to gain as many comforts and conveniences as you can without at the same time increasing the complications. Why, for example, make and maintain a path to the front door from the street if you must also have a driveway for the car from the street to the garage? Why not make the driveway serve both purposes? And why plant fruit trees down the garden if you have to buy climbers to disguise the hideously blank walls of the garage? Instead, train espalier fruit trees against the garage, where they will conceal and disguise the surface, save space and gain from the release of the warmth absorbed by the walls.

Plants belong to the great universal world of nature: they always look right. Use them to soften, to conceal, to disguise. But at the same time use a little intelligence in your building work. Use the same materials in making your drive, your patio or your garage as were used in the building of your house, or at least use a material that is

Patio containers have every virtue; hygiene, good drainage, size and a clean, clear-cut appearance.

compatible. If you have to employ new materials for reasons of economy, then hide the worst elements of the conflict by a lavish planting of creepers and climbers, making sure at the same time that you do not over-dress a wall and so use up space that should be open to the passage of people or vehicles.

Although the house and its garden should look right aesthetically, it is equally important that they should fit into their neighborhood and surroundings. The use of brick where everything is of stone is unsympathetic. The installation of modern plastic ranch-style fencing where hedges are the rule is again an unhappy lack of understanding. It is quite possible to indulge one's creative spirit and express one's personality in the making of a garden without at the same time violating the principles of unity and design that prevail in the neighborhood as a whole.

Privacy in the garden

As suggested earlier, the less open and public parts of the garden belong very much to the gardener and his family. They should be treated as another room of the house and, as such, afforded all the coziness and privacy that are needed. It is pleasant to be able to rest or drop asleep in the garden, or to have family meals on the terrace, with the knowledge that you will not be watched by curious eyes.

Happily, a dense screen is not necessary to provide privacy in a garden. The lacy branches of a silver birch, through which the sun can sparkle, can screen a garden quite satisfactorily from neighbors. A wall or fence need not be tall, for it can be topped with a lattice-work fence of timber or plastic slats, through which a silver fleece-vine can twine, its creamy foam of flowers cascading downwards. Too heavy a screen will darken a small garden and make it oppressive, even frightening.

Providing shade

Most of us are happy to have as much sun as we can, which will mean that our plant-

The silver-fleece vine, or mile-a-minute plant, is a rampant climber bearing a froth of creamy flowers.

ings must be made with the sun's journey through the skies in mind; but some, for reasons of preference or possibly health, will require a patch of shade in which to

21

rest. It is always wise, if not necessary, to carry out any significant planting of trees or shrubs with the orientation of the sun in mind. Work out the eventual spread and height of the tree and then gauge the movement of its shadow across the garden. It is possible to make use of this shadow to cool the patio at the hottest part of the day or to shade one of the rooms from the low and penetrating beams of the setting sun, but it is also possible to keep a room in deep shade all day or leave the terrace always hot and arid.

Never plant any tree so near to the house that it will significantly darken any room

The shade from small trees can be used to give a flower border a welcome respite from the hot sun.

for long. Trees too near a house can block roof gutters when the leaves fall. The roots of some trees can break walls and crack foundations. Other roots can enter and choke underground drains. If the local soil is heavy clay, roots will sometimes extract moisture from this until the soil cracks, moves and affects the stability of house or garden walls. It is pleasant to plant a small and immature tree where it can be seen and enjoyed from the windows of a house, but too many of these trees will grow too large, block out any other view and make a room so dark that you will have to prune the tree in order to let in light. The character and beauty of the tree will be spoiled and eventually the only thing left to do will be to remove the tree, always a considerable and unpleasant task.

Wind protection

Sunshine and light are not the only elements that we enjoy sometimes and from which we seek protection at others. On occasion it is very pleasant to enjoy a light breeze on a hot sunny day, but there are other days when the wind, cold or hot, can cause both irritation and damage. In most areas there is a prevailing wind, most frequently coming from one section of the compass. This being so, it is often possible to build a windbreak for protection from this prevailing wind. Like the sun screen, it need not be heavy, for a light screening is most effective in softening or breaking the power of the wind so that it filters through instead of rushing over a barrier.

But when making a windbreak, make quite sure that you are not creating a wind tunnel that increases the force of the wind into your own garden or that of a neighbor. Even as light a screen as wire netting can effectively break the force of wind without channeling it into narrower and more violent pathways. Some screening of this kind is most helpful for those parts of the garden normally much visited by the very young or the old, providing the warmth and comfort that they need.

Individual plants can be protected when young by a wire netting screen (two pieces of wire netting with straw between them).

The brilliant bed of begonias is easily tended from the stepping-stone path and is also protected from strong winds by a contrasting evergreen hedge.

4 Creating tiny backyard gardens

If your garden consists of a tiny backyard, with no more than about 270 sq ft (25 sq m) in which to create your elysium and perhaps raise vegetables, you will have to be the most creative and imaginative gardener of all. Your limitations are so severe that success will depend primarily upon your flair for design. As a general rule you will not be able to grow the same plants as are suited to larger locations, either for lack of space or lack of light. Almost certainly, the situation will be urban, with tall buildings blocking most direct light. Here, being entirely visible from the house, the garden area will more genuinely be an 'extra room' than in any other case.

Lawns, flower beds and shrubberies, tall, stately trees – all these are out of the

Always brilliant, mixed pansies (right) provide the concentrated mass of color that is essential in a large container. Soil should never be allowed to show.

Even in small spaces (left), almost everything from a full-sized garden can be included if grown in containers. Container plants are compact, easily cared for and can be moved according to season and the dictates of convenience.

question. Instead, everything must be miniaturized, each item selected with the greatest of care for its ability to grow under the poorest light conditions and to give of its decorative best where space restrictions are inevitable. In such circumstances, there can be no room for a sprawling plant, a tiny overflow of fallen leaves, a leaning branch or a drooping bough. Nor will there be anywhere to conceal such mundane but necessary items as garbage cans, oil tanks, compost bins and so on.

Unquestionably, the floor of the garden will have to be paved. There will be no room for grass, nor would it grow well under such conditions. There could be a tiny bed or border containing a flowering plant or shrub that will tolerate poor light conditions, and perhaps a climber or two growing up the wall towards the source of light. There could be a miniature pool, perhaps with its own little fountain. And there could be a number of plants in containers of various kinds. It may be possible in certain circumstances to remove these from time to time from the poor light of the garden to the brighter light of the roof or a

balcony. This will give them the opportunity to make good, healthy growth to sustain themselves during the periods when they enhance the true garden below.

Soil, light and artificial stratagems

Another drawback will probably be that the soil of town gardens or backyards is usually poor, undernourished, thin, sour and contaminated by years of deposits from the polluted air of the city. It would be wise to dig out 18 in (45 cm) or so of the top soil wherever plantings are to be made and replace it with fresh soil, either a prepared soil mixture bought by the sack or a natural soil made up of leafmold, loam, peat moss and sand. It will not be advisable, nor will it be helpful, to make this soil mixture too rich – the light available will not normally be able to balance the stimulus at the roots, and plants will find it difficult to grow as they would do under more normal circumstances. Watering will often have to be almost completely artificial.

Despite the difficulties and drawbacks in this type of gardening, the interested and intelligent gardener can only be stimulated

25

by the problems facing him. Obviously, everything possible should be done to overcome them. For example, walls can be painted white or a pale color to trap and reflect as much light as possible. A powerful but – for its gardening value – comparatively inexpensive artificial lighting system could be installed. Ample benefit will result from switching on only one or two floodlights or fluorescent tubes for the darkest parts of the day; it is not necessary to extend the hours of natural daylight.

The soil in which the few plants grow can be improved, and plants can be selected to decorate the space available without stealing too much space or light from other floral residents. You could even take advantage of the sheer artifice of your activities and paint murals on the walls, make a small dark moss-and-fern-encrusted grotto, or install a miniature pool, lit from beneath, which will glow gently in a spot not often in sunlight.

Coping with what a spacious garden can usually conceal – garbage containers, a compost bin, a place for gardening tools – is not such a problem in a small garden as it may appear, for the entire area is almost

26

certain to be paved, and much of it can be built up with raised beds and spaces for wall plants. If you can make what looks like a box-like bench against one wall, part can hold the necessary shovel and rake, and other parts can conceal the compost and garden debris – even the oil storage tank for the central heating, if necessary. If an ivy or a Virginia creeper is grown around the portions of the structure that do not have to be opened, the deception will be complete.

Advantages of a small, enclosed garden

Apart from temperature there will be little difference between the seasons. Because space is so limited, you could possibly allow yourself the luxury of changing the contents of the various pots, tubs, troughs and boxes more frequently than you might otherwise. A single box of early-season pansies bought from a nursery or a garden center can bring spring to the area when it still seems winter-bound. Instead of growing evergreens, concentrate on 'evergolds'

or 'everwhites' or grays – those plants that will reveal their strong and healthy foliage at all times of the year in some color other than a drab green.

One particular benefit of the small town garden is that it is unlikely to suffer from strong winds. So climbers, for example, need only minimal support, easily provided by wires attached to the walls. Taller trees, especially if young, will need no staking. The soil will not dry out as quickly as it would with a similar space on a roof, for example, and hence watering will be less necessary and need not be so thorough. The somewhat damp atmosphere will tend to encourage mosses and ferns – which is just what you want, for they will be natural to the surroundings. Plants of this kind will grow in comparatively shallow containers because of their root structure, and again this is an advantage because little watering will be required.

Frosts are less of a problem than in large gardens, owing to the proximity of heated buildings, so the range of containers nor-

The patio (left) should be a transition zone from the house to the garden. It is a place where both plants and living space can be happily combined.

A good rich soil in a town garden (right) will support a surprising array of flowers, such as marigolds, petunias and geraniums. Here, a constant succession of brilliantly colored flowers can be raised.

27

mally used for outdoor conditions can be extended. Glazed pots and tubs will bring an extra splash of color to brighten up the paving on which they stand, and white paint can be used to lighten pot stands or supports. Do not attempt elaborate architectural effects with your containers, however. Keep the area pleasant and unpretentious.

The front of this town house is richly and ingeniously decorated with simple, cottage-type flowers.

Tidiness

Under all conditions the tiny city garden must be kept meticulously clean and well groomed. Every trace of debris must be removed as soon as possible or the overall effect will tend to be slovenly and unkempt. To make the task easier, avoid using deciduous trees or shrubs, for they serve to emphasize winter gloom when their leaves drop, and the leaves themselves create untidiness. (In any case, in such a small area there would only be room for one or two plants of this type.)

Paving

The basic paving that is usually found to form the floor of a garden of this type is nondescript, dark in color and utilitarian rather than attractive. There are times when it might prove possible to move some of this paving – when electricity cables are installed, for example – and this could provide the opportunity to create a more exciting floor. Paving slabs when removed can be used to create raised beds or other features. With only slight reorganization it may be possible to repave a corner using glazed and patterned tiles, or some other more interesting and more attractive means of adding to the overall brightness of the scene. If you consider this to be carrying things a bit too far and making something resembling a bathroom in the garden, there is no reason why a dozen different textures cannot be imported. Paving slabs are available in many different shapes, colors and textures. It is possible to pour concrete into the space available and brush the surface to create an attractive pebbled finish. Cobbles or pebbled patterns can be laid in concrete, and bricks laid in many patterns. Any changes in the overall paving pattern will combine to add interest to the general effect of a garden of this nature. Whatever the type of paving, however, it should be laid so that there is a very slight slope to a drainage channel in one corner. It is important to keep the channel clean.

A large area of paving (above) is stark and harsh unless softened and made interesting by some plants. But where a paved area is comparatively small (below), keep it clear and uncluttered.

5 Furnishing the garden

Plants are not the only materials used to fill and furnish a garden: paths, terracing, sheds, compost bins, fences or walls – all these are practical aids to the creation and maintenance of the plot. It is possible to manage without any of these aids, and frequently new gardener-owners find they have to, either because there is insufficient time to organize their purchase and installation, or because after acquiring the house and moving into it there is too little money available.

Basic improvements

It is possible at first to do without paths and paved areas, but bear in mind the fact that the hardest gardening work of all is making a start. A wheelbarrow or garden cart travels much more easily on a path than on grass or muddy soil, and saves the soil from being churned up further. It may seem a simple matter merely to measure out the path or the paving and then order paving slabs, bricks, gravel or bituminous surfacing material. But it is not quite so easy as that, for the path or place to be paved must first be dug and possibly leveled. It must have a base or foundation installed and it must then be prepared to accept the type of final surfacing decided upon. This can involve ordering such materials as gravel, sand, cement and possibly timber. If foundation materials such as broken bricks, large stones, pieces of concrete and the like are not to be found in sufficient quantity on the site, a load may have to be delivered by a local supplier. It may be necessary to install a drainage system in the garden, which means buying agricultural drainpipes and installing them in underground channels of rough stone.

These basic improvements should be

carried out before any major planting scheme has been begun. Otherwise you may find yourself destroying work already done in order to install drainage or a path. The physical details of laying paving, installing drainage, building walls and so on are discussed in chapter 7.

Work centers

It is of the greatest assistance to have a work center (or at least a power outlet) in a new garden. The basis of this area should be a shed or other covered place where materials (tools, peat moss, lime, sand, insecticides, and so on) can be protected from the weather. Drainage from the roof of this shed can flow into a rain barrel to provide a water supply. A compost bin or mound can be built nearby, and all vegetable material can be placed there to turn into useful and rich garden soil.

It is not necessary to have electricity and water available at this center, but it is helpful. If you hope to install water pipes or electricity lines one day, the earlier the better, as the work can involve digging up the garden. Lines for electricity must be buried and specially protected to avoid injury in the event, for example, of a shovel being driven through the soil onto the wire. Always obtain an electrician's advice about this.

Garden sheds are inexpensive, often prefabricated or metal, and, if correctly installed and treated with moderate care, they should last many years. The shed must be erected on solid and level foundations, preferably of concrete or paving slabs. Choose a site that is level and equally accessible from all parts of the garden. If the shed has only one door, face it in the direction from which the shed will be most frequently

31

The working sections of the garden (a) should be grouped in a corner so that everything is conveniently accessible.

To receive the best light, a greenhouse (b) should be sited in a north-south direction.

Soil, sand and peat moss are best kept in convenient storage bins (c).

A compost bin divided into three sections (d) provides a constant supply of well-rotted humus.

approached, otherwise you may find that each time you go to the shed for a tool you have to walk right round it.

The way in which you lay out your garden shed will depend on several factors, such as its size, the number of appliances it will have to house, the number of windows, the type of flooring and other similar factors. Heavy machines such as mowers and cultivators will have to stand on the floor, of course, and if there are several it may well be worthwhile moving them about until you discover how they can be fitted together to occupy the least floor space. But remember also to make sure that the tool or implement you use most often will be closest to hand and that you do not have to wheel one machine out to get to another.

Hand tools such as spades, forks and rakes can be hung on a wall. Try to keep them neat and tidy and always in the same place, for this way you will know at a glance where a tool will be or which tool is missing if one has been left in the garden at the end of the day. Beside the hand tools keep a scraper of some sort with which to remove any mud adhering to them, and an oily rag with which to give the tool a final wipe after use, which will serve both as a cleaner and rust preventer.

Erect shelving to hold the cans, bottles or packages of weedkillers, insecticides, fungicides and other preparations that are helpful in the garden. Avoid confusion by grouping them according to category, all the herbicides in one place, the insecticides

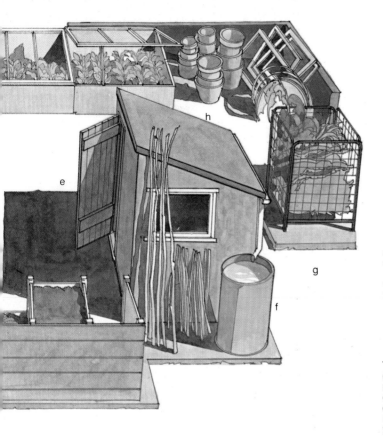

A garden shed (e) for storing tools, fertilizers and weedkillers is a key part of any work area.

Sheds and greenhouses, when adapted, are natural traps for collecting rainwater (f).

A small storage bin (g) is essential for keeping unwanted garden rubbish that cannot be used in the compost heap.

The area around frames (h) should be arranged to provide storage space for empty plant pots and extra frame covers as well as an area for standing young plants.

in another, and so on. If a package bursts or if a label is lost, always dispose carefully of the contents to avoid the danger of using the wrong substance on some occasion and causing damage. Always bear in mind that all insecticides are necessarily poisons. Keep them in the least accessible place and certainly where they cannot be reached by children. Never place any material, solid, powder or liquid, in a container that is not actually made for that material. In other words, if you have a little insecticide left over from a mixing, either use it up or throw it away; never pour it into, say, an empty soft-drink bottle. Examine your garden chemicals every month or so to make sure that no containers are broken or leaking. Garden sheds can become very hot in

summer and very cold in winter, and are sometimes damp, which can cause bottles to crack and cans to rust.

Outside the shed it is possible to have two or three bins, or a bin-like shelter for several sturdy plastic garbage cans. These are very useful for storing supplies of peat moss, sand, sifted soil, leafmold or similar materials. Beside them can be the compost heap. This can either be free-standing or contained in easily made wire mesh or plastic frames, or contained by homemade timber, brick or plastic walls. Homemade compost can be a vital source of good humus for the garden and it would be unwise not to establish your own supply. Ensure that the area is not adjacent to the clean compost.

6 Tools

A stainless steel shovel will slip easily through heavy soil.

An efficient digging fork must have strong tines.

A garden line is an invaluable aid for laying out straight rows and beds.

On heavy soil, a draw hoe must be used for most jobs.

The Dutch hoe is more useful where the soil is light.

garden line

Dutch hoe

spade

fork

draw hoe

Essential tools

The basic tools needed in order to garden efficiently will depend on the individual and the type of garden he intends to create. They will almost certainly include a shovel, a fork, a rake, a trowel, a hoe, a ball of strong twine and a garden hose, or at least a watering can, and the list can be extended from here.

Stainless-steel hand tools are best because they do not rust and hence tend to pick up less mud on their smooth surfaces. They should be selected with some care according to the size and physique of the gardener. Tools that are not too heavy and that fit the hand easily are a tremendous assistance in some of the heavier garden tasks. Never choose a large shovel, for example, in the belief that by moving a large quantity of soil at one time the task will be completed more rapidly. It will usually be found that a smaller shovel or the removal of smaller lumps of soil will enable you to work more quickly and with less expenditure of energy.

Power tools

Don't be in too much of a hurry to seek the assistance of a powered machine for your gardening. By the time a machine has been removed from the shed, filled with a fuel mixture as necessary, started, wheeled to the site and then set to work, many a small task could have been completed using a shovel or a fork alone.

A power mower is probably the most useful machine for the garden so long as the lawn is more than about 100 sq ft (10 sq m). The size of the mower can be increased according to the size of the lawn and, gen-

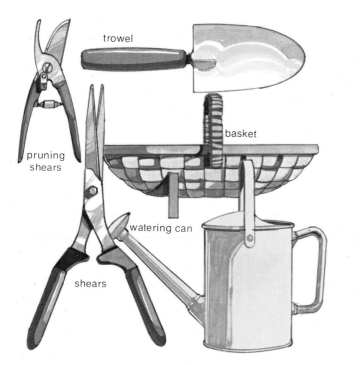

trowel

pruning
shears

basket

watering can

shears

Keep pruning shears blades sharp to avoid damage when pruning plants. Wipe and oil the blades of shears each time after using them.

A trowel is an essential tool for transplanting young plants and setting out bulbs.

A garden basket is useful when weeding or gathering vegetables, flowers and fruit.

A hand-held watering can is convenient for spot watering.

erally speaking, a small lawn is probably more easily maintained with an electric-powered machine than one driven by an internal-combustion engine. Electric mowers are almost foolproof, light in weight and nearly silent during operation, as well as being slower to deteriorate than fuel-powered mowers.

A powered cultivator or tiller is only justified in a garden where a comparatively large area – again, say 100 sq ft (10 sq m) – will require frequent cultivation, such as an intensively gardened vegetable plot. If the machine is required only for occasional but intensive use, as, for example, when a new lawn is being made and the whole area requires thorough digging more than once, then it will be found cheaper and considerably more convenient to actually hire a machine for a day or two and use it for all cultivating tasks in the garden at one time.

More likely to be of use are powered hedge trimmers and, possibly, powered chain saws, both of which can be obtained in different sizes according to the tasks to be carried out. There are trimmers powered by electricity and some models are available with a built-in rechargeable battery. Trimmers can also be obtained that run by means of a flexible drive and a power take-off point from some power tillers. Most chain saws are powered by miniature, but noisy, gasoline engines. This type is essential for use at any distance from the house or from a supply of electricity.

With all power tools, do treat them with respect – they are excellent aids to the gardener, but can be dangerous. All electrical tools should be periodically checked by a qualified electrician.

7 Creating the background

Establishing a lawn

Nothing makes a better background for your plants than a green lawn, and the sowing of grass seed or the laying of turf is often one of the first activities of the new gardener. Because the grass may be there for many years it is worth making sure that it is as perfect a lawn as is possible.

Dig the area thoroughly, removing all weeds and stones and leveling it roughly. After a few days another crop of weeds will be seen and these can be removed when the area is dug once again, this time breaking up the soil more finely and checking the level. Finally, rake over the surface several times, breaking down the soil even more finely and making quite sure that there are no hills or valleys. With this last raking it is helpful to rake in a layer of peat moss that covers the surface completely.

If you are sowing seed, make sure that the soil surface is just moist on a warm windless, spring or fall day. Sow the seed evenly on the surface, 1½ oz per sq yd (50 g per sq m), sowing half the quantity up and down the chosen area, and the other half across it. Rake the seed in very gently and sprinkle over it the finest layer of a peat and soil mixture. Some seed is pretreated with a chemical that will make it unpalatable to birds, but the fine soil is attractive to them for taking dust baths if it becomes dry. To prevent this and to speed germination, water the area often with a fine mist.

When the grass seed germinates with it are almost certain to be some more weeds, which should be pulled out by hand. Do not attempt to mow the grass until the spears are at least 2 in (5 cm) tall. Make sure your mower has sharp blades and that these are set high for the first three mowings. Only after the young grass has been growing for at least six months will it be wise to use chemical weedkillers on the lawn, and then only according to container directions.

If you prefer to turf the area, a process which will give quicker results but will cost appreciably more, the soil preparation is exactly the same as for seed sowing. The turfs will probably be delivered in rolls about 3 ft (1 m) long and 12 in (30 cm) wide. Lay them as soon as you can, depending on the weather, so that the joins fit alternately, like bricks. Keep each turf close to its neighbor and make sure that one is not thicker or thinner than another. If this *is* the case, adjust the soil level. When the area has been finished, sprinkle a mixture of fine soil and peat moss thinly over it and give the lawn a gentle watering. Make sure for the next few weeks that the lawn is not allowed to dry out or the roots will be killed and patching will be necessary.

Plan your lawn area with a view to the

Well-laid paving should never need attention again. Make sure that the ground is level (1), then put down an even bed of gravel and sand (2). Carefully place the concrete slabs in place (3) with even spaces (4) left around each. Brush cement into cracks (5) and water (6) so it sets in place and fills all the spaces where weeds might otherwise sprout.

mowing you will later have to do. Keep the site simple and uncluttered so that the mower can go over it freely and easily without having to stop to negotiate a tree or a bed. Make angles wide or, better still, substitute gentle curves.

Where paving joins the lawn, make sure that the levels are compatible so that the mower blades will not be damaged. If this is not possible, allow a space between lawn and paving.

Lawn mowing

The time and labor involved in mowing a lawn would be considerably cut if it were unnecessary to carry away the grass clippings to some convenient place. But this task can be eased by using several large plastic or burlap sheets placed at strategic points on the grass. If each is used as a dumping ground on passing, they can quite easily be dragged to the compost heap when the mowing has been completed.

Grass mowings can be used as a mulch in the vegetable garden, around the roses and at the base of trees and shrubs where there is space. Spread clippings quite thickly, to a depth of 2 in (5 cm) or so. The mulch helps keep down weeds and conserve moisture in the soil, and in time it will rot and improve the soil structure.

Laying paving

All paving should be laid on a foundation both for the sake of stability and for drainage purposes. This foundation should ideally consist of some 4 in (10 cm) of well-consolidated pebbles topped by 2 in (5 cm) or so of gravel or sand. Paving slabs can be laid directly on this, but it is generally more satisfactory to lay the slabs on a concrete foundation.

When marking out the area to be paved, remember that a very slight slope in one direction or another should be allowed for, so that rain water can drain quickly and

easily from the surface. It is essential that levels should be accurately worked out and the only way to do this is to drive pegs into the ground, their tops being leveled by means of a plank and a spirit level. If this is done carefully and all the work is carried out according to these pegs, much subsequent work will be saved.

Precast paving slabs come in several shapes and sizes and it is as well to work out in advance the pattern in which they will be laid so that you can order exactly the right quantity. Handle the slabs with care, for they can be surprisingly brittle if dropped. They are also exceedingly heavy, so do not try to save time and trouble by using slabs that are too large: 2 ft (60 cm) or so square is quite large enough, but they can be rectangular, hexagonal or round. A mixture of sizes produces the most appealing result.

If the paving is laid in concrete no weeds can grow through the cracks, but otherwise it is almost certain that weeds of one type or another will grow between the slabs, either up through the soil far below or from seeds caught in the shallow cracks between the stones. One way to avoid this without using

For an informal country garden effect, crazy paving is ideal. Always make sure that the surface is even and that the stones are firmly bedded in concrete.

a concrete base is to fill the spaces between the slabs with a sand and cement mix, applied dry. If it is mixed with water, it is certain to stain or otherwise disfigure the slabs on each side, but if brushed into the cracks while still dry, this will be avoided. After the dry mix has been carefully brushed into the cracks, water the area gently but thoroughly with a fine spray. The moisture will be sufficient to make the cement mix harden in a day or two.

Wall construction

As with paving, the most important element in the construction of other architectural or structural features, such as walls or pergolas, is the base or foundation. If the wall does not stand on a solid foundation it will be apt to crack, to lean or to fall, and equally if the pergola posts are not firmly anchored in suitable holes so that they are

This stone wall blends well with the shrubs growing above it and is attractively stepped to suit the sloping contours of the land as well as enhancing the appearance of the landscape.

meticulously vertical, the whole pergola will look unsightly and be exceedingly difficult to erect.

Walls can be of several types, whether they be retaining or free standing. A retaining wall is one that is built into the soil, as for example when a garden is on a slope and is terraced to give level areas one above the other. If a retaining wall is to retain or hold back a bank of soil, it must obviously be solid and secure; the foundation should therefore be of up to 4 in (10 cm) of concrete laid on a base of well-consolidated pebbles or broken-up stone in a trench dug well below the frost line in cold regions, or at least 6 in (15 cm) deep in other climatic regions. A retaining wall should also be

built with a slight batter or receding slope, which is to say that it should lean slightly into the bank, for added strength. During periods of heavy rain some of the moisture in the bank behind the wall will force its way outwards through the wall, and it is wise to make provision for this by allowing a few 'weep' holes in the wall while it is being constructed.

Materials from which a wall can be constructed are brick, stone and reconstituted stone. Unless your house is made of brick it is unwise to use this material for a retaining wall because it will look out of place. Stone can sometimes be difficult to obtain and expensive, but, fortunately, tremendous strides have been made in the preparation of reconstituted stones. These are now available in various colors and shapes.

A retaining wall is particularly suited to the growing of certain plants on its surface, and indeed so suited is it to this purpose that wild plants or weeds will find their way into the wall naturally after a time. It is possible to squeeze the roots of little plants such as sedums and sempervivums into cracks in the wall, but more satisfactory results can be obtained by inserting the plants as the wall is being built.

A free-standing wall has space on each side. This makes it easier to build, but also creates new difficulties. Again, a sound foundation is essential and the same materials for its construction can be used. However, whereas a retaining wall is supported to some extent by the soil, a free-standing wall has no such strengthening background. Where it is of a considerable height or length it will be necessary to insert at regular intervals a pier or buttress to give added solidity. A free-standing wall also requires a protective capping to keep water and frost from entering the interior of the wall and breaking it down.

It is best to make the foundation of a wall wider than the wall itself, so that weeds cannot grow through the soil immediately next to the wall – where they are difficult to remove.

8 Trees and shrubs

Apart from the more or less permanent or architectural parts of the garden, there are the plants, the real purpose or meaning of the garden as such. These vary widely, from trees and shrubs, some of which will outlive the gardener once planted, to the bright and brilliant little annual flowers, which will bloom for a few weeks. All of these can be raised from seed, even the largest tree. But it is likely to be so difficult to grow trees and shrubs that normally specimens between two and ten years old are bought from a nursery or a garden center and planted in the garden. These cost rather more than younger plants

would, but save the years of waiting.

The basic difference between a tree and a shrub is that the former grows on a single stem or trunk and the latter sometimes (though not always) rises from the soil with several main stems. Both can be evergreen or deciduous: evergreen kinds retain their leaves in winter, shedding them gradually all the year round; deciduous kinds shed theirs more dramatically, in autumn.

When buying a tree, you must first

Garden centers (above right), with their comprehensive selections of plants and equipment, are invaluable to beginner gardeners. They offer an inspiring array of flowering plants and trees ready to set out in the open garden or in containers (below).

decide on the type and variety of tree and its site. Should it be an apple or a pear? A conifer? A variegated-leaved maple? What should its ultimate height be? Spread? Where will it cast its shade? Will it block window light? Will its roots penetrate drains or wreck the foundations of walls?

Most of these questions will depend on the gardener's desires, the garden space available, and, possibly, his economic position in his decision whether or not to grow fruit. Ultimate heights and widths are frequently given in nursery catalogs and both are important, for a tree that is delightful in its young and immature state can prove a nightmare of obstruction when it begins to reach maturity.

Catalogs The gardener can choose his trees and shrubs from a catalog issued by a specialist nurseryman. The catalog entry, possibly illustrated, will probably give all the information necessary: the name, family, type, size and whether the plant likes an acid or alkaline soil or a mild and sheltered position. Unless the gardener has seen this particular plant growing, it may be difficult for him to picture exactly what it will look like growing on his own land. The nurseryman will always advise him, and tell him whether the plant is suited to his soil and his conditions. Having placed his order with the nurseryman, the gardener will be advised when it will be ready for pickup or delivery. This will usually be during the dormant season, when the leaves have fallen from deciduous trees and shrubs and when all plants of this nature are comparatively inactive. Some plants, such as evergreens, will be dug with a root ball, protected, staked and wrapped for a journey. Other plants will be shipped, well wrapped, with bare roots.

Garden centers For the new gardener or the gardener who demands immediate results or a year-round source of plants and supplies, garden centers are a real help, for here every type of gardening material may be seen, examined and bought, from alys-

41

sum to zinnia seeds and including many plants from annuals through to roses, trees and shrubs. It is possible to see many plants actually in full leaf or in flower, always a help to a new gardener. Plants can be bought in this state, taken home and planted without disturbing the root ball. Quite literally, it is possible to make an instant garden, a whole plot planted and growing in a single afternoon. So long as these plants receive the necessary early aftercare, they will grow well and quickly and several stages of gardening can be eliminated.

It only takes a visit to a botanical garden or a park to indicate that the choice of plants that can be grown in a garden is extremely wide. Most of us like trees and shrubs, but do not know the names of those we see frequently, to say nothing of those that we admire in the park. We may have a better knowledge of some flowers, but others, though attractive to us, are unfamiliar, and we may assume that those plants that we seldom see must be exotic or difficult to grow under normal circumstances. Similarly, we may fear that some plants we admire may grow too large for our gardens or demand a more equable climate than we can provide.

But all of this is merely a matter of finding out and checking, and, normally, nursery catalogs plus a visit to a good garden center will provide the answer to almost every question.

Planting trees and shrubs

Having chosen your plants with due care, it is only sensible to be just as thorough when it comes to planting them. Trees and shrubs are a major investment and it really does pay to give them a good start – then they will last in good health and fine appearance from some ten to twenty years to several hundred. In that time they will grow from only three feet (a meter) or so in height to maybe 60 ft (20 m) in the case of some of the lower species.

A tree on which one lavishes something like two hours' work can last a lifetime, which indicates the real value it can give. If it is planted with moderate care, it may require no further attention for the remainder of its life. It will seek its own water and its own food, will grow to ten times or more its original height, will provide shade in the garden, and in some cases will provide more fruit than can reasonably be consumed by the average family.

So a tree is worth planting well to give it the start in life it deserves. How far apart you plant your trees will be decided by the number that you can fit into the site unless you are prepared to remove some of them when they mature and begin to brush against each other. A very general rule about planting intervals says that one should add together the mature widths of two adjoining trees and divide by two. An example might be an autumn-blooming cherry, *Prunus subhirtella autumnalis*, which can grow to a mature height of some 23 ft (7 m) with a spread of 16 ft (5 m). Planted next to a hornbeam, *Carpinus betulus* 'Fastigiata', with a mature height of about 33 ft

Japanese maples, such as this *Acer japonicum* 'Vitifolium' (above), give us some of our brightest and most beautiful autumn colors. A hedge of mixed shrubs and small trees (left) is attractive where there is a suitable space in a garden.

(10 m) and spread of 20 ft (6 m), then the distance apart should be 16 ft (5 m) + 20 ft (6 m) divided by 2, or 18 ft (5·5 m).

No tree should be planted too close to a house, a major wall or drainpipes. In times of drought tree roots seek out moisture and some can penetrate drains and break them up. But the most frequent cause of damage is where the soil is heavy and made up mainly of clay, for here tree roots will absorb all existing moisture, causing the soil to dry out, to crack and to subside, thus causing cracks in walls and broken foundations. Poplar and ash are the most dangerous trees of this type.

Having chosen the site, dig the planting hole considerably deeper and wider than the root spread of the tree, and if the weather is dry, fill it with water. While this is soaking into the surrounding soil, examine your tree and trim away any broken or damaged twigs and any broken roots. Stand the tree in the hole to make sure that the roots can be accommodated comfortably. Place the stake in the planting hole to make sure that it will not damage the roots and then drive it in securely, making sure that it is absolutely vertical.

Now begin the actual planting. In the planting hole place and tramp down a layer of good soil mixed with peat moss and,

When a variegated maple sends out a branch that has plain leaves, cut it back to the main stem to keep the tree from going green.

if available, some rotted manure, thick enough to raise the soil mark on the tree trunk to the surrounding soil level. Then place the roots in position, following their natural direction as much as possible, and cover them gradually with the soil mixture, shaking the tree occasionally to make sure that no air pockets are formed. Tread down the soil at intervals. When the soil has reached the top of the hole, tread it down again. Leave a slight depression around the trunk so that rain water can be caught and absorbed, and fill the basin repeatedly with water to settle the soil. A final mulch with leafmold or compost will be helpful. Only after the tree has been planted and is in its permanent position should it be attached to the stake, preferably using a standard plastic tie. If string, rope or wire is used, make sure that the stem of the tree is protected so that this does not cut into the bark.

The method of planting a shrub is exactly the same except that a stake is not always necessary for a subject that is comparatively low and spreading. But both trees and shrubs should have close attention the first few weeks after planting, being sprayed daily in hot weather, perhaps even shaded and protected from strong winds and with the soil being kept uniformly

To space out two trees correctly, add the mature width of both trees and divide the total in half. This will ensure that each tree has enough room to grow without touching the other.

Heeling-in a tree gives the roots short-term protection from drying winds or surface frosts until permanent planting is done.

45

moist. After the first few months, which are critical, the tree will begin to look after itself but it will make little or no growth in the first couple of years while it puts down strong roots.

Some popular trees and shrubs

The following is a very brief list of trees and shrubs that are suitable for a small garden. They will, of course, be suitable for a large garden also, but no really large trees are included. The information is generalized and further specialized advice should be sought if in any doubt. The height and spread of individual varieties may differ widely. Where figures for a species alone are given, these indicate the maximum height and spread of which the group is capable. An asterisk indicates the plant is winter-hardy in mild climates only. Check in your catalogs or at local nurseries for detailed information.

Name		Evergreen	Planting Season	Mature height and spread (feet)
Acer palmatum Japanese maple			Spring, autumn	6–19; 10–13
Amelanchier canadensis			Spring, autumn	10–13; 6–10
Arbutus unedo strawberry tree		√	Autumn	15–19; 6–10
Aucuba japonica Japanese laurel		√	All year	6–10; 6–10

Name		Evergreen	season	Mature height and spread (feet)
Berberis barberry, many varieties		some	Spring, autumn	3–6; 3–10
Betula birch, several varieties			Spring	10–19; 13–15
Buddleia butterfly bush, several varieties		some	Summer	6–10; 6–10
Buxus box, clipped to size		V	All year	3–20; 3–10
Camellia japonica common camellia		V	Late winter, spring	3–10; 2–6
Chaenomeles flowering quince, many varieties			Spring, autumn	3–10; 3–10

Name		Evergreen	Season	Mature height and spread (feet)
Fatsia japonica castor oil plant		√	All year	3–10; 3–10
Hydrangea		some	Summer	3–6; 3–6
Laburnum golden chain, golden raintree, several varieties			Late spring, early summer	10–15; 10–13
Laurus nobilis sweet bay		√	All year	3–10; 2–3
Ligustrum privet, several varieties		some	All year	3–10; 3–13
Malus crab apple, many varieties			Spring, autumn	10–15; 3–10

Name		Evergreen	Season	Mature height and spread (feet)
Philadelphus mock orange, many varieties			Summer	6–13; 3–10
Prunus plum, cherry, almond, laurel etc., many varieties		some	Spring, summer, autumn	3–23; 3–15
Pyracantha firethorn, several varieties		√	Autumn, winter, Spring	6–13; 6–13
Ribes flowering currant		some	Spring, summer	10–13; 10–13
Syringa lilac, many varieties			Late spring	3–15; 3–13
Viburnum many varieties		some	Spring, summer, winter	3–15; 6–13

9 Coping with pests

Aphids (1) can produce millions of offspring in a matter of a few days.

Caterpillars (2) of many pests do untold damage to leaves and buds.

Leatherjackets (3) are the grubs of the cranefly or daddy-long-legs.

Slugs (4) can play havoc with lettuce and potatoes or leaves of many plants.

Just as a healthy person can quickly and easily shake off many of the infections that may attack him, so a healthy plant will frequently withstand the onslaughts of disease or insects. Your aim should be to grow all your plants so well that they remain strong and healthy for the whole of their useful lives. Unlike humans, however, any plant that is sickly and likely to infect others should be either cured or ruthlessly thrown away.

Owners of relatively small town gardens have fewer problems in the field of plant sickness than those who garden in the country. In the first place there is less chance of infection if plants in a locality are comparatively few in number, as they are in towns.

Secondly, if a garden is fairly small you can pay closer attention to individual plants than when you have large areas under your control. You can spot, identify and take action against any disease or pest attack as soon as it starts instead of overlooking the trouble until it has reached dangerous proportions and has affected many plants in one area.

There exist sprays or dusts to cure or prevent all plant illnesses – or almost all, for some diseases are so troublesome or so easily spread that it is better to destroy the plant than to try to cure it. Some treatments are quick acting and effective while some will merely alleviate the problem.

All reputable manufacturers subject

Earwigs (5) are scavengers that will feed on almost anything.

Pea moth attack (6) is most likely during a dry season.

The pretty cabbage white butterfly is preceded by a destructive caterpillar (7).

their products to long-range tests to ensure that they are as safe for the specified purpose as they can be made. They look for a product that is safe to handle when mixing or preparing, one that can safely be applied, one that will carry out its specific task without harming plants or beneficial insects, and one that breaks down quickly into harmless compounds without leaving dangerous residues on plants, in the soil or in the bodies of insects which it may have killed.

Apart from the trouble which arises from human error in growing plants, such as failing to water a thirsty plant or wounding a tree trunk by the careless use of a mower, nearly all plant troubles can be put down to pests or diseases. Most diseases arise from some form of fungus or virus.

This being so, you have only to kill or prevent insects and either prevent or cure fungus diseases to keep your garden plants in good health. Pests are usually biters, suckers or borers and if we apply a poison to the plant it is likely that these pests will be killed. Most fungus trouble can be prevented, and on the basis that prevention is better than cure we can apply fungicides to those of our plants which are susceptible to this type of attack. Virus-caused diseases are best prevented by controlling the insects, such as aphids, that carry them, or by buying certified virus-free fruits such as strawberries and raspberries.

51

Feeding, pruning and pest control

1 Basic techniques

For every gardener, there are certain techniques that can be said to lay the foundations of a beautiful, healthy and successful garden – the techniques that, being unglamorous in themselves, are rarely the subject of a special book: feeding plants, using compost, watering, pruning and keeping gardens free of weeds, pests and diseases. Yet these are the very areas in which many gardeners feel their knowledge could be improved. Among the questions often raised are:

Why should it be necessary to feed plants?

What is the difference between the various types of compost?

How much should plants be watered?

How do I know where, when and how much to prune plants, and why does it have to be done?

How can I keep my garden weed-free without hours of back-breaking labour?

How do I recognize what pest or disease is destroying my plants, and what can I do about it?

The general principles for successful garden cultivation remain the same whatever

Compost is invaluable; site the compost heap in the vegetable plot.

Choose trees of a suitable size for the garden so that they provide shade yet do not overwhelm the setting.

Bigger, brighter blooms and heavier crops will result from a program of balanced feeding.

A regular spraying or dusting program against pests and diseases will ensure that garden plants are well-protected against attack.

Weeds must never be allowed to compete with other plants, especially in the rows of a vegetable garden.

the type of garden, but unless gardeners know the whys and wherefores, their own actions (for example, overfeeding, over-watering, or cutting back essential new growth) may be as much responsible for poor results as the ravages of weeds, pests and diseases. These points and the answers to the questions listed above are dealt with here in detail chapter by chapter.

2 Feeding plants

Successful plant growth depends on good feeding. Soils differ widely in their content of foods or chemicals that are beneficial to plants but there must be adequate organic matter (humus) in the form of the compost to keep the soil in good condition. In addition, sufficient artificial or chemical feeds will be needed to maintain a balanced growth.

Even in an uncultivated garden, soil is manured or provided with organic matter by the action of worms, which bring decomposed leaves into the subsoil. There is also a natural process of decay or rotting down within the surface vegetation. However, where the soil is required for intensive cultivation, it is necessary to apply plant foods in a more concentrated form and more frequently, since plants quickly use up the food that is in the soil.

Most soils contain reserves of essential chemicals that slowly become available to plants by the action of soil organisms and weathering. It is still necessary, however, to add to these chemicals. In many cases, more of one chemical than another must be added in order to provide the plants with a good 'diet', to encourage sturdy, healthy growth, high crop yields and beautiful floral displays.

Frequent plant feeding is required for most garden plants so that they receive chemicals that can be used straight away by their root systems or that will be available in suitable forms, after some basic changes, in as short a time as possible.

Plant foods

Certain elements are essential to good plant growth. At the top of the list are three elements – nitrogen, potassium, and phosphorus. There are also some that are known as trace elements. These include calcium, magnesium, sulfur, iron, manganese, zinc, copper, boron and molybdenum. The first three elements are the ones gardeners need to supply to the soil, as many of the trace elements are probably already there in adequate amounts and are, in any case, only required in quite small amounts in comparison with the essential ones.

All the prime foods must be applied as a *balanced* feed to plants. Too much of one or too little of another will cause poor growth. By feeding back into the soil the correct proportions of plant foods the balance is restored. The results can be quite amazing.

Nowadays, it is possible to check the soil quite easily to find out what foods are lacking and how much of one particular food is required to bring the soil back into a balanced state. This is done with a soil-testing

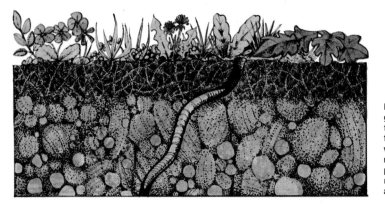

Even uncultivated gardens are enriched by the natural processes of fertilization. Earthworms work decayed plant matter into the subsoil, providing new organic material. Their tunneling also aerates the soil.

Pink-flowered hydrangeas are an indication of an alkaline soil, while blue-flowered hydrangeas indicate an acid soil.

kit, which costs only a few dollars and is a very good investment – especially when planting a new garden.

The test outfit provides a color code reference for small soil samples, which are treated with special chemicals in tiny test tubes. After shaking up the contents of each tube, the mix is allowed to settle and then a color comparison is made against a special chart.

The deficiency (if any) can immediately be read off, while a check-off column at the side of the chart tells how much of a particular fertilizer is required to bring the soil back to its correct balance. These tests are only relevant for vital plant foods – not for the so-called trace elements.

Acid and alkaline soils

When tackling the problem of plant foods it is also important to know whether the soil is acid, neutral or alkaline. This condition will have an influence on the fertility of the soil and on what types of plant can be cultivated.

Plants such as the heathers and rhododendrons will grow well only in soils

that are relatively acid. Cabbages and Brussels sprouts, on the other hand, will grow successfully only in soils that are neutral, slightly alkaline, or slightly acid.

Fortunately, there is a very simple way in which the acidity of soils is classified. This is by a scale that measures the soil's pH value. A reading of pH 7·0 indicates that the soil is neutral – neither acid nor alkaline. A reading above this figure indicates that the soil is alkaline, while below 7·0 the soil is acid.

The best values for most garden plants lie between pH 6·5 and 7·0. To make the soil more alkaline, lime must be added; to make it more acid, flowers of sulfur are applied. An example of the effect of an acid or alkaline soil is demonstrated in the case of colored hydrangeas. If blue flowers are produced all the time, this is an indication that the soil is acid. If, on the other hand, the flowers are pink, this is a sure sign that the soil is alkaline.

The degree of acidity or alkalinity of soils can be determined with a soil-test kit. A pinch of soil is mixed with the test chemicals and the resulting color matched against a standard chart. Each color indicates the degree to which a soil is acid or alkaline.

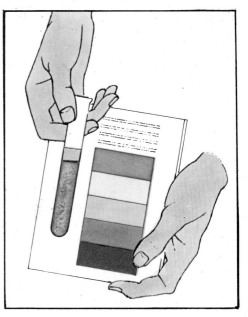

Let us now take a closer look at the individual plant foods that can be used to good effect in the garden. The nitrogenous feeds are generally very quick-acting and the effect on growth can be appreciated soon after application. The rate of growth increases, leaves take on a dark green color and become large and luscious (fleshy). By comparison, lack of sufficient nitrogen results in small, stunted plants and poor-sized foliage, which may also take on a pale bluish color.

Nitrogen promotes the rate at which plants grow. Leaves will become fleshier too.

Potash encourages better ripening and adds color to fruits and flowers.

Phosphorus is a plant food that produces a vigorous root formation, especially with root crops.

Phosphorus is needed to promote good root development, without which the plants cannot obtain enough good food from the soil. It is a very important substance for root vegetables too. The phosphorus content in the soil is vital for seedlings to form a vigorous root system – thus building up an excellent plant for planting out later on in permanent quarters. Phosphorus is also essential for the satisfactory ripening of fruits, as is potash – an even more important plant food in this respect.

Potash adds color to fruits, flowers and certain vegetables. It also encourages better ripening and enhances the quality of food crops in terms of flavor and storing properties. This is especially the case with apples, pears, potatoes and carrots. Plants deficient in potash become poor bearers and yield smaller crops. Leaf margins – especially those of fruit trees – can become scorched where potash is lacking.

The other top-priority food for plants is calcium, which already exists in many soils in adequate quantities. Calcium helps to stimulate essential bacterial action in the soil, which makes other foods readily available to the plants. It also helps to improve the physical condition of soils, corrects acidity and provides a good 'grounding', as it were, for other plant foods.

Foods can be purchased individually or they can be bought in pre-mixed bags.

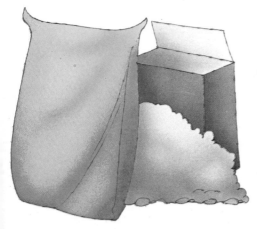

Fertilizer should be scattered along rows and should be raked in well.

Applying foods

Plant foods can be applied to the soil as individual types, or as balanced or specially blended mixtures that contain all the essentials, such as nitrogen, phosphorus and potash, and also contain several important trace elements. Nitrogen is available as a plant food in the form of such fertilizers as sulfate of ammonia, nitrate of soda and urea. Phosphorus can be obtained as superphosphate and as bonemeal, which should be of the steamed kind. Potash is supplied in the form of sulfate of potash. This is the best form of potash for the gardener as it is also relatively quick-acting.

Here is a checklist of some of the most popular plant foods. Others exist that may only be available locally. For instance, for those who live near the sea, gathering fresh seaweeds (a source of nitrogen and potash as well as humus) is perfectly feasible. Other fertilizers, such as cottonseed meal, which is popular with organic gardeners who avoid the commercial fertilizers, are often used in general purpose organic fertilizers as a source of nitrogen. Organic fertilizers are slow to break down, but usually less drastic than artificials.

Popular plant foods

Animal manures These include poultry, cow, horse, goat and others. They were once the main source of fertilizers and are still important in rural regions where they are most likely to be available. Cow manure is also usually available in dehydrated form from garden centers. Most manures, especially horse and cow, are valuable sources of humus as well as being general purpose fertilizers, especially when they are mixed with litter – straw, peat moss. Fresh manures are safe to incorporate with the soil in fall. Decayed manures are safest in spring.

Bonemeal Provides phosphorus (20–30 per cent) very slowly and a very small amount of nitrogen (1–4 per cent) fairly quickly. Steamed bonemeal is fastest acting. Apply at rate of 4–8 oz per sq yd (110–220 g per sq m).

Cottonseed meal Contains about 7 per cent nitrogen, 3 per cent phosphorus and 2 per cent potash. A long-lasting source of nitrogen, especially recommended for rhododendrons and its relatives. Apply 6 lb per 100 sq ft (2·7 kg per 9·3 sq m).

Dried blood May contain 12 per cent nitrogen. Fairly fast-acting but it is expensive. Save for salad crops. Use at rate of 2–3 oz per sq yd (56–84 g per sq m).

Limestone Not basically a fertilizer, although it is a source of calcium, it is used to counteract acidity. Limestone is slower acting than hydrated lime. Gypsum (calcium sulfate) is applied to soils to supply calcium but not alter the acidity. Gypsum is excellent for the physical improvement of soils, especially heavy clay types, as it helps to break them down.

Nitrate of soda This is a highly nitrogenous fertilizer (about 16 per cent nitrogen) that is quick-acting. It can be used very successfully during major growing periods and is ideal for leafy plants such as lettuce and spinach. Care must be taken when using it as it can burn plants, especially young ones. Rate of application is about ½–1 oz (14–28 g per sq m). It is perhaps easiest to apply diluted in water at the rate of ¼–½ oz per gall (7–14 g per 4 liters) of water.

Sludge This is the dried and pulverized residue from sewage disposal plants and may well end up the fertilizer of the future. The best known sludge that has been marketed with any success is Milorganite, a good all-purpose fertilizer high in nitrogen. Follow instructions on the bag.

Sulfate of ammonia Similar in use to nitrate of soda. This plant fertilizer is for boosting green growth. It is not so caustic as nitrate of soda and is best applied in spring and early summer. Can be mixed with sulfate of potash and superphosphate. It contains about 20 per cent of nitrogen. Apply at the rate of ½–1 oz per sq yd (14–28 g per sq m).

Sulfate of potash This contains about 50 per cent of potash and acts quite rapidly and is noncaustic. Can be used at any time of the growing season. Apply at the rate of ½–1 oz per sq yd (14–28 g per sq m). Muriate of potash, containing about 60 per cent potash, is similar.

Superphosphate For supplying phosphates to plants in the quickest form, this is the fertilizer to use. It is less costly than bonemeal. It should be cultivated into the soil at planting time at rate of 1–3 oz per sq yd (28–84 g per sq m). The amounts of phosphoric acid vary from 16, 20, 32 to 44 per cents.

Wood ashes A source of potash. The percentage varies but about 5 per cent of potash is typical. Use in spring or fall at rate of about 4–6 lb per 100 sq ft (1·8–2·7 kg per 9·3 sq m). Wood ashes can burn when first applied, so do not put on plants in active growth.

3 Compost

In gardening terms, there are two types of compost. The first is the special soil mixture that is made up for the cultivation of a wide range of plants. Then there is the compost we are concerned with here – the finished product, as it were, that results when waste vegetation is collected and allowed to rot. Both kinds are invaluable for soil and crop improvement.

Quite often compost is referred to as humus material. It is, without any doubt, a most important product and is essential if good results are to be expected from your garden, no matter what you are growing. It is something that is easy to provide because most of the ingredients for making compost

A garden can virtually feed itself. All the essential materials for making good compost can be obtained from the plants raised there. Trimmings from the vegetable plot can be used for compost as can leftover kitchen scraps.

Bracken, seaweed, leaves, dead flower heads and other trimmings can all go into the compost heap. Such material is a rich source of chemical nutrients.

actually come from the garden itself.

Any soft material can be used to form compost. This includes hedge trimmings, grass cuttings, trimmings from the vegetable garden, autumn leaves and many waste scraps from the kitchen – for example, tea leaves, peelings, etc. When the waste material is decomposed efficiently it becomes a dark brown, fairly friable mass.

Of course, if it is not made correctly, compost can become a rather nasty evil-smelling pile of slimy material that is pretty useless. In these days of natural manure shortages it is vital that as much compost as possible be made for the garden. Here is how to go about preparing your own.

Making compost

The amount of compost you will be able to make depends on the quantities of basic material you can obtain from your garden. It is surprising how many grass mowings can be collected over the cutting season. This material can form quite a large part of a compost-making scheme. If you have a busy vegetable plot there will be lots of 'bits and pieces' you can gather here, such as leaf trimmings from cabbages, lettuces and Brussels sprouts, and the tops of various root crops such as carrots, turnips and beets.

Then there are the bean and pea growths (haulms, as they are technically called) that can be added to the compost when the crop has been gathered. When you tidy up the garden, cutting off the dead flower heads, for instance, you can add the refuse material to your compost. In the autumn, there is usually a great clearing up effort made when the dead top-growth of plants, especially in the herbaceous borders, is removed. All this can be used to make compost.

Most weeds can also be incorporated. Try to place weeds in the compost before they have made their seeds otherwise you will be sowing more weeds in the compost, and once such compost has been dug in, a

It is amazing how much rich compost material can be obtained from the clippings gathered in a mower's collecting box.

The autumn fall of dead leaves can also be used in the compost heap. Hedge clippings, but not the woody twigs, are another valuable source of compost matter.

large proportion of the weed seeds it contains will grow again.

It is possible that you may be able to obtain other materials for your compost-making. Some bracken and seaweeds are useful but are best used in a moist condition, as they will not rot down easily if too dry. Small amounts of straw can be included too. This should be wet or watered before it is incorporated. Thoroughly made compost should not contain many viable seeds.

There are a few items that should not be used in making compost. These include tough stumps or roots, and bits of plastic. Very hard prunings or trimmings from hedges are not suitable either, as they do not decompose well. Nor should lawn cuttings from grass recently treated with a weedkiller be used.

Material for compost-making should be placed in a compost area or heap in order to rot down. The success of a compost pile depends to a great extent on the way in which the heap is made and contained. The use of special compost bins or containers is thoroughly recommended. These not only hold your compost heap neatly – this is very important in smaller gardens – they also encourage more efficient decomposition.

63

A simple compost bin can be made from wire netting attached to stakes.

Compost containers The material in a compost heap is broken down by bacteria and many other organisms that will only work well if there is adequate air, moisture, nitrogen, non-acid conditions and plenty of warmth. The modern compost bin is specially designed to promote the best conditions for the activity of bacteria. Holes in the sides of the container ensure adequate air penetration.

Of course, you can always make your own enclosure and this is what most gardeners do, using a portion of snow fencing, chicken wire or boards. The simplest container consists of wire or plastic mesh netting supported at four corners by strong posts driven into the ground. The smallest practical and efficient size is a little over 3 ft × 3 ft (1 m × 1 m). Usually a heap that is some 7 ft (2 m) in length and about the same in depth is the best size.

A compost heap should have a base made of coarse matter that permits proper drainage.

The first layer of material about 9 in (23 cm) deep is then laid in the bin.

The next layer is made up of manure or a rich fertilizer that serves to accelerate the decaying process.

The 'sandwich' effect is achieved by adding additional layers of plant matter and accelerator.

Avoid placing your compost heap in a low-lying damp location. Good drainage is important. Avoid deep shade or a place where there is no free movement of air, for here stagnant conditions may prevail. On the other hand, a place directly in the sun will cause the material to dry up too quickly and poor rotting will result.

Building the heap No matter what type of container is used, always start the heap with the coarsest or roughest materials so that they form a natural drainage system for the rest. This material will rot eventually but initially will do its work well. After this your heap is built up 'sandwich fashion' – that is to say, a layer of waste material followed by an application of a special compost accelerator and so on.

The accelerator is a special preparation that encourages a more rapid decomposition of the waste and ensures a better and sweet-smelling end product. The depth of

each layer should be about 9 in (20 cm).

Place the material lightly on the heap – ideally, scatter it over the surface with a fork. Also, try to balance the material so that the weight distribution is fairly even. This will prevent heavier areas from settling down more than lightly loaded ones. Also, decomposition will be encouraged if a balanced heap is made up.

The other big advantage with the use of special accelerators is that there is no need to turn the compost heap to ensure even and thorough decomposition.

Natural forms of accelerator include fresh manure – chicken, horse or farmyard manure. This can be applied on each 9 in

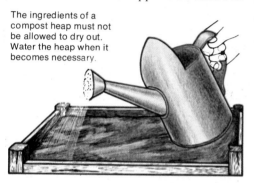

The ingredients of a compost heap must not be allowed to dry out. Water the heap when it becomes necessary.

Quicker decomposition in the heap is obtained by scattering an accelerator in with the plant material.

(20 cm) layer of material. Such a heap will need turning to ensure thorough rotting down. This can be done after some six to eight weeks. Throw the material to one side, making sure that the outer sections are placed towards the middle of the new heap to rot down better. Keep the heap tidy and compact by retaining it in a wire enclosure – the original one can be used.

You can make up your own compost accelerator by applying ½ oz per sq yd (14 g per sq m) of sulfate of ammonia to the surface, then covering it over with about 1½ in (4 cm) of soil. This should be done after each 9 in (20 cm)-deep layer of material has been laid down on the heap.

Rotting down will be much quicker in the warmer summer and early autumn months than in winter and early spring. A heap started in early spring will be ready to use

some time in the summer. With a good accelerator, many heaps of soft material will be well rotted after seven weeks. A heap started in summer should be ready in the late autumn. For spring use, a winter heap can be made up.

Keep an eye on the layers as they are built up. If they look rather dry, give them a light watering, using a fine nozzle on the hose or on the spout of a watering can.

If the weather is exceptionally wet, it is a

This specially designed container has removable sides.

65

Both light and heavy soils will benefit by digging in compost. This helps to retain moisture and aerates the soil.

heap has rotted down well, the bin can be removed and a new heap started.

The benefits of compost

Prepared compost will do many things for your garden. In the first place it is a soil conditioner. Light soils tend to dry out quickly, especially in the summer. If plenty of compost is dug in when the ground is being prepared in the winter or spring, and at any time when beds are being made ready for sowing or planting, the compost will act like a sponge and retain valuable moisture for the plants' roots.

Heavy clay soils are those that have their soil particles packed tightly together. If compost is worked in frequently it will help to space out these particles and make the soil easier to work or cultivate. It takes a little time for an improvement to be noticed but it is well worth doing.

Roots Compost also encourages the formation of vigorous roots, which in turn produce a healthy plant, one that is capable of taking in more food and water. Lining the bottom of planting holes or drills with compost is an excellent way to ensure a good start for plants. The larger holes for trees and shrubs can be treated likewise.

good plan to provide a temporary 'roof' over a heap in the form of a sheet of plastic or sheet of corrugated iron to keep off excess water. Some commercial bins or containers have a sort of top or roof. Some also have removable sides so that the progress of the heap can be judged and also so that the contents can be easily removed. When one

Rotted compost matter should be incorporated into the bottom of the trenches made while preparing a planting site, as it provides a source of nutrients.

Compost is ideal as a mulch or dressing along plant rows. It keeps the base of plants and their roots moist.

Quick-growing crops such as lettuce depend on a high moisture content in the soil. The inclusion of compost in the bed preparations for these crops will promote rapid growth, which in turn will result in crisp leaves.

Top dressing Compost is ideal as a mulch or top-dressing around plants or along plant rows. Applied to a depth of about 2 in (5 cm), the covering will reduce water loss from the surface of the soil and also suppress a lot of tiny weed seedlings. For many vegetable crops, mulching with well-rotted compost is an excellent idea. Crops that benefit especially from this system are peas and beans.

Root crops, such as carrots, benefit from a generous layer of compost in their drills at seed-sowing time. The compost retains soil moisture and encourages the formation of first-class tender roots.

Lawns Composted vegetable waste can be used for the preparation of lawn sites if the ground is enriched with the material by forking it in as the soil is cultivated. In light, sandy types of soil, this preparation is vital if the grass roots are to grow strongly and are not to suffer from very bad dehydration during hot weather.

Under glass Where plants are grown under glass – in greenhouses and cold frames – enriching of the soil beds is important, as they tend to dry out more quickly under glass owing to the persistent high temperatures. For pots or other containers that are used for tomato and cucumber cultivation, the compost can be mixed with soil at the rate of one part compost to three parts soil. This, and some basic fertilizers, will produce an excellent growing medium with which to fill the containers.

When preparing soil borders or beds, outdoors or under glass, The same proportion can be used. Wherever the soil is light and tends to dry out badly the compost ingredient can be increased by one part.

This also applies to the use of window boxes and larger containers or tubs for flower displays. The one-to-three mix has proved successful for a wide range of plants when used with fertilizers. (These will be discussed in chapter 4.)

Compost is also useful as a top-dressing for lawns, where it is applied in the autumn or spring. The material is scattered as evenly as possible over the surface of the grass at the rate of a small- to medium-sized barrow load to every 3–4 sq yd (3–4 sq m). Afterwards, the compost is carefully worked or 'rubbed' into the surface with to-and-fro motions using the back of a rake or a stiff brush. A large proportion of the compost will be incorporated in this way and the remainder will gradually be washed in by the rain.

The lawn will benefit from a dressing of compost worked into its surface, especially in sandy soils that tend to dry out rapidly and that tend to be relatively poor in nutrients.

4 Watering

One of the most important gardening operations is watering. A plant must have a regular intake of water in order to grow well. In the case of fruit-bearing crops water is essential in order to swell the fruits.

Watering is vital where plants are being grown under glass and where they cannot benefit from natural rainfall. Plants grown in containers under glass dry out surprisingly rapidly, especially in high temperatures. Without the correct amount of water all plants will suffer, since the nourishment that the plants are obtaining from the soil is in solution. Even cacti and succulents need plenty of water at certain times.

The art of watering Watering is something of an art, because too little will hinder good growth whereas too much can cause the soil to become waterlogged so that the plants' roots do not grow well. Too much water in the ground also cools the temperature and chills the soil, making for very poor plant progress.

If there is any 'golden rule' it is that the gardener should water little and often: the aim should be to keep the soil just nicely moist at all times. Remember that fruit-bearing plants such as tomatoes, cucumbers and melons need increasing amounts of water as their fruits swell.

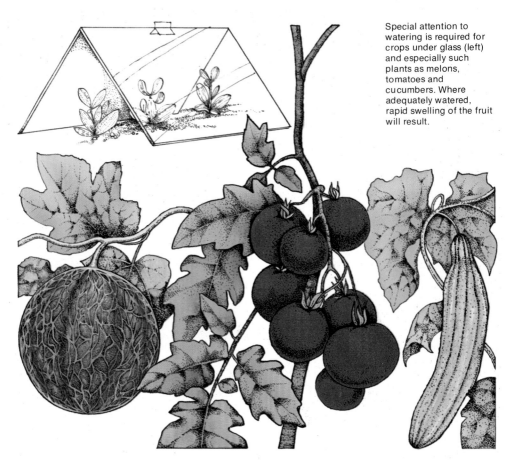

Special attention to watering is required for crops under glass (left) and especially such plants as melons, tomatoes and cucumbers. Where adequately watered, rapid swelling of the fruit will result.

In the greenhouse a good test for watering requirements is to pick up a pot and give it a tap. If there is a ringing note the pot needs watering. A dull ring, on the other hand, means that the soil is wet enough. This system applies only to the old (clay) type of pot. Unfortunately plastic ones provide no such practical clues.

However, a well-watered pot always feels heavier than a dry one, so this could be a fair means of gauging the condition of plants in plastic pots. It is now possible to purchase a special moisture indicator from your local garden shop or garden center. The probe of this device is pushed into the soil in the pot, and straightaway it will indicate whether conditions are wet, moist or dry. The device works from tiny batteries that will last many months. This is a very handy gadget, especially for house plants, which need constant checking for their watering requirements.

In the home the dry atmosphere of a

A moisture indicator (below) will reveal the moisture level of the soil at a glance.

In the warmth of the home, stand pot plants (above) on top of a water-soaked gravel bed in order to give them more moisture.

heated room quickly dries out the soil in plant containers. One method of overcoming this is to place plant containers in trays or dishes filled with small pebbles or gravel. Run in some water so that the level is just below the stones. If the pot is carefully placed on the stones its base will not rest in the water causing the soil to become water-logged. However, the air around the container will be kept cool and moist and will provide a better growing atmosphere for the plant.

Methods of applying water

The two most common methods of watering are by hose and by watering-can. For indoor use a smaller-capacity can with a long spout is much easier to handle. Some gardeners use their thumbs to control the force of water from a hose, but it is better to have a nozzle that can easily be turned to provide a spray or jet of water. It should never be so forceful that it washes soil from the roots.

With special connectors, a permanent hose system can be laid out for watering large gardens. Watering points can be attached so that all parts of the garden are watered at once.

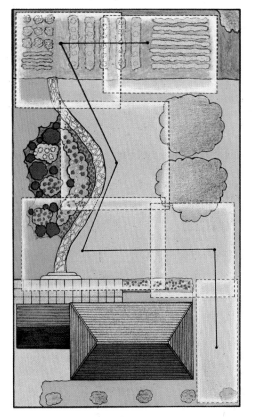

To conserve soil moisture, black polyethylene sheeting can be used as a mulch. Slits are cut for the plants to come through.

Sprinklers For watering large areas, such as a lawn or vegetable garden, sprinklers are a necessity. These range from the very simple stick-in-the-ground designs with a central hole through which the water is emitted in a spray pattern, to the more sophisticated adjustable sprinklers that move their spraying bar from side to side and whose direction is controlled by a switch system. The latter can be 'dialed' or set to water certain patterns. Their greatest advantage is that application can be controlled with accuracy.

Various kinds of irrigation systems using freeze-proof plastic pipes for above or below ground exist. Quite a complex layout can be quickly set up to reach various watering points in the garden. There, a tap can be attached so that only short lengths of hose are required to water any part of the garden.

Watering requirements can be reduced if the soil around plants is mulched. Rotted manure or waste vegetation from the compost heap can be used for mulching, applying it over beds or around plants to a depth of at least 2 in (5 cm). This prevents a lot of water evaporation from the surface of the soil. Black polyethylene sheets are also used for the same purpose. Turning a little soil over the edges as the sheets are laid down will hold them in place.

Watering under glass In the green-house, in gardens, and in frames automatic watering devices can play a useful role, especially during vacations. A simple system is one known as capillary matting. Capillary mats are capable of absorbing and retaining a considerable amount of water. If laid on the benching or staging with pot plants standing on top, each plant will be able to draw up its own water requirement.

The mat is kept supplied with water via a tank fitted with a simple float device. This piece of equipment is attached to the water trough, into which one end of the mat is placed. The mat absorbs water from the trough. To be completely automatic, the water tank can be attached to the main water supply. The floating ball valve in the tank will always keep it topped up with water.

For another simple system, a perforated hose or small-bore hose is used, fitted with an adjustable nozzle that can be regulated to provide a drip of water to plants in pots or in soil borders. This device can also be connected to a water-supply tank.

In a frame or among vegetables a trickle irrigation line with adjustable nozzles can be laid out and connected to a hose. The tap can be turned to slightly open to maintain a trickle of water to the system. Shading glass, whether in a greenhouse, or frame will reduce the amount of evaporation from the soil.

Watering times

Water should not be applied during the heat of the day. It is far better to water in the evenings or early in the morning before the sun is high. Make sure, too, that the outdoor soil is *thoroughly* watered. It may look wet and dark, but it may well be quite dry below the surface if you scratch down a bit.

Newly-bedded plants should be well watered, especially larger plants such as trees and shrubs. A good idea is to presoak the planting hole a few hours before placing the tree or shrub in position. As light soils tend to dry out more rapidly than others, they in particular *must* receive plenty of water.

In the open garden it is possible to apply a liquid feed at the same time as watering. This is accomplished by using a simple diluter attached to the end of the hose. The concentrated feed is put into the diluter and as the main flow of water passes through the hose the correctly diluted liquid is emitted from the end as a fan-like spray.

Capillary matting and a self-regulating water-supply device will provide an automatic watering system that is ideal for the greenhouse.

5 Pruning

Why do we need to prune? Basically, there are three very good reasons. The first is to produce the best possible fruits or flowers. The second is to maintain a tree or bush in good shape, and the third is to keep the plant as healthy as possible by removing dead or diseased growth.

There are, of course, several other advantages with pruning. It will keep a tree or shrub within predetermined bounds and will also maintain the attractive shapes that are so essential for fruit trees grown as cordons or fans.

The simplest forms of pruning are carried out purely to keep a tree or shrub in good shape. However, when fruit trees are pruned it is essential that certain rules be followed, as each type has its own special requirements. If these are not followed closely, a loss of fruit may result, simply because the branches that would have borne that fruit have been cut off.

Raspberry canes that have fruited (dark outlines) should be cut right back to soil level. In general, cut canes back after harvesting. Cut everbearers that fruit in summer, autumn and again the next spring, only after the second crop has been harvested.

Pruning is used to train such trees as this cordon apple. Unwanted shoots are pruned back to maintain the desired shape.

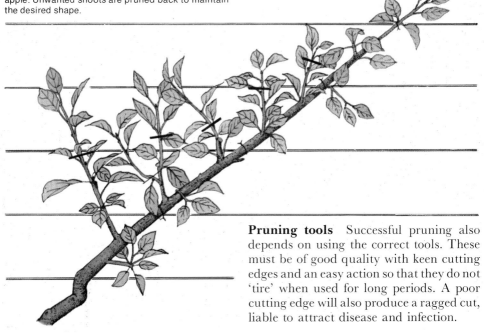

Pruning tools Successful pruning also depends on using the correct tools. These must be of good quality with keen cutting edges and an easy action so that they do not 'tire' when used for long periods. A poor cutting edge will also produce a ragged cut, liable to attract disease and infection.

There are two types of pruning shears. One has a so-called 'anvil cut'. Here the pruner has a sharp upper blade that comes down onto a bottom flat-edged blade. Pruners of this kind that have a slight sliding action are particularly good, as they produce a natural, knife-like cut. The other type of pruner cuts with a scissors action. The two blades cross over each other as the cut is made. Both upper and lower blades have sharp cutting edges.

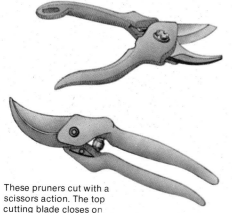

These pruners cut with a scissors action. The top cutting blade closes on the bottom anvil.

For taller trees and shrubs it is a good plan to have a special set of long-reach pruners. These have long tubular or flat metal shafts extending their handle, with a rugged cutting blade at the top. The blade is connected to a handle in the base of the shaft by a cable or rod. Some of the more sophisticated designs have extendable handles and can reach up high into a tree.

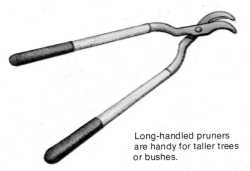

Long-handled pruners are handy for taller trees or bushes.

For tough wood, lopping pruners should be used.

There may come a time in a tree's or shrub's life when some large, tough branches must be removed. This is frequently necessary in neglected gardens. For this type of pruning special cutters, or 'loppers', will have to be used. These have short, thick handles and very strong blades. Some have a special action that gives the user extra cutting power.

Special saws are available for cutting thick branches.

For the removal of very large limbs or branches a saw will be required. The best ones have specially-shaped handles – many of them of tubular construction with a bow shape for easy handling.

Successful pruning depends on an appreciation of what a good pruning cut is and the ability to identify various types of buds, especially on fruit trees and bushes.

Pruning cuts These must always be made close to a selected bud with the slope or angle of the cut pointing away from it. The cut should never be made so that it slopes into the bud as this can cause moisture to lodge there and rot to set in.

Buds The difference between a fruit bud and a growth bud must also be recognized. The former is quite plump whereas the latter tends to be thinner and often lies a lot closer to the stem it grows on. The fruit bud is responsible for producing the blossom that in turn becomes the fruit. The growth bud, on the other hand, makes new shoots or growths and thus extends the size of the tree or bush.

Other pruning terms Leaders and laterals are two terms with which you should familiarize yourself before pruning. A leader, as its name implies, is a leading

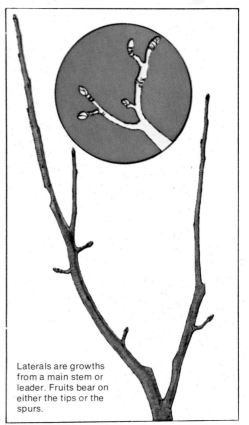

Laterals are growths from a main stem or leader. Fruits bear on either the tips or the spurs.

Bud identification: Plump buds (left) are the fruit buds. Thinner, pointed ones (right) are growth buds. The growth buds often lie closer to the stem.

shoot or branch of a tree or bush. A lateral is the growth or shoot that forms from the side of a main branch.

There are also the terms spur and tip. Some varieties of plant bear their fruits on short shoots or growths called spurs. Quite often, these spurs appear in clusters of more than one. Examples of spur bearers are 'Starkspur Lodi', 'Skyspur', 'Miller', 'Sturdy Spur Delicious', and 'Starkspur Winesap'. These varieties are all available as dwarf trees.

Although some plants bear their fruit on spurs, there are many that have their fruits at the tips of shoots that have been made the previous summer. These are the tip-bearing plants.

Ornamental trees and shrubs sometimes raise doubts too, but these are dealt with separately in the following pages.

Shrubs

Usually, shrubs need little pruning, except to maintain their pleasing shape or to remove dead or diseased wood. Where a neglected garden has been taken over, it may well be necessary to cut back shrubs quite ruthlessly if a lot of weak, straggly growth has been produced. The centers of the shrubs will most likely be very over-crowded and some drastic thinning in the area will have to be carried out. Crossing and badly-placed branches will need to be removed.

It is useful to know that some shrubs produce their flowers on new growths and others on the previous year's wood. In the case of the former, spring treatment is best, cutting all the previous year's growth back to three buds from the base.

For the latter type of shrub, pruning is carried out only after flowering. Seek out the branches that have just borne their flowers and cut back to about three buds from the base. There are some shrubs, such as clematis, that need 'sorting out' as far as their rather complex growth is concerned. This plant can get out of hand over the years unless the growths are cut back. For the large-flowered hybrids spring treatment is required, and for those varieties

Spring is the time for pruning climbing roses (below left). Strong shoots need cutting back by a quarter. Floribunda roses (above) are also pruned in spring.

that flower twice in a season, cut back lightly after the first bloom of flowers has finished.

Another rambling type of shrub is the wisteria. In July, cut back side growths to six leaves, and in August shorten them again to two or three buds.

Roses

New roses Plants that require no attention immediately after planting are ramblers, climbers and the species types. Old roses should also be left alone for the first year.

For others, such as the hybrid teas and the perpetuals, remove any damaged canes or tips. More drastic pruning is rarely required since the objective is to get the plant established and productive. The removal of too much top growth will weaken the plant.

75

Established roses Shorten the young shoots of hybrid teas to four buds. Medium-vigor shoots should be cut back to two buds. Do the work in spring, late spring being better in cold areas.

With floribundas study the different types of growth on each plant, distinguishing between strong-, medium- and weak-vigor growths. For strong growths, cut back to about six buds; for medium growths cut to four buds, and for the weaker ones prune to one or two buds. The latter treatment should encourage the production of sturdier shoots later in the year. Prune in spring.

Prune polyantha roses in spring also. Cut out all weak or thin shoots. Cut back other stems to about half their length.

Climbing roses must have all their old or diseased growths cut out in spring. Then cut the young branches back by approximately two-thirds their length. Prune the climbing 'sports', as they are called, in spring or late spring, cutting strong shoots back by a quarter, medium growths by a half, and weak ones by at least two-thirds in order to encourage stronger growths.

Prune shrub roses from autumn through to spring in mild climates. Elsewhere wait until spring. Thin out badly-placed growth and dead or diseased shoots at this time too.

Tree roses usually require very little pruning. For the most part pruning can be confined to the removal of dead or diseased branches and of any growths that are so badly placed that they spoil the shape or appearance of the tree. An open center to a tree – especially the round-headed types – should be the aim. For this reason some thinning out of the central branches may be required from time to time.

Trees

Deciduous trees (those that lose their foliage in the winter) should be pruned after their leaves have fallen. Evergreens (those that do not lose their leaves) should be pruned, if necessary, in spring.

Climbing roses (above) should have old and diseased wood cut out and thin wood removed. Make all cuts back to a good bud. Remove any old flower stems.

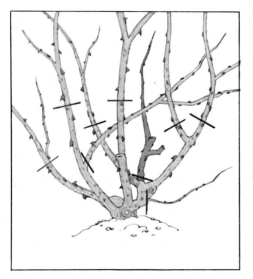

Cutting lines show how to prune an established hybrid tea rose (left). The extent of cutting depends on the vigor of each shoot. Remove dead and diseased wood.

76

6 Weeds and weed control

It is a great pity that weeds grow just as well as other plants in the garden. In fact, many weeds grow a lot *better*, and thrive in even the poorest growing conditions. Because weeds grow so prolifically, careful organization is needed so that they can be controlled with the minimum of effort and time.

Unless weeds are promptly dealt with, they will quickly seed themselves, thus adding to the misery of keeping them out of the garden. Weeds are generally vigorous

Care must be taken when applying weedkillers. They can be sprinkled onto vegetable plots by watering can or spread on lawns by special spreaders.

plants and will quickly smother crops if allowed to grow. Of course, they vie with other plants for food and moisture, often to the detriment of these plants, and ruin the garden's general appearance.

Weedkillers

Fortunately, there exists a wide range of chemicals that, if used sensibly, will greatly reduce the effort required in the battle against weeds.

A number of sensible and important precautions must be taken when using weedkillers. Keep them well away from children and animals. Always follow the instructions to the letter and always wash out containers thoroughly after use. Never use the same watering-can for ordinary watering as well as weedkillers. An *old* can, and one marked as such, should be kept especially for this purpose.

The use of weedkillers can be so complicated and fraught with risk for surrounding vegetation that many gardeners are returning to traditional methods of control: mulching and cultivation.

Chemicals do remain useful for eliminating weeds from lawns and paths and driveways, although in the latter case care must be taken that chemical run-off does not reach nearby growth and kill it too.

Lawn weedkillers are usually in dry form and applied with fertilizers by a spreader. Wax bars and spot weedkillers, such as the Killer Kane, can be obtained.

Lawn weeds

Chickweed This annual weed reproduces by seed. It has tiny heart-shaped leaves under 1 in (3 cm) in length. Use mecoprop or, for a recently-made lawn, a weedkiller specifically recommended for new lawns.

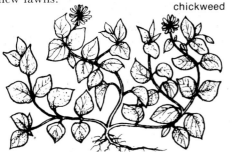

chickweed

Cinquefoil This is a perennial – in other words, a plant that continues to live for many years and that, in many cases, flowers time after time. Cinquefoil has a five-leaf pattern of a serrated form. Flowers are yellow with tiny reddish stamens. Cinquefoil seeds itself. Several applications of mecoprop should keep it in check.

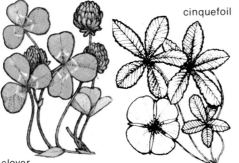

cinquefoil

clover

Clover Many lawns look lovely and green from a distance even in drought – but a closer inspection often reveals the fact that most of the growth is clover. This plant is a perennial with a three-leaf pattern formation (occasionally four-leaved). Clover has creeping stems and so spreads very rapidly. It has white ball-like flowers and also seeds itself. Use mecoprop or dicamba to control clover, and feed the lawn with a high-nitrogen fertilizer in the spring.

Creeping buttercup A perennial that, as its name implies, spreads quite rapidly by its creeping stems. It also seeds itself. It has triangular, serrated leaves and bright yellow flowers. Treat it by watering on a 2,4–D mixture. Dicamba is also used.

creeping buttercup

Buckhorn Perennial found in many lawns that have been uncared for. It has tapering leaves and rather insignificant brownish heads. Buckhorn seeds itself. Control it by using mecoprop or 2,4–D.

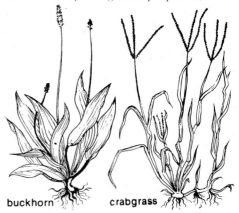

buckhorn   crabgrass

Crabgrass An annual grass weed common over most of the country, and a special nuisance in lawns. It is a creeping grass with rather wide blades. The best control is a pre-emergent chemical to prevent the seeds from germinating. Siduron (available under trade name Tupersan) has proved effective if applied at the right time in spring and used according to directions.

Dandelion This perennial has serrated leaves and bright yellow flower heads. The plant reproduces itself freely by seeds. Even if a new plant is cut down, its fleshy tap root will soon produce a new growth. Repeated application of mecoprop or 2,4–D should be effective in keeping down dandelions.

speedwell

dandelion

Pearlwort This perennial is a very common invader of lawns. It seeds a great deal, has very thin narrow leaves on spreading stems and tiny yellow flower heads. Use mecoprop, dicamba or silvex to control it.

Speedwell This is a perennial weed often found in lawns. It has pretty, tiny blue flowers and small, heart-shaped foliage. It takes root along its long stems and is generally quite fine in growth. Apply DCPA (a trade name is Dacthal) and use according to instructions.

Wild garlic or onion Also know as field garlic, this bulbous perennial can disfigure lawns with its tufts of typical onion-like leaves. Seeds itself and is also easily spread by its underground bulbs. Use 2,4–D with a wetting agent as a spray or use a wax bar such as the Ortho Weed Bar. A very persistent weed.

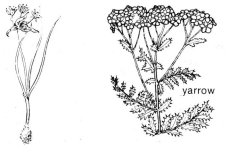

yarrow

wild garlic

Yarrow Another perennial, this plant has ferny-type leaves and tall heads of tiny white flowers. Several applications of mecoprop will control it. Sulfate of ammonia feedings will also help reduce infestations of this weed. Dicamba can also be used.

pearlwort

79

Flower and vegetable plot weeds

While you have been keeping an eye on your lawn weeds, other weeds have probably been settling in elsewhere in the garden. Let us take a look at the more common types that you may discover in your flower and vegetable plots.

Bindweed   A really nasty weed that can really take over a garden, bindweed climbs to fantastic lengths and smothers plants with its heart-shaped leaves. It can be recognized by its trumpet-shaped white flowers. Bindweed is a perennial that comes up early each year. It is easily spread by its fast-rooting underground stems. Concentrate the weedkiller application around groups of plants. Spot treatment, on the other hand, is a somewhat tedious but very effective method of attack. To spot-treat, take a paintbrush and dab concentrated weedkiller onto it. Use 2,4–D for this.

couch grass

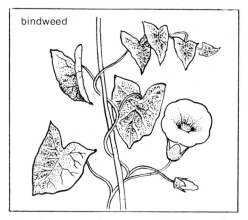
bindweed

Dock   The broad-leaved dock, which is a perennial, has long spikes of brown heads. It seeds only too easily. If the long tap root is cut off but left in the ground, this too will grow again and continue the infestation. Take your time and patiently spot-treat the weed. For large infestations, however, it is better to apply a watering or spray of dichlobenil, dicamba or silvex. Spot treatment should be done with 2,4–D.

Couch or quack grass   This is another nasty perennial weed that is difficult to deal with if it is allowed to get out of control. It makes life very difficult for a gardener, especially if he is taking over a new or neglected garden. It has broad, pointed leaves and green heads. Use dalapon to control it. Quack grass also has masses of creeping stems that can easily be rooted out before planting. Deep digging and then forking out and burning of roots is another method of dealing with this weed.

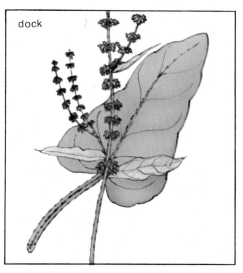
dock

Groundsel An annual weed that spreads by its seeds, groundsel has serrated foliage and bunches of yellow flower heads. There are many types of groundsel, which are all members of the Compositae family, also known as the sunflower family. Groundsel grows on dry plains and hillsides, particularly throughout the mountains of California and Oregon, where it blooms in the autumn. It is spread by the wind, and can be dealt with by applications of dichlobenil.

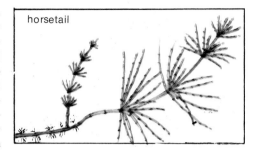
horsetail

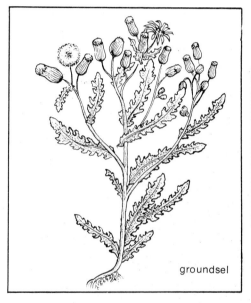
groundsel

Horsetail Another quite nasty perennial weed with fir-tree-like growths that start off as closed spikes of brownish shoots, horsetail is a non-flowering weed which gets its name because of its resemblance to a horse's tail. It spreads quickly by its root system. Usually growing on dry land, horsetail is able to spread downhill rapidly and is very difficult to eradicate. Repeated applications with dichlobenil will check it, although it is a very difficult weed to deal with and unfortunately there is no foolproof answer.

Nettle This plant is a real nuisance. Not only is it a perennial that seeds easily, but it has stinging oval leaves. Several applications of 2,4–D or 2,4,5–T are effective control measures. A spring application is always a good idea.

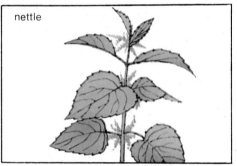
nettle

Oxalis A perennial that soon spreads by means of the tiny bulbs at its base, oxalis also seeds a lot. It has clover-like leaves and tiny pinkish flowers. Try 2,4–D plus silvex, following directions on container. Be careful when digging over the soil, for that's when the little bulbs break off and scatter. Try to remove it with surrounding soil.

oxalis

81

Poison-ivy This woody vine, with its compound leaves composed of three leaflets, is widespread over the eastern half of the country. A close relative, Pacific poison-oak, grows on the West Coast. Both are easily spread to home gardens by birds. All parts of the plants can cause a painful skin rash. Eradication is difficult. Both ammonium sulfamate (Ammate) and 2,4–D plus silvex are recommended.

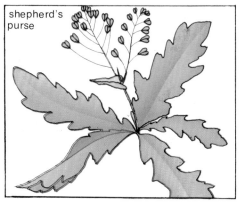
shepherd's purse

poison ivy

Shepherd's purse This plant is an annual with deep-toothed leaves and tall greenish heads. It seeds all too easily. Apply successive treatments of dichlobenil (trade name Casaron) to control it.

Plantain A perennial plant with broad leaves and spikes of brown heads, plantain seeds easily. It is controlled by mecoprop or by using 2,4–D.

thistle

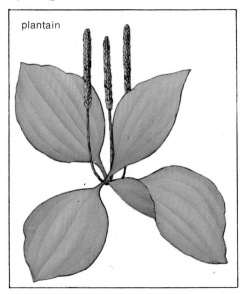
plantain

Thistle There are various types of perennial thistle, and they can be a nuisance in the garden, for they not only spread by seed, but also by vigorous creeping underground stems. Thistles have long serrated, prickly leaves and reddish or purple flowers. They should never be allowed to flower and roots should be removed when digging. Control with dichlobenil.

7 Controlling pests and diseases

One of the 'wars' all gardeners have to wage from time to time is against the pests and diseases that can attack your plants. The type of attack and its severity will vary considerably from season to season.

There are several pests and diseases that can be termed 'common' to the garden. It is well to be able to identify them early so that the best methods of control can be put into practice. Most pests and diseases you'll come across will be found in this book under the crops they may attack.

Spraying There is a lot to be said for taking precautionary measures in good time – even before an attack has begun. A regular spraying program can prevent

A powerful mist or spray is needed for trees so that a good penetration is assured.

A hand sprayer is useful when spraying smaller plants such as rose bushes.

troubles. With some types of preparation that are assimilated by plants early spraying can fortify the plants and make them reasonably resistant to attacks.

Successful control of pests and diseases also depends on spraying or dusting when conditions are favorable. Choose a windless day so that the material being applied is not blown all over the place. Care must be taken to reduce the drift of spray or dust to a minimum to prevent contamination of food crops (and your neighbors' gardens).

83

Garden flowers

1 Floral display

For many home gardeners the highest achievement is a garden full of flowers – a riot of floral color from spring to autumn, planted more or less according to the whim of the moment. Herbaceous borders, rock gardens, trees, shrubs and other permanent features all make their contribution.

Annuals and other plants, assisted by spring bulbs, raised and planted out twice a year in beds and borders, will produce the

A riotous mixture of colorful summer-blooming flowers for the herbaceous border here dazzlingly combines with flowering rock plants.

most colorful displays – the theme of this book. There is, however, a vast difference between a tasteful picture and the mere jumble of vivid floral color that random planting will produce.

Enthusiasm for shapes, colors and scents is not enough in itself. The importance of plant form, and of the shape, color and texture of foliage should not be overlooked. These aspects can help to modulate the

Above left: A more modest mixture of flowering plants can be equally pleasing if it is planned with care.

A cheerful bed of attractively arranged spring flowers puts an end to winter's gloom and heralds the warm days ahead.

Bedding plants graded in size and in contrasting colors relieve an otherwise austere design.

sheer brilliance of the blooms, and make possible tasteful arrays in which the different types of flower complement each other.

This can only be achieved by choosing good, healthy plants, creating for them the right setting in beds and borders that harmonize with the rest of the garden, and caring for them properly.

It is hoped that this book will help all gardeners to practice this popular form of gardening with understanding and inspiration. Better, more subtle effects can result from the same amount of effort and outlay (sometimes even less), yet will provide infinitely greater satisfaction. Working in this way, and knowing exactly what effects can be achieved, the gardener will be rewarded in ample measure by the results.

2 Making and preparing beds and borders

Sensible beds and borders in proportion to the surrounds and other features of the garden are the first essential. A few large beds are better than numerous small ones. They allow a greater range of plants to be grown without producing either a very flat or a top-heavy picture and usually a much better effect is obtained, often with fewer plants. After-care is generally easier, too.

Avoid making beds of intricate shapes

like those shown here. They add to the difficulties of preparing, planting, edging round, and mowing between, and produce no better effect than beds of simple outline.

Also, avoid narrow ribbon borders of 24 in (60 cm) or less wide skirting a path or lawn, or in front of the house. However planted, they will only emphasize straight lines; if a few plants make poor growth, the borders will look as if they are full of gaps, and they will also tend to dry out very quickly in times of drought.

When one display is over, the old plants should be removed as quickly as possible and the beds dug over the depth of a spade. Well-rotted farmyard manure, peat moss or compost can be incorporated at the same time, in fall for heavy and medium soils, in spring for those of a light, open nature.

Rake over the soil thoroughly several times to obtain a fine, level surface for planting. A light firming of the soil helps to eliminate air pockets, but excessive tramping of heavy clay or adobe-type soils can turn them into a cement-like texture.

Beds and borders should be finished slightly higher than the surrounding ground but should never be mounded up. The finished level after treading and raking should be concave, sloping down gradually to just below the level of the turf or path. It should never be left like a plateau with steeply sloping sides, otherwise the soil round the edges may erode.

Intricate shaped beds make for hard labor and do not necessarily add to a garden's beauty. Simple designs are usually best.

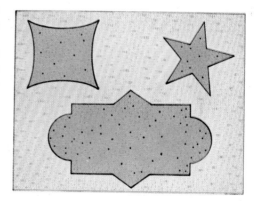

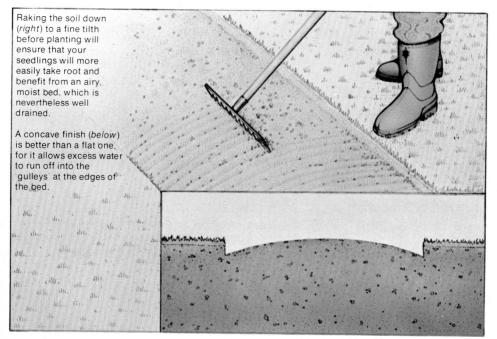

Raking the soil down (*right*) to a fine tilth before planting will ensure that your seedlings will more easily take root and benefit from an airy, moist bed, which is nevertheless well drained.

A concave finish (*below*) is better than a flat one, for it allows excess water to run off into the 'gulleys' at the edges of the bed.

3 Raising your own plants

A small greenhouse is valuable but not vital.

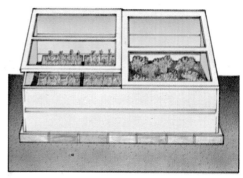

A cold frame is needed to harden off the plants.

Glass on flat or edge-side-up bricks makes a useful temporary frame.

Cuttings can be rooted and seedlings can be raised on a windowsill.

Anyone can raise at least some of the plants they require and thereby save some expense, and often disappointment, of purchased plants.

With the aid of a small greenhouse or a lean-to conservatory attached to the house, one can raise a wide selection of plants, provided these temporary occupants are not deprived of light by the other, more permanent plants.

A cold frame is essential for hardening off

plants. Even a knock-up frame constructed of boards nailed together or loose bricks with a plastic-covered sash can be invaluable. Frames should be placed in a sunny position.

Cuttings of bedding geraniums, fuchsias, and other plants can be rooted in a small propagating case and grown on a windowsill. Marigolds, asters, alyssum and other plants that do not need to be sown until March can be raised in boxes. Turn them

90

round each day to achieve balanced growth, eventually transferring them to the cold frame to harden off. If a sunny window is lacking, fluorescent lights equipped with special plant-growing tubes can be installed.

Suitable pans, pots and boxes will be required to accommodate plants, and compost in which to grow them. Rich seed and potting composts can be bought ready mixed or you can use a soilless compost, i.e. peat moss and vermiculite with nutrients added.

Put some suitable roughage over the bottom of each receptacle to assist drainage, and fill to the rim with compost.

Press down lightly with the fingertips and level off.

Lightly firm to just below the rim with a leveling board or an empty pot.

Stand receptacles in water before sowing and allow to drain off. Sift a little fine compost over the surface if fine seeds are being sown. Scatter seeds very thinly over the surface. Large pelleted seeds may be spaced out separately.

Sift sufficient fine soil over the seeds to just cover them, and lightly press down. Leave very fine seeds uncovered. Cover with glass or plastic, and shade until seeds germinate. Seedlings must be given plenty of light as soon as they germinate.

Prick out about 2½ in (6 cm) each way in other boxes as soon as large enough to handle. Lightly firm each seedling with forefinger and dibber. Handle by the seed leaves, never the stem, which is easily dam-

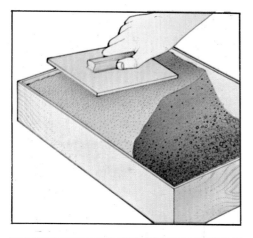

Left: First layer the bottom of the seed box with coarse material from the compost heap, then fill it to the brim with compost. Tamp down and smooth off.

Below left: Sow the seeds thinly in rows over the fine surface of the compost. Space pelleted seeds further apart. Cover both with a fine layer of soil.

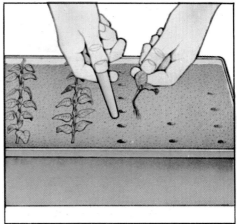

Above: To prick out seedlings successfully, pick them up carefully by the leaves to avoid damaging the delicate stems, insert the roots gently into holes prepared at regular intervals and press them gently in with the fingertips.

Above: Trim off the stem if you wish to make preparing the cutting easier but ensure that the main cut is made below a node to prevent rotting.

Below: Insert the cutting a reasonable distance apart in pots of peat and sand compost.

Above: Dahlia cuttings are best taken with the heel of the old stem.

Below: When the cuttings have rooted, pot them individually into separate pots.

aged. Lightly tap box to level the surface. Water in and keep as close to the light as possible.

Take cuttings of such plants as fuchsias, zonal and ivy-leaved pelargoniums, coleus, begonias and impatiens from plants in the beds at the end of August. Use a compost of 2 parts peat and 1 part sharp sand, and root under a propagating case in a greenhouse or on a shady windowsill. The pelargoniums do not need a propagating case and should be given very little water until

rooted. Give the young plants full light and the minimum of heat during the winter. Pot off separately into small pots after the turn of the year using a rich potting or a suitable soilless compost. Pinch if necessary to obtain bushy plants and harden off by transferring to a cold frame in spring.

To obtain dahlia cuttings, cover old tubers with peat or soil, water and give heat to start them into growth in spring. Take the cuttings with a heel of the old stem and root in a shaded propagating case.

Wallflower and forget-me-not seed can be sown outside in shallow drills, about 10 in (24 cm) apart, in a prepared seed-bed in late May and June. Pansies, English daisies, foxglove and sweet William are best sown in boxes at about the same time and germinated in a cold frame. Polyantha and most other hardy primroses should be sown in April and also need a cold frame for germination, transplanting into boxes and hardening off as for summer bedding plants.

As soon as they are large enough, plant out the young plants for the summer 10–12 in (25–30 cm) apart, in rows about 12 in (30 cm) apart on any spare piece of ground or corner where they will get full sun. Polyantha and other kinds of primroses can be planted in a more shaded position. Water in well and keep free from weeds. Daisies, pansies and other seedlings can be transplanted into larger flats if spare ground is not available.

Later, lift them carefully and plant in the beds and borders in the autumn when the summer bedding plants have finished flowering.

Polyantha and most other primroses are

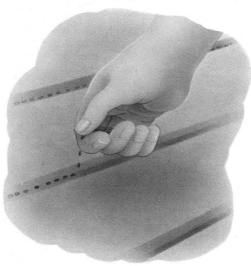

Sow spring bedding plants in shallow drills in the open.

perennials and last for years. When they have finished flowering, lift carefully with a fork, remove all old flowering stems and carefully pull them apart into single crowns, each with some root attached. Plant out as many of the best crowns as required on a shady piece of ground for the summer, and make sure they do not lack water at any time.

After flowering, propagate polyantha and primroses by dividing the roots.

4 Purchasing plants

It is not usually safe to set out summer bedding annuals before all chance of frost is past. Plants are rarely on sale in garden centers before this time. If a frost threatens – and weather reports usually carry such warnings – protect the plants overnight with newspaper layers.

Today home gardeners everywhere can look forward to buying a great variety of summer plants that are well-grown and easy to transplant into the open ground or special containers or planters. Among the available plants are petunia in a wide array of colors and types, marigold, zinnia, impa-tiens, coleus, ageratum, snapdragon, wax begonia, China aster, cosmos and many, many more. Containers include individual peat pots, in which case both pot and plant are set in the ground, or lightweight fiber, plastic or compartmentalized peat flats.

Plants should be set out reasonably soon after purchase to prevent their growth from becoming root-bound or stunted. Many plants, such as petunia, sweet alyssum, French marigold and *Phlox drummondii*, will be in flower. Pinching or snipping off the blooms will encourage new, bushy growth with more flowers.

5 Planting

The outer row excepted, slightly irregular staggered spacing is better than precise planting on the square system in straight rows or concentric circles. It is easier and quicker, and bare soil is not so obvious if the plants do not make their full growth.

Distances apart should be about 8–10 in (20–25 cm) each way for the dwarf edging plants; 12–14 in (30–35 cm) for salvias, petunias, intermediate antirrhinums, nicotiana and others of medium stature; 16–18 in (40–45 cm) for African marigolds, bedding geraniums, celosia, annual gloriosa daisies and the taller zinnias; and 24 in (60 cm) or more for bedding dahlias. Tulips and narcissus bulbs that are to grow up through forget-me-nots, etc., need be no closer than 14 in (35 cm) each way.

If the ground is dry, water thoroughly some hours before planting. Plant at the correct depth, being careful not to plant too shallow. Firm well by hand and/or the handle of the trowel, and level out the soil between plants as you go. Be sure peat pots do not protrude above the soil surface.

Water in thoroughly, preferably individually, using a watering can for small gardens, or a fine mist from the hose nozzle, avoiding treading on the beds. Water again as necessary until the plants are established. If the whole of the bed is watered, as the surface starts to dry, stir lightly to halt evaporation.

Above: Irregularly staggered spacing of the plants gives better coverage and promotes a fuller effect.

Below: An extension to the spout of the watering-can saves treading on the beds.

6 After-care

Careful hoeing on a dry day between the plants until they close up will keep down seedling weeds. When the plants meet they should effectively stifle most weeds; any that do survive should be pulled out by hand.

Specimen or accent plants such as standard fuchsias and geraniums may need supporting, as inconspicuously as possible, with single stakes and ties, especially if the situation is exposed.

The ground-covering plants seldom need any support, but if for some reason they start to flop about and become untidy they are best held up by inserting a few bushy

Hoe on a sunny day to keep down weeds.

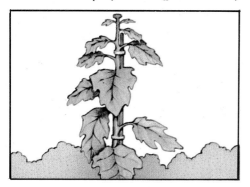

Support specimen plants with single stakes.

twigs that do not protrude above the plants.

Where practical, dead flowers or flowering heads are best removed as soon as they fade, for tidiness' sake and to prevent seeding and encourage continued flowering. This is very important in the case of antirrhinums, pansies, scarlet salvias, stocks and dahlias, where seed heads are conspicuous and soon affect flowering. It is not practical or necessary with alyssum, lobelia, impatiens, begonias and others with numerous small flowers. Marigolds, petunias and verbenas usually continue to flower without any such aid, while asters and nemesias tend to expend themselves in one long flush of bloom.

Spring bedding plants do not warrant this attention, as theirs is a comparatively short display with no follow-on. It pays, however, to snap off the flowers of tulips just below the head either before or when they are lifted from the beds, so that the formation of seed pods does not hinder the building up of the bulbs for another year.

Remove dead flowers for continuous blooming.

96

Insect pests are not usually much trouble. Aphids are an occasional problem and are controlled by applying systemic granules. Sometimes the greenhouse whitefly is brought out on geraniums and fuchsias and continues to breed in a hot, dry summer. Resmethrin gives a better control than a systemic insecticide. Some plants are damaged by these substances, so read the directions carefully. Earwigs can be troublesome, especially on dahlias. Spraying against the other pests may help to keep them at bay, or they can be trapped in pots with a little dry moss inside laid among the plants. Inspect daily, destroying any catches.

Diseases are not much of a problem and one does not generally have to take any

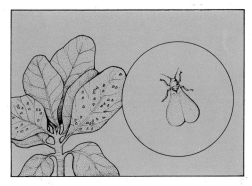

Whitefly

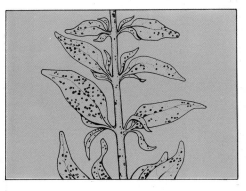

Antirrhinum rust

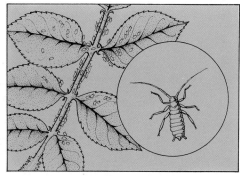

Aphis

active steps to keep them in check. However, in certain areas, the brown fruiting bodies of antirrhinum rust on stems and leaves can be very crippling. This can be countered by planting modern rust-resistant varieties such as those in the Tetra and Rocket strains. Wilt of China asters can mean the complete loss of plants. The stem blackens and shrivels just above ground level or a little higher, and the whole plant wilts and dies. Where it tends to be prevalent, it can also be countered by growing only resistant strains and varieties. These should always be grown in particularly difficult areas.

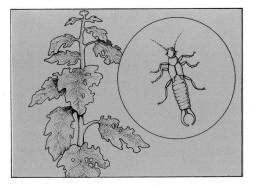

Earwig

7 Sowing hardy annuals in place

If you do not wish to raise or purchase plants to bed out in the usual way, you can still have a long display of summer flowers by sowing seeds of hardy annuals where they are to flower. However, this means forgoing an April and May show of spring-flowering plants and bulbs. Dig the ground in the usual way, firm and rake down to a fine tilth, and then mark out irregularly shaped patches to a preconceived plan, with the tallest kinds in the center – or at the back if the bed or border has one face only.

If necessary, thoroughly water the soil some hours before to ensure it is moist for sowing. Sow the seeds thinly from the end of March to early May. Either broadcast the seeds carefully over the surface and very lightly rake in; or sow in very shallow drills (little more than depressions in the soil) 10–16 in (25–40 cm) apart, according to the dimensions of each kind, carefully covering

To identify the flowers in the stylized border, see the diagram on the right:
1. *Clarkia* 'Salmon Queen' 2. *Linum grandiflorum* 3. *Phacelia campanularia* 4. *Chrysanthemum tricolor*
5. *Gypsophila elegans* 'Pink' 6. *Godetia* (mixed) 7. Cornflower 'Blue Diadem' 8. Candytuft (mixed) 9. *Calendula* 'Orange Cockade' 10. *Nemophila insignis* 11. *Nigella* 'Miss Jekyll' 12. *Layia elegans* 13. *Eschscholzia* 'Ballerina' 14. Shirley poppy 15. *Chrysanthemum* 'Golden Gem'

each drill with fine soil when complete. Germination is often better by this latter method if a dry spell follows.

Weed seedlings usually germinate before the plants; remove them carefully by hand when quite small. Thin the plants in two stages – the first, when about ¾–1¼ in (2–3 cm) high, to half the final spacing, according to each kind's ultimate size. At the second and final thinning some unwanted plants can, if necessary, be carefully lifted and used to fill any large gaps.

After-care consists of little more than hand weeding until the plants can take care of themselves, and supporting with bushy twigs if necessary. Sometimes these twigs can be confined to the perimeter of a group of plants merely to prevent them flopping over their neighbors. The removal of dead flowers often helps to prolong the display.

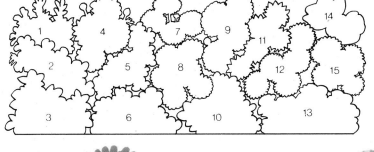

8 Window boxes, plant containers and hanging baskets

Even if you have only a backyard, or not even that, you can still enjoy the floral beauty of bedding plants by growing them in a variety of containers. If you have a garden, you may also like to decorate the house with window boxes and hanging baskets and have a few containers of plants on the terrace or patio.

along with the usual bedding plants such as wallflowers, forget-me-nots and pansies. Crocus, miniature daffodils, blue squills, dwarf iris and a host of other miniature bulbous subjects are very useful for window boxes. Aubrieta and arabis are especially useful plants for draping over the sides of such containers.

Above: A summer window box will brighten the barest window and is ideal for city apartment dwellers.

Many of the summer bedding plants lend themselves to this form of culture. Bedding geraniums, fuchsias, begonias, impatiens, heliotrope, marigolds, salvias and petunias are especially favored. Dahlias, antirrhinums, nemesias, pansies and some of the hardy annuals are less suitable. Ivy-leaved pelargoniums, trailing lobelia and *Mesembryanthemum criniflorum* and others of a low, spreading nature are invaluable for draping the sides of the containers. Annual climbing plants can be very successfully grown in containers that allow them to climb up supports on the house walls. Many permanent plants can be grown in large containers, on their own or associated with bedding plants.

In the spring hyacinths, daffodils (*Narcissus*) and the various tulips can be grown

Top: Brick pillars make attractive stands for plants.

Above: Group spring bulbs in containers.

9 Selecting plants

Summer bedding plants from cuttings

Note: Throughout the following pages botanical names are shown in italics. In some cases, for simplicity, only popular names are given.

As most of the half-hardy plants propagated annually by vegetative means require a start in a greenhouse, less emphasis will be placed on plants grown from cuttings than on those plants readily raised from seed. Some, in limited number, can be raised on windowsills and in lean-to conservatories including the popular zonal pelargonium or bedding geranium and its many forms, grown mainly for their colored foliage.

In most cases cuttings have to be rooted in late summer and over-wintered under glass. A few quick-growing subjects such as impatiens can be left until spring. Bedding dahlias can be raised as previously described but they are now very easily raised from seeds annually.

The hardy blue fescue grass (*Festuca glauca*) makes an excellent edging and foil for geraniums and other brightly-colored flowers. Stock plants can be lifted in autumn, divided and, for convenience's

Geranium (*Pelargonium zonale*)

Festuca glauca

sake, wintered in a cold frame. Other accent foliage plants, such as the modern coleus, whose multicolored, variously shaped leaves truly reflect a rainbow, are easily raised from late summer or spring cuttings. Equally quick and easy to root are cuttings of *Iresine lindenii*, with deep crimson foliage, and *I. herbstii*. Both species are known as bloodleaf. Always aim to have a few plants contrasting in shape and color.

Ivy-leaved pelargonium

accent plants in the beds or as specimens in large tubs. Varieties with a natural pendant habit are the most graceful when trained as pyramids or standards.

Ordinary bushy plants of many of the indoor varieties of fuchsia are splendid for window boxes and containers, for which purpose it is best to raise them annually from late summer cuttings. Compact growing, free flowering varieties should be chosen. The single-flowered are often more adaptable than the large doubles.

Many other plants that can spend the summer in the beds are within the reach of

The ivy-leaved pelargoniums are good value for those with the means for propagation and overwintering. In beds they can be well spaced out, as their trailing growths will cover quite a large area. This makes them excellent for hanging baskets and for draping over window boxes and other containers.

Those with a greenhouse can train up their own standard geraniums, fuchsias, heliotropes and lantana. This may take a couple of years, but, by lifting before frost does them damage, potting up and wintering in a cool greenhouse, and cutting back and shaping just prior to growth starting in the spring, they will last years.

Fuchsias in window box

Pelargonium crispum 'Variegatum', with small silvery, lemon-scented leaves, can be easily trained into close pyramidal form. Many fuchsias also make ideal pyramids, in which form they can be used as

those with greenhouses and some means of providing heat when necessary. For the majority of home gardeners, however, plants that can easily and cheaply be raised from seed will be more practical.

Summer bedding plants from seed

Throughout the succeeding pages the following abbreviations are used: H.A., hardy annuals; H.H.A., half-hardy annuals; H.B., hardy biennials; H.P., hardy perennials; H.H.P., half-hardy perennials. An asterisk (*) denotes plants that can also be sown where they are to flower.

Ageratum. H.H.A. 4–10 in (12–25 cm). First-class edging plant. Fluffy flowers mainly in shades of powder-blue, some with mauve cast. Also white variety. Sow February/March indoors.

Alyssum (also known as *Lobularia*) *maritima.* Sweet alyssum. H.A.* 3–4 in (8–12 cm). White, lilac, purple and rose-pink forms. Sow in March/April indoors, or outdoors while soil is still cool.

Amaranthus. H.H.A. 24–36 in (60–90 cm). Varieties such as 'Molten Fire' and 'Illumination' make spectacular accent foliage plants. Sow in February/March indoors.

Anchusa capensis. H.A.* 8–10 in (20–25 cm). Dwarf and compact. The variety 'Blue Bird' is intense blue. Sow in March indoors.

Amaranthus tricolor 'Molten Fire'

Alyssum maritima

Anchusa capensis 'Blue Bird'

103

Antirrhinum. Snapdragon. H.H.P. The old and still popular intermediate kinds ranging in height from 12 in (30 cm) to 18 in (45 cm) have been joined by such modern strains as the rust-resistant Rocket and Topper series. Entirely new types include the Coronette hybrids, with the first central spike surrounded by a cluster of laterals, the hyacinth-flowered, with wide pyramidal spikes, and varieties with open, penstemon-like flowers lacking the usual pouch.

The new Pixies, with open flowers on plants 6–8 in (15–20 cm) high, are an attractive addition to the other dwarf types.

Antirrhinum 'Floral Carpet'

Antirrhinum 'Madame Butterfly'

Taller varieties around 24–30 in (60–75 cm) in height include the original penstemon-flowered 'Bright Butterflies' and 'Madame Butterfly' (a variation with double, azalea-like flowers), base-branching varieties and others going up to 36 in (90 cm) in height.

Sow in January and February indoors.

Antirrhinum, penstemon-flowered

Aster. H.H.A. Bedding or China aster belonging to the genus *Callistephus* and not to *Aster* proper, which includes the popular Michaelmas daisies. There is a wide range of types and heights, including disease-resistant strains. All make an excellent display in beds from mid-summer onwards.

The flowers of the taller strains, 18–30 in (45–75 cm) high, vary in form from the neat rounded blooms of the Ball or Bouquet strains to the large shaggy flowers of the old Ostrich Plumes. Most, especially the single-flowered varieties, make excellent long-lasting cut flowers.

Aster Powderpuffs (Bouquet type)

The dwarf asters are ideal for formal beds. Modern strains such as Milady have large double flowers on bushy plants no more than 12 in (30 cm) high and as much across. Pinocchio is even more dwarf and has neat little flowers. Then there are the somewhat taller, pompon-flowered Lilliputs, the semi-double Pepite strains and others.

All the foregoing are available in well-varied mixtures, some of them in separate color varieties. Sow in March and early April indoors.

Aster, dwarf bedding type

Begonia semperflorens.
Wax or fibrous-rooted
begonia. H.H.P. 6–10 in
(15–25 cm). Many modern
strains and cultivars are
now available, either in
mixture or individual varieties in colors from white
through shades of pink to
deep scarlet, some with
deep purple/maroon
foliage. Continuous-
flowering in summer gar-
dens. In fall lift and pot for
indoor blooms. Sun or partial shade. Sow December/
January indoors.

Begonia, intermediate bedding. 8–12 in (20–30 cm).
Hybrids such as the Danica
series, which make rather
larger plants than *B.
semperflorens*, have a good
range of colors.

Begonia, intermediate bedding

Begonia semperflorens

Strains of tuberous
begonias and others, ideal
for hanging baskets and
window boxes, can now be
raised from seed to flower
the same season. Sow
December/January in a
greenhouse or in the house
on a sunny windowsill.

Cineraria maritima

Cleome spinosa

Coleus

Coleus. Flame nettle. 12–16 in (30–40 cm). Dwarf strains of these popular greenhouse foliage plants can now be had from seed and used to supplement flowers in the summer beds and in sunny windows. Sow indoors in February.

Cineraria maritima. (Also known as *Senecio cineraria*.) H.H.P. 6–12 in (15–30 cm). Not to be confused with the popular greenhouse annuals. Several varieties, all with silver foliage. Very useful for accent plants and for toning down bright colors. Sow in February indoors.

Cleome spinosa. Spider flower. H.H.A.* 36–40 in (90–100 cm). Unusual flowering plants for the centers of large beds, for use as accent plants or for large containers. They flower throughout the summer. Purple, rose and white forms. Sow February/March indoors or outdoors after soil warms.

Convolvulus tricolor

Convolvulus. H.A. 8–12 in (20–30 cm). Forms of *C. tricolor* are non-climbing plants allied to the bellbine. Trumpet-shaped flowers in a mixture of colors, including deep blue variety with white throat. Good for tubs and window boxes. Sow in February indoors in pots.

107

Dahlia. H.H.P. 12 in (30 cm) plus. Bedding dahlias of various heights with flowers of most of the popular types, i.e. single, double, cactus, collarette, pompon, etc., can now be so easily raised from seeds annually that it is not worth storing the tubers and raising plants from cuttings each season. Sow in February indoors.

Dianthus. Pink. 6–12 in (15–30 cm). Modern bedding strains derived from perennial species are grown as H.H.A., flower early and freely and produce brilliant displays in mixture or as separate varieties. Sow February/March and grow cool.

Echium. H.A.* Bugloss. 12 in (30 cm). Open flowers on bushy plants in a mixture of soft tones of pink, blue, lilac, purple and

Dahlia. Coltness hybrids

Dahlia, Unwin's hybrids

Dianthus chinensis 'Magic Charms'

Gazania splendens 'Grandiflora'

Echium, dwarf hybrids

white. Blue available as a separate variety. Sow March/April or while soil is still cool.

Euphorbia marginata. Snow-on-the-mountain. H.A.* 24 in (60 cm). Soft green leaves variegated with silvery white. Inconspicuous flowers surrounded by white bracts. Good accent plant. Sow April/May outdoors.

Gazania. H.H.P. 10–12 in (24–30 cm). South African daisies in brilliant mixtures of yellow, orange, pink, red and bronze shades, many attractively zoned. They revel in full sun. Good for window boxes and tubs. Sow in February indoors.

Euphorbia marginata

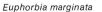

Geranium 'Sprinter'

Impatiens, mixed

Geranium. Zonal pelar-
gonium. H.H.P. 18 in
(45 cm). Now possible to
raise these popular bedding
plants from seed. New
dwarf early-flowering varieties such as Little Big
Shot, Carefree strains and
'Sprinter' are replacing the
original varieties and are
very free-flowering. Sow
indoors January/February.

Heliotrope. Cherry pie.
H.H.P. 16–18 in
(40–45 cm). Lavender to
deep purple flowers, some
varieties with purplish
foliage. Highly valued for
its sweet scent. Good for
window boxes and contain-
ers. Sow in February
indoors.

Impatiens. Patience plant.
H.H.P. 4–10 in (10–25 cm).
Dwarf, spreading and
continuous-flowering. Does
well in shade. Suitable for
window boxes and contain-
ers. Sold as mixtures or
separate colors, some with
striped flowers, some with
bronze foliage. Sow in early
March indoors.

Heliotrope 'Marine'

Lobelia. H.H.P. 4–6 in (10–15 cm). Along with sweet alyssum the most popular edging subject, especially the deep blue, Cambridge blue and blue/white eye varieties. Also available in white, red with white eye and a mixture of colors. The trailing forms are invaluable for draping hanging baskets, window boxes and other containers. Sow January/February indoors. Do not cover the seed when sowing and prick out in groups of 2–4 rather than individual seedlings.

Mesembryanthemum criniflorum. Livingstone daisy. H.H.A. 3–6 in (8–15 cm). Sprawling plants of a succulent nature specially suitable for a hot, dry position, thus ideal for trailing over the edges of window boxes and containers in full sun.

Lobelia 'Kaiser Wilhelm'

Mesembryanthemum criniflorum

Lobelia 'Sapphire'

111

Marigold. H.H.A.* The African or American marigolds have arisen from *Tagetes erecta* and are available in heights of 8–36 in (20–90 cm). Those of medium height are probably the most valuable for the home garden. All have large, almost globular, flower heads varying from pale primrose through lemon and gold to deep orange.

The French marigolds are forms of *Tagetes patula* and are smaller in all their parts than the Africans. Heights vary from the 6 in (15 cm) dwarfs suitable for edging to those around 14 in (35 cm). Mahogany-red, in whole or in part, is the latest addition to the color range and the flowers may be fully double, single or have a distinct central crest.

A new race of hybrids between the Africans and the French has been introduced recently. In habit and type of flower these hybrids more closely approach the French but the flowers are larger and the plants grow to 10–14 in (25–35 cm) high.

All these marigolds are quick to develop. To avoid them becoming tall and drawn before planting out, they should not be sown earlier than late March indoors.

Marigold, African 'Gold Coins'

Marigold, French 'Naughty Marietta'

Matricaria (*Chrysanthemum parthenium.*) Feverfew. H.P. 8–10 in (20–25 cm). Modern dwarf kinds may have ball-shaped flowers, or the boss of disk florets may be surrounded by a single row of flat florets. Sow in March indoors.

Nasturtium. H.A.* 8–12 in (20–30 cm). Non-climbing forms now available. Good for poor, dry soil and for hanging baskets and window boxes. Sow indoors in March in peat pots, one seed per pot.

112

Nemesia. H.H.A.* 8–12 in (20–30 cm). Most popular as a mixture but can be had in separate colors and bicolors. Flowers early and profusely. Sow in March. Difficult unless summers are cool and dry.

Pansy and viola. H.P. 6–8 in (15–20 cm). Can be had in mixture or in separate colors. Violas stand heat and drought better than pansies. Sow from January to March indoors or sow outdoors later for flowers the following year.

Nemesia hybrids

Pansy, mixed giants

Nicotiana. Flowering tobacco. H.H.A.* 10–36 in (25–90 cm). Available with white or crimson flowers; strains include pastel shades and lime green variety. Sow indoors in early spring or outside as soil warms.

Nicotiana affinis hybrids

113

Penstemon hybrids

Petunia Multiflora 'Pale Face'

Penstemon. Beard tongue. H.P. 18–30 in (45–75 cm). Sold as a mixture in mainly pink, red and purplish shades, some with white or striped throats. Long season of flowering and good for cutting. Sow January/February indoors.

Petunia. Multiflora type. H.H.A. 10–12 in (25–30 cm). These have smaller flowers and bloom more profusely than the Grandifloras. Also they are rather less susceptible to bad weather, so more reliable for bedding purposes. Good weather-resistant strains have been developed. Can be had in a wide range of brilliant colors. Sow January to March indoors.

Petunia Multiflora 'Starfire'

114

Petunia Grandiflora type

Petunia Multiflora Double type

Petunia. Grandiflora type. H.H.A.
10–14 in (25–35 cm). These have larger
flowers than the Multifloras, some with
waved petals, and are available as individual varieties in a range of brilliant colors – self, checkered or bicolor. They are
better for window box and tub culture
than for planting in the beds, but
weather-resistant strains are being developed. Sow January to March indoors.

Petunia. Double-flowered type. H.H.A.
12–14 in (30–35 cm). Both the Multifloras
and Grandifloras have double-flowered
strains with large, ruffled flowers up to
4 in (10 cm) across in a wide range of self-
and bicolors. Some strains are sweetly
scented. Generally used for pot culture
but also suitable for window boxes and
tubs. Sow from January to March
indoors.

Phlox drummondii. H.H.A.* 6–12 in
(15–30 cm). Both tall and dwarf strains
are available as individual varieties or
mixtures in a wide range of colors including blue and violet. Sow February/March
indoors, or outdoors as soil warms.
Transplant carefully.

Phlox drummondii, Beauty strain

115

Portulaca. Sun plant. H.H.A.* 6 in (15 cm). Dwarf and spreading with fleshy leaves. Like a hot, dry, sunny position so is very suitable for filling in on the rockery and for tubs and window boxes. Generally sold as a mixture of shades of reds, yellow and white. Sow February/March indoors, or outdoors after soil warms.

Ricinus. Castor-oil plant. H.H.A. Will reach 52 in (130 cm) or more when planted out. A splendid accent plant with large shiny leaves but suitable only for limited use in large beds. *Ricinus* 'Dwarf Red Spire' has red leaves and is lower growing; *Ricinus* 'Zanzibarensis' has green leaves with prominent mid-ribs. Sow singly in small pots January/February indoors.

Rudbeckia. Cone flower. H.H.P. 16–36 in (40–90 cm). Dwarf forms, such as the Rustic Dwarfs and 'Orange Bedder', make the best bedding plants. The Gloriosa Daisy type are taller with larger flowers. All are excellent for cut flowers. Sow in February indoors, or outdoors when soil is workable.

Rudbeckia, annual form

116

Salpiglossis. H.H.A. 18–28 in (45–70 cm). Delightful mixture of colors, many flowers veined and checkered with different shades. Must have plenty of sun and does best where summers are not too hot. Sow January/March indoors.

Stock. H.H.A. 10–24 in (25–60 cm). Ten-week and other summer-flowering stocks vary mainly in height, season of flower and size of spike. The Trysomic 7-week strain has proved the best variety for most northern areas where summers are very hot. Sow February/March indoors.

Salvia splendens. H.H.A. 6–12 in (15–30 cm). Several different scarlet varieties. Purple, rose and pink forms also available. Sow January/March indoors.

Salvia splendens

Tagetes signata pumila. H.H.A.* 6–8 in (15–20 cm). Differs from French marigolds in its finer foliage and its very small flowers in shades of lemon, yellow, orange or red. A useful edging plant. Sow in March.

Salpiglossis

Tagetes signata pumila

117

Verbena hybrida 'Nana Compacta'

Ursinia. H.H.A.* 6–8 in (15–20 cm). *U. anthemoides* is a South African daisy with orange flowers with reddish central zone. Other hybrid strains in lemon to orange tones. Sow February/ March indoors or outside later.

Venidium. Monarch of the Veldt. H.H.A.* 24–36 on (60–90 cm). *V. fastuosum* is a South African daisy with orange flowers with black centers. Hybrid strains have white, cream, lemon and orange shades. Sow February/March indoors or outside later.

Verbena. Vervain. H.H.A. 6–12 in (15–30 cm). Available in mixtures or separate colors including violet-blue; some have conspicuous white eyes. Sow January/ March indoors.

Venidium fastuosum

Zinnia 'Dahlia flowered

Zinnia. H.H.A.* Zinnias do best in warm, sunny summers. Weather- and disease-resistant strains are now being developed. The tallest varieties are suitable for large beds and cut flowers. They may have flat or quilled florets. The dwarf kinds range from the 'Lilliputs', 12 in (30 cm), with ball-shaped flowers; the 'Persian Carpet' type, 12 in (30 cm), with small double and semi-double flowers, many of them bi-colored; the compact 'Buttons' 10–12 in (25–30 cm), the newer 'Peter Pan' hybrids with large flowers on 10–12 in (25–30 cm) plants; down to the 'Thumbelina' varieties with small double and semi-double flowers on 6 in (15 cm) plants. Some can be had in separate color varieties. Sow in March indoors, or outside in warm soil.

Zinnia 'Lilliput'

Calliopsis

Calendula hybrids

Hardy annuals for sowing in place

Amaranthus caudatus. Love-lies-bleeding. 24 in (60 cm). Long, red, drooping racemes of flower like lambs'-tails. A form with greenish-white flowers also available. Best on a soil that is not too rich. Thin to not less than 14 in (35 cm).

Calendula. Pot marigold. 12–24 in (30–36 cm). An old favorite now available with double, quilled center and incurved flowers. Thin to 10–20 in (25–50 cm) apart. Sow in early spring in the North so that plants are established when the hot weather arrives.

Amaranthus caudatus

Candytuft. 10–14 in
(25–35 cm). One of the
most floriferous and popular hardy annuals, quick to
come into flower. Thrives in
most soils and will succeed
in sun or partial shade.
Available in mixture or
separate colors of white,
red, pink, rose, lilac and
crimson-purple. Sweetly
scented. Thin to 10–12 in
(25–30 cm).

Chrysanthemum. 6–30 in
(15–75 cm). Several different annual chrysan-
themums have excellent
garden strains. There are
the dwarf spreading *C. mul-
ticaule* with yellow flowers,
C. carinatum (Tricolor) varieties with zoned flowers in
bright colors, the garden
versions of the corn
marigold, *C. segetum,* and
the double-flowered *C.
coronarium* in yellow and
primrose. All have finely
cut elegant foliage.

Candytuft 'Mercury' ('Giant Tetra')

Chrysanthemum carinatum (Tricolor)

Calliopsis. Annual coreopsis.
10–20 in (25–50 cm). The
taller varieties have mainly
golden-yellow and orange-
yellow flowers, some with a
maroon zone. The dwarf
forms also include dark red
shades, some with a gold
border. Thin dwarf forms to
10 in (25 cm), taller varieties to 14–18 in (35–45 cm).

Cornflower. 12–28 in (30–90 cm). The dwarf – 12–16 in (30–40 cm) high – varieties are the most suitable, although the really tall ones can be used in a very wide border and their flowers are very useful for cutting. Both can be had in mixture or in separate colors, including white, shades of red, pink and rose, and true cornflower blue. Thin the dwarfs to 10–12 in (25–30 cm), the taller kinds to 16–20 in (40–50 cm).

Clarkia elegans. 20–24 in (50–60 cm). Long, slender stems of double flowers on bushy plants, which usually need a little support. Long season of bloom. Can be had in mixture or in distinct varieties with white, pink, rose, salmon, orange-scarlet, scarlet and purple flowers. Do not thin too closely: at 14–18 in (35–45 cm) apart, the plants should support each other without detriment to the display.

Cornflower (*Centaurea cyanus*)

Clarkia elegans

Dimorphotheca aurantiaca hybrids

Cynoglossum amabile 'Firmament'

Eschscholzia californica hybrids

Cynoglossum. Hound's tongue. 18–22 in (45–55 cm). Small true turquoise-blue flowers are freely produced, also a white form. Flowers throughout the summer. Thin to about 12 in (30 cm).

Dimorphotheca. Star of the Veldt. 10–14 in (25–35 cm). Large daisy-like flowers in yellow, orange, salmon-orange shades and white. Comes into flower quickly and continues throughout the summer if dead blooms are removed. Thin to about 10 in (25 cm) apart.

Eschscholzia. California poppy, 6–12 in (15–30 cm). Free-flowering plants with finely cut foliage and single, semi-double or double flowers in a brilliant range of colors. Likes plenty of sun and is not particular as to soil. Thin to about 8 in (20 cm) apart. Sow early.

123

Godetia. 8–24 in (20–60 cm). Long-flowering colorful annuals with single, semi-double or double flowers, many with frilled petals, in colors from white through pink and red shades to crimson plus lavender-blue, some composed of more than one color. Some are available as separate varieties. Thin the dwarfer kinds to about 8 in (20 cm), the taller ones to 12–18 in (30–45 cm) apart.

Helianthus annuus. Sunflower. The common annual sunflower growing to a height of 6 ft (2 m) or more is obviously much too tall for the average annual border. There are now dwarf forms no more than 24 in (60 cm) high, some with single, some with double flowers. They are good plant-makers, so thin to about the same distance as their height.

Gypsophila elegans. 18 in (45 cm). Graceful sprays of small white or pink flowers, which are also useful for mixing with larger flowers in floral arrangements. Thin to about 14 in (35 cm) apart.

Helianthus annuus 'Yellow Pygmy'

Lavatera. Mallow. 30–36 in (75–90 cm.) Suitable for large borders. Needs little or no support. Large rose, pink or white trumpet-shaped flowers. Good plant-makers, they should be thinned to stand not less than 24 in (60 cm) apart.

Leptosiphon. Stardust. (Also listed as *Gilea lutea.*) 4–6 in (10–15 cm) Finely cut foliage and masses of tiny star-like flowers in various shades. Very dwarf and ideal for the front of the border or for temporarily

Gypsophila elegans alba

filling bare spots on a rockery. Thin to 6 in (15 cm) apart.

Larkspur. Annual delphinium. 30–48 in (75–120 cm). Invaluable for the character of its long spikes of white, pink, salmon, rose, scarlet, lilac and blue flowers. A dwarfer form has recently been introduced. Available as mixtures or separate colors. They can be thinned to distances much less than their height. Must be sown very early in spring or in late fall for success in hot-summer regions. Annual delphiniums make good cut flowers.

Larkspur, 'Giant Imperial' mixed

Lavatera trimestris, mixed

Leptosiphon hybridus (Gilea lutea), mixed

Linum. Flax. 12–16 in (30–40 cm). *L. grandiflorum* in crimson-scarlet or white with crimson center is an excellent hardy annual. The slightly taller common blue flax is also well worth growing. Thin to 10–12 in (25–30 cm) apart.

Lupinus. 16–36 in (40–90 cm). The annual lupin can be had as a colorful mixture of tall kinds or as the dwarf Pixie strain; like the perennial kinds, it is a showy plant. Thin to 12–16 in (30–40 cm) apart.

Lupinus hartwegii

Lonas inodora. Sometimes called yellow ageratum. A South African daisy with small, tightly packed heads of yellow flowers on branching stems with finely cut foliage. A useful secondary plant when grown as an H.H.A. and also good for drying for winter decorations. Thin to 12 in (30 cm) apart.

Linaria. Toadflax. 8–12 in (20–30 cm). Spikes of small snapdragon-like flowers in mixtures of pink to red, purple and yellow shades, including bicolors. Suitable for the front of the border and for cutting. Thin to 8 in (20 cm)

Linaria 'Fairy Bouquet'

Nemophila insignis

Nemophila insignis. Baby blue eyes. 6 in (15 cm). Sweet plant for the front of the border. Sky-blue flowers with white centers. Likes a hot, dry situation. Thin to 6–8 in (15–20 cm) apart.

Nigella damascena 'Miss Jekyll'

Mignonette

Nigella damascena Love-in-a-mist. 16–18 in (40–45 cm). Cornflower-like flowers surrounded by ring of fine leaves followed by attractive inflated seed pods, but better succession of blooms if these are removed. Blue and rose-pink varieties, also mixture of these colors with lavender, mauve and purple. Good for cutting. Thin to 14–16 in (35–40 cm).

Mignonette (*Reseda odorata*). 12 in (30 cm). An old favorite valued more for its sweet fragrance than the form or color of its spikes of reddish or yellowish flowers. Attracts bees. Thin to 10–12 in (25–30 cm) apart.

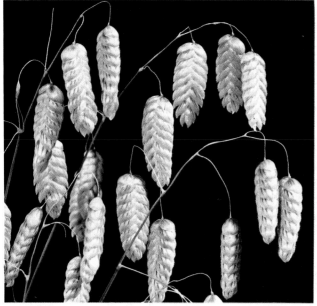

Ornamental grasses. Groups of annual grasses with ornamental flowering plumes can add to the distinction of the annual border and provide valuable material for drying for winter decorations. They may be used in mixture or, preferably, in distinct kinds. One of the most popular is the quaking grass, *Briza maxima*, with nodding spikelets. The cloud grass, *Agrostis nebulosa*, has broad feathery panicles, the hare's-tail grass, *Lagurus ovatus*, oval white downy plumes and the squirrel-tail grass, *Hordeum jubatum*, 2 in (5 cm) long silky tassels with barley-like awns.

Briza maxima
Hordeum jubatum

Poppy. 18–36 in (45–90 cm). The Shirley poppies with single, semi-double or fully double flowers, the carnation-flowered and the peony-flowered are all first-class, fairly tall, long-flowering annuals available in mixtures of bright warm colors. Thin to a little less than their height apart. Seeds must be sown in very early spring.

Poppy, Shirley mixed

Sweet William 'Indian Carpet'

Phacelia campanularia

Phacelia campanularia. 9 in (22 cm). Dwarf plant for the front of the rockery with true gentian-blue bell-shaped flowers beloved by bees. Thin to about 8 in (20 cm) apart.

Sweet William. 6 in (15 cm). Very dwarf forms of the popular early summer-flowering Sweet William flower very quickly when grown as hardy annuals. Thin to 6 in (15 cm).

Viscaria, mixed

Sweet sultan. 18–24 in (45–60 cm). Long-stemmed, sweetly-scented fringed blooms in a mixture of many colors. Good for cutting. Thin to a little less than their height.

Sweet scabious. 16–36 in (40–90 cm). Generally sold as a mixture of many colors from white to deep maroon. Thin to a little less than their height.

Viscaria (*Lychnis viscaria*). 8–16 in (20–40 cm). Single flax-like flowers in blue, pink, red and white in mixtures or separate colors.

Virginia stock. 9 in (22 cm). Useful little plant for the front of the border or the rockery. Small flowers in mixture of many colors. Thin slightly.

Sweet sultan

Morning glory (*Ipomoea*)

Annual climbing plants

Annual climbers are very useful for tub
culture on patios to grow up wires or
other supporting material.

Canary creeper (*Tropaeolum peregrinium*)

Canary creeper. H.A.
Fringed canary-yellow, it
flowers all summer. Grows
in sun or shade and is also
useful for draping window
boxes and tubs in addition
to covering fences or walls.
Sow in place in April or
early May or in pots for
planting out later. Sow one
or two seeds in each pot
and later thin to one plant.

Morning glory. H.H.A. A
lovely climber for a sunny
position, especially the variety 'Heavenly Blue'.
White, scarlet and blue-
striped white varieties also
obtainable. The flowers last
for a morning only, hence
the name, but are produced
in succession for many
weeks. Soak seed in water
before sowing in peat pots
indoors in March as for
canary creeper.

131

Nasturtium. H.A. The climbing forms have single or semi-double spurred flowers in a variety of colors. They are less rampant and more floriferous in dry, rather poor soils. They do well as hanging plants in window boxes and containers. Sow in place in April or early May or, if more convenient, in small pots as for canary creeper and plant out later.

Nasturtium (*Tropaeolum majus*), Gleam hybrids

Sweet pea. *Lathyrus odoratus.* H.A. Very popular, with numerous varieties and colors. Usually grown primarily for cut flowers but also make splendid plants for summer covering of walls and fences growing in the open ground or in tubs. Flowers must be cut off as they fade to maintain a succession of blooms. Soak seeds in water for two days before sowing in peat pots from January to March indoors or in very early spring in open ground.

Sweet pea, mixed

Spring bedding plants from seed

Bellis perennis 'Monstrosa White'

Aubrieta. H.P. 4 in (10 cm). This popular rockery plant makes an excellent subject for the spring beds with its low cushions of mauve, purple, pink or carmine flowers. Sow as advised on page 93 or lift after flowering, divide and plant out for the summer. Difficult in northern regions with hot summers.

Bellis perennis. English daisies. H.P. 4–6 in (10–15 cm). The Monstrosa type has flowers up to 1 in (2·5 cm) across. The Pomponettes are dwarfer and have smaller pompon-like flowers with quilled florets. Pink, rose-red and white flowers.

Cheiranthus allionii (syn. *Erysimum asperum*). Siberian wallflower. H.P. 12–16 in (30–40 cm). Slightly later flowering than the ordinary wallflower, extending its season into June. Colours are orange, gold or apricot.

Aubrieta

Myosotis. Forget-me-not.
H.B. 6–16 in (15–40 cm).
The only true blue spring
bedding plant. Pink and
white varieties are available
but these do not have the
same appeal. The taller varieties vary in the depth of
tone of their flowers. The
dwarf forms, including a
good rose-colored variety,
make very compact plants
ideal for edging or for small
beds.

Pansy. Heart's-ease. H.P.
6–8 in (15–20 cm). Numer-
ous strains and varieties are
available as mixtures or
separately. Some are com-
pletely self-colored, others
have the typical dark purple or purplish-black blotch
in the center. The most

Pansy
Pansy 'Clear Crystals'

Myosotis, dwarf type

popular spring bedding
plant over most of the country. Best treated as a biennial, with fresh seeds being
sown in midsummer, the
seedlings then wintered
over in a cold frame or carefully mulched in very cold
regions.

Polyantha primrose. H.P.

8–12 in (20–30 cm). Most
popular as a brilliant mixture in white, yellow, pink
to rose, red to crimson and
blue, many with yellow
eyes. Some colors are available separately, of which
blue is very valuable.
Beware of the very large-
flowered strains grown for
pot work; they are generally

Polyantha primrose, mixed

less profuse of bloom and do not always stand cold weather well.

Primrose. *Primula vulgaris.* H.P. 6 in (15 cm). Differs from the polyantha in that the flowers are produced singly instead of in heads. Generally a little earlier to flower. Now available in much the same range of color. Choose only the fully hardy strains for bedding.

Polyantha primrose, mixed

Primrose, modern strain of *Primula vulgaris*

Primula denticulata. Drumstick primula. H.P. 12–16 in (30–40 cm). Not used for spring bedding as much as it might be. Can be raised and treated in the same way as polyantha. The type has medium mauve flowers, but there are much deeper-colored versions. Daffodils and the earliest flowering tulips are its best companions. Not really suitable for container cultivation. Dislikes hot weather.

Wallflower (*Cheiranthus cheiri*). H.P. 8–18 in (20–45 cm). Spring bedding is incomplete without the seductive scent of wallflowers, but unfortunately they require cool, moist climates, such as in parts of New England and the West Coast. Many separate color varieties and types are known in the British Isles, where they grow to perfection and are available in white, primrose, yellow, orange, pink, scarlet, ruby, blood-red and purple shades. In the United States wallflower seeds are generally sold in a mixture of colors.

Primula denticulata

Wallflowers, mixed

Narcissus 'Flower Record'

Spring bedding bulbs

Hyacinths. May be planted on their own in beds or mixed with the usual spring bedding subjects. Ideal for colorful effects in window boxes and other receptacles. Choose bedding-type bulbs, i.e. those of second size, which are cheaper and produce rather smaller and more graceful flowering spikes.

Narcissus 'Sempre Avanti'

Hyacinths, mixed

Narcissus. All daffodils including the Trumpets, although these are generally less suitable for formal bedding than the groups with smaller trumpets, which are usually a little later to flower and are usually lighter in flower and foliage. The Tazetta or bunch-flowered and the double kinds are not suitable.

The larger-flowered daffodils usually look best in a natural setting – in grass, or on a rockery, for example. They can, however, be used in the beds with early-flowering subjects such as *Primula denticulata* and other primroses as companions. They are always acceptable in window boxes.

The bedding season begins with the large brilliant blooms of forms of *Tulipa fosteriana* and the Early Single tulips, which can be used either on their own or grown with primroses, pansies or candytuft. For the latter, the taller varieties of the Early Singles, such as 'De Wet', 'Dr Plesman' and 'Prince of Austria', should be chosen, all of which are sweetly scented.

Early Single tulip
'Pink Beauty'

Early Double tulips

The Triumph tulips flower second, and being of medium height are fine for growing with pansies. The Early Double tulips flower about the same time. Being quite dwarf, they are best used with a low ground covering of pansies, English daisies or dwarf forget-me-nots.

Lily-flowered tulips

Darwin tulip 'Queen of Bartigons'

The glorious Darwin and Cottage tulips and the elegant Lily-flowered varieties are the right companions for spring-flowering wallflowers and the taller forget-me-nots. The majestic Darwin hybrids and the Late Double or Peony-flowered group are very striking but only suitable for beds large enough to take their heights and 'weight'.

Those with a flair for the unusual can try the Parrot or Fringed tulips with waved and crested petals, the Rembrandts, which are flamed and feathered in different colors, and the Viridiflora tulips, which are blazed and feathered with green.

139

10 Plant associations

It is not difficult to put seasonal bedding plants together to form a colorful display. However, much of the satisfaction of this form of gardening lies in creating harmonious combinations of form and color, with the plants enhancing each other's beauty. Summer bedding can be divided into:

(a) main ground-covering plants, such as geranium (*Pelargonium*), petunia, snapdragon, large-flowered marigold and zinnia of medium height and perhaps salvia;

(b) secondary ground-covering plants, i.e., plants of open, slender growth with small leaves and flowers to percolate through the main cover plants. Examples include nemesia, *Anchusa capensis*, echium,

cynoglossum – all fine where summers are not too hot. However, in the North, more heat-tolerant annuals are desirable, such as French marigolds, the many small-flowered zinnias, impatiens, verbena, nicotiana and wax begonia;

(c) dwarf edging plants such as lobelia, ageratum and sweet alyssum;

(d) accent plants spaced at wide intervals to give height and character in proportion to the area, e.g., cleome, taller snapdragons, *Salvia farinacea*, tithonia and foliage plants of various habits, such as castor bean (*Ricinus*), amaranthus, coleus, dusty miller. In spring bedding combinations, tulips act as accent plants.

Bedding plants can be associated with the permanent occupants of the garden if beds and borders cannot be set aside for special bedding schemes. Although this style of planting is less formal, the harmonizing of plant forms and colors is equally important.

Left: the *Yucca* is the character plant of this display. Salvias, alyssum, lobelia, begonias and other permanent and seasonal plants are tastefully planted in association with both the spiky leaves and the plumes of creamy-white flowers of the *Yucca*.

When individual beds and borders are devoted to seasonal bedding, the happy associations created in them should also blend in with other features in the garden. Although personal taste will naturally enter into color blending, there are certain basic principles to follow. The color extremes are the soft tones of blue, mauve and pink and the harder tones of white, orange, deep yellow, crimson and scarlet. A soft tone can be used to relieve the intensity of a hard one, e.g. pale pink with crimson or blue with deep yellow; purple also requires some relief. Magenta is difficult to associate with other colors.

Foliage is particularly useful as a foil for floral color. Gray and silver especially will effectively break up and tone down bright and the less sociable colors. Golden and variegated foliage must be used with care: too much can produce effects that are either harsh or spotty. Foliage of a deep crimson or purple tone has many uses but must not be overdone, otherwise the picture will become somber. The surrounds of adjacent permanent plants may decide whether a quiet harmonious combination or something rather more vivid is needed. A dull situation will almost certainly call for a bright combination of colors.

Above: A bright association of scarlet salvias inter-planted with coleus 'Golden Ball', with the variegated *Abutilon savitzii* as an accent plant.
Left: A low and more subtle blend of the soft colors of pink fibrous-rooted begonias with white and violet alyssum and accent plants of the silver-foliaged *Cineraria maritima*.

141

Although the range of subjects is much more limited, spring bedding offers great scope for color planning. It is difficult to avoid a two- or three-tier effect in the beds but this seldom becomes boring. The blue of forget-me-nots (*Myosotis*) is invaluable as a main ground cover or in combination with any tone of wallflower. On their own, use wallflowers in a single color or mix two harmonizing tones. Fully mixed strains are seldom as pleasing as individual colors or planned combinations – either of wallflowers on their own or overplanted with tulips.

Polyantha and other primroses must be kept on their own, with tulips of suitable type as their sole companions – for they flower somewhat earlier than wallflowers *Myosotis, Bellis* and pansies. The last two subjects, together with the dwarf compact forms of *Myosotis*, make ideal edgings for wallflower combinations, providing blue, purple and white tones to offset the more dominant yellow and red shades of wallflowers. Alternatively, both *Bellis* and pansies make particularly good ground cover for the shorter-stemmed tulips in the smaller beds.

Left: 'Royal Blue' forget-me-nots filtering through the wallflowers make a suitable 'base coat' for the deep maroon of 'Giant' and the creamy-yellow of 'Niphetos' Darwin tulips.

Below: The brilliance of Darwin tulip 'Charles Needham' is softened by the pastel chamois-rose of wallflower 'Eastern Queen' and the ground cover of forget-me-nots.

142

The *Fosteriana* hybrids and the Early Single tulips are the best companions for primroses including *Primula denticulata*; the Triumph tulips blend well with polyantha; the Darwin, Cottage, Lily-flowered and other tall, late-blooming tulips are best for wallflower associations, and the dwarfer varieties of these together with the Early Double tulips look attractive over a ground-coat of pansies, *Bellis* or dwarf *Myosotis*. Purple and mauve tulips are particularly effective over yellow, primrose or white wallflowers. Separate varieties or a mixture of two to harmonize are more pleasing than full mixtures.

The more thought devoted to the initial planning of flower beds and borders, the more satisfying will be the finished result: a mere conglomeration of different plant colors and shapes can rarely be as pleasing in a garden as the beautiful, well-balanced picture that will emerge when the relationships of one plant to another have been thought out with care. Very little extra effort is needed – and the results will be infinitely more rewarding.

Above: A delicate combination of tulips 'Smiling Queen' and 'Northern Queen', with pink and white daisies interplanted with *Myosotis* 'Dwarf Royal Blue'.

Right: Pomponette daisies with *Myosotis* 'Dwarf Royal Blue' make a charming picture in a small bed or used to furnish a corner.

Balcony, patio and window box gardening

1 The pros and cons of container gardening

Diversity makes this patio a place of interest in all seasons, yet there is space left which is open and uncluttered.

Some people whose gardening activities are restricted to filling a few pots on a balcony, a few tubs on a patio or a roof, or to tending a window box might feel that they are underprivileged gardeners, deprived of their right to get their fingers into the real soil, to get mud on their boots and thorns in their fingers. But they would be very wrong.

This type of gardening could with advantage be called container gardening, for it must be carried out almost entirely in containers rather than in mother earth. Container gardening is probably the easiest, most rewarding, most exciting and most foolproof type of gardening there can be, for the gardener is in complete control over everything except the weather, and even this he can command to a certain extent.

The gardener can choose his own containers, their size, shape, color, material. He can decide where they are to be placed, in this corner or that, at this height or that.

He can decide what kind of soil he will put in them, sandy or peaty, acid or alkaline, heavy or light. He can decide which plants he wishes to grow and even though his residence may be in a belt of the most uncompromising lime, he can grow in his containers fine plants of rhododendrons, azaleas and ericas. He can change his display at will, moving his containers from place to place or emptying them according to season and replacing their contents with fresher, more colorful plants. If frosts come, he can even bring a container into the home for a night, or two, or place it where it will otherwise receive some shelter. He can plant spring-flowering bulbs in his containers at the end of the summer and overplant these with ericas, happy in the knowledge that he will have a certain amount of winter color and all the promise of a glorious spring, yet during the colder and darker months he need never step out onto his balcony, say, to tend his plants, for they will look after themselves.

What limitations, then, face the container gardener? What problems will he find? In the first place it will be apparent that he is limited by size. Almost any plant,

Geraniums (pelargoniums) provide vivid colorful bloom over a long period.

Contrast of color and shape on this balcony ensures a peaceful beauty with minimum attention

even trees of considerable size, can be grown in a container so long as it is large enough. But one cannot grow a tree in a window box, nor on most balconies, unless it be either one that can be kept under strict control – such as a clipped bay tree – or perhaps one of the dwarfed bonsai trees. The gardener is also limited by weight, for a container filled with moist soil can be heavy indeed, certainly too heavy to move about with ease, and sometimes too heavy structurally. There is, then, a tendency for gardeners to choose fairly small containers made from some lightweight material (rather than stone, concrete or other durable but heavy material) for the sake of convenience.

The fact that the containers used are mainly on the small side presents another problem, for small containers dry out very quickly and in warm or dry weather can require watering twice a day. This can be an awkward chore and a considerable tie, for it may mean that one is unable to go away for a weekend, for example, without making arrangements for the plants to be watered or without installing some automatic watering device.

But these are comparatively minor problems when one considers that no heavy digging, no constant weeding, no regular mowing of the lawn, no hedge trimming, and no carting away of piles of garden refuse are involved.

Although the three types of gardening mentioned here have been grouped together under the title of container gardening, certain minor differences exist, owing mainly to physical conditions. The balcony is larger than a window box, but probably smaller than the patio. So let us have a brief look at each of these locations.

Balcony gardens

With a balcony one must make up one's mind right at the beginning whether the

The use of masses of vivid color in containers is well-suited to hot and sunny climates.

garden is to be for the benefit of the residents or for the pleasure of passers-by. Are the plants to be enjoyed from indoors or are they to be placed on the exterior of the building so that they are hardly seen from indoors? A balcony is almost always bounded by a wall or a balustrade of some kind. Plants in their pots can be placed against this so as to leave as much room as possible, or they can be hung or otherwise fastened to the outside of the wall or railing. If both locations are used – growing plants *on* the balcony for the benefit of those indoors and at the same time *outside* the balustrade for the benefit of strangers – there will be problems of handling, reaching and stretching. There will also be problems of watering and the danger of debris falling into premises below or onto the street, something that must always be avoided.

On the whole it is probably better to create the balcony garden so that it can be seen at its best by the residents of the

Where the sun is strong the gardener seeks shade, but flowers will grow and cover themselves with bloom, delighting the eye with their decoration.

apartment. By using raised boxes, hanging baskets and the like there will be every opportunity of adding to the decoration of the building and the district at the same time.

There are several little problems that will face the new balcony gardener. For example, until one has experienced living high

A variety of containers: *from left*, an evocative urn; a classic trough; a coopered half-barrel; a shallow saucer; and a terra-cotta jar with planting holes.

149

above street level it is impossible to imagine how much more wind there is, not only in quantity and strength, but – more important – in unpredictability. One never knows from which direction it will arrive, regardless of prevailing winds. So it is vital to take this wind into account. In certain positions a hanging basket may swing so violently in the wind as to be a positive danger, yet moved further back or against a wall it may do no more than rock gently in the breeze. Dry soil or peat moss may be blown away and a jet of water from a hose can easily find its way into a neighbor's windows. Plants usually have to be well-staked or otherwise supported. Better still, they should be comparatively dwarf so they will not snap off or rock in their pots.

Another problem that can face the balcony gardener concerns the sun. Some balconies can be in full sun for almost the entire day, others can be so affected by shade that certain plants just cannot be grown successfully. There is nothing that can be done about this other than adapting one's style of gardening to the existing conditions.

There is also the question of weight. A box of pansies bought from a street market may weigh only a few pounds, but once they have been removed and planted in several pots or troughs of soil the total weight will have increased considerably, and when freshly watered they will be even heavier. Although this extra weight will not affect the structural safety of your balcony,

A built-in tray prevents problems with drips when hanging baskets are being watered.

you may find that if you have to move pots or tubs, they may be heavier than you can conveniently manage; and if they are to be lifted above floor level and fixed in position, you may find that soil and plants have to be removed first.

Debris can be a nuisance on a balcony. Dust and soil crumbs, fallen leaves, dead flowers, a broken pot, seed packets and labels – all these can be a nuisance, disfiguring an otherwise pleasant scene if they are allowed to blow about in the wind. For this reason it is always wise and helpful to maintain a covered trash can into which rubbish can be placed at the first opportunity so that the place is kept clean and tidy and so there is no likelihood of annoying neighbors.

Plants growing on a balcony should normally be in containers with drainage holes in them, although if they can be protected from rain this is not essential. Drainage holes will allow water to trickle through and onto the floor. However, this water can stain some surfaces, and it may linger in puddles and become a nuisance. Again, the copious watering needed at some times of the year means that fertilizers are constantly leached from the soil and require

Wooden window boxes are long-lasting, and a metal tray underneath will catch excess water.

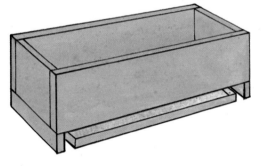

replacing. For all these reasons it is helpful to stand pots on the balcony inside a saucer or some other container or to fit drip trays underneath them to catch and contain any excess water. This can then be returned to the plant soil at the next watering and will help to reduce the fertilizer bill.

Window boxes

Window boxes offer rather less opportunity for gardening than the space of a balcony. They also offer additional problems, the greatest and most important of which concerns the actual box or container and the way in which it is fixed in position. There can be no half measures with window boxes; they must be sound and undamaged, they must be securely held in their positions and they must have means for the collection of excess water or for its safe removal. This water must not be allowed to drip down into the street because of the damage or danger it might cause.

There are restrictive clauses in the leases of some city buildings prohibiting window boxes and it is worth checking this out before installing any. Insurance policies should be examined, for if you are not covered for any possible damage or injury you could be open to heavy costs. It is therefore only prudent to make sure that if you do install window boxes they should both fit the windows for which they are intended and they should be securely fixed in place so that they cannot possibly fall.

It is this necessity for careful fixing that has led to the use of timber almost exclusively for the construction of window boxes, for this is a material that is easy to cut to size and easy to fix to walls or windowsills. The timber should be sound and not less than 1 in (25–30 mm) thick, and it should be well preserved with several coats of paint. The window box should be not less than 6 in (15 cm) deep and wide, preferably more. If possible, it should be fixed in position slightly above the actual sill so that a removable drip pan can be placed underneath it to catch any excess water. This should be of metal, and, once again, it should be either fixed in position or so secure that no wind or casual knock can send it

When constructing a window box, you should try to include the useful features shown here. The wood should be heavy and drilled for drainage. It should fit the space closely and safely, yet allow room at the sides for picking it up, and underneath for a drip tray.

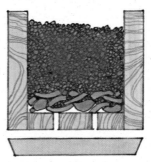

falling to the street below; yet it should be easily removed and replaced from inside the room, rather than being accessible only by means of a ladder in the front of the building.

A filled window box can be very heavy, so it is essential to fix it in position empty, and then fill it. It should have drainage holes in the base and there should be a drainage layer on the floor at least 1 in (2–3 cm) deep, with the soil above this. The soil mixture should be rich and well drained, yet with sufficient peat to hold moisture well. Too much peat or a soilless compost will almost certainly mean moisture loss by wind erosion.

Do not attempt to sow seeds in a window box, for uneven temperatures and the almost inevitable occasional dryness will inhibit their germination. Grow your plants indoors and then plant them out or buy ready-grown plants. Make sure that they are always at their best, for a shabby window box with half-dead plants is an eyesore. Any plant past its best should be removed and replaced.

152

Above: Window boxes need not be empty in winter. Evergreens such as English ivy, aucuba, ericas and skimmia can be underplanted with dwarf spring-flowering bulbs like crocuses, daffodils and tulips.

Below: Zinnias, mesembryanthemums and geraniums will flourish in a window box in hot sun if they are watered regularly.

Above: Where shade is a problem for part of the day, pansies can be persuaded to flower in spring and can be followed by wax begonias and calceolaria.

Keep window boxes going in winter as well as in summer. Use evergreens such as skimmia, winter-flowering ericas or heaths and ivy, dwarf conifers, possibly underplanted with spring-flowering bulbs. Choose dwarf varieties of daffodils and tulips, as well as smaller bulbs such as crocus and grape-hyacinth, for tall-stemmed kinds will almost certainly snap in the wind.

In summer the plants you grow will depend largely on whether the site is mainly in the sun or the shade. In the first condition use nasturtium, French marigolds, zinnias, and the always useful geraniums. If shade is a problem, try *Vinca rosea*, begonias and impatiens.

Patios and terraces

A patio or terrace is less likely to present shade problems, unless it conforms to the narrow definition of this site as a courtyard completely surrounded by buildings. The name has come to mean what is almost an outdoor room attached to the house, frequently linking the house and the garden,

153

lying as it does between the two. It has also come to mean the backyard of a town house, an area too small to be labeled a garden and probably paved overall, with perhaps a few gaps in which plants are grown. But having considerably more space than is available either on a balcony or in a window box, shaded parts of the patio can be used for shade plants and the sunnier portion filled with sun-loving plants. It is also possible to use light-colored paints to cover some or all of the walls, which will considerably increase the intensity of the available light.

Patio gardening gives the best of all worlds, for it makes it possible to plant some material directly in the soil, yet it also encourages the use of containers. The containers can be large and weighty. There is no need to worry about drips of excess water from any containers. Some plantings can be on a semi-permanent basis, while others can be as temporary as desired.

Unless one inherits a patio that has been used with intelligence and thoroughness, it is probable that the soil on the site will be cold, thin, sour and unproductive, so it will be well worth digging out the top layer where you intend to plant, and replacing it with some fresh and healthy loam. It is easy

enough to replace the soil in containers of growing plants, except where the containers are built-in or permanent structures, which might be more difficult.

Only in the most fortunate of conditions can a patio be made to look like a garden or even made into a green and pleasant retreat from the world. As a general rule, one cannot escape from a certain formality, from straight lines, from flat paving, from a built-in and slightly claustrophobic atmosphere. Yet on these bases it is perfectly possible to build an outdoor room of charm and beauty, to disguise the straight lines, conceal the flatness, and soften the surrounding walls with green growth.

It may be that the patio has to hold such unsightly objects as an oil tank or a trash can. It will probably have a pile of soil and perhaps some sand or a bale or two of peat moss, some tools and a roll of hose pipe. The thing to do is to build the patio in such a manner that these necessities can be concealed, yet readily available for use at any time. This is not a difficult thing to do so long as it is done right at the beginning and the work is carried out with the overall

'Before': It would seem impossible to transform this small, enclosed, obstructed place into a spacious and elegant garden.

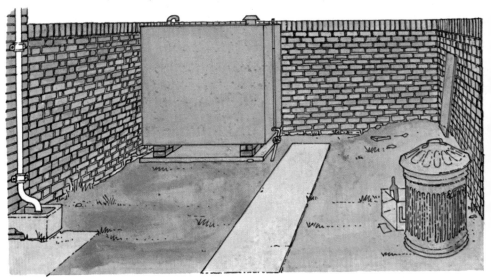

154

'After': Tank and trash can are hidden; the wall is lightened and heightened; and paving, plants and containers have been selected with care.

appearance in mind. A light screen can cover the oil tank, for example, with a rampant *Polygonum baldschuanicum* (silver lace vine, also listed as *P. aubertii*) growing on and through it, the plant's tendrils and creamy flowers concealing the functional interior. Seats with removable lids can hold tools. A wall with a built-in flower strip along the top can have concealed in its belly a cavity that will hold a good sack of soil. All this is a matter of good design and imagination, and where space is so limited it is essential that every square of it should be used both to give pleasure and to ease normal house- and garden-keeping. If the patio is made into an exquisite retreat from life at the expense of comfort in the home, or if it becomes unrealistic in its demands for constant clearing, it will be more of an irritation than a pleasure.

Planting in soil If the area has been paved overall and you want to make certain plantings direct into the soil, it will probably be possible without too much trouble to remove one or two paving slabs here and there. The soil beneath is certain to be poor and unproductive, so it should be removed to a depth of at least 6 in (15 cm) and more if this is not too difficult. In order to check that drainage will be sufficient or suitable, pour a bucket or two of water into the hole just excavated to make sure that it runs away satisfactorily. If the drainage is poor

155

and the water lies in the hole for more than a very few minutes, it will become necessary to dig out more soil and to break up the subsoil.

Fill the hole with fresh soil according to what you intend to plant. If you have in mind a small tree or a shrub, then fill the hole with a soil mixture that will provide nourishment to the plant over a long period. Place in the bottom of the hole a spadeful of well-rotted farmyard manure, if you can get it, and mix a few handfuls of peat with your loam or leafmold, which you sift in around the roots of your tree. Firm the soil well around the roots and then cover the naked soil with pebbles or something similar to give the finishing touch of

A pavement planting such as this should be bursting with plants, packed tightly so no soil shows through. This means a rich, well-fed soil, regular watering and constant dead-heading of the flowers.

smartness and to keep soil off the paving.

If you intend to grow something more brightly colored and cheerful, such as a little rectangle of vivid annuals, then plant these in a soil and peat mixture, about half and half, which has been well enriched with a slow-acting fertilizer, perhaps bonemeal or one of the proprietary types available. Make sure that the little patch is watered regularly and that all dead flowers are removed as soon as they begin to look faded. This will ensure that the bed always looks neat and it will help the production of further blooms.

When winter comes, the occupants of this summer bed will have to be removed and one is then left with a vacant space. It can be filled with some hardy material, such as heathers or ivy, but one cannot continually be lifting and planting in this manner, so a possible answer to this winter problem is merely to replace the original paving. This need not be done with any great thoroughness, for it will be a temporary measure, but it will help to disguise the vacant space until the spring comes around again.

Herb gardens It is possible on a patio to grow a few of the most useful herbs for the kitchen. Some can be grown in pots but, if there is space, most will do better in the soil. A tiny section can be marked out like a chess board and different herbs grown in each of the squares. In this way you can also help to provide the type of soil enjoyed by the different herbs, a deep, rich loam for the apple mint, a well-drained sandy soil for a little sage bush and so on. Some of the herbs will quickly outgrow the small space allotted to them, so use cuttings to replace a plant that has grown too large for its square, or continue to sow fast-growing herbs such as chervil, dill, or basil.

Raised beds Consider also making a herb garden on a raised bed at waist height, although lower beds, 12 in (30 cm) or 18 in (45 cm) high, the last permitting the gar-

A raised bed like this allows fragrant, colorful flowers and plants to be enjoyed with utmost ease.

lener to perch on the edge as he works, are also practical, and easier to build. Raised beds are useful for several reasons and they can give vast pleasure because the plants grow almost at nose level so one can pinch and smell easily. Waist-high gardening is also ideal for those who through age, accident or illness cannot bend to do their gardening at ground level. At this height they can plant and weed from a chair or even from a wheelchair, or they can stand, using a cane, to pluck out an invasive weed. In some cases the incapacitated can even perch on the broad side of an elevated garden and carry out simple operations from that position.

This last suggestion presupposes not so much a raised container as one that is built into a raised portion of the patio – in effect where there are two walls with an interior trough, usually planted up with bright plants to make a colorful band along the top of the wall. The actual soil container is seldom more than about 1 ft (30 cm) deep

and this rests on top of the otherwise solid or core-packed wall.

If a flower bed is to be raised to waist level, then it must be quite secure and there must be no danger that the sides will crumble and give way. For this reason the building of raised beds can be a somewhat lengthy business unless you choose the lower heights mentioned above. Even with a raised bed only 16–18 in (40–45 cm) high, it will be necessary to construct it carefully. One of the easiest materials to use today are railroad ties, which measure about 10 in (24 cm) high and about 8 in (20 cm) wide. However, railroad ties are heavy, bulky and difficult to cut apart without power saws, although most lumber yards and some garden centers can help here once you have determined your dimensions. Much easier to handle and cut apart are the lighter, smaller 'landscape'

157

ties, now carried by most lumber yards. They measure about 4 by 4 in (10 by 10 cm) and make handsome, long-lasting walls, edgings, and steps.

An attractive raised bed results if the walls are made from natural or reconstituted stone, although this is a more lengthy process, normally requiring a concrete foundation for the considerable weight of the stones.

Raised beds can also be made with strips of boards, cement blocks or, for a more formal effect, bricks. The last will require cement to hold them securely, as well as some skill to construct. Prefabricated patio blocks might be used, but their dimensions are more suited to paving uses, and to make a raised bed of much height would require many, many blocks.

Once the dimensions of the bed have

been decided and the ties or boards cut to proper lengths, the ground should be excavated to about 6–8 in (15–20 cm) deep on this size. The ties or boards can then be placed around the perimeter, outside the excavated area, which should be filled with pieces of broken pots, bricks, stones, pebbles, coarse coal ashes or whatever material is available as filling and draining matter.

The remaining space can then be filled with soil, preferably after placing some sealing material on top of the rubble to prevent the soil from trickling down too far. The type of soil used will depend on what is to be grown, and even more on what is available. City dwellers don't have much choice – the usual soil found in cities differing widely in quality and type. A big help are the soilless mixes, available under different trade names as Jiffy Mix, Redi Earth, Pro-Mix, Super Soil. These soilless mixes can be added to soils in varying proportions, and should greatly improve their moisture holding capacity.

A raised bed is easily made with regular paving slabs, which because they are strong and slim allow large areas of soil to be used. Natural stone walls are attractive but need a foundation and greater space.

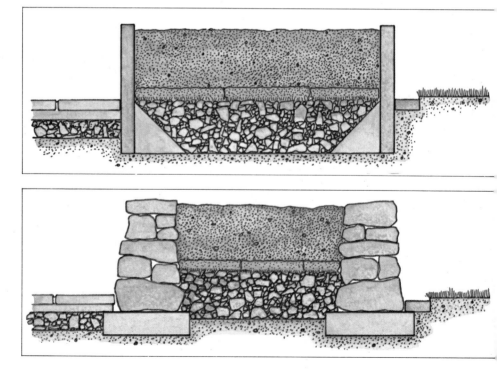

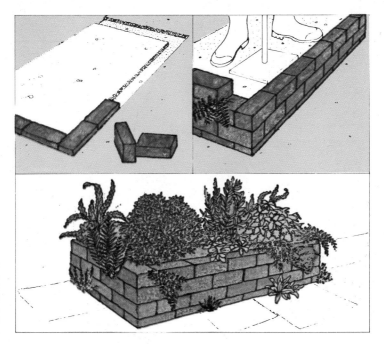

Peat bricks, occasionally used abroad, should be thoroughly soaked in water before being used to make a retaining wall. This makes them more stable and workable.

Electricity on the patio Try always to bear in mind the fact that a patio is an extension of the house, an outdoor room meant to be lived in, to be used and occupied. If you remove your furniture rather than leave it on the patio at all times and in all seasons, then make it easy to get out so that you waste no time and do not find it too much of a chore. Eat out of doors whenever weather encourages this activity. Install lighting, its type depending on the area available, but always bear in mind that glaring, overall flood-lighting will annoy or disconcert neighbors and will certainly not be attractive to anyone sitting out in it. It is far better to use just two or three smaller lighting units concealed among your plants, so that they are highlighted. At the same time you have a useful but not obtrusive lighting of certain parts of the patio while other parts are kept dim and mysterious.

If you are going to install exterior lighting on the patio, make sure that your electrical wiring is both safe and unobtrusive. Engage the services of a competent electri-

cian if you are not sure of what you are doing. You can either install a permanent system of electricity with one or two basic outlets into which you can plug your electric lights as and when you wish to use them, or, you can merely drape electric cable along the garden from the house for use on special occasions and remove it again at the earliest convenient time.

A permanent system will probably leave the house and travel through the garden to the required spots in a specially armored and insulated cable, which is expensive but safe and long-lasting. If a spade should accidentally descend upon cable of this type, it will do no damage. The outlets it is connected to would be of a special water- and weatherproof type, suitable under all conditions.

In fact, the possibilities open to exploitation by the possession of a patio are limited only by the amount of money and time available, and it has been known for a patio to be changed into a conservatory by the erection of a glass roof over the area, as the ultimate in garden luxury.

159

2 Containers

Materials

Under normal gardening conditions, when plants are grown in pots or containers of any kind, these look best if they have some affinity with the soil – that is, if they are of stone, clay, terra-cotta, wood, even metal. But gardening on a balcony, on a patio or in a window box is not normal gardening and this fact enormously widens the list of materials that are available for use as containers in these places.

Above: Containers are available in a wide variety of shapes and a large choice of materials.

Stone and concrete Stone flower containers are often prohibitively priced. They must be made by hand and, consequently, they are seldom produced today. Old models come from antique shops with price tags suggesting that the stone used is precious rather than mundane. Fortunately, the problem has been recognized and is being rectified by the use of reconstituted stone.

Its main virtue is that it can be molded, which means that many copies of a single model can be made instead of just one. Inevitably, this leads to a limited number of designs and the fact that one is likely to see one's own containers in a neighbor's garden, but this matters less today than it used to do. Designs are chosen that have a universal appeal and will suit most surroundings and conditions, and it is from these that the artificial stone duplicates are made. Sometimes they tend to be somewhat grainy, crumbly and soft at first, but normal weathering can be expected to harden and mature them so that they become safe under conditions of normal handling. Harder and tougher are those models that are cast in concrete rather than molded in stone; when new, these seem to have a somewhat unsympathetic surface texture, yet this again weathers to become a great deal more appealing.

Above: Unusual containers always appeal, but they should be practical enough to hold sufficient soil.

Below: Terra-cotta is used for all these containers.

All stone and concrete containers by the nature of the material are bound to be somewhat large and heavy, an impressive addition to patio design. They need to be placed carefully and are often improved if stood on a plinth or formal base. Various plinths, bases and balustrades are also available in reconstituted stone, as indeed are a range of statuary and ornaments that do much to bring back into the garden or even the patio a grace of decoration that was for a time lost because of the expense.

Asbestos A material similar in some respects to stone but lighter in weight and thinner in section is asbestos, used to produce containers that are pleasant in shape, comparatively light in weight, neutral in color and flexible in design. Being thinner,

Left: Half-sphere containers such as this are often available at reasonable cost.
Below: New shapes and materials are constantly being produced for the patio or terrace.

this material is particularly suitable for making smaller containers.

Wood The most common material for a window box is wood, and wood (redwood, cypress and others) is commonly used for tubs, square or rectangular planters and raised beds. This is because a wooden box can be made exactly to measure and, in the case of a window box, can be fixed in position with brackets or screws without trouble. If using wood, make sure that it is stout enough to last for more than one or two seasons. It should normally be at least l in (2–3 cm) thick and of a dense timber such as redwood. The exterior will probably be painted, but before this is done the entire surface should be coated inside and out with one of the copper naphthenate solutions, normally available as solutions in green, brown or natural. Do not use creosote, which is toxic to plants until it is old. If the box is painted, make sure that the paint has dried and all fumes have dissipated before doing any planting. The copper naphthenate solution will add years to

Above: Containers on a balcony should always be heavy or well balanced enough to avoid being blown over.
Below: Precast concrete and preformed asbestos will complement the brilliant flowers they contain.

Above: Choose containers to fit the style of the plant and the atmosphere of the site. *Below*: Always conceal the mouths of containers like this with plant growth.

the life of wood because it inhibits attack by all fungi and many insects.

Plastic and fiberglass Various types of plastic substances have been used for the production of containers, from the traditional flower pot to larger and more elaborate designs. Few of these plastic containers are suitable for window box use, mainly because of their lightness in weight and the fact that they are not easy to fix permanently and safely in position. A stronger material than most plastic is glass fiber, and apart from the fact that this again is dangerously light in weight, a fiberglass window box can generally be fixed securely in position. Fiberglass can be made in the widest possible range of shapes and designs, and finishes can also be controlled to some extent so that the completed container can look like plastic, timber or, most successfully, like antique lead. Fiberglass is not as cheap as most plastic, but, on the other hand, it is virtually everlasting, whereas some of the less expensive plastics tend to degrade under the influence of sunlight and lose their color and strength so that eventually they begin to split and must be replaced.

Choosing containers

Containers should be chosen carefully, partly for their suitability to the task and partly for aesthetic reasons. A little imagination and knowledge of what's available can be the keys to proper container acquisition. Antique and second-hand shops don't just offer expensive stoneware. Sometimes quite reasonable discarded farm feeding troughs can be found, or weathered wooden barrels can turn up. Don't overlook possibilities in pottery studios, where often not-so-costly ceramic containers are sold. Then there are also the prosaic tin cans,

Above: This plastic container is in the style of a coopered timber tub but is longer lasting.
Below: A few potted plants and a climber or two will quickly furnish an otherwise stark patio.

Where a container is unlikely to be moved, it can be as large as you like and hold anything up to a tree.

all containers have to be first transported to the spot where they are to be filled. This again suggests that, to say the least, lightness will be a convenience.

Clean colors suit balcony use because they fit into any decorative scheme. Plastic surfaces can easily be kept clean, wiped down quickly with a damp cloth or sponge. Some plastic surfaces will accept the growth of algae, molds and moss unless they are cleaned regularly. This may not be of importance in a garden or even on occasion on some patios, but, as a general rule, a soiled container like this would not be acceptable on a balcony.

Because a balcony is normally smaller than a patio it cannot accommodate the cumbersome containers of large plants that might be appropriate for the patio. So to get the same effect of flower and plant color on the balcony, one is forced to use a greater number of containers. There is nothing wrong with this so long as they are mainly massed together and not dotted about piecemeal. On a patio it is possible to cover an entire wall with a single plant growing either in the soil or in a large container. As far as the balcony is concerned neither the wall space nor the large container is available, so for concentrated impact a large number of pots must be massed together, some raised or banked to be easily visible.

Containers for growing crops

The plants grown on a balcony, in a window box or on a patio are nearly always purely decorative. The exception might be a few herbs grown on the patio. This is traditional, but there are a number of other, less traditional crops that are now being grown in these locations. Examples include lettuce, carrots, cress, Swiss chard, and mustard, which grow best in window boxes or planters. In tubs, large pots, even bushel baskets, grow tomatoes, eggplant, pepper and cucumber.

In comparatively recent years a new method of growing some of these crops has been developed in England and is just

discards from the kitchen. These can be sprayed with paint, punched with drainage holes, and used as hanging or stationary containers.

In addition, on a charming and sophisticated town patio, plastic containers would seem to strike a wrong note unless the design is also sophisticated. But plastic on a balcony seems much more at home, probably because it is functionally correct in its lightness and its easily cleaned surfaces. The balcony is more an extension of the house than is the patio, for it is connected to the home, whereas the patio proper is a link with house and with garden.

On a balcony it is almost certain that a container of growing plants will have to be moved on occasion. This means that it must be as light in weight as possible. One should also remember, when buying, that

advisable to use the bag for a second crop.)

It is a clean, easy and efficient way of growing, and one eminently suited to use on the patio or the balcony. The sacks are not, perhaps, attractive in appearance, but they can be disguised or hidden and it is, after all, the crop that is most important.

Hanging baskets

Hanging baskets are a useful and charming addition to a balcony display and they can

Left and below: Why empty the growing medium out of the sack into a container if you can use the bag itself as the container? These growing bags are used mainly for the convenient culture of vegetables and salads.

beginning to catch on in the United States, a method that for various reasons has proved so successful that it has been widely adopted by the commercial growing world, which we can accept as an indication of its viability. Basically, the idea is that instead of buying a special soil mixture and scooping this out of its sack into containers, the sack itself is used as the container. It is laid flat on the floor, and is slit open. Then the crop, such as tomato plants, for example, are placed in it just as they might be in a clay pot or in soil.

The plastic sack, sometimes called a 'pillow pak', is waterproof and the growing medium, normally a specially enriched peat mixture, is clean, sterile and balanced. All that is needed is the addition of water. Although these growing bags appear to be expensive and make the cost of the tomatoes or lettuces grown in them no cheaper than those in the shops, they are highly convenient and easy to use, and the growing medium can subsequently be used in the garden or to fill other pots. (It is not

provide color high on a wall, helping to make the most of the limited space available. They are unusual decorations, which bring welcome splashes of color where they are not normally expected.

The usual type of frame for a hanging basket is a half sphere of galvanized wire 12–18 in (30–45 cm) in diameter and provided with chains and a ring for hanging.

167

There are also types, usually made from some plastic material, which involve fewer problems. In either case the bracket from which the basket is to be hung must be strong and firmly fixed to the wall, for the basket, when planted and watered, can be very heavy indeed. Although they should be placed high enough to be out of the way of people walking below, they should not be so high that they are difficult to water, for they dry out quickly and will require water both morning and evening on a dry and sunny day. Make sure that any drips that might fall cannot harm other plants that are growing below, and, if the baskets are in a position over a street or sidewalk, see that they are hung so as not to drip on unwary passers-by.

When you are using a wire frame basket, it must have a lining to serve as a cup or container for the soil. Moss is the best material for this, but as this is not always available or easy to obtain, other materials will suffice. Thin sods of grass, laid so that the grass is on the inside and the soil on the outside, will be a useful substitute if you have access to them. Alternatively, pieces of burlap will usually last for a season and, if it is coarse enough, will allow shoots of some plants to grow through it and so clothe the basket in growing green, for the purpose will be to have flowers and foliage everywhere. Some wire and plastic baskets now come with a molded fiber liner. And it is possible to line the basket with plastic

sheeting, but remember that holes must be made in the bottom to permit excess water to escape.

Having lined the wire basket, fill the interior with a good, rich soil. Knock the plants from their pots and plant them in this compost, positioning them to trail prettily over the edges or even to grow downwards through the lining. Water the basket thoroughly and make sure that it is never allowed to dry out. You will find that on some days this will mean watering twice or even three times, so it may be worth your while to fix a hose on to a cane so that it can be lifted easily, to water from a window above or to have the hanging basket on a rope and pulley so that it can easily be lowered. In the last case it will sometimes be helpful to water the basket by immersion rather than by pouring water from above. Simply drop it into a bucket or basin and leave it there until uniformly moist, then allow to drain and restore it to its correct position.

Plastic hanging baskets will not normally allow plants to grow through the base, so it is more than ever necessary to have plants or trails hanging over the sides so as to conceal what might otherwise be a rather ugly naked material. On the other hand, plastic hanging baskets usually have a drip tray incorporated, which means that not only do you have fewer worries about water falling on other plants or on the heads of people, but a single watering will last longer, for the moisture that collects in this tray is more or less a reservoir for the main basket, the water being released slowly as it is needed.

Useful plants for hanging baskets include several varieties of the ever-popular pelargonium, some of the smaller-leaved ivies, sweet alyssum, lobelia, impatiens, nasturtium, petunia, thunbergia, and some of the begonias. Among the tender perennials choose from *Achimenes*, several of the more pendulous fuchsias, *Hoya bella*, the quick-growing plectranthus with its glossy leaves and some of the tradescantias and zebrinas. And, of course, ferns, both the tender house plant kinds and some hardy species, such as the Christmas fern, are graceful hanging basket subjects for shade.

Left: Line a hanging basket, then fill with a moisture-retentive soil. Allow some plants to trail.

Below: Fix hanging baskets securely and high enough to be out of the way of passers-by.

3 Techniques

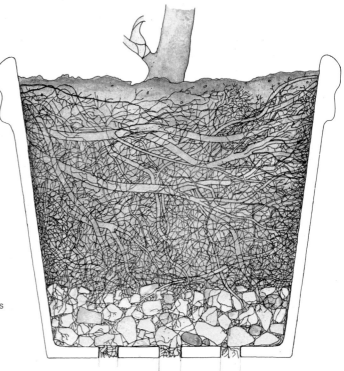

A plant's roots travel round in its container searching always for fresh moisture and fertilizer to keep it in good health.

With few exceptions, plants for patios, window boxes and balconies usually have to be grown in containers. A plant growing in a container can be killed in a day by neglect: it depends entirely on the gardener for its life because it cannot send its roots out in search of food and drink.

The soil in which plants grow is important. But this is not enough, for plants, like humans, need food and moisture, light, air, warmth and a degree of shelter. And the roots have as much need of these benefits as do the branches, foliage and flowers.

Aeration

Plants in containers need more water than plants in the ground, and this will affect the soil. Some of the soil is washed away, the fertilizer content is leached out, the surface may become brick-like, and the drainage holes may become clogged up.

Attention must be paid to the top and bottom of the soil. Scratch the soil surface lightly every now and then to open it up to the air. It also helps to mulch the soil surface once or twice a year with a rich leaf-mold, with a well-rotted farmyard manure, or even with a handful or two of moist peat.

Drainage

The base of the soil in a container cannot be reached, of course, but at the time of initial planting, before the soil is poured in, be

sure to include a layer of drainage material such as broken crocks, pebbles, or pea gravel. This will allow moisture to course through the soil quickly and easily. A spongy material, such as coarse peat or well-rotted farmyard manure, placed between the drainage layer and the soil will prevent over-quick drying out of the soil in larger containers.

Light and shade

It is not always easy to provide enough light when growing plants on an enclosed patio, on a shaded balcony, or in a window box on the north side of a building. Most plants will grow, but they cannot be expected to give their best. In some circumstances it may be possible to paint one of the walls in a light color, which will reflect more light. But the important thing is to choose plants that will grow happily and well under conditions of constant shade. It will also help where possible to give the container a quar-

Above: Poor light can be considerably improved by painting nearby walls a light color.
Below: If it is impossible to improve the light, grow only plants that tolerate shady conditions.

171

Roots can be kept at an even temperature by surrounding the plant pot with insulating material.

ter turn once a week or so to ensure that light strikes all sides of the plant, so that it grows upright instead of leaning towards the light. It is sometimes possible to move plants around so that, by rotation, each plant will have a chance of receiving some sunlight.

Temperature

Plants must be selected according to the climate and the situation or aspect in which they will be placed. Many plants like to have their head in the sun and their feet in the shade, and this should not be difficult to arrange. In hot sunshine the heat from the container may be transferred to the soil and then to the roots. To keep the soil cool, small containers can be placed inside larger ones, with the space between filled with dry peat or some other insulating material. Larger containers will have to be protected from the sun by some kind of portable shelter, such as a sun umbrella.

Pests and diseases

Container-grown plants are less open to trouble from pests and diseases than those grown in garden soil. We can quickly and easily clear our plants from any pest infestation with proprietary pesticides. Frequently, it is possible to pick off caterpillars from a plant, or to wash off aphids and red spider mites with soapy water.

Diseases can be brought by insect attack or can be the result of physiological disorder. They are less easy to cure than insect attack, but just as easy to prevent. Any plant susceptible to mildew or other fungal trouble should be sprayed before the disease is apparent, thus keeping it at bay.

Town sparrows can cause damage to town-grown plants, especially as they love to take dust baths in beds of fine soil sown with seeds. Large areas can have black thread strung over them, just 2–4 in (5–10 cm) above the soil. Small plants can be protected with a temporary dome of wire netting, and the sparrows can be kept off some plants by spraying or dusting the plants with one of the modern deterrents.

A wire netting dome can easily and quickly be slipped over a plant if it is being attacked by birds.

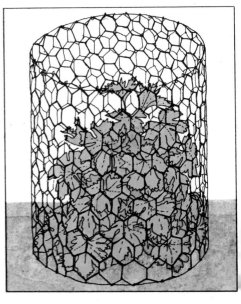

172

4 Plants

There are a lot of hybrid Japanese maples, many of them dwarf and suited to tub culture, and all particularly attractive because of the shape and color of the rich foliage.

The right plant for the right container

Any plant that will grow in the soil will grow in a container. Surprisingly large trees and shrubs will grow in comparatively small containers, but not for long. It is wise to try to match the size of the plant with the size of the container. Bear in mind the fact that the roots of a plant are roughly the same size as that part of a plant that grows above ground. A tree's roots will extend more or less to the same area as that occupied by the branches. This means that in a tub or pot the roots must coil round and

round, and this indeed they do until they just cannot grow any longer or find any more space open to them. They will then sometimes break the container, but more often they will begin to die.

However, really large trees or shrubs do not look right except in a container so large that it is fitted for a park, stately home or town square rather than the confined patio. Because so large a container cannot be fitted into limited space, we might be tempted to employ a smaller but lightweight container and here we will again run into

173

Camellias require an acid soil which is easily provided in a tub if they are to flourish.

trouble, for it will be found that the least puff of wind will overbalance the tree and send it over on its side. There is also the fact that a large or tall tree or shrub will probably require staking, and a stake in a container looks hideous and is exceedingly difficult to fix firmly into place.

Because any contained plant attracts more attention than a comparable plant growing in a bed or border in the garden, it should preferably be an evergreen.

Choosing plants for window boxes, balconies and patios

There are many non-woody plants that can be grown in containers on a balcony, in a window box or even on a patio. The choice must always be one of personal taste. It might help, however, to emphasize that, in all locations other than the garden proper, tall and floppy plants cannot be considered because they will need staking, and a stake in a container is an abomination. Certain other tall plants may be strong enough to

stand on their own in some situations but will look out of proportion when they are growing in a container.

Plants for the patio Some of the most useful plants for the patio are those that cover a considerable area yet leave the limited floor space almost entirely free – climbers. They take up little space yet give a vast return in providing leaves and sometimes flowers in abundance. They soften outlines, blur sharp angles and help to bring peace and quiet.

The most useful climbers are those that are both evergreen and self-clinging, but, unfortunately, there are only a few of these, especially in the North. Probably the best is the ivy, available in a wide range of varieties, colors and leaf sizes. The ivy will cling to a wall yet do little or no damage to it except after many years. It will make no demands in the way of special feeding or watering so long as it is growing in the soil and not in a pot. It can quite easily be trained to travel in any direction you choose and is quite simple to prune.

Among some of the other evergreen climbers there is *Eccremocarpus scaber*, the Chilean glorybower, with attractive fern-like foliage and, in the summer, orange-red tubular flowers, followed by unusual seed pods shaped like a small sack or bladder. This vine is only winter-hardy and evergreen in the south. Elsewhere it can be grown as an annual, but seeds must be started early indoors.

Berberidopsis corallina, the coral plant, has dark green, heart-shaped leaves, their undersides a glaucous blue-gray. It provides pendulous clusters of dark red flowers in summer.

Shrubs that are grown on the patio will have to be fairly small, whether they are grown in the soil or in a container. This is just as well, for if any shrub is to be grown in a space where its roots have little room to travel, it will tend to stay rather smaller than if given plenty of space. Although dwarfed to a certain extent by the environ-

The vivid scarlet berries of *Pyracantha coccinea* show at their best against a wall. Not strictly a climber because the plant needs support, the pyracantha responds well to training.

ment, there is no reason why most suitable shrubs should not live for some years.

Once again evergreens are useful because they are decorative at all times of the year. One that has several uses is the sweet bay, *Laurus nobilis*, which can be pruned into shape so that it becomes living sculpture. It also provides the occasional leaf for the kitchen pot when needed. It will grow in sun or shade, but in Northern regions must be grown in a tub so it can be brought indoors over winter.

Another evergreen that will stand shaping is the common box, *Buxus sempervirens*. Hardier in the North are the varieties of Korean box (*B. microphylla koreana*). These will grow in sun or shade.

If there is space for two or more plants of aucuba, you can have small, tough, evergreen shrubs that will grow in sun or shade and in grossly polluted air, and at the same time will provide glossy green and gold leaves and shining red berries. Aucuba is winter-hardy where temperatures don't fall much below 10°F (22°C).

There are a considerable number of deciduous or evergreen cotoneasters that will do well in soil or in containers on the patio, most of them bearing white flowers to be followed by scarlet berries, the flowers loved by bees and the berries by birds. Many of the cotoneasters are shrubs, some can be trees and there are others that either can be prostrate or will lean happily against a wall almost like a climber.

Two evergreen species of the normally deciduous euonymus, or the spindle, are *E. fortunei* and *E. japonica*, both with a number of varieties with differing leaf shape, size and color. Both of these are tolerant of soil, sun or shade.

An exceptionally hardy evergreen holly is inkberry, Ibex glabra, which bears black berries. This shrub of medium height is tolerant of city conditions and will grow in partial shade.

And, finally, consider the glorious pieris, hardy evergreens with the most dainty appearance. *Pieris forrestii* and *P. taiwanensis* are two species that come immediately to mind, but there are several more and a number of useful varieties. Some of these

produce pretty racemes of little white flowers like lily-of-the-valley and are noted also for their young springtime growth o' vivid scarlet shoots. The pieris like a moist and peaty soil together with a lightly shaded position.

Trees and shrubs

In the next few pages a number of trees and shrubs are briefly examined, most of them evergreen. It is suggested that, except under the most favorable circumstances, they are suitable only for growing on a patio. They are too large for all but the most magnificent balcony and, of course, unsuited to any window box. Plants suited to these sites will be discussed in detail later.

Some of the dwarf Japanese maples make first-class patio plants. Often gnarled and twisted they appear almost like bonsai and the vivid colors of their leaves attract immediate attention. They are deciduous. *Acer palmatum* 'Atropurpureum' is thickly

Top: The young foliage of *Pieris forrestii* is a vivid red, even outshining the little white flowers.
Above: *Euonymus fortunei*, the spindle, has several forms, green or variegated, prostrate or upright.

Useful because it flowers in winter, *Erica carnea* has many varieties with colored flowers and foliage.

covered with reddish-purple foliage. Keep them out of strong sun and drying winds.

An evergreen that will grow in part sun or shade is *Aucuba japonica*, available in several forms, large and small, with white, yellow or red berries and yellow and green splashed foliage. It is hardy up to about southern New Jersey and like regions. You must have bushes of both sexes in order to get berries.

If you have space and are prepared to go to a little trouble to find and select your plants, some of the Japanese varieties of evergreen azaleas can present you with rich and vivid flowers in late spring and early summer, and plenty of foliage color at other times of the year. Choose from a specialist catalog or go to a nursery or garden center to pick out your own. Give these plants a moist, peaty soil and a situation where they will not be baked by too strong a sun or blown by too strong a wind.

Box will grow on a balcony as well as a patio, for it can be clipped and controlled so that it does not grow too large. It can be rather fun clipping formal shapes in box,

and these plants grow easily. *Buxus sempervirens*, the common box, is plain green and evergreen. The Korean box is hardier than the common box.

There are a number of cotoneasters that grow well in containers and that give not only masses of little flowers in the spring but follow these with berries, usually scarlet. Bees love the blooms and birds the berries. There are many cotoneasters, both evergreen kinds for less severe climates and deciduous ones for more rugged regions that can be in the form of trees, shrubs or sprawling plants. Most can be trained to grow as you want them.

Most ericas or heathers must have a lime-free soil in which to grow, but this is not so with *Erica carnea*. Nevertheless, with container-grown plants, it is easy enough to tailor the soil to the plant, so ericas should be attended to very closely because so many of them will give excellent winter color.

A splendid architectural plant for the patio is *Fatsia japonica*, bearing large, dramatic, glossy green, palmate leaves.

Fatsia japonica makes an excellent pot plant, producing large, distinctive, palmate leaves.

Ruta graveolens, or rue, has a low, compact habit of growth and bright blue-gray foliage.

The flowers are insignificant and even the berries are subordinate to the foliage. Fatsia and the bay tree that follows are good container plants in the North, where they are not winter-hardy. Plants in tubs can be brought indoors to a sun porch or well-lighted but cool room until spring.

Culinary bay leaves are picked from plants of the sweet bay, *Laurus nobilis*, which is also decorative and useful. It is not a spectacular plant and is best grown clipped or pinched to familiar and formal shape. It will grow in sun or shade, and it is an evergreen.

Another subshrub, and barely evergreen in the North with a pearly-gray foliage, is the medicinal herb rue, *Ruta graveolens*. Keep the shrub trimmed back each spring and concentrate on getting good foliage by removing the yellow flowers, which begin to appear in the early summer, before they open.

Santolina is yet another silver, gray or almost white-leaved bush that will benefit from being cut back in the early spring, almost to the previous year's growth. The best form is *Santolina chamaecyparissus*, small, thick growing and producing masses of yellow flowers in midsummer. Remove these

flowers as they pass their best and you will achieve a constant succession almost all summer through.

There are so many hardy conifers suitable for containers and patios. They have great architectural value with their formal shapes: they can be upright, conical or low and spreading; they can be green, glaucous blue, gold or silver. They are easy, tolerant plants to grow so long as they are not allowed to become dry at their roots. There are dwarf and slow-growing varieties of conifer that will live for many years in a large pot. A golden conifer in the wintertime can be just as bright as a tree of flowers.

One of the slowest-growing conifers is the dwarf Alberta spruce (*Picea glauca* 'Conica'), which maintains a perfect cone shape year after year. At the other extreme in shape is the mugo pine (*Pinus mugo*), which in some choice forms grows like a pincushion.

If you are in doubt about the most suitable conifers for tubs and for your locality, consult your local nursery. They will have a wide knowledge of the best conifers for you. Conifers that grow too large for their containers can be a total disaster.

There are some good container possibilities among the evergreen barberries. Consider the warty barberry (*Berberis verruculosa*), which has spiny, lustrous leaves that are white on their undersides. In fall, the foliage takes on bronze tints. Among the evergreen privets are the Japanese (*Ligustrum japonicum*) and glossy (*L. lucidum*), both much grown in the South, but usually winter-hardy as far as Long Island.

An interesting deciduous shrub that is very hardy and that can be grown in a tub for a time is the winged euonymus (*E. alatus*). Its winter form is very sculptural.

Bonsai trees

Not suited to growing in a window box, but almost tailored to a life on balcony or patio are examples of the ancient Japanese art of bonsai, the art of dwarfing trees. Although

bonsai trees are sometimes thought of as indoor subjects, they are just as much outdoor trees as their fully-grown brothers. They can be brought indoors for brief periods to be enjoyed in the comfort of the home, but must be taken out again in a day or two, for the home is normally too hot and dry for them.

And even outdoors they must receive some protection against the elements. They must not, for example, be placed where the sun will be on them for more than a short period each day, for their root system is short and shallow. Even if the handful of soil around the roots is kept moist, this moisture cannot be taken up to the leafy extremities at the pace necessitated by the warmth of the sun. They must also be placed in a position where they do not stand in a strong wind. This can knock them over, break their sometimes frail leaves and once again lead to transpiration at a rate that cannot be compensated by the dwarf and delicate root system.

However, if you enjoy bonsai trees and wish to grow them on the patio or the bal-

The container is as important as the tree in creating a beautiful bonsai specimen, and the two should therefore be selected to harmonize with each other.

cony and can give them the necessary elementary protection, the following notes may be of assistance.

There are four basic ways of starting a bonsai collection, and in order of descending expense these are as follows. At the top is the purchase of genuine, old, trained examples of bonsai already planted in suitable containers. This can be a very expensive matter indeed and, unless you have some basic experience of handling these miniatures, it would seem to be unwise. But, on the other hand, the basic training work will have been completed and your tasks will simply be of maintenance. Any reputable dealer will guarantee your trees, give you advice and assistance, and some will take your tree annually for what could almost be called servicing.

It is often a good idea, by the way, to have this servicing carried out when you intend to take your vacations. Often, at such times, it is a worry to leave treasured

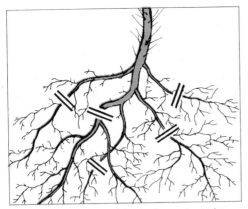

Above: Some of the heavy anchoring roots can be pruned away to save space in the bonsai container.

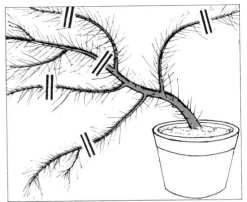

Above: With a careful eye to the final shape desired, cut away some of the excess stem growth.

plants with inexperienced people.

Next in order comes the purchase of trees some five to ten years of age, with a certain minimum of training already given to them. They will have been dwarfed and root pruned several times and their basic shape will have been decided and will be apparent. These trees will be comparatively inexpensive, although the price will reflect the work that has been carried out on them. They may or may not be planted in a decorative container, and may be growing in a flower pot and it will be up to the new owner to transplant them and to grow them on. Look for healthy growth with no signs of disease, damage or insect attack. Make quite sure that you see and understand the purpose and the shape of the preliminary shaping and training that have been done. See that any cuts made were cleanly done, without snags or shredding. Check that the soil in which the plant is growing is moist, yet aerated and well-drained, that no roots protrude above soil level and that the tree is held firm without any trace of rocking. If training wire is wound around branches, see that it is fulfilling its purpose without cutting into the surface.

Buy your container at the same time, making quite sure to choose one that the young tree will be able to grow in for many years and that conforms to the tree in shape as well as size.

Above: Use soft copper wire to bend and control the line of the branches, but never make this too tight.

You can buy young trees through the mail from specialist nurseries for suspiciously low prices, and by doing so you may waste your money. They are inexpensive because they are usually seedlings and are weak, quite incapable of traveling and being brought up in a completely different atmosphere.

If you wish to start from the beginning, it is much better to find and grow on your own trees. Any gardener will know that young oak trees, maples, pines and one or two others are constantly appearing in flower beds as the result of bird, mouse or squirrel activity. If these are carefully dug up, potted, cared for and gradually trained, they are likely to grow into something

180

which is both useful and attractive and which will give you pleasure.

The training of the bonsai tree consists of a somewhat complex balance of maintaining good growth and pinching out growing tips, of bending and splinting to shape, of pruning roots to keep them small in bulk yet capable of feeding the plant with the necessary food and moisture. Although the process could not be described as difficult, a certain talent and a certain sensitivity are necessary in order to obtain really good results with bonsai.

Flowering and foliage plants

The world of herbaceous plants (annuals and perennials) suitable for growing in containers on the patio, on the balcony and even in certain window boxes is a huge one, but it is necessary to be selective. In the first place one must turn down any plants that will grow very tall or will fall and flop about unless they are disciplined and staked. Secondly, one does not wish to make use of plants with so brief a life that they constantly need replacing. This can be the case with a number of herbaceous favorites if they do not get enough moisture at their roots. In general, it will be found that it is best to stick to just a few kinds. Too many plants of too many colors can tire the eye and give a restless, hot and over-busy appearance.

The following list comprises suggestions for plants that can be grown on the patio,

An old bonsai specimen makes a good patio plant.

on the balcony or, in many cases, in window boxes. The average growing height is given for each and there are occasional comments and suggestions. It is impossible to cope here with every combination of conditions that might be met and for this reason it is probable that certain varieties or species will not be successful in certain places. Little will be lost. Experiment will be helpful because it will reveal sometimes surprising results. Although some species or varieties will be suitable, others will not, and a choice must be made.

Ageratum

Names	Measurement	Comments
Achillea	10–20 in (25–50 cm)	Choose dwarf forms of this early summer-blooming perennial.
Achimenes	1–2 ft (30–60 cm)	Tender perennial grown from tiny tubers. Wide range of pink through purple flowers all summer. A trailer for baskets or window boxes.
Ageratum houstonianum	4–20 in (10–50 cm)	Annual that blooms and blooms.
Ajuga bugle	5–15 in (12–36 cm)	Perennial ground cover with blue flowers in spring. Will clothe a large tub.
Alyssum (syn. **Lobularia**) **maritima**	4–6 in (10–15 cm)	Hackneyed, perhaps, but easy from seed and excellent for carpeting, for odd corners and boxes. Fragrant.
Antirrhinum majus snapdragon	7–50 in (18–125 cm)	Tender perennial. Use dwarf varieties, such as 'Floral Carpet', for containers.

Asperula

Begonia

182

Antirrhinum

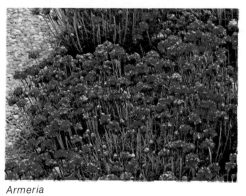

Armeria

Names	Measurement	Comments
Arabis rock cress	6–10 in (15–25 cm)	A perennial that may take over a tub or window box, but only spring-blooming.
Armeria thrift	2–13 in (5–45 cm)	Perennials with flowers of long and lasting life in early summer. Needs full sun and good drainage.
Asperula odorata sweet woodruff	8 in (20 cm)	Dainty-leaved ground cover for partial shade. Perennial.
Begonia		Wide range of shapes, sizes and colors. Among the best for containers and patio decoration.
Bellis perennis English daisy	6 in (15 cm)	Annual or biennial, blooming from spring to early summer.
Campanula bellflower	10–60 in (25–150 cm)	A wide choice, but rock garden types best, except for temporary effects possible from Canterbury bells. Grow *C. isophylla* (Italian bellflower) in hanging baskets.

Bellis

Campanula

Cheiranthus

Chrysanthemum

Names	Measurement	Comments
Cheiranthus wallflower	10–20 in (25–50 cm)	Dwarf and colorful. Spring flowers only.
Chrysanthemum	12–24 in (30–60 cm)	Wide choice of types and varieties, all long-lasting. Late summer-autumn.
Coleus blumei	8–24 in (20–60 cm)	Tender perennial, easy from seeds and cuttings. Varicolored foliage.
Dahlia, Dwarf	10–24 in (25–60 cm)	Tender tuberous perennial. Dwarf types bloom from early summer to frost, and are excellent in tubs.
Dianthus	6–20 in (15–50 cm)	Many sweet-smelling pinks that will do well as long as they have good sun and well-drained soil.
Eschscholzia californica California poppy	24 in (60 cm)	Seeds must be sown in early spring or fall during cool weather. Then needs full sun and good drainage.

Gaillardia

Iberis

Dianthus

Eschscholzia

Names	Measurement	Comments
Fuchsia	3–5 ft (90–150 cm)	Tender shrubs, almost solely pot and tub subjects in the North. Procumbent types fine in hanging baskets in partial shade.
Gaillardia	18–36 in (45–90 cm)	Perennial needing full sun and good drainage. Summer-blooming.
Heliotropium arborescens heliotrope	2–6 ft (60–180 cm)	Tender shrub long popular for baskets, as standards in tubs or for bedding around a patio, where its fragrant purple flowers can be enjoyed.
Hemerocallis day-lily	24–72 in (60–180 cm)	Choose the lower growing varieties of strong fragrance for tubs on a patio.
Iberis sempervirens candytuft	10–20 in (25–50 cm)	Several useful evergreen varieties with mostly spring flowers. Require full sun and good drainage. Plant around the edges of raised beds.

Impatiens

Lysimachia

185

Pelargonium

Petunia

Names	Measurement	Comments
Impatiens wallerana patience-plant	12–24 in (30–60 cm)	Popular indoors as well as out in its many new varieties. A tender perennial easy from seeds and cuttings. Fine in hanging baskets, boxes or in ground beds around patio. Endures semi-shade.
Lysimachia nummularia moneywort, creeping Charlie	1–2 in (3–6 cm)	Perennial trailer that can be weedy in lawns but is safe if confined to a pot. Glossy foliage and yellow flowers all summer.
Pelargonium geranium		Variable height according to how the plant is grown. This is perhaps the best-known and most used container plant in many parts of the world. It is also one of the best.
Petunia	9–24 in (23–60 cm)	Many types, many sizes, many colors, all of them good.

Sedum

Sempervivum

Phlox drummondii

Saxifraga

Names	Measurement	Comments
Phlox drummondii	6–15 in (15–40 cm)	The annual phlox provides a wide and useful range of plants for many locations.
Saxifraga saxifrage	6–12 in (15–30 cm)	There are many kinds and many colors.
Sedum stonecrop	2–8 in (5–20 cm)	Stonecrops of many kinds, shapes, textures and colors are natural inhabitants of troughs and tubs. They are tolerant of neglect.
Sempervivum houseleek	4–12 in (10–30 cm)	Sometimes difficult to differentiate from the stonecrops.
Thymus thyme	2–8 in (5–20 cm)	There are a large number of thymes, mainly creeping or mat-forming, most in vivid colors and all easy to grow.
Viola pansy and viola	4–8 in (10–20 cm)	The biennial pansy is a worthy plant for window boxes and planters in spring.

Thymus

Viola

187

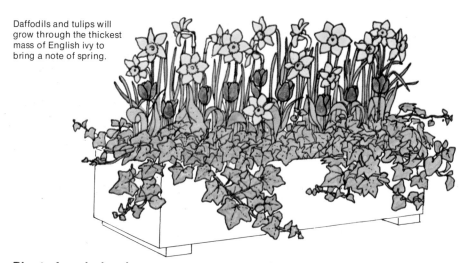

Daffodils and tulips will grow through the thickest mass of English ivy to bring a note of spring.

Plants for window boxes

Some of the preceding plants will grow well in a window box, but circumstances vary here and it is difficult to make recommendations without knowing details. Sun and shade, wind, size of box and depth of soil, all these and other matters affect what plants can most successfully be grown. There is also the personality and the courage of the owner to be taken into account, for some growers will attempt anything and will frequently succeed, whereas others will grow only the tried and tested plants and even then will fail. Window boxes are always tricky because their situation makes them liable to freak winds in some locations, which can either break and batter the plants or can sear them and burn them so that they either die or at the best fail to grow as they otherwise could.

In winter, window boxes can be planted with winter heaths (*Erica*), with the broad-leaved green of skimmia, with ivy and some of the dwarf conifers. These will not give much color other than a pleasant green and they will have to be washed or hosed down every so often to remove from the foliage the gritty dust that is almost certain to settle on them if they are being grown in a city. They will, nevertheless, be growing plants and they will be evidence that life still exists in a cold and bleak world.

Before installing your winter plants anticipate spring by underplanting with bulbs. Snowdrops, crocuses, daffodils, tulips and others will grow quite successfully in window boxes, and as they appear, the drab winter occupants can be removed

Below: Petunias are excellent window-box flowers so long as faded flowers are constantly removed.

188

or allowed to stay with the green leaves of the bulbs growing through them. When choosing your bulbs, make sure you select only the dwarf kinds. Do not attempt to grow any daffodils or tulips with long stems in a window box, for they will almost inevitably snap in the strong winds.

As the bulbs die, so the fear of frost becomes less and when all danger of this has passed, you can prepare for the glory of summer. Trite and commonplace they may be, but the magnificent, easy and showy pelargoniums, or geraniums, take a lot of beating and will last the whole of the summer until the frosts come again. There is the widest possible choice of color, shape and form, including some of the fancy-leaved types that look so well when seen at close range and have aromatic foliage.

If the site is sunny and the soil can be watered frequently, you will find that dwarf zinnias and dwarf or French marigolds will flourish. Petunias will grow colorful and

Above: Clematis can make a good foil for a window box, if correctly trained around the window.
Below: Geraniums will grow well almost anywhere.

189

lush if you feed and water them well. Lobelia, sweet alyssum, verbena and the new strong, dwarf and rust-free varieties of antirrhinum will all remain in constant bloom.

Where the boxes are on the shady side of the house, you will probably have more success with wax begonias and impatiens, all of which will give you tremendous amounts of color.

If you are both keen and ambitious, as well as willing to take a chance against the elements, it is quite possible in many circumstances to grow one or two climbers to surround the window frame, particularly the quick-growing climbers and trailers of the tropaeolum family, which gives us

Canary creeper and the nasturtiums. Make sure that supports are available and that the tendrils are secured at all times, for it only needs a single long trailer to break free and the whole plant will be in peril from the winds.

If you are not concerned about the view from the window or even the light that enters, it is perfectly possible to grow in the window box a series of climbers that will cover the entire space. A number of examples have been seen of pole beans that have been grown mainly to conceal the view of the house next door, and have also presented the growers with several meals of vegetables. In a case such as this, make sure that supports are firm, that the plants are secure in their growth and that you can get at them for attention and for picking without damage to the plants or danger to you.

Lobelia, geraniums, petunias, tagetes, alyssum, and begonias all in a container of some kind, are centered round the window box to make a vivid display.

190

Tomatoes in window boxes or small containers require watering two or three times a day in hot weather.

Food crops

It is perfectly possible to grow certain of the smaller food crops, mainly salads, in a window box. Lettuce, radishes, and carrots are examples of this, and certainly strawberries can be grown. If the appearance of the window box is of major concern, then these crops can be grown between flowering plants or, if there is space enough, they can be grown at the back (i.e., the window side) of the box. It is not suggested that any major contribution towards feeding the family can be made by this means, but it is always pleasant to have a freshly cut lettuce plant or crisp radishes straight from the soil.

The secret of all vegetable-growing is to hurry the plants along, grow them quickly, for they are then tender and succulent. To do this it is necessary to have a richer than ordinary soil and plenty of moisture, so incorporate plenty of humus-making material in your soil mixture and use frequent liquid feeds.

Little more can be grown on most balconies than one can raise in a window box, but a patio is a different matter and here, depending on size and inclination, it is possible to have one or two fruit trees, a miniature vegetable patch, a herb garden and other culinary crops.

5 Roof gardens

The main advantage of a roof garden over other forms of gardening above ground level is one of sheer space. On a roof the sky is literally the limit – at least in one dimension, and other boundaries depend on the size of the building. Yet all plants will have to be grown in some container, which means watering will be a constant exercise. Winds can be a problem on a roof, but shade will probably cause less trouble.

Preparation

Before beginning any roof garden it is vital that the actual roof surface be examined to

Rich soil and copious watering will result in lush growth on the roof garden, and this in turn will help to keep the roots always cool and moist.

make quite sure that it cannot be damaged. The structure of the building should also be investigated because if the garden is to be extensive in any way, the extra weight that will be placed on the load-bearing sections may be very considerable. When it is wet, soil can be very heavy indeed. Where the roof is composed of some bituminous material, take care that all containers placed on it have rounded edges, rather than sharp ones, for sharp edges can easily work into sun-softened bitumen and can cut and pierce it.

On some roofs it is possible to make beds around the circumference by containing soil with bricks. Most roofs have a low retaining wall around them for safety reasons and soil can be placed against this wall and held in position by the bricks. Here it is especially necessary to make quite certain that the roof surface is sound and, in particular, that the junction of roof and wall is free from any cracks or faults. The roots of plants will easily find their way into any crevice or crack and quickly enlarge the opening until water can seep through and cause damage.

Beds of this type present the greatest opportunities for effective roof gardening. One advantage is that with complete beds, all plant roots will have a wider area in which to roam. Also, the soil will take longer to dry out, so watering will be less of a problem. And because it is possible to

The larger the size of the bed on a roof garden, the greater the moisture reservoir there will be and the less watering that will be necessary.

have a greater depth of soil, taller trees can be grown without the danger that they will be blown over. Aesthetically, it is more satisfying to grow plants in a long and comparatively wide bed than in a series of small containers.

It is possible, too, to install special soils for special plants. Azaleas, which require an acid soil, grow well on rooftops, and so do various pinks and carnations, which prefer a more alkaline mixture. It would be unwise to try to grow bog plants on a roof, but the location admirably suits the drier and sandier soils demanded by cacti and other succulents. Herbs for the kitchen can quite easily be grown, as well as an occasional lettuce, some radishes and perhaps even some carrots. If there is space to spare, it is quite possible to grow pots of tomatoes, so long as you can find a place for them that is protected from strong winds.

Watering

The greatest problem on a roof garden, as with gardening on a balcony or in a window box, is watering. Whether plants are being grown in containers or in artificial beds, neither has any quantity or depth of soil, which means that evaporation in the sun and air is quick. Watering must be thorough and frequent, sometimes twice a day. Not all roof gardens have facilities for such frequent watering, but with a little ingenuity it is usually possible to rig up a hosepipe from some convenient spot on the floor below and lead this onto the roof. Take care when watering that gusts of wind do not send showers into open windows nearby or onto the streets below. Make sure also that all drainage pipes are kept free of fallen leaves or other debris that might block them and cause trouble.

Other roof garden features

Every roof garden should provide space for leisure. Arrange plantings so that at the hottest part of the day the leisure area is in shade. A strategically placed tree or a vine-covered pergola, both perfectly possi-

Below: Succulents grow well on a roof because there they get the hot sunshine they need.

ble on a large roof, can provide shade and add interest to the area.

Some roof gardens have space for a small greenhouse. These are especially useful for the raising of seedlings and for the restoration of ailing house plants. Failing a greenhouse, it is almost always possible to install a frame or even a Hotkap in which to bring on seedlings or protect tender plants.

If attention is paid to their watering, vegetables and herbs will grow well and quickly on a roof. When you are harvesting your crops, make sure all city dust and grime are washed away.

All gardening produces waste vegetable matter. This can be converted into soil or compost and stored in a roof garden. With the necessary care, rooftop gardening, like other kinds of gardening in containers, can offer new and rewarding possibilities.

195

Fruit growing

1 Planning the fruit garden

Fruit-growing is a satisfying occupation and by careful planning it is possible to enjoy home-grown fruit all the year round and have sufficient in the freezer for out-of-season use.

Both dessert and culinary apples should be grown, for they are the most useful of all fruits. Where space is restricted, choose dwarf fruit trees, which usually bear sooner and are easier to care for. Ten or twelve apple trees will provide fruit from August until March if it is stored carefully.

Pears, even in standard sizes, grow upwards rather than spreading their branches, so are ideal lawn trees. They can also be grown as espaliers (horizontal-trained), on a sunny wall or along a path, and in this way will take up little space.

Of the stone fruits, peaches are the most sensitive to low winter temperatures. The blossoms that open on bare branches before the leaves unfurl are also very vulnerable to late frosts. Standard-size peach trees fit most home properties because the trees can be pruned to restrict growth. They can also be grown against a sunny wall or fence as fan-shaped trees. Full sun is essential. Reliance and Sunapee are two peach varieties that are suited to cold climates.

Most of the plums are very hardy and can be grown as part of the home orchard, as lawn trees or against a wall as fan-shaped trees. Among plums are the Damson types, used for jellies and preserves, the Gage varieties, considered superb dessert fruits as well as jam sources. In the home

The plan makes the best use of a small area and takes into consideration the climatic aspects. For instance, on the sides where cold north-easterly winds are prevalent, blackberries are grown as a hedge and the hardy damson plums act as a windbreak. Horizontally trained grapes and pears may be planted alongside a path to conserve space; and beneath, plums and peaches, gooseberries and strawberries are grown, for they flourish in semi-shade. Red currants and raspberries are planted in full sunlight. Make the rows north to south so that all parts of the plants receive maximum sunlight.

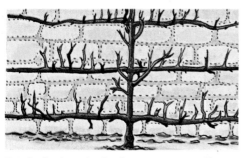
Espalier (horizontal-trained) tree on a warm wall.

fruit orchard it is possible to intercrop among young fruit trees, especially dwarfs, with vegetable crops or other bush fruits. Examples of neat, fairly low bush fruits are currants and gooseberries. Blueberry bushes, although eventually too tall-growing for intercropping, are ornamental enough to serve as an informal hedge.

Although strawberries can be set in double rows between bush fruits, they are usually confined to their own 'bed', often at one end of the vegetable garden. While some home gardeners, mostly because of space restrictions, plant strawberries quite close together, 12 in (30 cm) it is better to set them 15–18 in (37–45 cm) apart in the row.

The cane fruits bear later than the soft fruits, and the hardiest are blackberries, which may be used as a hedge, trained along wires, or alongside a path. Varieties include Darrow, Bailey and U.S.D.A. thornless. All freeze well.

The loganberry is simply a dark red blackberry, the result of a cross between blackberry and raspberry. They also require full sun. Plant blackberries apart, raspberries at 8 ft (240 cm) 18 in (45 cm). Newburgh is an early raspberry, followed by Latham and Taylor. The autumn-fruiting varieties will prolong the season, and September and Heritage are both suitable for this purpose.

There should be a place for a grape vine, against a trellis or trained along wires. Grape varieties vary greatly in their winter hardiness. For those in the colder regions, there are now several varieties of high quality, including Interlaken, a golden seedless variety that ripens early, and Beta, a super-hardy variety for jelly and juice.

One thing that is important today is to plant healthy, virus-free fruits. Avoid well-intentioned handouts from neighbors' gardens that may be carriers of diseases. Two sources for fruits are J. E. Miller Nurseries, Canandaigua, New York 14424 (catalog free), and the New York State Fruit Testing Association, Geneva, New York 14456. Membership in the latter is inexpensive and is refunded if orders are sent.

Apples (culinary)	Apples (dessert)
Greening d	Golden Delicious d
Haralson d	Jonathan d
Mutsu d	Macoun d
Rome Beauty d	McIntosh d
Wealthy d	Stayman Winesap d

Plums	Pears
Burbank	Bartlett d
Damson	Duchess d
Green Gage	Maxine
Santa Rosa	Parker
Standley d	Seckel d

Cherries, Sour	Cherries, Sweet
Early Montmore d	Black Tartarian
North Star d	Napoleon (Royal Ann)
Meteor d	Van d
Montmorency	Vista d

Strawberries	Currants
Dunlap	Red Lake
Geneva e	Wilder
Ogallala e	
Ozark Beauty e	Gooseberries
Sparkle	Pixwell
	Welcome

Raspberries	Blueberries
August red e	Berkeley
Cumberland	Blueray
Heritage e	Collins
September e	Earliblue
Sodus	Lateblue

Peaches	Apricots
Hale Haven d	Early Golden d
Polly d	Moongold d
Redhaven d	Moorpark d
Reliance d	Scout
Sun Haven d	Sungold d

Key: d – usually available as dwarf and can be grown in tubs; e – everbearing variety (bears two crops).

199

Types of fertilizer used in fruit cultivation.

Preparing the ground

Though each fruit requires somewhat different treatment as to soil and climate, the ground should be given a general preparation, so that if each fruit is planted at the right time, the minimum of attention will be needed to bring the soil into just the right condition for maximum crops.

Site and situation are important, for where frosts are troublesome, those fruits flowering early should be omitted unless their blossom is frost-tolerant. If you are thinking of planting only a few dwarf apple trees or a hedge of raspberries, the chances are that the correct site can be found. This means an open, sunny situation free from shade cast by buildings or nearby trees. However, if an actual orchard is contemplated, the site must be chosen with care. Here there will be a substantial investment in cost and time and starting off with the wrong site and soil conditions is folly. The wrong site might be the bottom of a slope reached by cold air draining from above, or the top of a wind-buffeted hill. Avoid any low spots where late frosts in spring can settle in and kill the flower buds. There are few fruits that will grow in wet soils –

blueberries, elderberries and cranberries being the exceptions – so make certain that the soil is well-drained. Sandy soils can be improved by adding humus, as suggested below. For reliable and heavy crops, select varieties to suit the district and the soil of your garden. Blackberries require a heavy soil, containing potash. Plums and cherries do well in a limestone soil if given plenty of nitrogen; apples and pears do not, for they are often troubled by chlorosis (caused through iron starvation), in which the leaves turn yellow and the trees are stunted in growth.

Alkaline soils are usually shallow soils and need liberal amounts of humus, as do sandy soils, such as material from the compost heap, composted straw or decayed manure. If the latter is in short supply, it may be augmented by some peat or by 'green' manuring, in which seed of quick-growing plants, such as winter-rye, vetch and buckwheat, is sown thickly over the surface in fall and the plants dug in when 3 in (7 cm) high.

Except for the use suggested later in the case of heavy clay soils, adding lime to

Below: raking in fertilizer. *Opposite:* essential tools.

Manures and humus materials are shown here being incorporated into the trench.

When digging deep, soil is removed to a depth of at least 16 in (40 cm) or two spades' depth.

decrease the high acidity of soils is not generally recommended. If your soil is heavily acid, you may have the ideal situation for blueberries. It's a good idea to obtain the opinion of local authorities on soil problems. Your county extension agent can advise you on how to get your soil tested.

Heavy clay soil may be broken up quickly by treating it with lime obtained from a builder's supply house. If applied during the early winter just before digging the ground, the action of the lime works to break up the clay particles of the soil. Then, in March, when frost has left the ground, dig in some peat moss, compost or decayed manure before any planting is done.

Soft fruits require plenty of moisture to make growth and for the fruit to swell. To supply the plants with humus, dig in whatever materials are available, such as clearings from ditches, straw composted with an activator, leaf mold and peat. Wool and cotton waste, used hops (obtainable from breweries) and farmyard manure have the advantage over other forms of humus in that they contain greater amounts of nit-

rogen, which is necessary for the plants to make plenty of new growth. Other forms of nitrogenous manure are alfalfa hay, poultry manure and fish meal. Chopped seaweed is also valuable.

Working the soil

No amount of care in supplying the correct fertilizers will be of any value unless they are worked well into the soil. Clear ground is essential, for most fruits are permanent crops and it is difficult to clear the ground after planting without damaging the roots.

It is best to bring the ground into condition in autumn, while it is still dry and in a friable condition. Deep digging is necessary in order to work in the humus to a depth of at least two 'spits' or spades, about 16 in (40 cm).

As the digging is done, it is advisable to treat the ground for wireworms and millipedes, which feed upon the roots of raspberries and strawberries in particular. Everything must be done to ensure that the fruits are given the conditions necessary to bear well over a long period of time.

2 Apples

Apples are the most important of all fruit crops, for they have so many uses and can be stored or prepared for use all year. They are also the hardiest fruit, bearing well in cold climes where, apart from the gooseberry, little else would grow so well.

Apples are available as standard or dwarfs. Dwarfs can be trained to be cordons or pyramids. Although cordons take up little space, making them useful in the small garden, the training and timing to maintain these forms – and to obtain fruits – puts them beyond the ability of the average gardener. The new Malling rootstocks developed at England's Malling Station, have the ability to keep the variety grafted to it. On Malling IX, the trees will come quickly into heavy bearing. They bear fruit rather than make wood, which means growers should know how to prune them and provide the trees with a balanced diet. Dwarf trees on this rootstock may be planted 8–9 ft (240–270 cm) apart; pyramids 6–7 ft (180–210 cm); cordons 3–4 ft (90–120 cm). Plant dwarf trees apart; standards 10 ft (3 m) apart; standards 15 ft (4·5 m) apart.

Trees on the dwarfing rootstocks need careful staking, for they do not produce such large roots as on the more vigorous stocks. Stake the trees immediately they are planted, using strong wooden stakes driven well into the ground, about 12 in (30 cm) from the roots and at a slight angle. Use one of the patented ties, or strips of rubber 12 in (30 cm) long cut from the inner tube of a tyre. The stake must not be in contact with the bark of the tree, or it may rub against it during windy weather.

To obtain heavy crops from limited space, plant cordons and train against wires, Spur-forming apples may be grown in this way, or as small trees.

Soil requirements

Apples require a balanced diet with plenty of humus in the soil to retain moisture – without which the fruits will not make any size and will lack juice. As apples require magnesium in the soil, it is best given, if lacking, when the ground is prepared, as magnesium carbonate, about 1 lb per sq yd (525 g per sq m). Apples also require potash; for heavy soils give 1 oz per sq yd (33 g per sq m), doubling this amount where the soil is light and the potash easily washed away. The amount of nitrogenous manures will depend on variety. The most vigorous apples will need little, for they require no assistance in making new wood. But those of more compact habit need as much compost or farmyard manure as can be obtained, and cooking apples need more nitrogen than dessert kinds. Nitrogen will intensify the green coloring of the cooking apples, whilst potash will bring out the scarlet and crimson colorings of dessert apples. Where possible, use organic nitrogenous manures, which will supply the necessary humus.

Young trees will suffer a shortage of nitrogen if planted directly into grass. In its nitrogen requirements, grass will be in competition with the trees, so it is important when planting in grass first to make a

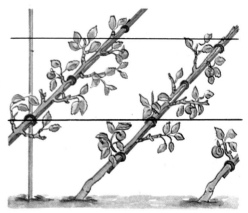

circle of 2 ft (60 cm) diameter and to remove the turf from this area before preparing the soil. In areas of low rainfall, all apples will benefit from a thick mulch of garden compost or farmyard manure given in June to check moisture evaporation. Trees growing in dry districts will also require more nitrogen, and if after two years they have made less than 12 in (30 cm) of new growth, give each tree a 2 oz per sq yd (66 g per sq m) application of sulfate of ammonia early in spring when growth recommences.

Lack of potash may be shown by the leaves turning brown at the edges and becoming crinkled, while the fruit will be small. Potash will also release the phosphates in the soil, which are so important in building up the size of the fruit and stimulating root action. So in spring give each tree a 1 oz per sq yd (33 g per sq m) dressing of sulfate of potash. Magnesium deficiency, which causes the leaves to turn pale green, is corrected by spraying the foliage with magnesium sulfate (Epsom salts) at a strength of 4 oz to 1 gall (25 g to 1 liter) of water.

As suggested earlier, a soil test before planting and then follow-up tests after the trees have been growing, is wise. If any of the deficiencies described above occur, consult a county extension specialist.

Pollination

This is important and it is little use planting several trees of 'Macoun', just because it is one's favorite apple, without a pollinator. Since almost all apples are self-unfruitful (meaning that the pollen of another apple variety is needed for pollination), don't plan on ordering just one apple variety or several plants of the same variety. There are a few exceptions, however! The 5-in-1 apple, available as a standard (full-size) tree or dwarf, should offer no problem because five different apple varieties have been grafted on to one tree. Two other exceptions are 'Golden Delicious' and 'Rome Beauty', which tend to be self-

Standard apple trees bear heavily, but dwarf and semi-dwarf trees bear as well, and sooner.

fruitful. Generally speaking, most apple varieties will pollinate each other – *if* they bloom at the same time, that is – so the bees can work among them.

Triploids will not set their own pollen, nor will they pollinate others, so two pollinators should be grown with them to ensure heavy crops.

Planting

Apples may be planted in early spring or fall. The former is better for extremely northern regions. The soil should be in a friable condition to allow for treading it around the roots when covered over.

Select a tree with a good head and a strong sturdy stem if planting a standard. But for dwarf apples, plant maidens – i.e. one-year-old trees, which are readily established and may be trained and pruned to the requirements of the grower. They are also less expensive to buy than older trees. Cordons are usually planted in trenches, made perhaps on either side of a path; the rows should be 4 ft (120 cm) apart. The trees are tied in to strong wires held in place by strong stakes at intervals of 8–9 ft (240–270 cm).

After making the hole, which must be of ample size, plant by spreading out the roots. Shorten with the pruners any that are too long. This will encourage them to make more fibrous roots. With a grafted fruited tree, especially a dwarf apple, it is important that the graft (a knobby, swollen area low on the trunk) is above ground. If it becomes covered with soil, the scion may put out its own roots, thus eliminating the desirable dwarfness of the understock. Before replacing the soil, which should contain the necessary humus and plant food, sprinkle some damp peat moss over the roots; tread in the soil as it is replaced. Fix the stake in place, tie, and water in if the soil is dry. Before doing any training, select an efficient pair of pruners that feel comfortable in the hand; the pruners will have to be in constant use.

Training and pruning

Training to the required shape will depend on the type of tree to be grown: standard, bush, dwarf pyramid or cordon.

For a **standard**, a 'feathered' tree should be obtained. This means the small 'feathers' or lateral shoots will have been removed by the nurserymen all the way along the stem. A full standard will have a 5–6 ft (150–180 cm) stem, a half standard a 3–4 ft (90–120 cm) stem. The formation of the head, which will be the same for **bush** trees, will be by one of two methods, the 'open center' plan, or the 'delayed open center'.

For the first plan, a bush tree should have a good 'leg' and, like standards, be allowed to grow unchecked the first year, during the winter 'heading' back the main shoot to 3 ft (90 cm) above soil level. This will persuade the tree to 'break' and form two or three shoots, which will form the head. Shoots appearing on the lower 18 in (45 cm) of stem with bushes should be removed. The following winter, the new shoots should be cut back to half way, and the next year the newly formed extension shoots cut back

Cordons may be used alongside a path where space is limited. Plant them 3 ft (90 cm) apart in the rows.

Dwarf pyramids give the heaviest crops in the quickest time and take up little room. Plant 4 ft (120 cm) apart.

Standards produce the heaviest crops over a long period but take several years before bearing heavily. Plant 12 ft (360 cm) apart.

Semi-dwarf trees are somewhere between the pyramid and standard forms, have a long life and bear heavily. Plant 10 ft (3 m) apart.

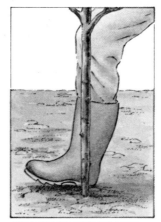

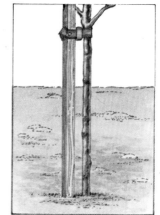

Spread the roots well out, removing any damaged roots before covering.

After covering with soil, tread firmly if the soil is friable, and water in if dry.

To make the tree secure, place a stake close to it and use a rubber tie.

half way, to about 9 in (22 cm) of their base. The head will now have formed.

The delayed open center is made by removing only the top 6 in (15 cm) of the main stem. Then, along the entire length of the stem, buds will form from which new growth will begin and the tree will be built up. Remove any laterals where there is overcrowding, or if several close together are facing in the same direction.

The **dwarf pyramid** form will produce the heaviest crop in the shortest time. Unlike apples in the bush and standard form, there is no waiting several years. For the tree to make as much wood and as many fruit buds as quickly as possible, bud growth must be stimulated by making a nick in the bark just above each bud on the main stem. The shoots formed from the buds are pruned back to half the new season's growth each year to encourage the formation of fruiting buds. Throughout its early life, until well established, the central main shoot must be pruned back each year. This enables the tree to concentrate its energies on the formation of side shoots.

Cordons are single-stem trees, planted at an angle of 45° to restrict the flow of sap and prevent the trees from making too much growth. Maiden trees should be planted 3–4 ft (90–120 cm) apart, and tied in to wires stretched at intervals of 12 in (30 cm) above ground. Here, the main or extension shoot should never be pruned, only the laterals, which in August should be pinched back to 6 in (15 cm) of the main stem. This will ensure the formation of fruiting spurs as quickly as possible. When the main stem has reached 6–7 ft (180–210 cm), it should be cut back to persuade the tree to direct its energies to the side shoots. The removal of surplus fruiting spurs will maintain the quality of the fruit.

The trees should be allowed to grow away in their first year untouched, to form plenty of wood while making root growth. The next winter, pruning will begin.

There are three methods: the 'established spur' system, for the more restricted or artificially trained trees; the 'regulated' system, for trees of vigorous habit; and the 'renewal' system, for keeping the tree in continuous new growth.

In the established spur system, wood formed in summer is cut back to four buds. During the following summer, the two top buds will make new growth while the lower will develop into fruiting spurs. From the cut made above the top buds, two laterals will form, which in turn should be cut back

Left: When renovating old fruit trees, use a tree saw to cut away dead wood. Remove entire branch so that the wound will callus over.

Right: To build up a healthy spur system, cut back wood formed in summer to four buds. The next year, the two uppermost buds will make new wood and the two lower buds fruiting spurs.

to two buds. Thus the balance is maintained while the tree channels its energies into making fruiting spurs. With trees over ten years old, some spur thinning is necessary to maintain the size of fruit.

The regulated system mostly applies to bush and standard trees. The idea is to keep the tree 'open' at the center by removing crossing branchlets and all in-growing laterals. Begin by shortening the laterals to a third at the end of each summer. Then cut them back as described for the spur system. The tip bearers (those that fruit at the ends of the laterals) are left unpruned until they have made excessive growth, when some wood must be removed.

The renewal system involves the replacement of old wood by new, thus maintaining the tree's vigor over many years. The side shoots are cut back to two buds from the base. These will produce two more shoots that will bear fruit. Afterwards, each is pruned back to two buds and the process continues indefinitely.

Old trees may be made more productive by removing all dead wood, using a tree saw. Where there is overcrowding at the center, entirely remove any branches, to let in sunlight. Make the cut close to the bark so that it will heal (form a callus) quickly. To leave even a few inches of the branch will enable brown rot to take hold. Paint the wound with a fungicide or with white lead paint to guard against disease.

De-horning will also increase the yield of old trees. It is the top branches that are de-horned, cutting them back by a third of their length. Make a sloping cut so that moisture will drain away, and treat with a fungicide to heal the cut as described.

If you need to restrict a certain bud, make a notch in the bark just below it. To encourage a bud to 'break' into growth, make the notch above it.

Harvesting and storing

Knowing when to harvest calls for a degree of skill. Do not remove the fruit too soon: it will keep longer if you let it stay on the tree until it is fully mature. The apples should never be ripped from the fruiting spur but gently removed with the stalk intact.

An attic, shed or cupboard is suitable for storing fruit. It must, be cool, about 40°F (50°C), dry and frostproof. Place the fruits on a layer of straw, making sure that they do not touch each other. Do not store fruit with vegetables.

Varieties

The apple varieties listed below are available as standard (full size), semi-dwarf and dwarf trees, although no one nursery is likely to offer all in every category. Some shopping around will be necessary. When buying dwarf fruits, it is sensible to ask what kind of dwarfing understock is used, since there are several and some are more dwarf than others.

It is often the case that certain varieties thrive in some areas better than others. A few varieties may not be so hardy, while others, such as the well-known Cox's Orange Pippin, are susceptible to diseases in damp areas.

Therefore, take the opportunity to consult your local nursery or horticultural advice center if you are in doubt about the best varieties for your local soil and area. Because fruit trees are a long-term crop, do select the right varieties.

Beacon Not of the highest quality, but recommended for far north regions. Ripens early, bears heavily, has good red color and is not as perishable as some early apples.

Cortland Known for both dessert and culinary qualities. A large red-striped fruit with white flesh. For storage, pick five days after McIntosh.

Cox's Orange Pippin One of the most popular apples ever introduced. It is a weak grower, susceptible to frosts, and bears well only where everything is in its favor. Yet the fruit has a more subtle blending of aromatic flavor and crispness than any apple, and is good for eating from fall to late winter. Not generally available from nurseries.

Left: In the regulated system of pruning (mostly for semi-dwarf and standard trees) crossing branchlets and in-growing laterals are removed to keep the tree open at the center. Shorten the laterals to a third at the end of summer, then cut back the laterals as for the spur system. Leave the tip bearers unpruned until they have made excessive growth, then remove some of the wood.

Above: In the renewal system of pruning, old wood is replaced by new to maintain vigor. Cut side shoots back to two buds from the base. These will produce two more shoots, which will become fruit-bearing. Then prune each back to two buds, and so on.

July Red Early summer apple for most of the Northeast. Fruit is blush colored with red splashed stripes. A new variety that is much praised for its eating quality and superior keeping properties for an early variety.

Left: One of the best dessert apples, Cox's Orange Pippin is offered in both dwarf and standard-size trees by a few fruit specialists.

Fireside A very hardy apple for Minnesota, North Dakota and like climates. Fruit is red and large, juicy, sweet and crisp, and keeps well. A late variety that stores for three months.

Golden Delicious Retains its popularity and, with its evenly shaped fruit and clear yellow skin, it is a favorite of the supermarkets. A high quality fruit.

Haralson Deep red apple that stores for 4–6 months. Late variety recommended for cold climates.

Jonagold An apple prized for dessert and culinary qualities. Attractive fruit has scarlet stripe over a yellow background. Good keeper – until spring at storage temperatures of 33°F (1°C). Will probably replace Golden Delicious.

Macoun Outstanding dessert apple, red and of medium to small size (hand or chemical thinning may be necessary to prevent over-bearing and small fruits). Reminiscent of McIntosh in its crispness, but better flavored. Popular in the Northeast.

McIntosh One of the most popular dessert varieties, famous for its sparkling red color and crisp white flesh.

Below: A well spaced and heavily laden branch, the result of good pruning and cultivation.

Right: Golden Delicious, one of the most reliable dessert apples, bears heavily in both dwarf and standard trees.

Mutsu A very large yellow apple that is late. Fine dessert and culinary qualities. One large fruit can yield a bowl of sauce.

Spigold A triploid, so can neither pollinate itself or other varieties. A red-striped, very large apple, excellent for cooking uses.

Wealthy A fine apple known for its hardiness. The fruit is yellow and striped with scarlet. It makes excellent eating right from the tree in the fall and also cooks well.

Winter Banana A variety for the South and mild climates of the West Coast. Fruit is large and pink-fleshed.

3 Pears

Natives of the warm regions of the Mediterranean, pears require greater warmth than apples for the fruit to ripen correctly and so attain their full flavor and keeping qualities. Pears require the sunniest places in the fruit garden, where they may be grown as standards or bush trees, and in the pyramid and cordon form, requiring similar culture to the apple in their pruning.

However, if pruning is neglected, pears continue to bear well. Pears are at their best where grown as espaliers or in horizontal tiers, the arms being either fastened to a wall or to strong galvanized wires supported by posts at intervals of 8 ft (240 cm). Espaliers may be grown in the open, possibly alongside a path, or to divide one part of the fruit garden from another.

Espalier trees

A maiden tree will form one pair of arms each year, which can be grown on to any length. Espaliers can also grow to any height and will often be seen covering the entire wall of an old house to a height of 30 ft (9 m) or more. Long ladders must then be used for picking fruit and pruning at the top. In the garden, the topmost arms should be about 7–8 ft (210–240 cm) from soil level so that cultivation can be readily carried out.

After planting the young tree, make a nick in the bark above two buds, one on either side of the stem and pointing in opposite directions, to make them 'break'. These will form the first arms or tier. The leader shoot is allowed to grow away. Next season, in early spring, another two buds are selected on either side of the stem, and so on, selecting a pair of buds each year that are spaced about 16–18 in (40–45 cm) above each other.

At first, the new wood growing from the main stem will tend to grow upwards. It is advisable to fix canes to the wires, first at an angle of 45°, to which the shoots are fastened. The canes are gradually brought to the horizontal position, then fastened to the wires.

The first tier will grow to about 3 ft (1 m) on either side of the main stem in a year. The following year, early in August, to encourage the formation of fruiting spurs, which will bear fruit the next year, all shoots growing from the arms should be pinched back to 4–5 in (10–12 cm) of the main stems. The plant will then form fruiting buds instead of making excess wood. As the arms continue to grow, at the end of each summer, cut back the new season's wood to about half way, to a bud that will form the extension shoot to grow on next year. This process may continue for several years, until the arms are approximately 6 ft (180 cm) in length; therefore, with espaliers it is desirable to plant them about 12 ft (3·5 m) apart.

As pears bloom about two weeks before apples, many varieties should not be planted in frost-troubled gardens unless they are planted against a warm wall. Varieties for colder regions have been developed by the University of Minnesota and the South Dakota State University, and include Parker, Patten and Luscious. The disease fire blight can be serious with pears (see page 256).

Pollination

Pollination is as important for pears as for apples. Though several will be in bloom at the same time, they are unable to fertilize each other. The fertile Conference is unable to pollinate Beurré d'Amanlis; neither will Seckel fertilize Louise Bonne. They need another pollinator, such as Marguerite Marillat or Durondeau.

Certain pears, such as Duchess, are self-fertile, setting fruit with their own pollen, but they will set heavier crops with another in bloom at the same time. The variety

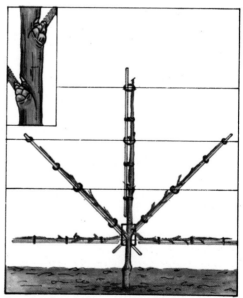

Opposite: Doyenne du Comice, also known as Comice, requires a warm garden. It is one of the most popular of the dessert fruits.

Above: Buds on fan trees can be induced to develop or remain dormant by nicking either above or below the buds.

Gather pears dry, before they're frosted.

Wrap in greaseproof paper, stand on end.

Magness has sterile pollen and should be planted with Duchess for cross-pollination to set fruits.

Early and mid-season varieties, and mid-season and late pears may be planted together, for their flowering times will overlap. Thus Conference and Bartlett will fertilize each other. However, two superior pear varieties that might appear to be a suitable planting combination in the home fruit garden, Bartlett and Seckel, will *not* fertilize each other. A third variety must be included.

Rootstocks

There are several rootstocks for pears that are grafted on to quince stock. Quince B is comparable to MII of apples, making large trees that crop heavily but take longer to come into bearing than the more dwarf stocks (such as Quince C, which is used for pyramids and cordons). Also, those pears that are slow to begin cropping, e.g. Comice and Beurré Hardy, should be worked on this stock. Quince A comes somewhere between these two stocks and is the rootstock mostly used.

Where a large standard tree is required, pears are worked on wild pear stock and this is also used for the weaker growers. It is the most vigorous rootstock.

Trees on quince stock must be planted with the graft at least 3 in (8 cm) above soil level so that scion rooting does not occur. Dig a large hole so that the roots can be spread out well, making it a depth such that the graft is comfortably above the soil after treading down. Sprinkle peat moss over the roots and mix in compost before replacing the soil, treading it well down. Then stake the trees as for apples.

Pruning

As to their pruning, pears are divided into two sections: those of vigorous upright habit, and those of weaker, drooping habit. In the former group are Comice, Conference, and Bartlett.

When pruning, the upright growers should be cut back to an outward-facing bud and the droopers to an upward bud. This will correct the 'drain-pipe' habit of the second, weaker group and the 'umbrella' habit of those of the first group. Those of weeping habit are mostly tip bearers and light croppers and so require little pruning.

Each shoot or lateral will form both fruiting and wood (foliage) buds. The latter lie flat along the stem and are more pointed. Several years after planting, the spur bearers may need to have some of their spurs removed so as to maintain the size and quality of the fruit.

212

Harvesting and storing

Pears require more care in their harvesting than apples. They bruise easily and are harmed by frost, while they deteriorate quickly if overripe. They will be ready to gather if, when you take the fruit on the palm of the hand and lift it, it parts from the spur with its stem attached. They require a temperature of 45°–50°F (7°–10°C) to store well and should be kept in a darkened room or a cupboard or drawer. Pears will sweat and quickly deteriorate in a too cold place, such as a refrigerator. However, if they are carefully stored, some pears will keep until Easter.

Varieties

When selecting the varieties, remember to choose varieties that fruit at different times. Nothing is more annoying than to wait all year for fresh pears, then to have them all at once and many of them to be wasted. Most catalogs will give an indication as to the expected date of fruiting.

Aurora Bright yellow pear with russet blush. Large with juicy, aromatic flesh that is sweet. Early (late summer in most Northern regions), the fruit storing well until early winter. Vigorous tree but not resistant to fire blight.

Bartlett Possibly the best all-round pear ever raised. It makes a compact tree and bears heavily, the white flesh retaining its quality after preserving. It ripens early (mid- to late summer) but is not resistant to fire blight.

Beurre d'Anjou Large, greenish fruits considered comparable to Comice in quality. Hardy to southern Vermont and like regions. Late ripening; the fruit stores well into winter in a cool cellar. Moderately resistant to fire blight.

Beurre Hardy The rose-tinted flesh has a pleasant rose perfume. It makes a strong, upright tree. Hardy. Offers some resistance to fire blight.

Clapp's Favorite An old pear of vigorous, upright habit. It bears heavily, the pale yellow fruit, striped crimson, ripening early (midsummer). A good pollinator and resistant to fire blight.

Colette The large fruits are yellow with a red or pink blush and are of superb quality. Very hardy. The fruits ripen over several weeks, beginning in mid- to late summer. Vigorous but not resistant to fire blight.

Conference Although well known to pear fanciers, finding a source for this variety may be difficult. It is hardy, a valuable

Possibly the best all-round pear ever, the Bartlett makes a compact tree and bears heavily. The flesh retains its quality after canning.

213

pollinator and known for its reliable harvests. The dark green fruits, heavily russeted, are of excellent flavor.

Doyenne du Comice This is the finest of all pears, its melting cinnamon-flavored fruit having no equal. It requires warmth and a long growing season, conditions best met in a few regions of the Pacific Coast.

Duchess A famous French pear nearly as revered for its flavor as Comice. The russet fruits are ripe in fall. This is a hardy variety resistant to fire blight.

Gorham Forms a neat, upright tree that is slightly resistant to fire blight. The fruits are bright yellow, similar to Bartlett, and fine for dessert or canning.

Magness Green-yellow fruits, slightly russeted, juicy and sweet. Ripens about 3½ weeks after Bartlett. Its pollen is sterile, but it is highly resistant to fire blight.

Maxine A yellow pear with a rating of only fair quality, its flesh being coarse. It is hardy and ripens late. It is quite resistant to fire blight, an important asset.

Moonglow Pale yellow fruits that ripen before Bartlett, but are rated as being of only medium quality. Very resistant to fire blight.

Parker Fruits, which are somewhat similar to Bartlett, ripen in early fall. It is a very hardy variety recommended for Minnesota and like climates. Patten is very similar, but later.

Seckel A small brown pear of magnificent flavor. Ripens in early fall. Resistant to fire blight.

Sirrine Yellow fruits slightly blushed of high dessert quality, being sweet and juicy. Bears about the same time as Bartlett but is much more resistant to fire blight.

Conference is a pear famous for its quality among fruit fanciers. It is a valuable pollinator.

4 Plums

After apples, plums are the next most widely grown fruits, for they have both dessert and culinary uses. Plums do not keep for long but, by planting for succession, they may be enjoyed from early summer to fall.

Americans are fortunate in having a wide choice among plums. There are the best varieties from Europe, including the famous Green Gage and Damson types, the Japanese varieties, and various native species and hybrids. These plums all vary, not only in their fruits, but also in their hardiness and tolerance of climatic differences. The prune is a kind of plum. Commercial production of prunes is concentrated in California and a few other Western states where the proper conditions for drying the fruits exist.

Some of the native plums make small trees or shrubs and even some standard-size plums such as Green Gage possess a habit dwarf enough for a small garden. However, some European plums are grown on dwarfing understock. Both the dwarf and standard plum comes quickly into bearing.

The Damson is such a special plum that

Plums can be enjoyed from early summer to fall.

it deserves extra attention, if only to forestall its neglect by future plum growers. The trees are among the hardiest of fruits and able to bear heavy crops when growing in shallow soil and rocky outcrops. For cold, exposed gardens they will bear more heavily than most other plums. However, when provided with moderately fertile soils containing moisture-retentive humus in the form of peat moss, compost, leafmold, decayed straw or whatever is available, the size and quality of the fruit will be much enhanced. They will need almost no pruning, as they make only small twiggy growth. Although considered self-fruitful, damsons will bear better if another European plum is planted nearby. Damsons are not suitable for eating out of hand, but they make delicious preserves and pies with their own unique flavor. Planting distances for standard trees is about 8–10 ft (2½–3 m) apart.

Training and pruning

It does not require the same degree of pruning attention as either the apple or pear. The plum fruits mostly on the new wood and, apart from the removal of any dead wood, excessive pruning must be avoided. Stone fruits suffer from 'bleeding', which weakens the tree and enables disease, especially silver leaf, to enter where cuts or wounds have been made.

216

In spring, cut back any unduly long shoots, and early in July, pinch back to half way all side shoots, which will have made new growth. Plums form their fruit buds along the entire length of the branches and a well-grown tree may be allowed to carry a greater amount of wood than any other top fruit.

The pyramid, budded on to the dwarfing St Julien A stock, is ideal for small gardens. Maiden trees are planted 8–9 ft (240–270 cm) apart in November. On about April 1 the trees should be cut back to 4 ft (120 cm) above soil level and all lateral shoots pinched back to 9 in (22 cm) from the main stem. In mid-July the laterals should be shortened again, to 6 in (15 cm), and the following April the leader shortened by about one-third of the past season's wood. Then, in July prune back the laterals again to 6 in (15 cm) and in this way the tree will concentrate on making fruit buds rather than wood.

To form the fan-shaped tree, which may be planted in the open and trained against strong wires or against a wall, cut back the leader to an upwards bud and on the lower portion of the stem, about 10 in (25 cm) above the scion, to two buds, one on either side of the stem. Make a nick in the bark above the buds to persuade them to 'break'. When the two buds have made 18 in

(45 cm) of growth, cut the leader back to just above the topmost shoot. Then tie two shoots to canes at an angle of 45°. At the end of summer, cut back these side arms to a bud about 9 in (22 cm) from the base; then, during next summer allow laterals on the upper part of the two arms to grow on. Cut back the arms to the laterals furthest from the base. The framework will then be established.

The only pruning necessary will be to pinch back the newly formed shoots when they have formed seven or eight leaves. Do this in early July and tie the shoots in to prevent wind damage.

Root pruning

Often fan trees, and, indeed, all types of plum tree, begin to form suckers. These are shoots that arise from the roots below the scion and they must be removed. Uncover the roots around the stem and, taking care not to damage the scion, cut away the suckers with a sharp knife before covering the roots again and treading firm.

At the same time, root pruning may be done. This is the best way of restricting growth with plums, for there will be no 'bleeding'. It is usually fan-trained trees growing against a wall that are root-pruned. Scrape away the soil to a distance of 4–5 ft (120–150 cm) from the wall to uncover the roots and cut them back to about 3 ft (1 m) of the stem. This will encourage more fibrous roots to form. Scatter peat around the roots before replacing the soil and tread firmly. Then give the roots a good soaking.

The choice of rootstocks is not large. Dwarf trees are grown on Common plum or Brompton stock and in the United States on sand cherry, Nanking cherry and St Julian A plum. Standards are grown on the Myrobolan stock. This is mostly used for heavy-bearing orchard trees. Owing to their 'gumming', plums are budded, as with roses, and not grafted.

Plums enjoy best a heavy loam. They will grow well in a limestone soil provided there is plenty of humus present, but they require a moisture-retentive soil and one that receives plenty of nitrogen, preferably of an organic nature. In light soils, work in plenty of farmyard or poultry manure, peat moss or compost. At planting time, give a handful of bone meal or superphosphate to each tree, mixed well into the soil as it is placed over the roots. The trees should also be given a liberal mulch of organic manure in spring each year, augmented by 1 oz (28 g) of sulphate of ammonia.

Harvesting and storing

Plums must be allowed to remain on the trees until fully ripe. The best test will be to remove one when it is thought to be ripe and taste it. If it is soft and juicy and the stone readily parts from the flesh, it is ripe. Most plums will store for several weeks in a dry, airy room if removed from the plant with their stalks and placed in cotton in trays.

Pollination

As with apples and pears, some thought must be given to pollination.

The flowering time of plums is from eighteen to twenty-one days, so that the flowering period of many plums will overlap. Only the very early and very late do not overlap, for plums are in bloom for only ten

Plums bear on both the old and new wood, hence they crop heavily. A number of plum types exist, including varieties from abroad and the native kinds.

Opposite: All of the 'Gage' plums are prized for their fruits. This is Mirabelle Gage.

days, and not until the early plums have finished do the late ones come into bloom.

While some plums do not require cross-pollination, even these will probably bear more abundantly if another plum variety is in bloom nearby. One point to keep in mind is that American plums do not pollinate European or Japanese varieties, nor do European or Japanese varieties pollinate each other.

Varieties

DeMontfort Old European plum of high quality prized by fanciers. Dark purple, round fruit of medium size with sweet, juicy flesh. Ripens in late August in Northeast.

Early Transparent Gage European plum that makes a dwarf tree and sets a heavy crop with its own pollen. The skin is so thin as to show the stone and has an apricot flavor when fully ripe. Excellent for the home garden because it ripens over several weeks.

French Damson European oval-shaped plum, large and tart, ripening in midsummer. The Damson is famous for preserves and jams.

Golden Transparent Gage Similar to Early Transparent, though ripening later. The bright yellow fruit, speckled red, has a peach-like flavour.

218

Green Gage One of the most famous of European plums. With another European variety blooming at the same time, it crops heavily. Its greenish-yellow fruit is juicy and sweet, and unsurpassed in flavor. It forms a neat, compact tree. Ripens mid-season.

Ozark Premier Japanese plum popular in the Midwest. Large, bright red fruits ripening in midsummer.

Santa Rosa Japanese plum, large and dark red-purple in color. High quality. Ripens midsummer on. Trees grow large except in dwarf sizes.

Shiro This golden plum, a Japanese variety, begins to ripen in midsummer. Forms a low tree.

Stanley European prune type for dessert or preserving. Dark blue fruit with heavy bloom. Very productive. Ripens mid-season.

Underwood An American plum of exceptional hardiness, suitable for colder states and into Canada. Red-purple fruit in midsummer.

Superior Japanese plum acts as pollinator for other Japanese varieties. Red fruits ripen in midsummer.

Yellow Egg European plum, oval with yellow skin and flesh. Sweet and juicy and self-pollinating.

Green Gages make delicious eating if removed when just ripe.

219

Wild plums native to America

There are, of course, species of the plum family that are native to the North American continent. In fact, the genus *Prunus*, which encompasses both the plums and cherries, has over 200 different species of trees and shrubs widely distributed through the North American Temperate Zone – and a few even extend into the tropics.

The American Plum, *Prunus americana*, is a relatively small tree, about 20 to 35 ft (6–10 m) high. It bears ill-smelling flowers, with round, red fruits which are about 1 in (2·5 cm) in diameter. The flesh is tart and yellow.

The Mexican Plum, *Prunus mexicana*, bears dark, purple-red fruits about 1½ in (4 cm) long, with thick and sweet flesh. It is a taller-growing tree than the American Plum.

Much further north, the Canadian Plum, *Prunus nigra*, displays white flowers, with yellow-fleshed, orange-red plums just over 1 in (2·5 cm) long. It is a tree with distinctive bark that is gray-brown and peels off in layers.

Native to the West Coast is the Klamath Plum, *Prunus subcordata*. Growing to 25 ft (7·5 m) high, it produces tart, dark-red or occasionally yellow fruits about 1 in (2·5 cm) long.

The Flatwoods Plum, *Prunus umbellata*, which heralds from the Southern states, produces tart plums that are purplish-black in color although they are on occasion yellow.

Coming from around the New England area is the Allegheny Plum, *Prunus alleghaniensis*. It somewhat resembles the Flatwoods Plum, but the slightly larger leaves are narrower. Globular plums are produced, with dark reddish-purple skins and yellow flesh. The Allegheny Plum is a smallish tree, with bark that is scaly and dark brown.

From the lower Ohio and lower Mississippi valleys come the Wildgoose Plum,

Damson plums are untroubled by cold winds or frosts and so may be planted as a windbreak.

Prunus munsoniana, with palatable plums of good quality. The red fruits are just under an inch (2·5 cm) in length.

The Hortulan Plum, *Prunus hortulana*, with leaves 4–6 in (10–15 cm) long and slender orange stems, produces red, or occasionally yellow, fruits.

The Chickasaw Plum, *Prunus angustifolio*, is an interesting plum, originally a native of the South Atlantic and Gulf states. However, it is now naturalized throughout many areas, where it often forms impenetrable thickets in old fields and waste areas. Numerous horticultural varieties have been developed from the Chickasaw Plum for use in southern orchards, but, unfortunately, the fruits are seldom of a really good quality.

Originating from southeastern Texas is the Larissa Plum, *Prunus tenuifolia*. The fruits have very thin flesh.

5 Cherries

Though always in demand for dessert and culinary use, being the first of the fruits to ripen, sweet cherries are now rarely planted in the amateur's garden. They do well only as standard or half-standard trees, on which they take about ten years to bear a prolific crop. Again, there are pollination difficulties, for only cherries of certain groups will pollinate each other and several must be planted together for best results. A standard cherry needs ample space to develop and in a small garden several of the more compact apples, occupying the same amount of ground, will be a better proposition. Nor are most cherries, notably sweet varieties, as cold-hardy as apples. Birds, too, are always troublesome, for even where the fruits have set well, birds can take half the crop. But early cherries, sweet or sour, are always appreciated and where space permits, two or three varieties may be planted together. These two or three varieties might be placed in a shrub border if bush cherry varieties are ordered. Bush cherries are hybrids from an American species (*Prunus bessyi*) that are found from Manitoba to Kansas, and only grow 4–6 ft (1·22–1·83 m) tall. The bushes are of such a size that nylon netting can readily be thrown over them to protect the fruits from birds. Bush cherries are very hardy and can be grown in regions too frigid for most standard cherries. Bush cherries do require pollination from another bush cherry variety, so plant two or more different varieties.

Cherry trees do well in a variety of soils so long as they are well drained. They can not tolerate wet soil. Since growth is started so early in spring, and if there is any choice in the matter, sandy loams might be preferable because they warm faster. Avoid sites where the flowers can be injured by late frosts. Cherries do not require excessive fertilizing, although if the leaf color is washed out and pale green, it may be a sign that the tree needs feeding.

Planting of cherries is done in the fall. Take care not to damage the bark, for that would permit bacterial canker or silver leaf disease to enter at the wound. If planting in grass, first remove a circle of 2 ft (60 cm) diameter, and if planting standards, allow

Cherries are best grown as standards, and will bear well in a limestone soil. They take several years before bearing heavily, and they need suitable pollinators.

Morello cherries are hardy and may be grown as a windbreak or against a north wall in the fan-trained form. Most home gardeners, however, grow them as regular standard trees. The dark sour cherries are later than Montmorency.

at least 20 ft (6 m) between them. For a fan tree, provide a 16 ft (480 cm) frame of horizontally fixed wires. Plant bush cherries about 3–4 ft (90·5–120 cm) apart.

Pruning

Follow much the same pruning procedure as for plums. Fan trees are formed in the same way. Afterwards, pinch back the side shoots to about six leaves early in July; in September, pinch back to four buds. If the leader shoots are making excessive growth, bend them down as far as possible and tie in, releasing them after twelve months. Root pruning may also be done as for plums.

With standards, cut the leader shoots back to half way in April, at the same time removing any dead wood but nothing more. Eventually, cherry branches that become too tall or are outgrowing the side branches can be headed back as necessary.

Standard cherry trees are budded on two rootstocks, mazzard (*Prunus avium*) and mahaleb (*P. mahaleb*). Mazzard rootstocks are preferred for sweet cherries, although it may take the tree longer to come into bear-

ing. Work is continuing to find suitable dwarfing understock for cherries that would limit the size of the trees and bring the trees into bearing earlier. A promising development is the genetic dwarfing of rootstocks obtained from crossing *Prunus avium* and *P. cerasus*.

Pollinating

Cherries have a flowering period of eighteen to twenty days, twice that of plums, and except for the very earliest and latest, they overlap. Yet this plays little or no part in their pollination and only certain groups will prove fertile with each other.

One way to surmount the pollination problem is to plant the true dwarf variety North Star, which will pollinate itself. Another sour cherry, Montmorency, is also self-pollinating, as is Meteor, another natural dwarf.

There is no sweet cherry that is self-pollinating. Most catalogs give pollinating information for the cherries they list. Help can also be obtained from the fruit specialists at state agricultural experiment stations or county extension associations (listed in the telephone book under the county government). Good pollinators for most sweet cherry varieties are Merton Bigarreau (but will not pollinate Windsor, Van and Venus), Sam and Van.

Varieties

Black Beauty A bush cherry with very glossy maroon-red fruits for eating fresh or using for pies and preserves.

Brooks A bush cherry with red fruits nearly as large as standard varieties. All bush cherries are very hardy.

Emperor Francis Early-blooming sweet cherry with large, high quality fruits. The dark red fruits ripen in midseason.

Golden Bush This bush cherry has attractive yellow fruits. Bush cherries all bear in early summer.

Jubilee A variety from California that is replacing Bing. Sweet black cherries ripen in midseason.

Merton Bigarreau A sweet cherry tree too large for most backyard orchards. A very productive variety, the large, dark red fruits ripening in midseason.

Meteor Semi-dwarf tree with tart, bright red fruits. Tree remains at 8–10 ft (2·45–3 m), making it useful in small gardens. Also self-pollinating.

Napoleon Also called Royal Anne. Old sweet cherry variety with yellow fruits with a red cheek or blush. Use Black Tartarian, Van or Vista to pollinate the flowers. Moderately hardy.

North Star A naturally dwarf variety that remains 6–7 ft (1·80–2·14 m) in height. The early, bright red fruits are excellent for pies. Very hardy.

Royal Duke All Duke varieties are hybrids between sweet and sour cherries. This variety has red cherries which are considered quite sweet. Another variety must be planted for cross-pollination.

Cherry trees have a flowering period twice as long as the flowering period of plums.

6 Apricots, peaches and nectarines

These are plants of the East, able to survive a cold winter but requiring a long, dry summer to ripen the fruit and the wood, without which they will bear little fruit the following year. Both apricots and peaches are good fruit crops for backyard gardens. The trees are available as both standards and dwarfs, and even the standards can be kept in bounds by pruning. There are a few peach varieties that can be grown in tubs. Most apricots and peaches are self-pollinating.

Apricots

Apricots are very tolerant of heat. They grow well in a variety of soils but they must have good drainage. Humus-forming materials, such as compost and peat moss, can be mixed in the planting holes, especially if the soils are very sandy. After planting, cut back young trees to about 2½ ft (75 cm).

Plant in autumn. Apricots can be grown as fan-trained trees against a wall. Plant at least 18 ft (5·5 m) apart, for they make long shoots. Allow the main shoots to grow on, pinching back the side growths in summer to about 2 in (5 cm).

For non-fan-shaped trees, the usual practise is to develop a main branch, or 'leader', with the lateral branches being cut back as necessary to maintain this pyramidal form.

Though self-fertile, apricots will set a better crop if hand-fertilized. This is done by dusting each flower with a camel-hair brush as they open. Apricots flower early and if they are grown against an outside wall, it is advisable to hang muslin over the plants as soon as the blooms begin to open if a late frost threatens.

When the fruits have set and have started to swell, thin them to three in a cluster and to about 3 in (8 cm) apart as they make size, removing perhaps the center one. Allow the fruit to become fully ripe before removing it.

Apricots fruit on old and new wood. To prevent overcrowding, remove the old spurs after the plants have borne fruit on them for two years.

The plants will benefit from a mulch of strawy manure each season in early summer. Once the fruit has set, you should never allow the trees to go short of moisture at the roots.

Varieties

Alfred A hardy apricot that bears bright orange, slightly blushed fruits in late July in the Northeast. Fruits are juicy and rich in flavor.

Early Golden Orange-gold fruits of good size and with virtually fuzzless skins on vigorous trees.

Hardier apricot varieties are now available for the North. Both dwarf and standard trees exist and are well-suited to the smaller fruit gardens.

Above: Prune peaches by the replacement system.

Right: Peaches crop heavily without a pollinator.

Goldcot Large golden-yellow fruits on strong trees. Cold-hardy and tolerant of humidity in summer.

Henderson Large yellow apricots with pink blush. The tree is strong and highly productive.

Moorpark Large golden-yellow fruits with pink cheeks. Considered very hardy.

Moongold Golden fruits in late summer. Originated especially for cold climates. It requires cross-pollination. The companion variety below is recommended for this purpose.

Sungold Bears a little later than above. Plant with Moongold for pollination.

Peaches

Outdoors, peaches are grown as standards or fan-trained trees against a wall; in pots on a terrace or verandah; or as dwarf trees, like apples, when they will come into fruit two years after planting. Plant in fall or early spring, allowing just over 18 ft (5 m) for fan trees and just under 6 ft (2 m) for dwarfs. They require a well-drained soil containing organic matter, a sandy loam being preferred. Peaches are budded onto seedling peaches or special dwarf stocks, and when planting, make sure that the union is above soil level. Tread in the roots firmly and water well if the soil is dry. Each year, in May, give a liberal mulch of strawy manure to conserve moisture.

Reliance Medium-sized yellow fruits, early ripening, recommended for very cold climates.

Sun Haven Bright red peaches, medium to large in size, and nearly fuzzless. Very early to ripen, about 10 days before Red Haven.

White Champion Old variety of fine quality with white flesh that ripens in midsummer. Fruits large and tree vigorous.

Nectarine

This is a smooth-skinned peach and requires similar culture in every way, plenty of sunshine to ripen its wood, and in spring a thick mulch to conserve moisture – without which the fruits will not swell to a good size.

225

Varieties

Nectacrest Good-sized, fine-flavored fruits with white flesh in early fall.

Nectarina A genetic dwarf like Flory and Bonanza peaches, suitable for tubs.

Mericrest A very hardy nectarine ripening in midsummer.

Pruning

At the beginning, give dwarf trees the same treatment as in the renewal system for apples, i.e. shoots that have borne fruit are grown on until they are 18 in (45 cm) long. Do the same for fan trees. Fasten them to the wall and pinch the tips back to a wood bud. This will produce the wood that will bear next year's crop. The wood buds are small and pointed, the blossom buds round and fat.

Pruning of established trees consists of, in early spring, cutting back the leaders to about one-third and, in early June, pinching back the side shoots to about 2 in

Nectarines are smooth-skinned peaches that need similar culture.

(5 cm), to a single wood bud at the base. This is grown on as replacement for next season's crop. Those shoots that have fruited are removed at the end of summer. This continuous formation of replacement shoots on which the crop is carried will keep the trees free from old wood, which often causes 'gumming' when removed.

Peaches are self-fertile and need no pollinator, but a heavier set of fruit will be obtained if the open flowers, when dry, are pollinated with a camel-hair brush, especially those in a greenhouse.

Do not thin the fruit until after 'the June drop'. This is a natural falling of the fruits when about the size of fully grown cherries. There should be about 5 in (12 cm) between the fruits left to mature.

The fruit ripens from the end of July until early October, depending on variety. To determine the ripeness, place a hand beneath a fruit and lift gently upwards: it should come away easily with its stalk. Or gently press the base of a fruit: if ripe, it will be slightly soft. Ripe fruits can be kept in the refrigerator for a few days.

Varieties

Bonanza A dwarf peach that does quite well for a time in tubs. Large, yellow, freestone fruits.

Crawford An old variety whose red-tinted fruits ripen in late September in northern New York.

Elberta Famous variety with large, yellow, freestone fruits. Hardy, with fruit ripening in fall.

Flory A naturally dwarf Chinese peach with large, decorative foliage and small white-fleshed peaches in fall.

Golden Jubilee Large, yellow, freestone peaches of excellent quality in midsummer.

Red Haven Large, red peaches nearly fuzzless, of medium size. Early ripening.

7 Grapes

There is no other crop for the home fruit garden that requires the skill and dedication demanded by proper grape culture.

Where space is a problem, there is the grape arbor, a structure that was once a part of every backyard and supplied fruits and summer shelter. Or a row of grapes can be grown alongside a vegetable garden, the vines being trained on wires between posts. They can also be grown horizontally against a wall or fence. European grape varieties are sometimes grown on posts, planted 4 ft (120 cm) apart.

There are three kinds of grape vines grown in North America, each group

Though grape vines require an open, sunny situation to ripen, they are hardier to cold than imagined.

having many named hybrids and varieties. The European grape (*Vitis vinifera*), the basis of grape culture in Britain and Europe, requires mild climates and is grown in California and a few other Western regions. In the South the native Muscadine grape (*Vitis rotundifolia*) is grown. In the North where grapes are grown, the varieties are derived from the native fox grape (*V. labrusca*) crossed with European varieties.

Planting

The latest information on culture, training and varieties for each region can be obtained from state agricultural experiment stations and county extension agents. The vines require a sunny site that is not

227

Grapes are usually planted outside, but grow well in a cold or slightly warm greenhouse, trained over the roof.

prone to late frosts in spring that can damage the flower buds. The soil should be well-drained, deeply prepared and rich in humus. A sandy loam is best, but most soils are adequate. Add compost, peat moss or rotted manure and about 10 lbs (4·50 kilograms) of superphosphate to each row of 25 ft (7·63 m). Plant in fall or early spring, spacing the vines from 6–8 ft (180–240 cm) apart. Cut back to two buds.

Training American Grapes

Unless grown over an arbor where pruning is reduced to thinning out older woody canes every few years, vines are trained to the four-cane Kniffen System, both com-

mercially and in the home garden. The System can be used for European varieties, but they are usually trained somewhat differently (see below).

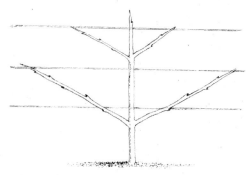

Above: A grape vine may be planted against a trellis in a sunny place. Tie in stems as they make growth.

For the System, strong posts are set every 10 ft (300 cm) and strung with two rows of wire, the bottom 30 in (75 cm) from the ground, the second about 36 in (90·5 cm) above it. The vine is kept to a single stem with two canes trained along the wires in each direction (four canes in all). Since grapes are borne on shoots from one-year canes, the annual pruning during winter dormancy involves removing excess growth so the vine retains its fruiting vigor but does not overproduce. There are other Systems; the Umbrella Kniffen System is also popular. Southern grape varieties are grown on arbors and are only pruned as needed to restrain growth.

Pruning European grapes

Pruning calls for some thought. A shoot will grow 20 ft (6 m) in a single season, and every eye along the entire length is capable of bearing a shoot that will produce one or more bunches of grapes. In addition, a vine is able to bear fruit on the older wood, though this would prove too much for its constitution. If new shoots are encouraged, the eyes on the old wood will not be sufficiently vigorous to bear fruit, and the fruit on the new wood will be better.

There are two main methods of pruning, the long rod system and the spur system.

The long rod system This name applies when one or two new shoots or rods are allowed to grow on and all other growth is restricted.

With vines, pruning is done in the depths of winter, the first days of January, before the sap begins to rise, being most suitable. For greenhouse plants, allow the vine to form stems or rods; train these as far apart as possible and tie in to wires stretched across the roof. The stems will grow 20 ft (6 m) or more their first year. In early winter, cut the weaker stem back to two buds near the base. On the other, stronger stem will be borne the next season's crop, and the stronger stem from its two buds will be grown on to produce the crop for the season

By the long-rod system, one or two shoots only are grown on and other growth is restricted.

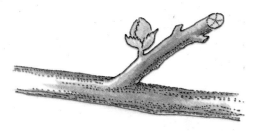

From these stems, select alternate buds on either side of the stems to produce short laterals.

after that. To prevent the formation of too much foliage, pinch back all laterals to two buds – one to bear the fruit, the other the foliage, which should be stopped at two leaves. Do this pinching back in summer over several weeks so as not to check the plant too drastically.

For vines in the open, growing vertically, follow the single rod and spur system, retaining the strongest shoot of two basal buds to bear fruit. Then, after fruiting, cut back to a single eye or bud to produce next year's rod, or stem.

The spur system From the stem that has grown away unchecked, select alternate buds on each side of the stem to produce short laterals. These bear fruit and should be stopped one leaf beyond. Then cut back each shoot to two buds in winter, one of which will form the grapes, the other the foliage. This will build up a system of spurs. Stop fruit-bearing laterals at the first joint after the bunch has formed, and pinch back non-fruiting laterals to 2 in (5 cm).

Vines growing horizontally against a wall should receive the same treatment as espalier pears. Cut back to the lower three buds in winter, the upper forming the extension shoot while the lower buds, one on either side of the stem, will form the lower arms. Train them first at an angle of 45°, tying them to canes, then gradually bring them to the horizontal position. The following year, cut back the extension shoot again to three buds, the two lower ones facing in opposite directions to form the next pair of arms, about 16 in (40 cm) above the lower pair and so on until the vine reaches the required height. Each arm or stem should be treated the same as for the spur system.

When the fruit has set it must be decided how many bunches the vines can mature. This depends upon age. Probably the stems will carry ten bunches in their second year, twice that number next year and so on. Should there be overcrowding, nip out a few grapes with pointed scissors, as well as any damaged fruits.

Varieties

American

Buffalo Blue-black early grape.

Concord Blue, midseason grape, famous for juice and jelly.

Golden Muscat Large, golden grape clusters. Late.

Himrod Seedless Golden-yellow grapes of medium size. Early.

Interlaken Seedless Amber grapes on

hardy vines that rival Thompson Seedless. Very early.

Ontario White grape. Disease-resistant vines. Very early.

European

Cardinal Dark red grapes. Early.

Emperor Purple-red grapes. Late.

Muscat of Alexandria Green fruits for fresh and raisin use. Late midseason.

Southern

Burgaw Reddish-black grapes. Midseason. Self-pollinating.

Scuppernong Red-tinted green grapes. Early.

Tarheel Black grapes. Self-pollinating. Midseason.

Below: White and yellow grapes have a distinct flavor. They are usually hardier than the black varieties.

230

Above: Grapes growing against a wall.

Right: The Black Hamburgh grape is a famous European variety that is still grown to some extent in greenhouses. The fruit possesses a rich muscat flavor.

8 Figs

The fig is hardier than is generally believed. Though a native of the Near East, it crops well and will ripen its fruit almost anywhere in an average summer. In the East and in the warmer parts of the USA, it bears two to three crops a year, being continuously in bearing.

Figs do well close to the sea where the salt-laden atmosphere and sea mists give protection from frost. They prefer an average garden soil that retains moisture and is slightly acid. Avoid too much fertilizer, for figs make plenty of leaf without it. They need a sparse diet and this means restricting the roots so that they cannot go far in search of food.

Planting

Obtain pot-grown plants and either plant the vine in the pot, burying it below soil level, or remove from the pot with the soil ball intact, and plant over a layer of stones. These should be rammed well down to make a solid base after the soil has been removed to a depth of 18 in (45 cm). If you are planting the figs against a wall, which is a good site for them, place pieces of slate on the other three sides of a hole made 18 in (45 cm) wide, to restrict the roots still further. Then when planting the soil ball, make the soil around it as compact as possible and water in.

Growing figs in tubs is a common practice in much of the North. The tubs act to restrict root growth and make it easier to move the plants into more sheltered areas over winter. Or plants are wrapped in straw and burlap which serves as protection against freezing temperatures.

Figs are planted in spring and require copious amounts of water through summer. They should also be given a thick mulch in May each year. They grow well in the horizontal form planted against a west wall, leaving a south-facing wall either for peaches or for pears.

Figs ripen well when planted against a warm wall.

Pruning

The fruit is carried on the previous year's wood. The replacement shoot is stopped at the fourth leaf, at the end of July – not before, as the fruits expected to manure the following summer will form too quickly at the expense of new wood. Yet if the shoot is not stopped, the tiny figs will lack nourishment, turn yellow and fall off.

The fruits form at the leaf axils the previous year and begin to swell in spring. If the shoots are pinched back late in July, new fruits will form at the axil of each leaf and will be next year's crop. If the tree begins to make too much wood, some of that which carried the previous season's fruit should be thinned.

Figs in greenhouses, growing in gentle heat, will bear two crops yearly. The fruits formed the previous year will swell early in spring and be ripe by early summer, then those formed in spring will mature by late

January. The base is dipped in hormone powder to encourage rapid rooting, before being inserted in a small pot containing a gritty compost. It should be placed over a radiator or in a propagating unit, for bottom heat is necessary; it will root in three months. Re-pot into a large pot before placing outdoors in May, in a sunny position to ripen the wood. Plant it in its permanent place the following spring. Or the plants may be moved to larger pots in which they will fruit. They should be 6 ft (180 cm) apart, for they will soon reach that height and will grow to the same width.

The method by which plants are grown on from suckers is the easier way. These should be detached with their roots and grown on in pots.

To harvest figs, remove them before they split but not much before. Place them in trays lined with cotton. They may be kept for several months in a frost-free room.

Varieties

Brown Turkey The best all-round hardy fig, good under glass and outdoors, bearing heavy crops of large purple-brown fruits of excellent flavor.

Brunswick Good under glass, it needs a sheltered, sunny position outdoors. The large green figs have white flesh.

September. The shoots formed in the last weeks of summer will bear next spring's crop.

Propagation is a simple matter. It is either by cuttings or by suckers. By the former method a well-ripened shoot 8 in (20 cm) long should be removed in

Plant in a tub, or remove with soil ball intact and restrict roots by planting over a layer of stones.

Fruits form in the leaf axils the previous year. Pinch back the shoots in July to encourage new fruits to form.

9 Raspberries

A cane fruit to follow strawberries as the chief soft fruit of summer with everbearing types producing fall harvests, too. It freezes well and with its unique flavor makes excellent preserves. The plants flower later than strawberries and are rarely troubled by frost.

Raspberries require an open sunny situation. To enable the canes to receive the full amount of sunshine, plant the rows north to south. A plantation will be permanent, although raspberries fruit on the previous

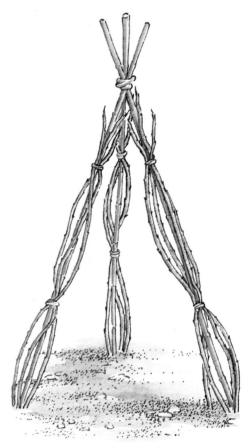

Above: Raspberries ripen after strawberries, fruiting on the previous year's canes.

Left: Raspberries bear well in a humus-laden soil if not planted too deep.

year's canes and it is necessary to provide the plants with a moderately fertile soil in order to enable them to make plenty of growth.

Raspberry plants also need humus in order to retain summer moisture, without which there will be few new canes and the fruits will be hard and seedy.

234

Preparing the ground

Dig in all the humus possible, including some peat moss together with manure or rotted compost. Use large amounts if the soil is of a sandy nature. At planting time, rake in 1 oz of sulfate of potash. per yd (30 g per m) of row, or of wood ash that has been stored under cover.

It is important to plant into clean ground, for it will be difficult to clean after planting without damaging the roots, as this fruit is surface-rooting. Rather than hoe too near the plants, give a mulch of compost and rotted straw in early June each year. This will suppress weeds and preserve moisture in the soil.

Planting

Plant the canes in spring in the North so that they are established before the frosts, although planting can be done at any time until mid-March if the soil is in a friable condition. If not, dig a trench and spread out the roots before covering them with soil until planting can take place. As with all fruits, purchase from a reliable grower who offers virus-free stock, very important with raspberries.

Plant the canes 24–30 in (60–75 cm) apart, the black and purple varieties needing slightly wider spacing; allow 4 ft (120 cm) between the rows. Do not plant too deeply, for this is the cause of failure of many plantations. Just cover the roots and tread in the soil over them. Then after a few days, cut back the canes to 6 in (15 cm) above ground level. There will be no fruit the first summer, though the autumn-fruiting kinds will bear a crop. This cutting back will cause the buds at the base of the canes to produce new canes on which will be borne next year's crop.

As the canes make growth, tie them to wires stretched along the rows at intervals of 18 in (45 cm). This will prevent the canes being broken by winds. At the end of summer, remove the tips of the canes, which will then have grown about 6 ft (180 cm) tall. After fruiting, cut out the old canes to about 3 in (7 cm) above ground and tie in the new canes for next year's crop. Burn the old canes and leave each root with six to seven new fruiting canes.

With autumn-fruiting kinds, the canes that fruited in fall can be headed back to force branching and a bigger crop on the same canes in early summer. The new fall crop is borne on canes which are produced that summer. In all other respects, the culture is the same for them.

The fruit ripens quickly, and if the weather is warm it may need picking twice daily so that it will not get too ripe and become 'mushy'.

To propagate, lift a root or two in spring or fall and separate the canes, holding them near the base and pulling them away with the roots. Re-plant as soon as possible so that the roots do not dry out, treating them as described.

Varieties

Allen Black fruits, large and glossy, firm and juicy. Begin to ripen in early July in the

When planting raspberries in rows, fasten canes to wires, cut back to 6 in (15 cm) above ground after fruiting. New canes will fruit next year.

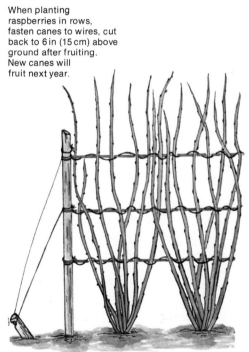

Northeast. The fruits tend to ripen at about the same time, an advantage for commercial growers and perhaps for some home fruit growers, too.

Black Hawk Black raspberries, large and sweet. Very productive with berries ripening for several weeks.

Bristol Black berries, large, glossy, of high quality. Midseason ripening.

Clyde A purple-fruited variety developed by the New York Experimental Station at Geneva, New York. A late variety, the fruits start to ripen in mid-July.

Fall Gold Large, golden-yellow berries, appearing in early July and again in the fall until frosts arrive. Very vigorous.

Fall Red Everbearing, the first red berries appearing about July 1, the fall crop starting in mid-August and continuing until frosts arrive.

Early to ripen, Malling Promise bears heavy crops.

An early variety which is widely grown in Europe, where it produces heavy crops.

Heritage Everbearing, the red fruits appearing early and again about September 1.

Newburgh An older variety that tends to be virus-resistant. A good midseason bearer.

Sentry A high-quality red raspberry from the University of Maryland and recommended for the Middle Atlantic region. Described as early-midseason.

September Everbearer with medium-sized red fruits, first ripening the end of June in much of the Northeast, with the fall crop ripening the beginning of September. Vigorous, highly tolerant of dry conditions and always bears well.

Sodus A purple-fruited variety popular in the Midwest.

Taylor Large-fruited red berries of exceptionally high quality, these are vigorous, hardy plants with sturdy, upright canes. They ripen midseason, continuing for about three weeks.

10 Blackberries

Blackberries rarely appear in the market these days as the berries are too fragile for shipping. The commercial production goes into jams and jellies. So the only way to savor these sun-ripened, juicy berries at their peak of perfection is to grow them in the home garden. Although blackberries are not as hardy as raspberries and can be damaged by long periods of below-zero winter weather as well as late spring freezes, they do well over much of the country. A few plants can be very productive. The berries freeze well and make excellent tarts and preserves.

There are various ways of growing the plants. They can be grown along a fence or wall, or used as a hedge, possibly to divide one part of the garden from another, with a central archway for access. Or plant in rows and train the stems along wires held in place by strong stakes at intervals of 8 ft (240 cm). Plant in early spring 8 ft (240 cm) apart in the rows and allow 5 ft (150 cm) between the rows. Where possible, plant thornless varieties, which are easier to tie in

and to pick the fruit from. Set the roots only 3–4 in (7–10 cm) deep.

Another method is to grow them up 10 ft (3 m) poles, or posts driven well into the ground with 8 ft (240 cm) above ground. Tie in the shoots as they grow, and when they have made too much old wood, cut away the ties and lay all the shoots on the ground. Then cut the older wood and tie in against the new shoots. In this way, the plants will be kept healthy for years. The time to do this is in fall or early spring; at this time any old or dead wood is removed from plants grown as a hedge or in rows.

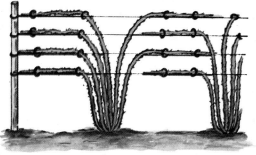

Above: Where growing on wires, space wires 18 in (45 cm) apart, using strong stakes to support them. Plant blackberries 8 ft (240 cm) apart in the rows.

Left: Blackberries may be grown against a trellis to serve as a hedge, or along wires or against a north wall.

Preparation of the soil

The plants require plenty of humus to retain moisture and produce large and juicy fruits. Give the ground some peat moss and whatever humus is available, such as garden compost or old manure. The plants will also benefit from a yearly mulch of lawn mowings or compost, to conserve soil moisture. In spring 28 g (1 oz) of sulfate of potash should be scattered on the surface around each plant. Or apply a sprinkling of 5–10–5 complete fertilizer. This will improve the quality of fruit. Blackberries will benefit from an occasional watering during wet weather of dilute liquid manure – as indeed will all soft fruits. This should be given from July until September and will not only enhance the quality of fruit but will also increase cane growth.

After planting, which should be done in spring in the North, in fall or winter in the South and other mild climates, if possible, cut back the canes to 6 in (15 cm) above soil level. New canes will appear in spring and these should be tied to wires horizontally, or vertically if they are growing against poles. Blackberries bear fruit on second-year canes.

Propagation

Named varieties are propagated by rooting the tips of the branches or canes. They are bent down from the wires in July and the ends inserted into the soil to a depth of about 3 in (7 cm). Tread firmly and keep moist. By November they will have rooted and may then be severed from the parent plant with about 6 in (15 cm) of cane attached. They should then be moved to their fruiting quarters and the parent cane should be tied in again. Nothing could be easier.

Varieties

Bailey Large black berries that begin ripening in early summer.

Blackberries can be grown against poles in the same way as rambler roses, tying in the long shoots.

Boysen or **Boysenberry** Large mulberry-colored fruits, the result of a cross between a dewberry and loganberry. The plants are vines, which are growing vigorously, and they need support. They are best in the milder climates, such as the South and Pacific Coast. There is a thornless form of boysenberry available.

Darrow Probably the best variety for most Northern regions. Bears a little later than Bailey.

Snyder Rust-resistant variety.

Lucretia Lucretia is a dewberry which has fruits that are larger and milder-flavoured than those of the blackberry.

Thornfree An origination of the US Dept. of Agriculture. Black fruits appear later than Darrow. Its advantage is its lack of thorns. Smoothstem is similar, but more upright growing and a week or so later than Thornfree in ripening.

Other members of the blackberry tribe

There are, of course, many other members of the blackberry tribe, including the loganberry, which is discussed on the following page. Some of these have their ancestry in America. For instance, the Parsley-leaved blackberry was formerly known as the American blackberry, although it is not actually of American origination. It is a variety of one of the British native wild species and initially was found growing wild in the county of Surrey. It was probably the species *Rubus fruticosus*, which is notable for its elegantly cut leaves and large, sweet, juicy berries. When ripe, these are distinctively black.

Another berry-bearing bramble is the species called the Himalaya berry, which does not have any connection with Himalaya but is said to have originated in America. It is exceedingly rampant, making shoots 8 to 10 ft (2·5 to 3 m) long in a single season. When established it is a very heavy cropper.

The Kugo Acre berry is supposed to be a variety of the American blackberry, bearing long berries which are black in color when ripe. It is not so vigorous as the Himalaya berry.

The Laxtonberry is of British origin, and reputed to be a cross between the loganberry and the raspberry. The berries are large, round, and raspberry-like and they are excellent for use in either jam or jelly-making.

The Veitchberry is a hybrid between the old variety November Abundance raspberry and a blackberry, and was introduced as far back as 1902 by the firm of Messrs. James Veitch and Sons.

There are many other berried plants to be found in North America, a number of which were put to very good use by the early settlers and were subsequently cultivated in gardens.

The hybrid berries fruit in autumn and are excellent for preserves and for freezing, to use in pies during winter.

11 Loganberries

Above: Loganberries, a blackberry for mild climates.

Farmyard manure, poultry manure and composted straw are all valuable, or dig in some peat moss and garden compost and give a handful of bone meal for each plant. In April, give the rows 1 oz per yd (30 g per m) of sulphate of ammonia during wet weather. This will increase cane growth, on which next year's fruit will be borne.

Plant any time between November and early March, 6 ft (180 cm) apart, only just covering the roots. In March, cut back the canes to 6 in (15 cm) above ground, and tie in the new canes as they grow. Like raspberries, this fruit will not bear a crop the first year. Should the cane tips have been caught by frost, remove them in spring when the plants are given a heavy mulch. During August, they will be laden with large crimson berries, which do not part from the core and so freeze and bottle well.

Propagation is by rooting the tips of the canes as for blackberries.

Loganberries can be increased quite easily by rooting the tips of the branches or canes. These shoots are bent down and the ends are inserted into the soil to a depth of about 3 in (7 cm). Firm the soil well around the tips, and keep them moist. The shoots will have rooted by November, and can be severed from the parent plant, with about 6 in (15 cm) of the cane attached. They can then be moved to their fruiting quarters.

Below: Train the canes against wires like raspberries.

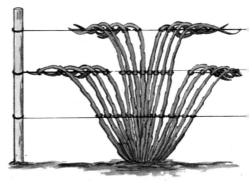

Believed to be a red-fruiting form of the blackberry, or the result of a chance cross between a blackberry and a raspberry, the loganberry was discovered by Judge Logan at Santa Cruz and named in his honor.

Loganberries do not like cold winds and the canes are more frost-tender than either raspberries or blackberries. Hence they are grown only in California and the Northwest.

Provide the plants with a soil containing plenty of humus, for they fruit only on the new season's canes and as much new cane growth as possible must be produced.

12 Gooseberries

Gooseberries are the hardiest of the soft fruits, cropping well where few other fruits would. They are troubled neither by frost nor by cold winds.

One of the hardiest of the soft fruits, the gooseberry prefers cool conditions to ripen. It does better where cool, moist conditions prevail. It crops heavily for the area of ground it occupies, and no amount of frost or cold winds will trouble it. It is one of the few soft fruits to do well in semi-shade. It may, therefore, be planted between apples and other top fruits, thus making the best use of the ground. It is also a very permanent plant and with the minimum of attention will continue to produce fruit for fifty years and more. In addition, the fruit will hang on the bushes for several weeks so that it may be picked when there is plenty of time to do so. But it should not be left until the fruits begin to crack and fall from the plants. The fruit is used for preserves, and it will freeze better than any, keeping for two years. Fresh, ripe gooseberries have no equal for flavor eaten from the plant, a treat unfortunately known to few Americans, since gooseberries are rarely grown today. Reasons for their lack of popularity are the very thorny plants and, in common with the currant, their susceptibility to white pine blister rust, of which they are an alternate host. If there are no white pines within 1000 ft, it should be safe to grow gooseberries and currants.

Gooseberries will ripen early in midsummer in the North. What is more, a

pound of gooseberries can be picked in a few minutes (but wear gloves!) and the fruit does not turn mushy, however warm the weather. It is the foolproof fruit with a distinctive flavor all of its own.

Preparing the soil

Gooseberries, which fruit both on the old and new wood, bear so heavily that it is necessary to maintain a balance between the production of new wood and fruiting. The soil in which gooseberries grow needs humus to maintain moisture in summer. Without this the fruits cannot swell and will lack both weight and flavor. So dig in plenty of peat moss or garden compost, or rotted manure.

If dry conditions prevail, water the plants as often as possible, preferably in the evening, giving the roots a good soaking. All soft fruits, especially the gooseberry, require plenty of moisture for the berries to grow large and juicy. An occasional application of dilute manure water given in early summer will help the fruits to swell and increase the flavor.

Watering should commence as soon as the fruits have formed and should continue until ripe. If left until the berries have grown large, heavy watering will then cause the skins to crack, as with tomatoes.

Planting

Plant in the fall when there is no frost. But where the ground is heavy and not well-drained, early spring planting is better. Plant 4 ft (120 cm) apart in rows, with the same distance between them, for a fully grown plant will cover an area of just under a square yard (square meter).

During the first three or four years, little or no pruning is needed. Afterwards, begin to remove some of the old wood and thin out the shoots if there is overcrowding, so that the plants do not grow into each other. Those of spreading and somewhat drooping habit should have the shoots cut back to an upwards bud to counteract this tendency. Those of upright habit are cut back at an outwards bud in order to prevent overcrowding at the center.

Propagation

Gooseberry cuttings are difficult to root, for

the wood is relatively hard. Because of this, use only the new season's wood and insert as soon as possible after removing it from the plant. Cuttings are removed early September when about 6 in (15 cm) long. Remove all but the top three buds so that the plant will form a 'leg' and insert the

Gooseberries are grown on a 'leg', with the lower buds being removed before the cuttings are rooted.

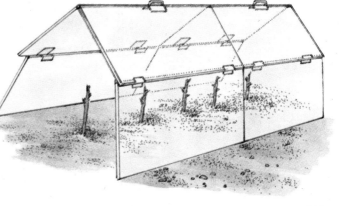

Cuttings can be rooted in a cold frame or in the open ground, where they can be protected over winter by a mulch or by a plastic adaptation of the cloche.

243

Home-grown gooseberries are delicious, and are excellent for preserves and the freezer.

base in hormone powder to encourage quicker rooting. Then insert the lower 1 in (2 cm) into the soil either in trenches outdoors into which peat has been incorporated, or in a frame, the soil having been prepared in the same way. Those in trenches can be covered with cloches.

Plant the cuttings 3 in (7 cm) apart and make the soil firm around them. Water in and keep the soil comfortably moist. They should have rooted by early the following summer, but keep growing them on until October when they should be moved to their fruiting quarters and planted at the recommended spacing. They will begin to fruit the following year, but strawberries may be grown between the rows until such time as the gooseberries have made some growth.

An alternative method of propagation for gooseberries, perhaps easier than the above, is mound layering. This is the method used commercially, but it is a perfectly feasible one for the home gardener. Select one bush (or more if needed), cut

back to about 6 in (15 cm) in spring. Then, in early summer, mound up soil over the entire bush, but leaving the tips of the shoots uncovered. By the next spring, the shoots covered by soil will be rooted and can be cut from the old plant and replanted. If only one or two new plants are wanted, this can be achieved by simple layering: select a branch, bend it to the ground and bury in the soil, about 1 ft (30 cm) from the tip. Fasten it securely in the soil with a U-bent wire or stone. The branch should be rooted the following year and can be cut from the parent plant.

Varieties

Fredonia Large, dark red berries in mid- to late summer. Vigorous and productive.

Pixwell Pink-red (when fully ripe) berries that hang freely from the underside of canes for better stripping.

Poorman The fruits are large and judged to be of excellent flavor.

Welcome Large, dull-red berries. The plants are reputed to be nearly thornless and are highly disease-resistant.

Growing Giant Gooseberries

Many people like to produce, either in competition or for their amusement, very large gooseberries.

These are produced by pruning each bush to several fruit-bearing shoots, feeding the bush more than normal, and thinning the berries through several stages to just a few berries.

The fruits, of course, will have to be protected from pests, especially birds, which could soon destroy the champion-sized fruits.

If bird damage is usually bad in your area, you should delay pruning the bushes until early March. By that time, there will be other berries about for the birds to attack and eat.

244

13 Currants

The currant, though revered in Britain and Europe, is of minor importance in the USA. The fruits (red, white, or black) are borne on bushes only 3–4 ft (90–120 cm) high that can readily be fitted into even the smallest property, but they are tart and at their best only in jelly and jam.

Probably a more important factor in the currant's lack of popularity is that the bushes are alternate hosts of the disease white pine blister rust. Although the currant bushes can survive the rust when both sides of the leaves are sprayed weekly with zineb or maneb after buds form and up to flowering, the white pines usually succumb, and many states prohibit the growing of currants to protect their white pine forests. The black currant, considered an even more effective transmitter of the rust to white pines, is virtually an outlaw and not offered by any fruit nurseries.

Those who wish to grow red- or white-fruited currants should first check with state and local authorities (state agricultural experiment stations and cooperative extension associations, the last listed under the county government in the telephone book) to find out about restrictions against currants.

Not all is bad with the currant, though. For those who can grow them, the fruits offer much for those interested in culinary arts. In addition to jellies and jams, there are sauces and syrups to be made and conserves to have with meats.

Soil requirements

The plants are very hardy and exceptionally long-lived. They will grow in most garden soils – from light (add plenty of humus to the planting holes) to medium and heavy. They will even bear well in light shade, unlike most fruits, but they should not be exposed to prevailing winds.

Planting and pruning

Fall planting is best. Set the bushes about 3–4 ft (90–120 cm) apart and cut back to about 3 in (7 cm) of their base. It is recommended that bushes be set slightly deeper than their original depth to force new shoot growth rather than allowing the bushes to grow with a single stem. No more pruning will be required until the bushes reach three years; then each autumn, all those canes which are over three years old should be removed.

The fruits begin to show color in midsummer, when they should be covered with netting to protect them from birds. Fruits for jelly possess the most pectin just before they are fully ripe. Fully ripe berries, sprinkled with sugar and wine, can be eaten fresh.

The black currant is a continental favorite.

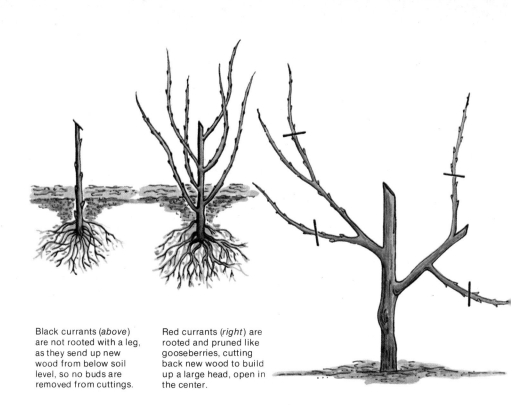

Black currants (*above*) are not rooted with a leg, as they send up new wood from below soil level, so no buds are removed from cuttings.

Red currants (*right*) are rooted and pruned like gooseberries, cutting back new wood to build up a large head, open in the center.

Training

Although white currants and red currants are usually grown as bushes, they can also be positioned against a wall. In such positions they can be formed into single, double or even triple cordons. When set against a wall it is far easier to protect them from birds than if positioned as bushes in the middle of the fruit plot. Nets can be secured to the wall and draped over the cordons.

Red or white currants can also be formed into fan-trained trees, when they are best set 6 ft (2 m) apart. Cordons can be 1 to 1½ ft (30 to 45 cm) apart. Often, these soft fruits can be advantageously positioned along walls between young wall-trained apple or pear trees. Then, after a few years when the apple and pear trees have grown, the currants can be removed.

Varieties

Minnesota 71 Large clusters of large red berries of excellent quality.

Red Lake Popular and prolific with large red berries.

White Imperial A white currant.

Wilder Large red fruits that remain in good condition on bushes after ripening if protected from birds.

Where did currants originate?

When the currant was first cultivated is difficult to say. There is no doubt that the Dutch cultivated both the red and the white currant, and that this was a long time before they became popular throughout the British Isles.

The word currant is derived from the name 'Corinth'. Currants, of course, did not originate in Corinth, which is too warm for their successful cultivation. But a variety of small grape was grown in Greece, and its likeness to the currant gave the latter its name.

The white currant is but a simple variety of the red currant, which botanically is known as *Ribes rubrum*. The black currant is a quite distinctive species, *Ribes nigrum*, and was formerly known as the Quinsy berry. It gained this name because its fruits were used to ward off, and to act as a remedy for, various infections of the throat and also for colds.

Medicinal uses of currants

The currant has for a long time been considered by herbalists to have special curative qualities.

Its uses have ranged from a cure for oral and throat ailments to strengthening gums. Also, it has been used in the treatment of fevers, especially in infants and children. Its use has even been extended to attempts at preventing miscarriages and curing anaemia. It is also proclaimed to be useful against all disorders of pregnancy. And, amazingly, its use in the past also extended to a remedy for dysentery.

However, in modern-day times the currant's merit is as a useful source of vitamins especially vitamin C.

Red currants require a warm, sheltered garden. The fruit ripens July and August and should be covered with muslin to protect from birds.

The red currant is thought to be a better and more powerful laxative than the black species, although it does not seem to possess the same curative powers for the throat and mouth. According to old herbals, the red currant is said to be of value for all fevers, constipation, jaundice and all disorders of the liver. The dosage is normally one cupful of the berries twice daily. But for disorders of the liver or jaundice, a brew of the leaves is recommended. This is made by boiling the red currant leaves in water, and then taking a morning cupful of the resulting liquid.

247

14 Strawberries

The most popular home garden fruit, always prominent on special summer occasions, to be enjoyed in shortcake or with cream or sprinkled with wine. Strawberries freeze well and, of course, are famous for jams, preserves and sauces.

They are popular with home gardeners because they are quick to bear compared to most fruits. Everbearers (strawberry varieties that bear two crops a year) planted in early spring will yield a crop the following fall. June bearers (strawberry varieties that bear one major crop in early summer) will give a good crop the second year (they will bear the summer after planting but all flower buds are picked off to build the plant's strength for the following season).

Yet the strawberry ripens quickly, needing constant attention with its picking, and its blossom is more liable to frost damage in some regions than other fruits. The plants are more troubled by pests and diseases. Finally the fruits may be spoiled by prolonged rainy weather when ripening. Even with these disadvantages, the strawberry remains America's favorite home garden fruit and commercial production is constantly heavy.

Most home gardeners choose everbearers today, of which there are several good varieties that do well over much of the North. Everbearers perform less successfully in the South, where June bearers are usually selected. Whatever variety is ordered, make sure the plants are certified as being virus-free.

Although winter hardiness varies among varieties, the main problems are due to alternate freezing and thawing of the soil, which heaves the shallow-rooted plants out of the soil; and to injury to flower buds from late spring frosts. Avoid planting in low ground where frost can settle.

Preparing the soil

Strawberries grow best on light land; if

Strawberries are the most popular of summer fruits.

heavy, it will tend to be badly drained in winter when the roots may decay because of red stele, turning red at the center and causing the plant to die back. But light land will need plenty of humus and this may be given as peat moss, garden compost, and rotted manure. Strawberries bear better in a slightly acid soil and peat will encourage this. With it, mix in any other form of humus to bind the soil.

Clean land is essential, for the plants send out in all directions runners that take root, and it is impossible to clean round the plants later. Also, in weed-infested land the weeds deprive the plants of moisture and soon the strawberries begin to die back. If you are planting in newly turned turf land, you should treat for wireworm and grubs before planting.

Planting

Allow the ground several weeks to consolidate before planting. Before planting, rake in 1 oz per yd (30 g per m) of 5–10–5 or a similar complete fertilizer.

The Hill System or a modified version is most successful in home gardens, especially with everbearers, which form fewer runners. In this System, plants are set out 15–18 in (37–45 cm) apart in rows with about 18–24 in (45–60 cm) between rows. Keep the plants mulched, either with straw (from this use of straw the plant took its name), pine needles, leaves or, except in the South, black plastic. In winter the plants must have extra mulch applied right over the crowns to protect them from freezing temperatures and to prevent the plants from being uprooted by fluctuating soil temperatures.

The plants must be kept moist if they are to make plenty of healthy foliage and the berries are to be large and juicy. Therefore, in dry weather give plenty of water, though ample humus in the soil before planting helps retain moisture. Mid- to late summer is a good time to apply a fertilizer high in nitrogen. Any lawn fertilizer will do, especially one containing nitrogen in the urea form. Apply at the rate recommended for lawns and water in, washing any fertilizer off the foliage.

If the land is heavy and not well-drained, it will be advisable to plant on ridges or on a raised bed to allow winter rains to drain away. Also, plants on raised beds are less liable to be damaged by frost. This type of bed is made 6 in (15 cm) higher than the surrounding land and 5 ft (150 cm) across to allow for picking without treading the bed. Plant 15 in (37 cm) apart in rows 16–18 in (40–45 cm) apart.

Runners begin to form towards the end of summer, and in the Hill System are removed before they begin to root. This will enable the plants to concentrate on fruit production and in this way the plants may be productive for four or five years. A few plants may be allowed to form runners, which are removed when they have formed roots. These are used to make a new plantation each year, to take over when the original plantings begin to bear poorer-quality berries.

When planting, use a blunt-ended trowel and make the hole large enough to take all the roots and to enable them to be spread out. Only just cover the roots, with the crown of the plant at soil level. Use a garden line to make the rows, which should run north to south. Tread the plants in and do so again in spring for some may have been lifted by frost.

When the green berries have turned white, inspect them daily for they will soon turn pink and then scarlet, this taking only

Where the ground is not well-drained, plant strawberries on ridges or on a raised bed.

Plant with a blunt-edged trowel, being careful to spread out the roots before covering with soil.

a few days, or less in warm weather. Pick them with the calyx attached if possible and place in a refrigerator to cool. Then remove the green tops, sprinkle with sugar and replace until required.

Growing in tubs

Good crops can be obtained by planting in tubs or barrels used by cider and vinegar makers. They need drilling with drainage holes at the base, and also round the side at intervals of about 15 in (37 cm). Make the holes large enough to take the roots with the foliage outside the hole.

The tubs and barrels can be of any size and may be placed in a courtyard where there is no garden. They need as much sunshine as possible. First treat the tubs with wood preservative (though being of oak, they will usually be long lasting) and the iron bands with paint or a rustproof material. Then place a layer of broken-up pieces from clay pots or pebbles at the bottom, to cover the drainage holes and to permit surplus moisture to escape. Over these pieces, place some coarse compost, then fill up to within 1 in (2·5 cm) of the top with prepared loam, peat and decayed

If there is no ground available, heavy crops may be obtained from strawberries grown in barrels or tubs. Be sure to prepare the soil well before planting.

manure, mixed well together. Also, give a handful of superphosphate to each tub; twice that amount to each barrel.

Plant 6 in (15 cm) apart in a tub and put a plant in each hole in a barrel. Water from the top and, from spring, keep the plants well supplied with moisture, for they will obtain only limited amounts naturally.

Varieties

Black Beauty Large, dark red June bearer, that is a flavorful novelty for the home garden.

Geneva This is a large, high-quality berry. The plants bear well in June, through the summer and into early fall. A fine everbearer from the NY Agricultural Experiment station.

Ogallala An everbearer from the University of Nebraska. A large and productive strawberry.

Ozark Beauty Popular everbearer of fine-flavored berries to use either fresh or for freezing.

Premier An early June bearer, this old variety retains its popularity.

Sparkle June bearer, midseason to late. Attractive fruits of good flavor.

Surecrop This is a June bearer that lives up to its name. It has deep red berries of sweet flavor.

Where did strawberries originate?

Unquestionably, the strawberry is one of the most delicious of our hardy fruits. It is also one of the most adaptable – being used in jams, pies and perhaps best of all being eaten on its own with cream.

In its wild state it can be found in many parts of the world, on hedge banks and in woods. It is especially abundant in northern Europe. In fact, the wild strawberry is often appreciated more than the cultivated

250

Everbearing strawberries provide a second harvest beginning in midsummer.

At that time, the North American strawberry, the Scarlet or Virginian strawberry, *Fragaria virginiana*, was introduced into Europe, and the Chili strawberry from Chile. They were, however, considered to be not as good as the native European strawberry, the Wood strawberry.

During the beginning of the eighteenth century, the present-day strawberries were developed by crossing the Virginian or Scarlet strawberry with the Chili strawberry. From these have developed the modern large-fruiting varieties which are now in cultivation.

Today, there appear to be three main types of strawberries in cultivation. The first is the Alpine, or small-fruiting types; the second the Large-fruiting varieties; and thirdly the Perpetual types.

The Alpine ones are noted for their free and continuous fruit-bearing quality, and also for their ease of cultivation. The Large-fruiting varieties are esteemed for their size and flavor. The Perpetuals are valued for their ability to supply berries throughout the summer and autumn. The Perpetuals, by the way, are a result of a cross between the Alpine and the Large-fruited kinds, and these strawberries are particularly popular.

Medicinal use of strawberries

Like the currants, strawberries have great medicinal value. They are said to be useful in the treatment of impure blood and also anaemia, to improve low vitality or a low appetite, and for bowel and stomach disorders. But whatever their value to the body, they are certainly good to eat.

one. Its taste is less watery than many modern-day varieties.

As far back as the thirteenth century in Britain mention was made of them. They were mentioned in the Household Roll of the Countess of Leicester. And by the time of King Henry VIII, the fruit was valued at fourpence a bushel – a good sum of money for those days.

The strawberries grown at that time were the Wild strawberry or Wood strawberry, botanically known as *Fragaria vesca*. Also, the Hautbois strawberry, *Fragaria elatior*, is mentioned by the well-known botanist of the sixteenth century, Gerarde. In the eighteenth century, the Alpine strawberry, *Fragaria alpina* was introduced from the continent of Europe into Britain and was subsequently grown extensively in gardens.

Rooting strawberry runners

16 Blueberries

Blueberries bear well in acid soils and have a long life.

These plants, also called whortleberry and bilberry, are present in acid moorland soils of North America, the British Isles, and across northern Europe and Asia, growing to 6–8 ft (2 m) tall and in large plantations. Wild berries are harvested, but are small. Modern cultivated blueberries are as large as small black grapes and begin to color early in summer, lasting for several weeks.

The fruits require an acid soil, like the azalea and rhododendron, so work plenty of peat moss about the roots at planting time, which is early spring. The plants also require plenty of nitrogenous manures to encourage the formation of a continuous supply of new wood upon which high quality fruit is obtained. Dig in rotted manure or composted straw. And in spring each year scatter on the surface around each plant 1 oz (28 g) of sulfate of potash and the same of superphosphate, mixed together. This will increase the quality of fruit. They should always be mulched.

Plant deeper than other fruits, as reproduction and new growth are by underground suckers, which may be detached and replanted to increase.

Set the plants 4 ft (120 cm) apart, for they grow bushy and at least 4 ft (120 cm) tall. Plants have a long life and bear heavily. The plants crop better if helped with their pollination, so plant two varieties together, one to give early crops, the other later. Three plants of each will provide worthwhile pickings. Blueberries turn from green to red then pale blue before turning black.

Varieties

Berkeley Huge berries of good quality. Ripens in midseason after Earliblue.

Bluecrop Bright colored, high quality berries. Requires pruning to slow down its remarkable productiveness. Midseason, ripening before Berkeley.

Blueray Large light blue berries of good flavor. Midseason, ripening about one week after Earliblue.

Darrow Medium-sized light blue berries. Fruit is very late, ripening one month after Earliblue.

Earliblue One of the earliest blueberries of high quality.

Herbert Very large berries produced in generous clusters. A later variety, ripening about 25 days after Earliblue.

Cranberries

This twiggy shrub grows to 2 ft (60 cm) tall in acid boglands. The plants form a dense mass of long wiry stems, and in September and October the fruits ripen to brightest crimson with a delicious sharp taste.

Plant only in low ground, for during summer its roots should be continually submerged in water. Plant 4 ft (120 cm) apart as it spreads quickly. Propagation is by lifting and dividing the roots in winter.

17 Rhubarb

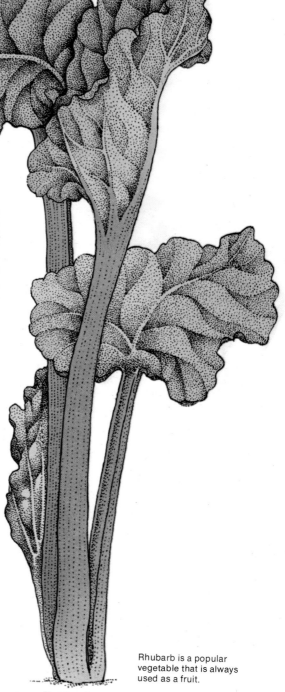

Though a vegetable, rhubarb is always used as a fruit. As it can be forced during winter in warmth or in the open, it is one of the most valuable crops, and the first outdoor rhubarb always enjoys a welcome. It may be grown in light shade where little else will grow. It will also grow well in any soil. It requires plenty of humus to maintain summer moisture if it is to make those thick, juicy sticks so much in demand for stewing or for pies and tarts. So dig in plenty of rotted manure or garden compost and give the roots a mulch in summer.

Many gardeners treat rhubarb as a decorative feature, positioning it where the large leaves can be seen, and also where the stems can be harvested without the need to tramp over wet soil.

In addition, why not set a clump of these plants as exclamation marks at the ends of rows of asparagus? Here, again, they will be easily accessible when harvesting time comes around. Fortunately, the soil preparation for asparagus exactly suits the needs of the rhubarb – making a happy combination.

Rhubarb roots, or thongs, must contain an 'eye', which will produce a stalk. Without this there will be no plant. The roots are planted in fall or spring while dormant, for they begin to grow with the first warm spring sunshine. Plant 2 ft (60 cm) apart with the 'eye' or bud just below soil level,

Rhubarb is a popular vegetable that is always used as a fruit.

but make the hole deep enough to take the long root.

At planting time, give a 4 oz per sq yd (132 g per sq m) dressing of basic slag, which rhubarb loves, for it releases its nitrogen content over a long time.

Pull no stalks the first year and only a few in the second year. By then, the roots will be established and a dozen stalks or more can be removed in the year.

After four years the roots will have grown to 18 in (45 cm) across. To prevent them becoming too hard and woody, lift in fall and divide with a knife or spade, remembering that each piece of root must have at least one 'eye'. Treat the cut parts with lime or flowers of sulphur before replanting.

Producing early crops

If there are several roots, one or two can be lifted and forced in a garage or beneath the greenhouse bench. But first allow it to remain for a week or two in the open after lifting during cold, even freezing, weather; this will make it force all the better. Half fill a deep orange crate with a friable soil (a mixture of loam, peat and decayed manure is ideal), and in it place the root with the 'eye' at soil level. Water in and place a sheet of cardboard or a sack over the top to exclude light. If planted in December, the stalks, reddish-pink in color, will have reached to the covering by the end of January. They will be about 12–15 in (30–37 cm) long and are then removed as required by pulling. Use the largest first to allow the others to grow on. When cropping has finished, turn out the roots, divide them and re-plant in spring to grow on, but do not remove any stalks that year.

Another way to obtain early stalks is to cover a mature root in the open where it is growing. This is done by placing over it a deep box or upturned bucket. The previous year's stalks will have died back during winter. Before covering, place over the root some fresh strawy manure or composted straw, which will provide some warmth. About March 1 is the time to cover the roots, and the first stalks will be ready to pull about mid-April.

Uncovered roots outdoors will produce stalks to use in early May and they will continue for a few weeks. Rhubarb freezes well. Late in autumn, remove the old stalks and foliage, dig over the soil around the roots and give a strawy mulch.

Varieties

Canada Red It forces well outdoors and bears large, thick, red stalks right through summer.

Valentine Known for its bright red stalks.

Victoria Stalks are red on the outside, green within. Very vigorous.

Below left: Divide long-established rhubarb roots in winter before re-planting into well-manured ground.

Below: Rhubarb can be forced by covering the roots in January with pots or boxes in order to draw up the stalks.

18 Pests and diseases

Apple (pages 202-9)

Aphid It feeds on the young shoots and leaves, causing them to curl up, and early in winter it lays on the spurs. To control, spray with malathion after petals fall.

Codling moth A serious pest, the tiny white grubs of which burrow into the fruits leaving a pile of brown dirt at the entrance hole. Spray with rotenone each month after petals fall from June to September to control.

Scab It attacks shoots, leaves and fruits as black blisters. The home gardener should select varieties least susceptible to the disease. Spraying with captan, manels or ferbam as part of a regular spraying will help.

Blackberry (pages 237-9)

Cane spot Attacks all cane fruits, usually in a cold, wet summer, as brown spots on canes and leaves, which fall. Spray in spring, before flowers open, with Bordeaux mixture.

Cherry (pages 221-3)

Canker It affects mostly black cherries, first as yellow leaf spots, causing leaves to fall, later as brown areas on branches. Spray with Bordeaux mixture – 1 lb (500 g) copper sulphate and ¾ lb (375 g) slaked lime to 6 gall (30 liters) of water in spring before buds open.

Cherry (cont.)

Aphid The tiny black eggs winter on the twigs; the grubs, on hatching in spring, feed on the leaves and new growth. Control by routine spraying with malathion as part of general spray program.

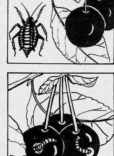

Fruit moth The small green caterpillars enter the flower buds and later bore into the fruits, making them uneatable. The fruits fall, the moths emerging in spring to lay their eggs on the blossom. Dust with rotenone just before the blossom opens.

Fig (pages 232-3)

Scale It also attacks vines, apricots and peaches, appearing as white scale-like insects, clustering on the stems and sucking the sap. To control, spray with malathion in early March.

Peach (pages 224-6)

Leaf curl The most troublesome disease, attacking the leaves and causing them to curl. Later, they take on a powdery look and die. Spraying with ferbam or 8-8-10 Bordeaux before buds begin to swell will control to some extent.

255

Peach (cont.)

Borers Borers infest trunks and branches, often after winter injury or pruning scars have been made. Borers can be removed with a wire or knife. Borers in the trunk are killed by paradichlorobenzene crystals applied around the base of the trunk.

Pear (pages 210-14)

Fire blight Also attacks apple and quince. New growth appears to be scorched by fire, the change often occurring very quickly. Plant resistant varieties. Cut off infected branches; spray with an antibiotic, Actidione.

Scab Though the symptoms are similar in appearance, scab on pears takes a different form from that which attacks apples. Spray with captan or ferbam early in May and again after blossom set, early in June.

Plum and gage (pages 215-19)

Brown rot It attacks the fruit spurs, the blossom (as blossom wilt) and later the fruits, causing them to mummify on the trees. To control it, remove mummified fruit in winter. Spray with captan after petals fall.

Sawfly As well as plums and gages, it attacks apples and gooseberries when in bloom, laying on the flower buds, the white caterpillars causing the buds to die. Spray with methoxychlor; apples at petal fall, plums ten days later; or use rotenone and a spreader.

Plum and gage (cont.)

Silver leaf Its presence is shown by the leaves taking on a silver appearance and the trees soon die. It enters through cuts. For this reason, pruning should be completed by mid-July so that the cuts will 'gum' quickly. There is no known cure.

Raspberry (pages 234-6)

Raspberry beetle It also attacks blackberries and loganberries, laying its eggs on the flowers. After hatching, the white grubs eat into the fruits. To prevent, dust with rotenone as the flowers open and again when the fruit has set.

Raspberry moth It winters in the soil and emerges in spring as a silver-brown moth to lay its eggs on the flowers. The caterpillars eat the fruits, often entirely. To prevent, dust with rotenone as for raspberry beetle.

Red and white currants (pages 245-7)

Aphid Can be common on currants. Spray with malathion as leaf buds are unfurling.

256

Strawberry (pages 248-7)

Aphid It feeds on the sap and reduces vigor, allowing virus diseases to enter at the punctures. To control, spray with Malathion before the blossoms open.

Mites Most troublesome of strawberry pests, both the cyclamen and two-spotted mites can infest plants. Severely stunted plants should be destroyed. Spraying with Kelthane, making several applications 10–14 days apart, will check the mites before they cause serious damage.

Botrytis (mildew) Both are forms of mildew, botrytis attacking the fruits, mildew the foliage, as a powdery white fungus. Dust with 10% captan, as soon as the first green fruits have set.

Red stele Caused by a fungus that attacks the roots, causing them to turn red at the center and the plants to die back. There is no cure, so, in low-lying, badly drained land, plant in raised beds or plant resistant varieties.

Note: The best way to control the various pests and diseases of fruit trees is to use a general purpose fruit spray several times during the growing season. Directions for the timing of the sprays are usually on the container, but such information, along with information on the pests common to a particular region, can be obtained from the county extension specialist.

Although regulations regarding pesticides are being constantly reviewed, the major chemicals in fruit sprays are malathion, captan, methoxychlor and sometimes carbaryl.

The US Department of Agriculture has published a booklet, *Control of Insects on Deciduous Fruits and Tree Nuts in the Home Orchard Without Insecticides*. It is Home and Garden Bulletin No. 211 and can be obtained from the Superintendent of Document, US Government Printing Office, Washington, DC 20402.

Vegetable Growing

1 Soils and digging

Before you can grow anything the soil has to be cultivated, and different soils need different treatment. The gardener has to understand and make the best of his soil, because although it can always be improved its basic character cannot be changed.

Types of soil

Heavy or clay soils These are wet and sticky in winter, drying to hard clods or a cracked surface in summer if wrongly treated.

Dig early in winter, exposing a rough surface to frost, which shatters the clods into a fine tilth ready for sowing in spring. Work in bulky organic manures when digging. Never tread on the soil when it is wet. If the soil should be waterlogged when you wish to dig, try spreading some peat on top. This will make digging easier and save you getting embedded in mud.

Sandy or light soils These are easy to work, warm up quickly in spring and so are good for early crops. They dry out in summer and are often poor because plant food is quickly washed out.

Dig in moisture-holding material – manure, compost or peat. Apply complete fertilizers shortly before sowing. During the growing season top dress with fertilizers and water them in, or apply liquid fertilizers. Mulch with peat or compost.

Loams These are generally fertile soils, lighter than clays but holding moisture better than sands. A good loam has a naturally high humus content and when it derives from, for instance, old pasture-land, it should support crops well for several years with little manure or fertilizer. But if you are lucky enough to have such a soil you should treat it generously from the start, otherwise the initial fertility will be lost and take years to rebuild.

Alkaline soils Often grayish in color, these dry quickly after heavy rain. This natural drainage makes for an early start in spring, but alkaline soils need the same attention to watering and mulching to keep crops growing in summer.

Alkaline soils rarely need lime and benefit from all the organic manure and peat that you can give them. Crops such as potatoes, which dislike an alkaline soil, do much better if plenty of peat is worked into the planting site.

Get to know your soil and the way it is affected by differing weather conditions. In a new district, learn about its peculiarities from gardening neighbors.

If certain crops fail persistently, change varieties, substituting those likely to suit the soil better: stump-rooted carrots for long varieties on clay soils, for instance, or snap beans on sandy loams.

hardcore   topsoil

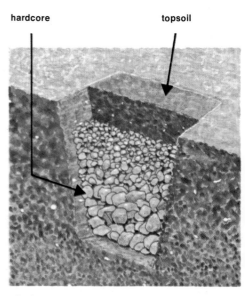

Drainage: to improve waterlogged soil, construct a soakaway. Dig a hole about 3 ft (1 m) deep, fill with hard-core topped by gravel, and replace topsoil.

1. Place one foot – left or right – on a shoulder of the blade and drive it *vertically* into the ground using just the weight of the body. If you drive it in at an angle the digging will be less effective.

2. Pull the spade handle back to lever the chunk of soil loose, lift it with one hand well down the shaft at the point of balance.

3. Throw it gently forwards, twisting the spade slightly so it slips from the blade. Repeat this in a steady rhythm. When you reach the far side of the plot walk back and begin another row.

The why and how of digging

Digging is the first and most important part of cultivation. It breaks up the soil so that the surface weathers into a friable tilth in which seeds can be sown, it allows the penetration of water and air, both necessary for the health of soil and plants, and it permits the removal of weeds and the incorporation of manure and compost.

Digging is the hardest physical work in the gardening routine, but at the right tempo and in reasonable stints it need not be tiring. Start at a left-hand corner of the plot to be dug and work from left to right. Use a spade rather than a fork unless the soil is hard to penetrate, and dig only when the surface is fairly dry or lightly frozen.

Pick out all perennial weed roots and consign them to the bonfire. Annual weeds may be buried if completely covered, but are best taken to the compost heap.

Right: basic soil preparation. In plain digging the spade goes one spit deep and the soil is thrown forward, leaving only a narrow trench. In double digging a wider trench is first taken out and the subsoil is dug with a fork. The first trench is then filled with soil from the second, and so on, the first soil excavated being barrowed to the end of the plot and used to fill the last trench. In ridging the soil is thrown forward to form a ridge-and-furrow pattern, exposing it to frost and improving drainage.

Plain digging

Double digging

Ridging

2 Planning your vegetable plot

Make the most of your vegetable garden by planning ahead. The easy and obvious course is not always the best in the long run.

Give the vegetables the most open position possible, cutting back tall hedges on the south and west sides. Avoid sites overshadowed by trees. A few dwarf fruit trees can be included in the larger home vegetable garden, since they cast little shade.

Try to arrange things so that the crop rows run north-south, giving equal sunlight on both sides of a row and reducing the extent to which short crops are overshadowed by taller ones. Remember that good paths between beds and to the garden shed and compost heaps make for ease of working. The grass path is the worst, having to be mown and trimmed in the summer while in winter it becomes bare and muddy. One of the best and most quickly laid is that made of cement paving slabs with non-slip surface. Kitchen garden paths need not be more than 24 in (60 cm) wide.

Planning the crops

Decide at the start of the season on the crops to be grown and the space to be allotted to each, otherwise you may realize too late that some varieties you particularly wanted have been crowded out.

Crop rotation The object of 'rotating' crops is to ensure that the same crop, or a similar type of crop, does not occupy the same ground year after year, which encourages the build-up of pests and diseases and depletes the soil of particular nutrients. Divide the vegetable plot into three roughly equal areas or beds and the crops into three groups, growing each group in a different bed over a three-year period. The groups are roots (including potatoes), brassicas (all the cabbage tribe) and miscellaneous, which includes peas and beans.

The manurial treatment of the groups is different: the brassicas should receive most of the organic manure and the miscellaneous crops any left over. Root crops are not manured. All the beds get fertilizer dressings before sowing or planting. It is not, of course, possible to keep to the rotation in every detail. There is always some overlapping, and quick-growing crops such as lettuce and spinach may be fitted in wherever space is available.

Successional crops

Achieving maximum yields from your garden depends on making the fullest use of the ground. This does not mean cramming rows and plants closer together than the recommended distances, which often means a lower total yield, but ensuring that that group is not left unused or cluttered with the remains of a previous crop.

Wherever possible, follow a main crop with a successional one, usually quick-maturing and harvested the same season, sometimes the following spring. Clear away the old crop immediately it finishes, and lightly fork over or rototill the surface. Most successional crops are started in the summer, when everything must be done to conserve soil moisture. Don't dig deeply, because this releases moisture and brings up intractable clods. Leave the roots of early pea and bean crops in the ground, to release the nitrogen accumulated from the atmosphere in the root nodules. Just hoe the topsoil. Work in a complete fertilizer at $1\frac{1}{2}$ oz per sq yd (50 g per sq m), water drills thoroughly in dry weather before sowing, and keep germinating seeds and young plants watered until well established. Follow broad beans and early peas with broccoli, snap or lima beans, or summer squash.

Catch crops Some vegetables with a short growing season can be 'slotted in' between other crops to make the most of the ground. Radishes can be sown together with slow germinating seeds such as parsnips.

Three-year rotation

First year **Second year**

Final distance between:
plants **rows**

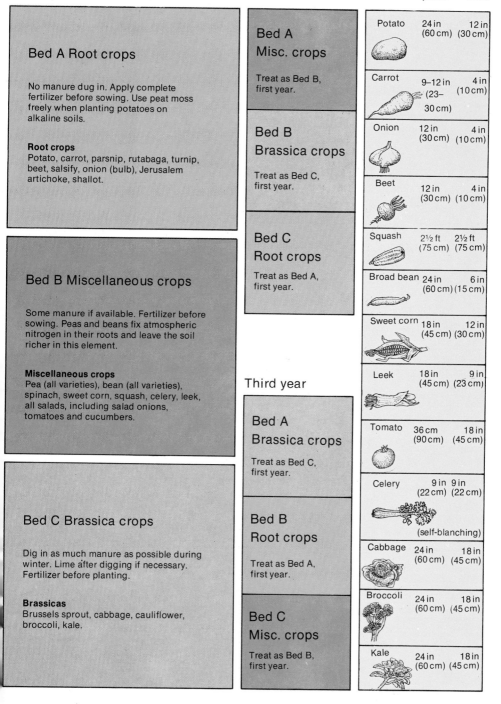

Bed A Root crops

No manure dug in. Apply complete fertilizer before sowing. Use peat moss freely when planting potatoes on alkaline soils.

Root crops
Potato, carrot, parsnip, rutabaga, turnip, beet, salsify, onion (bulb), Jerusalem artichoke, shallot.

Bed B Miscellaneous crops

Some manure if available. Fertilizer before sowing. Peas and beans fix atmospheric nitrogen in their roots and leave the soil richer in this element.

Miscellaneous crops
Pea (all varieties), bean (all varieties), spinach, sweet corn, squash, celery, leek, all salads, including salad onions, tomatoes and cucumbers.

Bed C Brassica crops

Dig in as much manure as possible during winter. Lime after digging if necessary. Fertilizer before planting.

Brassicas
Brussels sprout, cabbage, cauliflower, broccoli, kale.

Bed A
Misc. crops
Treat as Bed B, first year.

Bed B
Brassica crops
Treat as Bed C, first year.

Bed C
Root crops
Treat as Bed A, first year.

Third year

Bed A
Brassica crops
Treat as Bed C, first year.

Bed B
Root crops
Treat as Bed A, first year.

Bed C
Misc. crops
Treat as Bed B, first year.

Crop	plants	rows
Potato	24 in (60 cm)	12 in (30 cm)
Carrot	9–12 in (23–30 cm)	4 in (10 cm)
Onion	12 in (30 cm)	4 in (10 cm)
Beet	12 in (30 cm)	4 in (10 cm)
Squash	2½ ft (75 cm)	2½ ft (75 cm)
Broad bean	24 in (60 cm)	6 in (15 cm)
Sweet corn	18 in (45 cm)	12 in (30 cm)
Leek	18 in (45 cm)	9 in (23 cm)
Tomato	36 cm (90 cm)	18 in (45 cm)
Celery	9 in (22 cm)	9 in (22 cm) (self-blanching)
Cabbage	24 in (60 cm)	18 in (45 cm)
Broccoli	24 in (60 cm)	18 in (45 cm)
Kale	24 in (60 cm)	18 in (45 cm)

3 Sowing and planting

Buying seeds

Obtain catalogs and send in your seed order very early in the year. Latecomers are apt to find the varieties they want out of stock. Seedsmen usually specify an average length of row or number of plants to be expected per packet of seeds, and quantities ordered may be based on your plans for the season.

Buying plants

Some vegetables are transplanted to their final quarters and not sown where they are to grow. If you intend to buy plants rather than raise them yourself, it pays to get the best obtainable, preferably from a local nurseryman. Avoid brassica plants that are leggy and drawn from crowding in the seed-bed, long-stemmed tomato plants with bluish foliage, and yellowing squashes. The best plant is not the largest, but the one in vigorous growth, short-jointed, with leaves of a healthy green.

Seeds and sowing

Seeds in sealed vacuum packs may be kept for a year after the packeting date if the packs are unopened. In ordinary packets, brassica seeds remain viable for several years but the germination of others cannot be relied on after a year. Sowing defective seed means losing irreplaceable time.

Conditions for sowing To germinate, a seed must have moisture, warmth and air. The temperature must not be too low, the soil must be in the right condition, and the seed not sown too deeply.

Recommended sowing dates are only approximate and vary from region to region. Do not begin the first sowings of the year until the soil starts to warm up and signs of growth are evident.

Soil preparation Lightly fork in a pre-sowing fertilizer dressing about a fortnight before starting to sow. If the surface, left rough after winter digging, is dry enough to walk on without soil sticking to your boots, rake it down to a fine, crumbly tilth. If still wet, wait until just before you are actually ready to sow.

Left: stocky, leafy cabbage plant grown in seed-bed with plenty of room.
Right: leggy plant grown in overcrowded row.

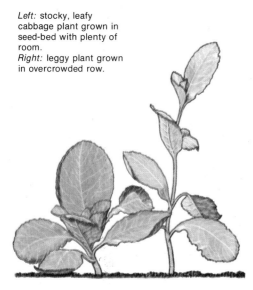

Rake the seed-bed in both directions, to ensure the soil is well broken up.

Sowing

To make a drill, put the garden line in position and make sure it is taut. With the draw hoe, make a shallow furrow, guided by the line. For small seeds, make the drill V-shaped with the corner of the hoe blade; for large ones, such as peas and beans, take out a wide flat-bottomed drill with the full width of the blade. Measure the distance to the next row and move the line.

To sow small seeds such as lettuce or carrot, tip some from the packet into the palm of the hand and deposit them evenly and fairly thinly along the drill from between thumb and forefinger. Beans are placed individually but peas may be scattered liberally (but not touching) in a wide drill.

Pelleted seeds, which are made larger by being covered with a protective coating, are all spaced individually to facilitate thinning.

Cover the seeds by pulling the soil into the drill with the hoe or the back of the rake, leaving the surface level. Tamp it down gently with the flat of the hoe blade or by *light* pressure of the foot.

In dry weather water the drill thoroughly before sowing and continue to water until emergence of the seedlings. Moisture is absolutely vital, and pelleted seed especially may fail if the seed-bed dries out for a short period. As a general rule, early sowings are covered less deeply than those made later in the season. In the first case the soil is warmer just below the surface, in later sowings moisture is conserved better around the seeds by placing them a little deeper.

Planting out

For planting out tender subjects such as tomatoes and squash choose a warm spell when all possible danger of late frosts is past. Unless you can protect with Hotkaps nothing is gained by being too early.

Water pot- and flat-grown plants an hour before planting. Brassica and similar plants grown in a seed-bed should be well-watered the day before planting out and lifted with the trowel, ensuring that plenty of soil clings to the roots. Make planting holes with the trowel, setting all types of plant a little deeper than they had been growing previously. Firm the soil, making sure that the roots are not left in a cavity at the bottom of the hole. Water after planting and keep watered until established and growing.

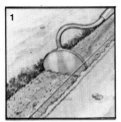
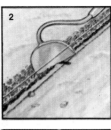
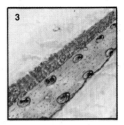
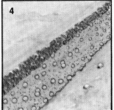
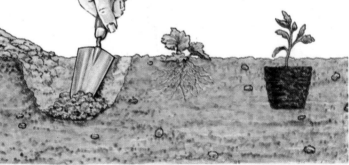

Types of drill

1. Wide drill, made with full width of draw hoe.
2. Narrow drill, made with corner of hoe blade. Used for all small seeds.
3. Beans in staggered double row in wide drill.
4. Peas scattered liberally (not too close) in wide drill.

Firm the soil with flat of hoe blade (or light foot pressure). Water seedlings when transplanting and continue until they are established.

Use a trowel rather than a dibber and make the hole large enough to take roots easily.

Plant with the lower leaves just clear of the surface and no bare stem showing.

Plants in peat pots are planted pot and all, the top of the pot being just covered.

265

4 Caring for growing crops

Thinning

Plants growing in a row must have enough room to develop properly. If crowded together, normal growth is impossible; if too far apart, space is wasted and the row yields less than its potential. There is therefore an optimum distance for best results.

Plants raised in a seed-bed or cold frame are planted at their final distances in the row, any thinning being done at the seedling stage in the seed-bed. Peas and beans are spaced when sowing and are not thinned. Pelleted seeds are spaced about 1 in (2·5 cm) apart and subsequent thinning is easy. Early and adequate thinning is most necessary in sowings of small seeds, which invariably come up too thickly.

Thin in three stages. First, as soon as the seedlings are large enough to handle, to about 1 in (2·5 cm) then to double this distance as the seedlings grow, and then to the final distance for the crop to mature. Never thin to the final distance in one operation; a few seedlings are always lost from pests or climatic conditions and if this happens after thinning to the full distance the row will be depleted and 'gappy'. Also, if seedlings are

allowed to grow between thinning stages the thinnings in some crops will be of usable size and will not be wasted. Among root crops, small carrots and golf-ball-size turnips and beets are pulled as required while the rest of the crop is left to reach full size. Spinach seedlings of a fair size are usable if the roots are trimmed off and the thinnings of lettuce are a salad ingredient long before the plants have heads.

Thin only when the soil is moist, to minimize root disturbance of the remaining plants. In dry weather give a good soaking the day before thinning: the work is easier if the tops of the seedlings are dry. Patience is needed to 'single' the crop, to reduce each clump of seedlings to one plant, but this is essential. Beet is especially difficult because each 'seed' is really a fruit containing several seeds, but monogerm seed producing only one plant per seed is now becoming available.

Weed control

This is a vital part of cultivation. Weeds compete with the crop for moisture and nutrients and, if allowed to get out of hand,

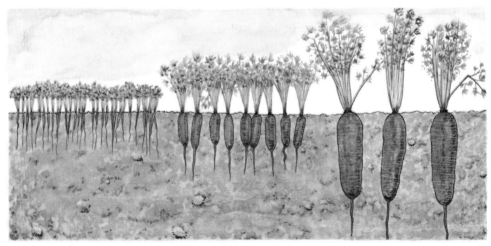

1. Carrots after initial thinning, still crowded.

2. After second thinning: every other one now removed for use.

3. Carrots growing on to full size after final thinning.

Types of hoe: The draw hoe (*left*) is drawn towards the operator, who moves forwards. The Dutch hoe is pushed away from the operator, who walks backwards avoiding ground already hoed.

A contact herbicide may be used on weeds between crop rows. It should be applied with a can and sprinkler bar and should be held close to the ground to avoid splashing crop foliage.

may smother it completely. Deal with them before they become a menace.

Hoeing and hand-weeding Hoe between rows regularly when the surface is dry. Do it even if no weeds are visible and you will destroy weed seedlings before they appear. Keep the hoe blade just below the surface and do not chop or jab close to the row. A rototiller may be used with the blades set very high, provided there is sufficient inter-row space and room to turn at the headlands without damage to the crop. Remove weeds to the compost heap if rain is likely or the small ones may re-root.

Weeds actually growing among crop rows must be pulled up by hand with as little disturbance to the crop as possible. Large weeds with a strong root system should be eased out of the row with a trowel. Hand weeding is essential for close set crops where other methods could damage plants and weeds alike.

Weedkillers Both state and federal authorities are becoming increasingly critical of chemical weedkillers, and especially

their use by non-professional gardeners. Most home owners today would do well to stick to the hoe as a means of eliminating weeds or the lazy gardener can apply a mulch (see page 296), which has the additional benefit of contributing humus to the soil as it decays.

If you have a large garden and wish to try using chemical weedkillers, here are a few that are not yet restricted: Dacthal, a herbicide applied to the soil before weed seeds germinate, which can be used with many vegetable crops; Dymid or Enide, and Vegiben, all used as above. Always follow directions on the container.

Using weedkillers
Your local garden center and your county extension agent have information on which chemical weedkillers are licensed for use in your state.
Follow directions on the container *exactly* to avoid injury to yourself, to adjacent plants and to the environment in general.
Mix only enough for immediate use. Store out of children's reach and *never* put surplus solution in soft-drink bottles.

5 Watering and mulching

The soil is a reservoir in which the rains of winter are stored for use in the growing season. The better cultivated it is, the more spongy humus it contains, the greater its water-holding capacity and the more accessible is the moisture to the plant roots.

Soak drills thoroughly before sowing in dry weather. Continue to water until germination.

Conserve moisture by spreading 3 in (7·5 cm) of mulch along both sides of crop row.

Water intake
1. When fully grown, the plant takes much more moisture from the soil than is lost by direct evaporation from the surface.
2. Repeated small waterings only moisten the top of the soil and do not reach the feeding roots, which may be attracted upwards as a result.
3. Well-cultivated soil encourages a good

root system which collects more moisture.
4. A subsoil broken up during digging permits moisture to be drawn up from deeper levels.

In the summer, moisture is lost faster than the rainfall can replace it, partly by evaporation from the surface but even more by plants transpiring from their leaves the water taken up by their roots. Crops in full growth are the ones most likely to need additional supplies of water.

How much water? It is worse than useless to give little drops in dry weather. You cannot slightly moisten the soil all the way down, for water penetrates to the dry soil below only when the upper layers are saturated. Inadequate watering causes the roots to spread upwards to the saturated layer, where they are more vulnerable to the inevitable periods of drying out.

Average summer rainfall is from 2 to 3 in (5 to 7·5 cm) per month, and in a dry spell moisture reserves are quickly used up and the crop begins to suffer. Remember that 2 in (5 cm) of rain is the sort of quantity needed to be effective after a few weeks of summer drought.

Crops that respond most to watering are early potatoes and carrots, lettuce, spinach, squashes, peas and snap beans. Whether you water by watering-can, hose or sprinkler, give an adequate quantity to a limited area at each watering rather than a little to every crop.

Mulches A mulch is a layer of organic material such as peat, compost or well-rotted manure applied to the soil to reduce moisture loss by evaporation. It should be spread to a depth of 2 in (5 cm) on both sides of the row when the crop is past the seedling stage and the soil is thoroughly moist. As an alternative, black polyethylene sheet may be used, which also suppresses weeds. Simplest of all is the soil mulch, the layer of loose topsoil created by regular hoeing, which prevents moisture being drawn to the surface.

6 Harvesting and storage

Harvesting at the right time is an important factor in the quality of vegetables and sometimes in the size of the crop. Many vegetables can be stored in the freezer, and for successful freezing they must be harvested in perfect condition and at the right stage of growth. The advice that follows is, however, concerned only with harvesting for immediate use and storing those vegetables that keep without freezing.

Potatoes
Earlies are dug as required and the shorter the time between digging and cooking the better the flavor. Dig later crops when the tops have died down and the skin of the tubers has set and cannot be rubbed off. Avoid damage when lifting. Store in a cool but frost-free place in complete darkness. Frost destroys the tubers and light turns them green and renders them inedible.

Turnips and rutabagas
Lift in October or November and store in a cool place. A few degrees of frost will not hurt them. Green top turnips are very hardy and may be left in the ground for much of the winter, any not used producing edible tops for greens when growth starts in spring.

All root crops should be stored as clean as possible, soil being rubbed off without damaging the skin.

Carrots and beets
Pull young roots during the growing season. Lift for storage in October, remove tops (twisting off rather than cutting beet tops), and store in boxes covered with slightly moist sand or peat.

Parsnips
Leave in the ground and dig as required, but lift remainder of crop in spring before they start new growth.

Squashes
Butternut squashes, pumpkins and winter squashes keep for several months if well ripened.

Leave them on the plant until the skin is absolutely hard and sounds like wood when tapped. Store where they are safe from frost and inspect frequently for signs of deterioration.

Onions
Lift when growth finishes and dry very thoroughly spread out in shed. Hang up in nets or tied in bunches in a dry, airy and frost-free place. The chief enemies of long storage are warmth and dampness. Shallots are stored in the same way but are usually harvested much earlier than onions.

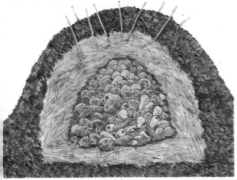

Twist off beet tops

Potatoes spread out for drying

Making an onion rope

Left: clamps are used for storing beets, carrots or potatoes.

Ropes of onions are attractive, space-saving and easy to make, as the above diagrams show.

269

7 Pests and diseases

Plants have a natural resistance to their insect and fungus enemies. The more vigorous a crop, the less likely it is to be attacked and the quicker to recover.

Health hints

Maintain soil fertility and keep crops growing steadily by watering and cultivation. A stunted plant is the first to suffer infection or insect damage.

Prevent overcrowding of crops by early and adequate thinning and the removal of weeds, which compete for food and moisture, and harbor pests.

Watch over garden hygiene. Trim waste and weedy corners and long grass where slugs take refuge. Clear away remains of crops, especially the stumps of Brussels sprouts and winter cabbages, which carry the cabbage troubles into a new season.

Inspect crops frequently and deal promptly with any trouble. A puff of insecticide today is worth more than a full-scale blitz next week.

Practice crop rotation, i.e. avoid growing similar crops always on the same ground.

Buying and using pesticides

Suitable pesticides may be bought in liquid form to be made up into a solution for use in a sprayer or syringe, but for the small garden the most convenient forms are the aerosol and hand duster.

The safest preparations are those based on pyrethrum and rotenone, both non-toxic to humans and animals and reasonably effective against a wide range of insect pests. Dusting packs containing a combination of pyrethrum and piperonyl butoxide, or aerosols containing pyrethrum and lindane are also perfectly safe, and with one of each you are equipped to deal with most of the pests likely to be encountered.

Precautions in using pesticides Read the instructions. Note that certain plants such as squashes and cucumbers may be sensitive to the spray. *Never* use household fly-killers on plants. Keep to the recommended time between using the pesticide and harvesting the affected crop. Don't spray young seedlings or flowering crops in strong sunlight – wait until evening.

Common insect pests

Black aphids
Attacks broad beans and occasionally runner beans. Like all aphids, multiplies and spreads very rapidly. Pick out the growing points of broad beans as soon as enough pods have set and spray with malathion as soon as clusters of aphids are noticed. On runner beans they frequently appear first on the flower buds and these should be examined occasionally for any sign of them

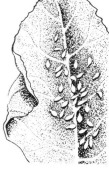

Cabbage aphis
Especially troublesome on cabbages and sprouts if it gets into hearts and other sheltered spots. Look for clusters of grayish insects and spray or dust immediately. In bad cases an aerosol may be ineffective and you should use a syringe and a solution of malathion to penetrate the crevices.

Cabbage caterpillars
The larvae of cabbage white butterflies, these ravenous creatures can be extremely destructive. All brassicas may be affected in summer. Use a pyrethrum dust or Sevin, or *Bacillus thuringiensis* as soon as they are noticed, and repeat the treatment as more hatch out. For a consideration, the children may be persuaded to pick them off by hand and deposit them in a jar of salt water.

Flea beetle
Very small, punctures and
seriously damages seed-
lings of brassicas, tur-
nips, rutabagas, egg-
plant and radishes. Keep
plants well watered
and dust frequently with
pyrethrum or rotenone.

Cabbage root fly
The larvae particularly
attack cauliflowers, eat-
ing into the roots and
causing the plant to col-
lapse. Dig up affected
plants with nearby soil
and burn them. As a pre-
ventive, apply diazinon
dust round each young
plant.

Carrot fly
The insect is attracted by
the scent of crushed
foliage during thinning,
where it will lay its eggs.
Use pelleted seed to
reduce thinning to a
minimum.

Slugs
Use pellets containing
metaldehyde under a
slightly raised tile to keep
them away from birds and
pets. Or sink saucers in
the soil, and fill them
with beer.

Common diseases

Only two bother most gardeners' crops.

Potato blight
Spray maincrops with Bordeaux mixture or maneb in
July if the season is wet. At the end of the season cut
off blighted tops and burn before lifting the tubers.

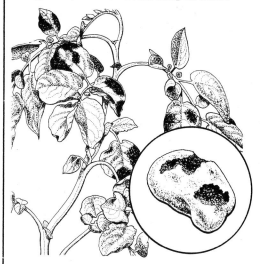

Club root
This disease of the cabbage family can become a serious nuisance. If you see any signs of swollen and dis-
torted roots among brassicas, stop growing them on
that piece of ground for two or three years and give
it a heavy dose of garden lime after winter digging,
followed by a lighter one the next year.

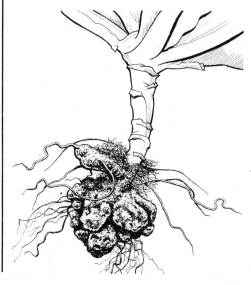

271

8 The vegetable garden month by month

January

Order seeds, seed potatoes and onion sets, keeping mainly to well-tried varieties, but including a few new ones as well.

In the South and milder climates of the Southwest and Pacific Coast continue clearing spent crops. Begin digging and adding compost if the ground is workable and not too wet. Apply garden lime if a soil test shows it is necessary for the crops to be grown in that space.

Harvest winter greens such as kale. There will also be leeks, and in mild regions Savoy cabbage, Brussels sprouts, spinach and cauliflower. Seakale and chicory forced indoors will be ready now. Dig up Jerusalem artichokes and parsnips as required. If prolonged frost threatens, cover root crops in the ground with layers of newspapers or straw so that lifting still remains possible.

In a heated greenhouse you can now sow onions, leeks, and cauliflowers.

Check over vegetables in storage and throw away any that are beginning to rot.

February

Set up seed potatoes in trays in a light, frost-proof place to sprout.

In the milder, coastal areas of the Northeast, much of the Southwest, Pacific Coast and upper South it may be possible to sow peas and broad (fava) beans.

Toward the end of the month in a sunny window, under fluorescent lights or in a heated greenhouse sow broccoli, cauliflower, celery and cabbage.

In mild climates continue harvesting cabbages, leeks, parsnips, and celery. If the ground was not dug last month, do so now, turning under cover crops and applying lime where necessary. Apply a complete fertilizer, such as 5–10–5 to ground intended for planting in March, but rake it only when the surface is dry. Do not apply lime and fertilizers at the same time.

At the end of the winter it is very important to check vegetables in storage for any that may be rotting. You should also rub sprouts off potatoes in store.

March

Pull up old broccoli, cabbage and Brussels sprouts stalks and spent kale plants. All the brassicas are prone to diseases and can harbor overwintering insects.

Turn under cover crops such as rye sown in the fall.

Throughout this month in most of the North, earlier in milder regions such as New York's Long Island, sow peas, broad beans, spinach, cress (all kinds), roquette, broccoli raab. Toward the end of the month sow radishes and lettuce.

Cold frames need special attention in all areas. Unseasonably warm weather – and quite the reverse – can occur.

Continue to plant onion sets.

If your last frosts should end in about 8 weeks, it's a good time to sow seeds of various tender vegetables, such as tomato, eggplant and pepper indoors.

In the warmest regions of the South and Pacific Coast, outdoor activity is well along with the setting out of such seedlings as tomatoes and eggplants.

In much of the North the harvest can start with lettuce from the cold frame or lettuce thinnings from the open ground. When thinning spinach, use the thinnings in salads. Cress sown earlier should be ready. An asparagus bed makes a good place for sowing all the cresses as their shallow roots can't interfere with the deep-rooted asparagus plants. A few radishes, either from a frame or open garden, should be ready; spring onions should also be ready now.

Prepare and plant new asparagus beds. Prepare a place for celery plants to be set out the following month.

Put down bait to combat destructive slugs. Do this especially around lettuce plantings.

Sow sweet corn and snap beans in milder regions. Indoors in the North, sow 1 or 2 seeds per pot of squash, cucumbers, melons in individual peat pots. If a sunny window is lacking, grow under artificial lights. They should be planted outside in about 3–5 weeks.

Thin early crops as soon as the seedlings are large enough to handle.

Sow snap beans about the middle of the month in most Northern regions or anywhere as soon as the soil has warmed. Don't rush this if the weather remains cool and wet. Snap beans revel in heat. This same advice holds true for sweet corn. Sow as soon as possible any crop mentioned in two preceding months if first sowing has failed or been delayed by weather, also lettuce and radish for succession. Make first sowings of rutabaga and winter squash for winter use.

Plant tomatoes, peppers and eggplants under Hotkaps or improvised cloches.

Harvest asparagus from established buds, cutting all shoots including thin and deformed ones. Harvest summer cauliflowers, bending leaves over the curd to prevent discoloration by the sun.

Plant celery seedling and water well. Cucumbers and squash can be sown in place.

Hoe regularly and water growing crops in dry weather.

June

Regularly pick peas and broad peas so later pods continue to fill. If you find your pea harvest is ready all at once, you may want to plant one of the less commercial varieties next time that ripens its pods more gradually. In New England and other cool-summer regions, another pea sowing is possible. Plant the variety Wando.

Sow squash and cucumber seeds; continue to set out tomatoes, eggplants and peppers (under Hotkaps in the far North if weather remains cool and wet). Sow all beans except broad – bush and pole snap beans and bush and pole limas. If space is limited, choose the pole types.

In some regions the two-month harvest of asparagus is close to final cutting to allow ferny top growth to develop and build up roots for next year's crop. Sprinkle a complete fertilizer such as 5–10–5 over the bed toward the end of the month and if the soil is dry, water it in.

Mulch all crops with compost, pine needles, rotted manure, best applied on wet ground.

Remove the growing points of staked beans when they reach the tops of the poles.

Stake and tie tall-growing tomatoes and rub out sideshoots as soon as they are seen. Earth up the stems of potatoes to keep upright.

Keep a close watch on maturing vegetables such as green beans. Gather them while young and in top condition for immediate use or freezing. A few days too long in hot weather can make a serious difference to quality. Early tomatoes that may be ready include Early Salad, Early Girl, Springset, Presto, and Small Fry. Also ready are cucumbers, zucchini and other summer squashes, globe artichokes and early potatoes.

For harvesting this fall sow quick-maturing endive and snap beans. Make further late sowings of spinach, carrots, lettuce and winter radishes.

Make final plantings of kale and broccoli, doing all you can by careful planting and watering to establish quickly.

Watch for pests, especially worms. Dust with rotenone or Sevin.

August

Bend over the tops of fully grown onions to encourage ripening of the bulbs. Harvest shallots, breaking up the clusters and storing when dry.

In mild climates sow cabbage, spinach, onions, broccoli for winter,and spring harvesting. In most Northern regions it is still not too late to sow radishes and quick-growing lettuce for autumn use. The lettuce can be left in the open ground where the fall season is long and mild. In colder areas transplant seedlings into a cold frame.

Gather runner beans before the pods swell with developing seeds; once seeds are allowed to form the plants cease to produce. In hot weather they may need picking every two days. Sweet corn should be tested by squeezing kernels and using before contents are solid and starchy. Use or freeze cobs as soon as possible after harvesting, as conversion from sugar to starch continues.

Start earthing up celery that needs blanching at the end of the month.

Lift and store unused early potatoes as the tops die down.

September

Cut off and burn potato tops infected with blight. If the skins of the tubers are set lift them immediately; if not, leave them for another week or two until the skins are too tough to be easily damaged in lifting.

Pull up tomato plants with unripe fruit if frost seems likely, hanging them under cover for ripening to continue.

Complete harvesting of squashes, cucumbers and broccoli. Lift onions and garlic and dry thoroughly before storing. Pickling onions will be ready for harvesting.

There will also be cauliflower, the ever-present cabbages, self-blanching celery, and the first Brussels sprouts and savoy cabbages.

Transplant seedlings of cabbage and other crops for winter harvesting in mild climates. Continue to transplant lettuce sown last month in frames.

Cover late-sown snap beans with tunnels of polyethylene stretched over wire frames to prolong cropping.

Earth up celery for the second time, leeks for the first.

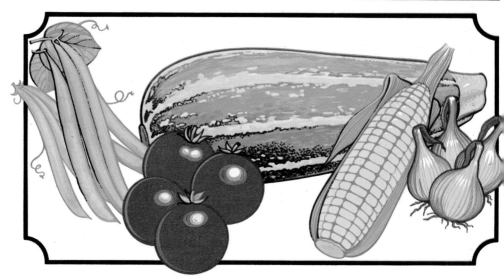

Harvest and store all root crops for the winter: carrots, beets, rutabagas, turnips, and winter radishes. Handle beets carefully when lifting. Left in the ground and pulled as required are Jerusalem artichokes, parsnips, celeriac, horseradish, and possibly turnips.

Complete earthing up of trench celery and leeks. Start forcing chicory and blanching endive. Cut down asparagus 'fern' when it turns yellow and lightly earth up the bed or row. Mulch with manure or compost.

Continue picking Brussels sprouts, which will be improving in quality, and remove dead leaves from the plants. Do not on any account take out the tops. Remove dead foliage from seakale and cut down the stems of Jerusalem artichokes to keep them from being blown down.

Sow winter cover crops such as cereal rye, if this wasn't done last month. The grass will make an attractive 'lawn' for the vegetable garden during the dreary months and will continue growing even under snow. In spring the rye can be spaded over to supply humus to the soil.

Complete lifting of all root crops to be stored under cover. If very wet and dirty, spread them out in a shed to dry and rub off soil before storing.

There are still many other vegetables to take from the garden, including blanched celery, leeks, Jerusalem artichokes, cauliflower, Brussels sprouts and cabbages. The first blanched endive and forced chicory will also be ready; lift all remaining chicory roots and seakale to force as desired.

Clear away remains of spent crops. Take the yellowing leaves off Brussels sprouts, heel over cauliflowers to protect them from frost, and put a layer of straw over the crowns of globe artichokes.

Press ahead with winter digging whenever the ground is fit to work and not planted to a cover crop. Do not try to dig when the soil is so wet that it clogs on your boots. That does more harm than good and makes the work harder. Manure for next year's peas, beans, onions, leeks, celery, and spinach.

This is the month for general garden maintenance – for tidying up after the preceding year's work and preparing for the next growing season.

Keep a check on cold frames if they contain lettuce sown earlier in the fall. This year you will still have celery, leeks, Jerusalem artichokes, cabbages, parsnips, and broccoli from the garden, as well as blanched endive and forced chicory – if you planned carefully!

There will also be many root crops stored indoors, including potatoes, onions, turnips, carrots, rutabagas, and beets. Keep them in a frost-free, warm place.

Make sure overwintering crops like globe artichokes are protected with straw over their crowns.

Place manure and compost in convenient heaps in the garden for use in spring.

Cover compost heaps with soil and add additional material such as leaves.

Order catalogs for new season unless already on their mailing lists.

9 Cabbage family (brassica crops)

Brussels sprouts

One of the hardiest and most valuable of winter greens. Two rows of sprouts, say about thirty plants, will yield good weekly pickings from fall to early winter.

Soil
Like all the cabbage family, sprouts are fairly greedy, but only moderate amounts of manure or compost should be dug in during the winter. Over-feeding tends to produce lush, leafy growth which suffers in severe weather, and too many 'blown' or open sprouts. The crop often does well on land manured the previous season, provided any lime deficiency is corrected and digging is done early to allow the soil to settle. Loose ground produces poor sprouts. Rake in 3 oz per sq yd (100 g per sq m) of a general fertilizer when leveling the site for planting.

Right: Tight, medium-sized sprouts of the type preferred for kitchen and freezer. Loose, 'blown' sprouts often result from loose, over-manured soil.

When to sow and plant
Not too early in most Northern areas with hot summers, since the sprouts should begin to form in the fall during cool weather. Best time is late spring to early summer.

How to sow and plant
Plants are sometimes available from local outlets in the spring. Or start from seeds. Sow in a seed-bed in the open or sow thinly in drills ½–¾ in (2 cm) deep and 6 in (15 cm) apart, and thin to about 1 in (2·5 cm) apart as soon as possible. When about 3 in (7·5 cm) high, lift carefully with a trowel after watering and plant out 24 in (60 cm) each way. Water in and keep watered until established.

Above: Well-filled stem of Brussels sprouts. Pick them from the base so that the upper sprouts will develop.

Below: Plant seedlings out at 24 in (60 cm) intervals.

Time to germination
10–14 days. Germination is good, and if pelleted seed is used, it may be safely spaced at almost the final seed-bed distance.

Season of use
Fall to early winter.

Good varieties
The best variety for the home garden is Jade Cross Hybrid. Second to that is Long Island Improved.

Special note
Avoid those commercial varieties in which all the sprouts develop simultaneously. Pick systematically, taking the larger sprouts from the lower part of the stem and removing the top only when crop is finishing.

Cauliflowers

Cauliflower is not the easiest crop because the plants need a long growing season that should be cool when the plants start to form heads – in the fall in most regions.

Soil
The better the soil, the better the cauliflower. Dig in as much organic matter as possible, which can be home-made compost, leafmold, peat moss, rotted manure and any other humus-building materials available locally. Before planting, rake in the standard dose of a complete fertilizer, such as 5–10–5, using 3 oz per sq yd (100 g per sq m).

When to sow
For most Northern gardens, where the harvest will be in the fall, sow seeds indoors in early to mid-spring and plant resulting seedlings outdoors about 6 weeks later. In the South and other mild-winter regions, seeds should be sown from late summer to late fall.

How to sow and plant
Sow a small quantity of seed very thinly in a flat or special seed tray, covering the seeds lightly and keeping moist until germination. A minimum temperature of 50°F (10°C) is required. Transplant the seedlings, as soon as true leaves appear, into peat pots and grow on a sunny windowsill or about 6 in (15 cm) from fluorescent tubes. Set plants outdoors 5 to 6 weeks later, either first into a cold frame for gradual hardening off or set in the open ground under Hotkaps for a few weeks. The seedlings will endure some frost once properly hardened off. Space seedlings in the garden from 18 in (45 cm) to 24 in (60 cm) apart. The plants should be watered as necessary and a second feeding of fertilizer given when the heads start to form. White varieties of cauliflower require blanching: tie the leaves over the head when it is about the size of a tennis ball.

Time to germination
7–10 days.

Season of use
According to climate – from summer through autumn, winter and spring. Freezer life: 6 months.

Good varieties
In the South: February, November–December and Mayflower. Elsewhere Snow King Hybrid, Snowball types. Purple Head requires no blanching. Its purple heads turn green when cooked.

Protect young cauliflower seedlings with an adjustable garden frame.

Cauliflowers of the Snowball type are grown throughout North America.

Cabbages for summer and fall

The cabbage addict can have this vegetable all the year round. Here we deal with those sown from late winter to spring, and cut from early summer to fall.

Soil
Dig well and incorporate some organic manure. Dried poultry manure, which has a fairly high nitrogen content, is a good choice. Before planting, rake in 3 oz per sq yd (100 g per sq m) of general fertilizer. If at any time the plants seem to be 'standing still', top dress with 1 oz per sq yd (33 g per sq m) of sulphate of ammonia, hoed and, if necessary, watered in.

When to sow and plant
Varieties listed as summer-maturing should be sown as early in spring as possible, preferably in February indoors. Autumn varieties are sown in April or May. Plant from early April to June. Plants are usually quite easy to buy during that period.

How to sow and plant
The early summer cabbages are sown in seed trays indoors if no greenhouse is available. Prick out, harden off, and plant out in April. Or sow in shallow drills, 6 in (15 cm) apart, outdoors in mid-spring and thin out early. The larger and later summer varieties and the autumn types are sown in a prepared seed-bed a few weeks later in drills ½–¾ in (2 cm) deep and 2 in (2 cm) apart and thinned to at least 1 in (2·5 cm). Many varieties are obtainable as pelleted seed and this is one way of ensuring well-spaced seedlings. Plant out when about 3 in (7·5 cm) tall. Planting distances

are: early small-headed varieties, 18 in (45 cm) either way; larger and later ones, 18 in (45 cm) in the rows and 24 in (60 cm) between rows.

Time to germination
7–14 days. Cabbage seed, like that of other brassicas, remains viable for several years and a surplus should not therefore be thrown away.

Season of use
June to August for the earlies, August to November for later varieties.

Good varieties
Earliana (60 days), Early Jersey Wakefield (63 days), Copenhagen Market (72 days), Stonehead Hybrid (70 days), Emerald Acre (61 days), Hybrid Emerald Cross (63 days). The last is reputed to stand a long time without splitting.

Above: Small cabbages will form on the stump of a cut spring-maturing cabbage.

Left: Fine summer cabbages. They need good soil and adequate watering.

Below: A fine specimen of a spring-maturing cabbage.

Broccoli

Broccoli matures in most home gardens in late summer and fall. Even the smallest plot has space for a few plants of this high-quality crop.

The tender autumn-maturing broccoli is becoming increasingly popular. The picture shows the central head, which is harvested first, and the smaller sprouts which follow it.

Soil
Any reasonably good soil will do, but the best quality broccoli is produced on soil treated as advised for summer cauliflowers. If planted in succession to early peas or lettuce, a dressing of 3 oz per sq yd (100 g per sq m) of complete fertilizer should be hoed in before planting.

When to sow and plant
Indoors in early spring, following same method as for cauliflower. Or sow in a seed-bed in April or early May and plant out in June. Or sow direct where it is to grow in June.

How to sow and plant
Sow in the seed-bed as advised for other brassicas, planting out 18 in (45 cm) between plants and between rows. Or sow where the plants are to grow in early June in a drill ½–¾ in (2 cm) deep in groups of seeds 18 in (45 cm) apart. Thin by stages to one plant per group. Water the drill thoroughly before sowing in dry weather.

Brassica seedlings frequently need protection from birds, and where this is the case, protection by nylon net is more easily given when the plants are grouped closely in a seed-bed than when strung out sparsely in a long row. Where bird damage is likely, the seed-bed/transplanting method may be preferable to direct sowing for seedlings liable to attack soon after sowing.

Time to germination
7–14 days, according to time of year.

Season of use
August to November and possibly later in a mild autumn. Broccoli freezes well, the sprigs having a freezer life of six months.

Good varieties
Green Comet, a very early single-headed type with few side shoots. Premium Crop, similar to Green Comet but matures later. De Cicco, producing a central head followed by a large crop of side-shoots.

Special note
The plant normally forms a central cluster of buds like a rough green cauliflower. Earlier types produce many lateral shoots when the central head is cut, and such varieties still give the longest-lasting crop. Recent hybrids, however, have been bred to form a larger head at the expense of the side-shoots, and these varieties do not furnish pickings over a long period.

Protect young seedlings by grouping them closely in a seed-bed and covering with nylon net.

Kale

Because of its extreme hardiness kale is regarded as a 'coarse' vegetable. In fact, if the more tender inner leaves are harvested, it is one of the best of winter greens.

Soil
Dig deeply and leave the soil in a condition to ensure good drainage. This should have been done for the crop preceding kale, which is usually sown or planted after snap beans or peas. A light dressing of complete fertilizer, raked in when clearing and lightly cultivating the ground, is advisable to give the kale a good start, but the crop needs no other feeding.

When to sow and plant
Seeds may be sown in the seed-bed in April and planted out in June, or sown where they are to grow in June or early July.

How to sow and plant
In the seed-bed, sow thinly in shallow drills 6 in (15 cm) apart, thinning to give plenty of space to the seedlings. Plant out 18 in (45 cm) apart with rows 24 in (60 cm) apart. When direct sowing, take out a drill ½–¾ in (2 cm) deep, flood it if the weather is at all dry, and drop groups of seeds at 18 in (45 cm) intervals, thinning the seedlings by stages to one at each station. Gaps may be filled by transplanting. There must be no lack of moisture during or after germination; if the July sowing fails it may be too late to try again.

Time to germination
5–10 days. Very rapid in summer – watch for bird attacks on emerging seedlings.

Season of use
Fall, winter and spring.

Good varieties
Green Curled Scotch (55 days), Dwarf Blue Curled Vates (60 days), Dwarf Siberian (65 days).

Special note
Young leaves can be eaten in salads, either alone or mixed with lettuce and other ingredients.

Dwarf curled kale. Like all kales, this will do well in colder areas where winter cabbage and broccoli are not very successful.

Cabbages for winter and spring

From the gardener's point of view the main difference between these cabbages and the sorts grown for summer and autumn consumption is in the matter of hardiness. A wrong choice of variety can be disastrous.

Savoy cabbage. Very hardy and succeeds on poor soil.

Soil
All cabbages are heavy feeders. Follow the recommendations given for summer and fall on page 307. On sandy soils dig in some manure or compost and apply a light dressing of complete fertilizer. On stronger land, especially when the cabbages follow a well-treated previous crop, additional manuring is probably unnecessary.

When to sow and plant
Sow winter varieties in May and transplant in June and July. Sow spring varieties at the end of July to mid-August in mild climates and the South. Transplant between mid-September and mid-October.

How to sow and plant
Sow in a prepared seed-bed as advised for late summer and autumn varieties, moving to permanent quarters when about 3 in (7·5 cm) tall. Winter varieties are spaced at 18 in (45 cm) in the row and 24 in (60 cm) between rows. Spring cabbages are spaced at 9 in (23 cm) in the row and 18 in (45 cm) between rows. The close spacing allows every other cabbage to be pulled for 'spring greens' as soon as a fair amount of leaf has developed, leaving the remainder to reach full size and heart up.

Time to germination
7–10 days.

Season of use
Fall to spring. Solid hearts may be frozen, keeping for six months.

Good varieties
Savoy types: Chieftain Savoy, Savoy King. Winter types: Danish Roundhead, Penn State Ballhead, Premium Flat Dutch, Autumn Marvel.

Special note
In addition to the main cabbage crops listed here, some others are worth growing. There is the red pickling cabbage such as Ruby Ball, useful for purposes other than pickling.

January King, probably the best all-round mid-winter cabbage.

281

10 Peas and beans

Broad or Fava beans

An easy vegetable to grow, not a universal favorite but rich in proteins and giving back more to the soil than it takes out.

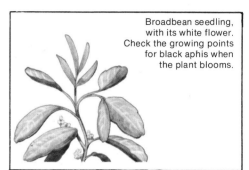

Broadbean seedling, with its white flower. Check the growing points for black aphis when the plant blooms.

Soil
Preferably a cool, moist, rather heavy one, deeply dug well before sowing. On light sands dig in some well-rotted manure or garden compost. Fertilizer is unnecessary.

When to sow
Spring sowings should be made as soon as the soil is dry enough to be raked down to a reasonable condition. The sowing must get established in the cool, damp conditions of early spring. Even quite sharp frosts will not harm the young plants. This is a good crop for many Northern regions because it utilizes garden space in early spring to early summer, and can be succeeded by other crops. Best grown in New England, southern Canada, and similar climates. Grow in winter along the Gulf Coast.

How to sow
In drills at least 6 in (15 cm) wide, 2 to 3 in (5 to 7·5 cm) deep and 24 in (60 cm) apart. Sow two rows in the drill, both the rows and the seeds in each row being 6 in (15 cm) apart in staggered formation. Make the soil firm after covering the drill.

Time to germination
14–21 days.

Season of use
Spring to early summer. Freezer life: 1 year.

Good varieties
Not much choice. Long Pod is usually offered.

Special note
The broad bean has one serious insect pest, the black aphis. It starts in the growing point when the plant is in bloom and may spread down over the pods. Pick out all growing points when a fair number of pods have set. This checks the aphis and speeds up the growth of pods. Or spray with malathion.

Below: A prolific crop of Longpod broad beans. Plants as loaded as this must sometimes be supported by running a length of string along both sides of the row.

Snap and lima beans

Snap beans, formerly called string beans, are available in both bush and pole, or climbing, varieties. Their pods are nutritious and freeze well. Old or mature pods can be shelled and the beans can be cooked fresh or they can be dried.

The lima bean pod must be shelled. It too has both bush and pole varieties, and requires a longer growing season.

The picture below shows just how prolific dwarf beans can be.

Soil
Average garden soil is satisfactory. Apply a complete fertilizer along the rows after the pods form to prolong harvesting.

When to sow
Sow both beans after the soil and temperatures have warmed. Seeds will rot in cold, wet soils. These beans are heat lovers.

How to sow
In drills 2 in (5 cm) deep. The seeds should be 4 in (10 cm) apart and may be sown as a single row in a narrow drill with rows 18 in (45 cm) apart; or as a double row in a wide drill as described for broad beans, the double rows being 24 in (60 cm) apart. Pole beans require support. Set poles 18–24 in (45–60 cm) apart in a row or circle teepee fashion, tying the tops together. Allow 1 seed per pole. Sow extra seeds at one end of the row for filling up any gaps later.

Time to germination
14 days. If no emergence in 21 days, dig up some seeds to discover if seed has rotted owing to low soil temperature.

Season of use
July to September or longer in mild winter climates. Freezer life: 1 year.

Good varieties
Snap bush beans: Improved Tendergreen (56 days), Greensleeves (56 days), Royalty (51 days) has purple pods that turn green when cooked, Goldcrop Wax (54 days), Roma (53 days) has flat pods. Pole snap beans: Kentucky Wonder (65 days), Romano Italian Pole (60 days), Blue Lake (60 days). Bush lima beans: Henderson Bush (65 days), Kingston (70 days). Pole lima beans: King of the Garden (88 days), Prizetaker (90 days).

Special note
Germination is sometimes erratic owing to sowing too early or too deep. Sowing at 2 in (5 cm) is the maximum depth, though the later sowings in light soils dry out rapidly at this depth and should be kept watered until the beans are well up.

283

Peas

Garden peas, so called to distinguish them from the very different asparagus and sugar peas, are a most important summer crop, both for immediate consumption and for freezing as well.

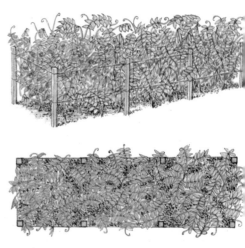

Soil
A medium or heavy moisture-holding soil is preferred, but peas do quite well on lighter land if some manure or compost is dug in during the winter. They do not like acid conditions, and if there is any doubt on this score lime should be applied after digging. Fertilizer is not necessary where manure or compost has been used.

When to sow
Early varieties, February to March indoors, March and April in the open and again in June for the latest crop. Maincrops, March to May.

How to sow
In drills 6 in (15 cm) wide, 2 to 3 in (5 to 7·5 cm) deep and 24 in (60 cm) apart. Early sowings are made in the shallower drills, late ones in the deeper. The seeds need not be spaced individually but should be scattered evenly and generously in the drill so that a good plant population is obtained. Make sure that the soil of the drill is moist for the late sowings, if necessary by a thorough watering before sowing.

Right: Peas supported by strings along both sides of the row. The crop may be damaged if allowed to lie flat on the ground in a wet season.

Below: Early peas Kelvedon Wonder, one of the best for the earliest sowing of the year, indoors or in the open.

Time to germination
10–21 days. Be prepared to protect from birds, which often discover the emerging seedlings before they are visible to the human eye.

Season of use
June to September from successional sowings. Year-round when frozen.

Good varieties
Indoors, Histon Mini, Feltham First, Hurst Beagle. Early outdoor sowings, Pioneer, Kelvedon Wonder. Maincrops, Early Onward, Onward, Hurst Green Shaft. Latest sowing, one of the first three earlies given above.

Special note
Only dwarf varieties are recommended but even these need some support. Short, twiggy peasticks are excellent but are now rarely obtainable. A neat alternative is to drive in wooden stakes or canes at intervals of 6–7 ft (2 m) along both sides of the row and close to it, running two or three strands of stout garden twine tightly from stake to stake and enclosing the row in a string fence to prevent it flopping sideways.

Asparagus peas and sugar peas

The asparagus pea is not a true pea but a relative of the climbing cowpea. It is half-hardy and must not be exposed to frost. It does not grow in a thickly sown row but as separate bushy plants with attractive pinkish flowers. The sugar pea or mangetout is grown like the garden pea, but the edible parts are the pod and the seeds. The same applies to the asparagus pea.

Season of use
July to September.
Freezer life: 1 year.

Good varieties
Dwarf Gray Sugar (65 days) and Sweetpods (68 days). There are no named varieties of asparagus pea.

Special note
Edible podded peas must be harvested at the correct stage or they are simply uneatable. Sugar peas must be picked when well grown and fleshy but before the seeds have developed. Asparagus peas are gathered when the pods are about 1 in (2·5 cm).

Below: Sugar peas picked at the right stage. The pods must not be left until visibly swollen.

Soils
No special preparation is needed for soils in good average condition, but any lime deficiency should be remedied by a dressing of garden lime after winter digging.

When to sow
Sugar peas are sown from late March to May. Asparagus peas may be started in peat pots indoors in early spring and planted out in May when frost is no longer expected, or sown in the open in early May.

How to sow
Sugar peas are sown in drills 2 in (5 cm) deep exactly as advised for garden peas. Asparagus peas may be sown in seed compost in small peat pots, three seeds to a pot and 1 in (2·5 cm) deep, and started in the frame or on the windowsill. Reduce the seedlings to one per pot and plant out in late May. Alternatively, they may be sown in small groups in a narrow drill and reduced to one seedling at each station by thinning in stages. Whether planted out or direct-sown the plants should stand finally at 18 in (45 cm) apart.

Time to germination
10–21 days. Asparagus peas are rather erratic in germination outdoors though more consistent in pots.

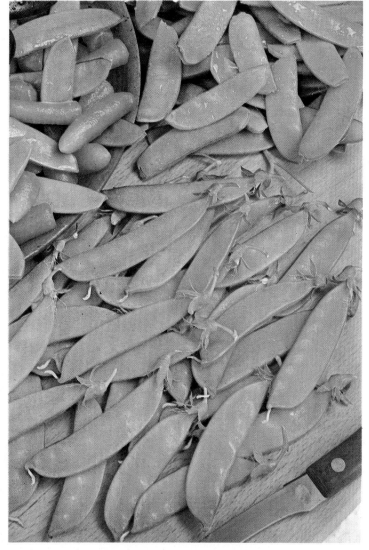

Runner beans

Most Americans know this bean as an ornamental vine grown for its attractive flowers, responsible for its name, scarlet runner. In England and on the Continent the vines are more prized for their edible pods and seeds, which can be used like lima beans. As a vegetable, the vines require a long growing season, about 120 days.

Soil
Some organic materials should be dug in during spring, and supplemented with 3 oz per sq yd (100 g per sq m) of a general fertilizer, raked in 14 days before sowing. Biweekly feeds of liquid fertilizer from the time the plants start to bloom, watering and overhead spraying in hot weather, and mulch, are as important as the initial state of the soil. Just as important too is a situation sheltered from strong winds.

When to sow
In the North sow seeds indoors in peat pots in early spring. In mild climates sow seeds outdoors when the soil has warmed sufficiently.

How to sow
In narrow drills 2 in (5 cm) deep, with the seeds 4 in (10 cm) apart. For growing up poles, sow two rows 12 in (30 cm) apart, placing a row of poles along the outside of both rows of beans and tying the poles together at the top to form a stable inverted V-shaped structure. Sow a few extra beans to provide transplants for gaps.

Time for germination
14 days.

Season of use
Summer to fall if all the pods are picked when young.

Good varieties
American catalogs list only one variety, Scarlet Runner.

Special note
Runner beans, like all leguminous plants, should not be pulled after cropping. Tops should be cleared away and the roots left in the ground to release their accumulated nitrogen.

Above: how to stake a continuous row.
Left: "wigwam" staking for small groups. Use bamboo canes, which last for many years.

Heavy-cropping runner beans like this are produced by good soil, watering and mulching.

11 Permanent crops

Asparagus

This semi-luxury crop is not difficult to grow and an established bed remains in production for up to twenty years. It is now usually grown on the flat rather than on raised beds.

Soil

Asparagus may be grown in any type of soil, though the crop is easier on light land. Eliminate all perennial weeds by thorough cultivation, as it is impossible to do so after planting without damaging the asparagus roots. Dig deeply and if necessary break up the subsoil to ensure good drainage. Work in some manure or compost and about a month before planting fork the soil over and break up any clods.

When to plant

Mid-March to mid-April.

How to plant

Order one-year-old plants early in the season from a good nurseryman. Do not unpack the roots until you are ready to start planting and never leave them exposed, even for an hour, to sun and wind. Take out a trench 12 in (30 cm) wide and 8 in (20 cm) deep. Plant the roots 18 in (45 cm) apart in the trench, sitting each clump on a small heap of soil so that the fleshy roots have a downward slant. Cover carefully with fine soil and fill the trench in.

Cut no shoots the first year but encourage growth by watering freely and also by giving an occasional feed of liquid manure.

During the season all shoots should be cut – thin and deformed ones as well as fine spears like these.

Season of use

April to June. Spears may be cut for a short period in the second season after planting and a full crop cut the following year. All cutting should cease in early summer to allow strong growth of the 'tops' and strengthening of the plant for next year's crop. Freshly cut asparagus will freeze well. Freezer life: 9 months.

Good varieties

Martha Washington. The strain is more important than the variety. Order from a specialist nurseryman.

Special note

When hoeing near a row draw the soil towards it, creating a low ridge. Cover with a layer of compost or rotted manure or compost in winter, top dress with 3 oz per sq yd (100 g per sq m) of complete fertilizer in February or March and after harvesting.

Newly planted asparagus crown, arranged on a little mound of soil at the bottom of the trench so the roots spread downwards.

287

Globe artichokes

The globe artichoke requires a lot of space to produce its edible flower buds and so is not an economical crop for the small garden. It is, however, an impressive plant, and individual specimens may be dotted about and look quite decorative if a row is out of the question.

Left: Cut off suckers as close as possible to where they start growing.

Soil
It must be well-drained and the site open and free from tree-drip. Plants that die in the winter are usually killed by a combination of cold and wet. Work in manure, compost and any available bonfire ashes during digging. Before planting rake in a dressing of general fertilizer.

When to plant
Plant in April, ordering the plants in advance from the nursery. They may be grown from seed but this is rather a long business.

How to plant
Globe artichokes are often planted much too closely. Allow 3 to 4 ft (1 to 2 m) between plants in the row and between rows. Plant very firmly and water after planting in dry weather.

Season of use
Late summer. In the first season there will not be many heads worth using and the plants will be getting established and making growth. Normally, the large terminal buds form first and should be picked before the scales on them begin to turn purple. They are followed by smaller buds on lateral shoots. The artichokes deteriorate rapidly when cut and should be used or frozen as soon as possible after harvesting. Freezer life: 1 year.

Good varieties
Not much choice, but Green Globe is a common variety.

Special note
The plants remain profitable for three years and must then be replaced. Propagate by taking suckers or offsets from the base of adult plants and establishing a new row in April of the third year. Protect plants in winter by covering them with straw.

Below: Harvest heads of artichoke before the scales begin to turn purple.

12 Salad crops

Celery

Blanching or trenching celery is grown in a trench and earthed up to blanch the stems and render them edible. Self-blanching types are grown on the flat and not earthed up. They are mild in flavor and of good quality, but cannot be left in the ground after the beginning of winter frosts.

Above: Plant celery in the bottom of a trench leaving the excavated soil on either side for earthing up.

Below: Blanched or trenching celery. Self-blanching are usually shorter and sometimes green.

Soil
Dig in plenty of moisture-holding organic matter, compost, manure or peat before planting. For blanching varieties the trench should be prepared at this time and manure dug into the bottom of it. Make it 18 in (45 cm) wide and 12 in (30 cm) deep and leave the excavated soil in a ridge beside it for earthing up.

When to sow and plant
Sow seed indoors about 10 weeks before night temperatures reach 50–60°F (10–16°C). Plants are available from the nurseryman in May and June.

How to sow and plant
It is much simpler to buy plants than to raise them, especially as only a limited number are required. If, however, it proves difficult to order the variety you want, sow seed *very* thinly in a tray or flat. Enclose the flat in a plastic bag until the seedlings appear. Prick out the seedlings 2 in (5 cm) apart as soon as you can handle them, using more plastic to cover them for a few weeks. Plant out when 3 in (7·5 cm) tall, one row down the center of the trench, 9 in (22·5 cm) apart, and the self-blanching varieties should be the same distance, both in and between the rows.

Season of use
Late summer to late fall, and longer in mild climates. Celery can only be frozen if it has been cooked and used as a vegetable. Freezer life: 1 year.

Good varieties
Summer Pascal, Golden Self-blanching.

Special note
The growing plants need lots of water. Earth up trench varieties in mid-August, tying the stems of each plant loosely together. Pack soil carefully round to half its height. Repeat monthly until the trench is a ridge with only tips showing.

Chicory

This valuable winter salad is generally neglected by the amateur gardener although it is an interesting crop to grow. The home-grown product will not equal the solid white heads of imported chicory in appearance but it will be fresh and crisp.

Chicory is a biennial plant, making growth and a substantial root one year, dying down and shooting up to flower the following year. The part eaten is the beginning of the second year's growth, grown in darkness so that is blanched and cut before the leaves unfold.

Special note
The chicory roots should be lifted very carefully when the tops die down in autumn, placed in a shallow trench and covered with soil or peat so that they may be withdrawn a few at a time for blanching. Remove dead leaves but take care not to damage the crown.

To blanch, place a number of roots close together in a deep pot or plastic bucket, fill with soil-less compost or a mixture of soil, sand and peat to the level of the crowns, and place in a *completely dark* cupboard or cellar. Keep the compost uniformly moist and so long as the temperature is over 50°F (10°C) the heads will develop.

Fine heads of Witloof chicory, showing the type of root necessary to produce them.

Soil
Any good garden soil, well dug to allow good root development and easy lifting. Wild chicory is a chalkland plant and a dressing of lime should be given if the soil is at all acid.

When to sow
May or June. The latter month is best as a number of plants from early sowings usually bolt and send up premature flower stems.

How to sow
In shallow drills 12 in (30 cm) apart. Sow thinly and thin the seedlings to a final distance of 9 in (23 cm). This distance is a minimum for the development of good plants, as overcrowding and shortage of moisture are two more causes of bolting. So thin rigorously and also water freely in dry weather.

Time to germination
10–14 days. The seedlings are too bitter to suffer much from birds or from insect pests.

Season of use
December to March.

Good varieties
Witloof

Cucumbers

Here we are concerned with cucumbers that can be grown outdoors with or without some cloche protection.

Bottom: One of the improved types of outdoor cucumber, which is of excellent quality.

Below: Prepare continuous mounds of soil and compost on which to plant out rows of cucumber.

Soil
Cucumbers require sun and good drainage, and, at the same time, plenty of moisture, best supplied by incorporating generous amounts of organic matter – rotted manures, compost, peat moss, leafmold – in their growing areas. If there is any doubt as to whether the soil is well-drained, form the planting site into a low mound before sowing seeds or setting out plants. A mulch helps.

When to sow and plant
Cucumbers grow quickly from seeds sown in the open ground after frost danger is passed. However, for an early harvest seeds can be sown indoors about 4 weeks before outdoor sowing is safe. Grow under fluorescent lights or on a sunny windowsill.

How to sow and plant
Sow two or three seeds to a small pot, reducing to one seedling if more than one germinates. Sow in seed compost and preferably in peat pots so that there is no root disturbance in planting out. If the plants are to trail on the ground the planting areas should be 3 ft (90 cm) apart, but if they are to be trained up a trellis or other support only 18 in (45 cm) apart. Water in when planting and do everything possible to shelter plants from cold winds.

Time to germination
Cucumber seeds germinate quickly, but only if a temperature of about 64°F (18°C) can be

maintained. A propagator is useful. Sow ½ in (2 cm) deep, placing the seeds on edge.

Season of use
July to October.

Good varieties
Burpee's Hybrid, Victory Hybrid, China, Burpless.

Special note
When grown as ground trailers the plants should be stopped at six leaves to encourage the growth of laterals. In climbers, the main stem is tied to the supports and pinched off when it reaches the top. Laterals are also tied. Only they are allowed to fruit.

Endive

Endive is a popular salad ingredient in fall and winter. Since it is more tender and flavorful after blanching, a process that requires time and effort, it may not be a crop that appeals to every home gardener.

Soil
Plant in a soil rich in organic matter – rotted manure, compost, peat moss – and add a complete fertilizer before sowing as recommended for lettuce.

When to sow
July is the best month if only one sowing is to be made.

How to sow
In narrow drills ½–¾ in (2 cm) deep. As this sowing takes place at the hottest time of the year the drill should be thoroughly soaked beforehand and kept damp until germination. The seedlings will also need watering in dry weather. If more than one row is grown they should be 12 in (30 cm) apart, and that should also be the final spacing of the plants after thinning. The plants must not be allowed to overlap or the dense, curly foliage will start to rot. Seed may be sown thinly as there are usually few losses of seedlings from birds or other causes.

Time to germination
10–14 days.

Season of use
Fall and winter.

Good varieties
Green Curled, Batavian Broad Leaved, Florida Deep Heart, Witloof Chicory.

Special note
The blanching of endive is essential; the leaves are bitter and inedible until they have lost their green color. About three months after sowing, start tying the outside leaves over the hearts. Or cover the plants with a long board or buckets, flower pots with the drainage holes covered, or anything to keep them warm and dry and completely in the dark. Plants can be packed in a cold frame and blanched as needed through much of the winter.

Curled endive before blanching. The delicate leaves are liable to decay under damp conditions.

Lettuce

One of the most important ingredients of the salad bowl, lettuce is easy to grow but less easy to grow well. The secrets are a fairly good soil, adequate moisture in summer, and frequent small sowings.

Soil
Choose a sunny site (some shade in summer is acceptable) and a soil that is rich in organic matter. Add peat moss, rotted manure and compost before sowing or planting.

When to sow
Spring is the big season for lettuce in most of the North. Sow seeds outdoors as soon as soil can be worked, usually in late March-April. Sowing indoors 3–4 weeks before then or in a cold frame or heated frame speeds the harvest. Make small sowings every 10 days or so until early summer. Start sowings outdoors again in late summer for fall use. In mild climates, lettuce grows best in cool weather – fall, winter, spring.

How to sow
In short drills or broadcast over seed-bed ½–¾ in (2 cm) deep. Start thinning when first true leaves appear, or transplant 5–10 in (12·5–25·5 cm) apart, according to variety.

Season of use
Spring, summer, fall and through winter in mild climates.

Time to germination
10–14 days.

Good varieties
A wealth of variety is available – consult seed catalogs. Choose from among butterhead or cabbage, looseleaf or head types. Bibb, Buttercrunch, Tom Thumb are all butterhead types that are small and mature in about 75 days. A larger butterhead is Dark Green Boston (80 days). Among looseleaf varieties are Ruby, Oak Leaf and Salad Bowl (see below), all fairly heat tolerant. Among head lettuce varieties are Great Lakes and cos or romaine types.

Special note
A new development has been the advent of the leaf lettuce, a non-hearting type from which leaves are taken as required without cutting the whole plant. A good variety is Salad Bowl.

Above: Modern varieties of cos lettuce are self-folding and do not need to be tied.

Below: The other main type is the cabbage group of lettuce, and there are many varieties from which to choose.

Radishes and salad onions

These two salad crops are useful short-term fillers of the odd space as well as being essential to the complete salad list. They sometimes disappoint for want of a little care.

Radishes and spring or salad onions. Grow them as catch crops on any small area available.

Soil
Any soil in reasonably good heart, as one manured for a previous crop, will do for these crops. The worst soils, especially for radishes, are very poor, dry ones. A little garden compost forked in before the ground is leveled for sowing is a help, but do not use large quantities of organic manures or fertilizers.

When to sow
Radishes, as early as the ground can be worked in the spring, and thereafter every 10 days or so up to early summer. Sow again in late summer for fall crops. Radishes do not withstand heat. Onions, March to July, remembering that if you are growing onions for storage there should be plenty of thinnings for a time in May or June. A final sowing of onions for spring use may be made in September, wintering unprotected in mild districts.

How to sow
Both crops are sown in drills ½–¾ in (2 cm) deep and 6 in (15 cm) apart. Sow thinly and thin the radishes further if the seedlings are at all crowded. The commonest cause of failure with radishes is not giving the roots room to develop. Salad onions may be left fairly thick and withdrawn for use as soon as they are large enough.

Time to germination
Radishes, 5–10 days.
Onions, 14–21 days.

Above: Oval radish French Breakfast. An old variety, unbeatable for quality.

Season of use
Spring to autumn.

Good varieties
Radish: Scarlet Globe, Sparkler, Cherry Belle (globe-shaped), French Breakfast, Summer Grass Hybrid, a giant white oriental type that remains crisp and mild. Onions: White Lisbon. The pickling onion, White Portugal, is grown like salad onions, sown in spring, and lifted when the roots are as big as marbles.

Below: unthinned radishes, roots unusable. (*left*): properly thinned or sown very thinly (*right*).

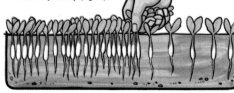

Special note
It is far better to sow salad onions than to rely entirely on the main onion bed for the supply of 'spring' onions. This leads to onions too large for the salad and too crowded, owing to delayed thinning to make good storage bulbs.

294

Tomatoes

The tomato ranks as the most popular home garden vegetable. Culture can be complicated and laborious, or a few plants from the local garden center can be stuck in the ground and produce a miracle harvest. Study catalog descriptions of varieties suitable for containers on terraces as well as greenhouse and garden growing.

Some top-quality varieties of miniature tomatoes make decorative pot plants.

Soil
If possible, select a position on the south side of a wall or fence and dig thoroughly. Rake in 3 oz per sq yd (100 g per sq m) complete fertilizer before planting. When plants are fruiting, feed regularly with a high-potash liquid fertilizer.

When to sow and plant
Buy plants from a local nursery and plant out in late spring. Alternatively sow seed in early April, harden off and plant out under Hotkaps in mid-May.

How to sow and plant
Sow in seed compost in trays in the greenhouse, on a light windowsill or anywhere maintaining a temperature of 60°F (16°C). Prick out seedlings into peat pots of potting compost after the first true leaves appear, grow on to 15 cm

(6 in) under fluorescent lights to ensure sturdy growth, and harden off in the frame before planting out. Tall varieties are planted 18 in (45 cm) apart, and each is tied to a stout cane. Bush or dwarf varieties, are planted 24 in (60 cm) apart.

Time to germination
10–14 days in the right temperature. Very early pricking out of the small seedlings is essential.

Season of use
July to November. The last of the crop is ripened indoors. Tomatoes for cooking may be frozen; storage life, 1 year.

Good varieties
Early Girl Hybrid, Big Girl Hybrid VF, Better Boy Hybrid VFN. Small-fruited bush varieties: Small Fry, Pixie, Early Salad.

Special note
Tall varieties are grown as a single stem. Nip out all side-shoots as soon as they show in the leaf axils. Remove the growing point after the third or fourth truss has set. Restrict the number of branches on bush varieties to three or four.

Good full-size tomato specimens.

Pot-grown tomatoes on a patio. Keep them to a single stem by pinching out side-shoots (see inset) as soon as they appear in the leaf axils. Pinch out growing points of outdoor plants when three trusses of fruit have set.

295

13 Root crops

Beets

Beet succeeds on most soils provided its growth is not checked by cold or drought, which may cause it to bolt instead of forming a proper root or to produce roots that are tough and woody. Do not sow it too early in spring and be prepared to water it on light, dry soils.

Certain varieties of beet are grown for their edible leaves and stems instead of for their roots (see perpetual spinach).

Soil
A complete fertilizer may be raked in well before sowing at the rate of 3 oz per sq yd (100 g per sq m) but on land in good heart after manuring for a previous crop this may not be necessary.

When to sow
Beets are very hardy. Start sowing in early spring (about April 1 in most Northern areas) and make successive sowings, where space permits, up to early summer to maintain a supply of small beets to use fresh (with their tops) as well as older beets for storage.

How to sow
In drills 1 in (2·5 cm) deep and 12 in (30 cm) apart. For midsummer sowings in dry weather, water the drills before sowing and keep watered until seedlings emerge. Beet 'seeds' are usually clusters of seeds, so don't sow too thickly. Protect from birds with netting or black thread if necessary.

Time to germination
10–21 days according to season and soil temperature.

Season of use
Fresh and stored, late June to late February. Freezer life: good condition for six months.

Good varieties
Golden Beet, good for tops and roots; Lutz Green Leaf, Winter Keeper, for greens and roots for storing; Detroit Dark Red Medium Top, for greens and roots for storing; Cylindra, long roots for slicing.

Special note
Start thinning beet as soon as the first true leaves appear. Thin in stages to 1, 2 and 4 in (2·5, 5, and 10 cm) using sizeable roots from the last stage. At the first thinning, take care to reduce to one seedling the little clumps that often emerge from each seed.

Above: Golden Beet. This new variety does not bleed like the ordinary red types. Its quality is excellent and the leaves may be cooked like spinach.

Left: Globe beet, best for winter storage. Semi-flat early-maturing beet.

Carrots

The carrot is one of the most useful of root vegetables, pulled young and tender from successional sowings in summer, kept in that condition in the freezer, or stored naturally when mature for use throughout the winter.

Soil
Light land produces the finest long carrots, but the stump-rooted and cylindrical varieties do well on heavy land well dug and left rough to weather through the winter. The crop responds to the standard fertilizer dressing of 3 oz per sq yd (100 g per sq m) raked in about two weeks before sowing. No organic manure is needed.

When to sow
From early spring to early summer, choosing a short, quick-growing variety for the latest sowings. Carrots are a useful crop to succeed early peas or spinach.

How to sow
In drills ½–¾ in (2 cm) deep and 9 to 12 in (23 to 30 cm) apart. Monthly sowings will ensure young roots for immediate consumption and freezing over a long period and plenty of full-sized ones for winter storage. Thin by stages to a distance of 3 in

(10 cm), using the later thinnings.

Time to germination
14–21 days.

Season of use
Freshly pulled and naturally stored, June to March. Freezer life: 1 year.

Good varieties
On deep soils, Imperator, Gold Pak. On all types of soil, Danvers Half Long, Royal Chantenay. Recommended for freezing, Goldinhart, Nantes.

Special note
The major pest of the carrot is the carrot fly, whose larvae scar and distort the roots. It is controlled more by management than by pesticides. Choose an open and exposed site for the carrot bed as the fly prefers a sheltered habitat. It is attracted to the crop for egg-laying by the smell of the carrots, frequently when they are disturbed during thinning. Thin on a dull day or after sunset, firm and water the seedlings after thinning and, best of all, use pelleted seed sown ½–¾ in (2 cm) apart and reduce thinning to a minimum.

Left: Forked carrots are caused by manuring the ground with manure just before sowing.

Right: The long, cylindrical type of carrot which gives its best performance on deep, well-cultivated soils.

Above: Carrot Chantenay. An intermediate variety, red-cored, early and fine for freezing.

(30 cm) apart in the row with 18 in (45 cm) between rows. Water before lifting and plant so that the roots are covered but the small swelling at the base of the stem rests on the surface. Water carefully after planting to settle the plants.

Time to germination
14–21 days.

Season of use
October to March from the ground and from storage. Not much point in freezing.

Good varieties
Marble Ball, Alabaster, Large Smooth Prague.

Special note
Celeriac is grown on the flat and dries out more than trench celery, although it needs water just as much. Keep it hoed, watered and if possible mulched with peat.

Left and below:
Improved types of celeriac. Modern varieties have better-shaped roots than the older forms.

Celeriac

Also known as turnip-rooted celery, this rather unattractive-looking root serves a useful purpose. It is a celery-flavored vegetable and may be used in cooking as a celery substitute, or parboiled and marinated, then served as a salad. It will grow where celery consistently fails, is less trouble to cultivate and may be lifted and stored for winter like other root vegetables.

Soil
Well-manured soil that will hold moisture is essential for succulent roots. If manure is short, dig in plenty of peat on the site of the row and rake in a dressing of general fertilizer before planting out.

When to sow
Start seeds indoors as for celery, or in the open during late spring. Celeriac plants, unlike celery plants, are difficult to buy.

How to sow and plant
Sow thinly in very shallow drills lightly covering the seed with fine soil. Outdoor sowings must be watered in dry weather. The seedlings, like those of celery, are apt to look crowded and fragile, and if you do not want the trouble of pricking out, they may be thinned and left to grow on. In this case you must sow a sufficient length of drill to give the required number of plants when thinned to 2 in (5 cm) apart.

Plant out when the young plants are big enough to handle, 12 in

298

Jerusalem artichokes

The Jerusalem artichoke has no associations with Jerusalem; its name derives from the Italian *girasole*, a sunflower. Its knobbly tubers are not universal culinary favorites but it has the advantage of being extremely easy to grow.

Soil
Neither manure nor fertilizer are normally used. The ground should be well dug before planting and forked over again before planting to leave it loose and open.

When to plant
April to May as soon as the soil is workable.

How to plant
In separate holes or a continuous trench 6 in (15 cm) deep, spacing the tubers 12 in (30 cm) apart. Planting tubers may be bought from the seedsman or you can use those bought from the greengrocer for culinary purposes. It is unlikely that more than one row will be required, and as the plants grow a good 6–7 ft (2 m) tall this should be sited where it will least overshadow other crops. In a windy situation it may be necessary to support the tall stems by running a strand of wire or twine, attached to poles or stout canes, along the row.

Time to emergence
Shoots will appear 3–4 weeks after planting.

Jerusalem artichoke tubers bear no resemblance to the globe variety and are cooked quite differently. They take up less planting space than the globes and are a much underrated vegetable – the globe variety being considered a glamorous starter to a luxurious dinner.

Season of use
November to March, the tubers being lifted as required, or stored in a cool place covered with peat if hard frost seems likely to make lifting impossible. The tubers may be frozen but the high-quality storage time is only 3 months, so freezing in the autumn is pointless. The season of use may, however, be prolonged a few months by freezing the tubers in late fall or before growth restarts.

Varieties
There are not any varieties of Jerusalem artichokes which are distinct.

Jerusalem artichokes make a good screen for less attractive items – such as a compost heap.

Special note
This is a difficult plant to eliminate from the garden once you introduce it since every small and broken tuber left in the ground proliferates like a weed. It is better to leave it out of the rotation and confine it to some corner of the plot where it may be grown for several years running.

Onions

This concerns bulb onions for storage. Salad onions are dealt with under that heading.

Soil
Choose an open, sunny site and dig it deeply during the winter. If the onions form part of the root-crop section in the rotation, no manure or compost need be used, but some may be dug in if a special bed is prepared. Onions are one of the few crops that may be grown on the same ground for years if free from disease. Complete fertilizer should be raked in at the rate of 3 oz per sq yd (100 g per sq m) as soon as the soil dries in early spring. Then tread it until quite firm and rake it again to a fine, level tilth.

When to sow or plant
Sow seed as soon as the soil is workable in early spring. Plant sets in April.

How to sow or plant
Seed is sown in drills ½–¾ in (2 cm) deep and 12 in (30 cm) apart. After covering the seed, firm the soil by lightly treading the drills. Thin the seedlings by stages to a final distance of 4 in (10 cm). Use the later thinning for salads but do not be tempted to delay thinning to ensure a supply of 'spring' onions.

Onion sets are small bulbs whose growth was checked the previous season. When planted they start growing again and mature more quickly than seed-grown plants. Take out drills the same distance apart as for seeds, press the sets into the bottom of the drill 4 in (10 cm) apart, and fill in the drill so that only the necks are visible.

Time to germination
14–21 days. Sets begin to root in 14 days.

Season of use
July to March. Chopped or sliced onions may be frozen for two months.

Good varieties
Seed: Early Yellow Globe, Ebenezer, Southport White Globe. Sets: Ebenezer, Stuttgarter.

Special note
Onion seedlings are small and fragile and should be carefully hand weeded from the time of emergence. If weeds are allowed to get established they can soon smother the young crop. Many mail order nurseries and seed houses, and local garden centers, now offer onion seedlings in the spring. These seedlings will supply mature onions faster than your own seedlings.

Flat onion. The Stuttgarter variety shown here is one of the best to grow from sets.

Globe onion, the most popular type for growing from seed.

Onion sets

Parsnips

The parsnip is a hardy and undemanding vegetable, but perfect long specimens are only grown on deep loams or similar soils. Heavy clay soils must be deeply prepared before sowing parsnip seeds.

Perfect long-rooted parsnips. On heavy clays stump-rooted varieties give better results.

Soil
Dig deeply, breaking up the subsoil if possible, though without bringing any of it to the surface. Try to complete digging early in the winter, leaving the ground rough. If it was manured for the previous crop no fertilizer need be used when preparing to sow. Rake the surface down to a fine tilth.

When to sow
March or April in all districts, when the soil is in workable condition. This crop is not expected to mature until autumn. Always buy fresh seed each year, as old seed will not germinate.

How to sow
Sow in narrow drills ½ in (1·25 cm) deep and 12 in (30 cm) apart. The seed is large enough to be sown quite thinly, but is also very light, and when sowing in a strong wind the hand should be held close to the drill. Thin seedlings by stages to 6 in (15 cm) apart.

Time to germination
14–21 days, but in early spring you should allow 4 weeks before assuming a failure.

Season of use
October to March. Parsnips are left in the ground and lifted as required during the winter. They should not be stored in the freezer.

Good varieties
All-America, broad and somewhat short roots; Marris Model, medium long roots; Hollow Crown, long tapered roots.

Special note
Parsnips do not store well out of the ground and so are better dug only when needed. This becomes difficult during prolonged hard frost, and it pays to keep the row covered with a thick layer of peat to reduce the depth to which the ground is frozen. Lift all unused roots when they begin to grow out in late February or March and store in a cool shed in a box of peat moss.

Potatoes

Early potatoes are a semi-luxury and should be grown if room can be found. Later varieties are only worth growing in the larger garden.

Even crop of potato tubers.

Soil
Potatoes prefer a slightly acid soil rich in humus. Compost or well-rotted manure may be used in the trench when planting but a combination of peat and fertilizer is almost equally good, especially on light sandy soils. The ground should be dug in fall or early spring and forked over again before planting. Potatoes do not need a fine tilth but do best in a loose soil not settled and compacted.

When to plant
Earlies, late March to mid-April. Maincrops, April and early May. Much depends on the frequency of late frosts in your district and nothing is gained by early planting if the growth is cut off. Gain time by getting the 'seed' tubers at least a month before planting and setting them up in trays in a light, frost-proof place to develop sturdy green shoots.

How to plant
Take out a trench 5 in (12·5 cm) deep with the spade. Space the potatoes in it 12 in (30 cm) apart, with the rows 24 in (60 cm) apart for earlies and a little more for maincrops. Cover each tuber with a double handful of peat or compost. Sprinkle complete fertilizer along the trench at the rate of 2 oz per yd (66 g per m) of row. Fill in the trench with the rake or draw-hoe.

Time to emergence
2–4 weeks according to soil temperature. Watch for the shoots and draw soil over them if frost threatens at night.

Season of use
June to the following May. Apart from normal storage of the mature crop, new potatoes may be frozen partially cooked and will keep for up to a year.

Good varieties
Buy certified seed potatoes that are free from disease and are varieties which are recommended for your region.

Special note
Potatoes should be earthed up to encourage tuber formation and prevent tubers greening from exposure to light. Draw the soil up to the stems to form a ridge when the plants are about 8 in (20 cm) tall. If growth seems to have been slow a further light dressing of fertilizer may be scattered near the plants before starting to earth up.

Earthing up: tubers are protected from light and given friable soil in which to develop

Seed potatoes set up to sprout.

Left: Tuber wrongly sprouted.

Rutabagas

The rutabaga is a useful vegetable and although related to the turnip is different and distinctive in flavor and texture.

Soil
Heavy and loamy soils are better than light ones. As with most crops in the root section of the rotation, the ground should not be manured when dug in the winter, but 3oz per sq yd (100g per sq m) of general fertilizer should be raked in before sowing. Rutabagas are an excellent crop to follow early peas, beans or potatoes.

When to sow
Not early. From late spring to early summer so that roots will mature in the fall.

How to sow
In drills ½–¾in (2cm) deep and 18in (45cm) apart. Sow thinly and start thinning as soon as the seedlings get their first true leaves. Continue thinning in stages to a final distance of 6in (15cm). The thinnings are of no culinary use, as rutabagas do not develop their proper flavor until nearing maturity.

Time to germination
7–10 days. Germination of the later sowings is very rapid.

Season of use
October to March from storage. Rutabaga purée keeps for a year in the freezer.

Good varieties
Purple Top Yellow (90 days), Macomber (92 days). The latter variety is particularly recommended both for its keeping qualities and also for its mildness of flavor.

Right and below:
Purple-topped rutabaga. This unjustly neglected vegetable does best sown in late spring or early summer.

Special note
It is a mistake to sow rutabagas too early. The roots are not wanted in the summer and early crops are often badly affected by mildew. Sown in June or early July following the clearance of early peas or potatoes, the crop has plenty of time to mature and is usually healthy. In dry weather, water the drills before sowing and keep the seedlings watered until well-established.

Turnips

Turnips flourish in most gardens, given a consistent supply of moisture. Drought and erratic watering may cause them to bolt and form no root at all or to produce roots strong in flavor and stringy in texture.

Purple-top Milan turnip.

Soil
Give turnips a reasonably good garden soil that contains organic matter – compost, rotted manure. Rake in 3 oz per sq yd (100 g per sq m) of complete fertilizer well before the early crop is sown. The late crop should follow peas or spinach and for this a dressing of 1½ oz per sq yd (50 g per sq m) should be hoed in.

When to sow
Turnips are fairly fast to mature and make best growth in cool weather. Sow seeds of Tokyo Cross and Early Purple-Top Milan in early spring in open ground. For fall and winter crops sow seeds about 8 weeks before first expected hard frost.

How to sow
In drills ½–¾ in (2 cm) deep and 15 in (37·5 cm, apart. Turnips should not be crowded at any stage of growth and the leaves need plenty of room to spread. Start thinning when the first rough leaves appear and thin by stages to a final distance apart of 4 in (10 cm), using the small roots from the later thinnings.

Time to germination
5–14 days. June and July sowings, if kept moist, may emerge in 4 days and careful watch must be kept to see that the

small seedlings are not being pulled up by birds. Protect with netting or black thread if necessary.

Season of use
From the ground or storage, June onwards and for most of the winter. Freezer life: 1 year.

Good varieties
Early sowing, Tokyo Cross Hybrid, Early Purple-Top Milan. Later sowings, Just Right Hybrid.

Special note
A productive late crop may be obtained from a broadcast sowing. Select a strip about 24 in (60 cm) wide, hoe up weeds and incorporate fertilizer. Rake level, scatter seed thinly over area and cover lightly with fine soil, keeping watered. Thin where crowded.

Milan turnip, a flat variety. Globe varieties are usually better for earliest sowings.

14 Miscellaneous crops

Leeks

The leek is not only one of the hardiest of the onion family but also the most delicately flavored. Nothing quite replaces it as a winter vegetable.

Soil
Good soil produces large, plump leeks. Dig deeply in spring, working in some manure or compost. Before planting, apply 3 oz per sq yd (100 g per sq m) of a general fertilizer, forking it well into the topsoil.

When to sow and plant
Sow in a seed-bed from early March to mid-April. Plant out from May to July. Give leeks the longest growing season possible.

How to sow and plant
Sow in the seed-bed in shallow drills 6 in (15 cm) apart. Thin the seedlings to 2 in (5 cm) and plant out when about 8 in (20 cm) tall. Well-grown plants are easier to transplant than thin, grassy ones, and for that reason it pays to allow them plenty of space.

Water before lifting, and trim back the longest leaves of the seedlings by about one-quarter of their length before planting. Plant 9 in (23 cm) apart in rows 18 in (45 cm) apart. Make a hole with a dibbler, not quite as deep as the leek plant is long, drop the plant in it, and fill the hole with water. Do not fill it with soil, either then or subsequently. Enough soil is washed down to cover the roots and the stem is left with room for expansion.

Blanch the stems, beginning in late summer when plants are about 6 in (15 cm) high, by pulling soil against the plants up to where the green part of the stem begins.

Time to germination
14–21 days. May be rather slow. Seedlings are practically immune to insect and bird damage.

Season of use
Autumn to spring. Plants are kept in the ground and lifted as required. Leeks may be frozen for use in summer.

Good varieties
Broad London, Conqueror.

Special note
Although leeks survive hard frost, they are almost impossible to lift without damage when the ground is frozen. One solution is to lift the plants and pack them upright in boxes of damp peat moss and soil, and store these in a cool cellar or shed.

Far left: Leek seedlings planted. The holes are filled with water after planting but are not filled up with soil.

305

Squashes

This is a large and varied group, which also includes zucchini and pumpkins. They all need basically the same treatment and the same humus-rich soil. They are all tender and must not be exposed to frost.

Soil
These vegetables cannot be grown without some organic manure or compost. They do not respond well to inorganic fertilizers. Use the manure or compost to prepare stations for the plants, digging the manure into the soil at each site and raising it into a low mound. Do not leave manure and soil in separate layers. A barrowload of manure is enough for three plants.

When to sow and plant
Indoors: 4 weeks before last frost is expected. Outdoors: A week before the last frost.

How to sow and plant
Sow in seed compost, preferably in peat pots. Squashes dislike root disturbance in planting out. Sow two or three seeds per pot at a depth of ½–¾ in (2 cm) keeping only the strongest seedling. Do not sow earlier than suggested or the plants will be starved and pot-bound before it is safe to plant them out. Alternatively, sow in the same way on each prepared mound in the first week of June, placing the seeds in little pockets of compost or sifted soil and watering daily if necessary. The prepared sites should be spaced as follows. For bush squashes and zucchini, 2½ ft (75 cm). Most squashes, 3 ft (90 cm). Vining winter squashes and pumpkins, 4 ft (1·2 m).

Time to germination
10–14 days, provided a

Right: Zucchini, a productive bush type which may be cut as courgettes or left to grow to full size.

Below: Summer squash.

Below: Squash Vegetable Spaghetti. One of the best of the squashes, with flesh of a distinctive texture.

night temperature of 50°–55°F (10°–13°C) is maintained. In temperatures below this seed is likely to rot.

Season of use
Summer squashes, July to October. Ripened Butternuts, pumpkins and winter squashes, from October to January.

Good varieties
Summer squashes: Vegetable Spaghetti (a vining variety – boil and scoop out center), Baby Crookneck, Seneca Butterbar Hybrid, St Pat Scallop, Greyzini, Aristocrat Hybrid. Fall and winter squashes: Bush Acorn Table King, Butternut, Hubbard.

Melons and watermelons

Melons (cantaloupes and muskmelons) and watermelons do best in mild climates with long growing seasons. Gardeners in the North can be successful if they start the seeds indoors and choose early-maturing varieties.

Soil
Like squashes and cucumbers the melon must be grown on a prepared site. For each plant mix a good pailful of rotted manure or garden compost with the soil taken from a hole about 12 in (30 cm) square. Loosen the soil at the bottom of the hole to promote good drainage and replace the mixture, shaping it into a small mound. The same procedure applies whether the plants are in the open, or in a frame. Distance between planting sites should be 24 in (60 cm).

When to sow and plant
Seed requires a temperature of 60°–70°F (16°–21°C) for germination, and the plants cannot be transplanted to the garden until late May or to the open ground until early June. Therefore, sow seeds indoors about 4 weeks before it is safe to plant outside in peat pots.

How to sow and plant
Raise seedlings as described for cucum-

bers, remembering that melons are a little more tender. Plant out with the least possible root disturbance, choosing the sunniest, most sheltered site you can find for the unprotected plants. Never allow the plants to suffer from lack of water, using it tepid for young seedlings and watering newly-planted outdoor plants before sunset. Plant under Hotkaps. Mulch with black plastic.

Time to germination
7–10 days in the right temperature.

Season of use
August to October. Freezer life: 1 year.

Good varieties
Muskmelons: Gold Star, Harper Hybrid; Watermelons: Sugar Baby, Yellow Baby.

Special note
The trailing shoots are stopped after the fifth leaf and the laterals they produce are stopped at the third leaf. The fruits are borne on these laterals. Rest the fruit on pieces of tile or polyethylene as they ripen and harvest when they develop the characteristic melon scent and the fruit slips readily from the stem.

Top and left: Cantaloupe melon. Several varieties may be grown in frames, under cloches or even in the open.

307

Swiss chard

This rather neglected vegetable is another leaf beet, related to perpetual spinach. The edible part is the broad leaf stalk and midrib, pure white in most varieties and pink in the variety Rhubarb. This is a delicious vegetable and should be better known. It is a good summer greens, as it withstands heat well.

Soil
Treat it as for the growing of spinach. The only difference is that Swiss chard is slower in reaching maturity and has time to respond to weekly feeding with liquid fertilizer in addition to regular watering. In well grown plants the edible stems should be 2 in (5 cm) wide.

When to sow
Early to mid-spring. This is a late summer and autumn crop and too tender to carry on into winter.

How to sow
In drills 1 in (2·5 cm) deep and 18 in (45 cm) apart. Thin the seedlings to 4 in (10 cm) apart as soon as they can be handled. A week or so later remove every other plant and leave the remainder at twice this distance. Swiss chard, in both white and pink forms, is quite a decorative plant, and clumps of it may be grown in the shrub or herbaceous borders if kitchen garden space is limited.

Time to germination.
14 days.

Season of use
July to October.

Good varieties
Fordhook Giant, Rhubarb Chard, Lucullus, Perpetual.

Special note
The outer leaves are cut at ground level when large enough and the plant continues to produce more from the center. The leaf is stripped from the midrib and may be cooked like spinach if there is enough of it. Leaf stalks and midribs, which are the main part of the crop, can be cooked separately.

Bottom: Ruby Chard, the red form of Swiss chard. A valuable addition to the menu and so decorative that it may be grown in the flower border.

Below: The production of Swiss chard can be prolonged with protection in frosty weather.

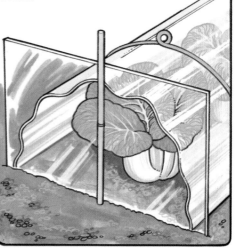

Spinach

Spinach is one of the fastest vegetables to mature. A March sowing is often ready for cutting in late May and sowings at intervals of three weeks will maintain a continuous supply in regions where summers are cool and moist. Elsewhere it is only a spring and fall crop, as it has no heat tolerance.

Soil
Spinach is a leaf crop and must have plenty of moisture and adequate nitrogen to produce abundant foliage. Its worst feature is a tendency to run to seed, and the warmer and drier the soil, the quicker it does so. On heavy clays and very light soils dig in all the humus-forming material you can spare, even if it be only peat. Then, before sowing, rake in 1 oz per sq yd (33 g per sq m) of sulphate of ammonia.

When to sow
Early spring and late summer for fall harvest.

How to sow
The largest crop from a given area is obtained by sowing in a drill about 6 in (15 cm) wide and rather less than 1 in (2·5 cm) deep. Sprinkle the seed thinly and evenly over the bottom of the drill, first soaking it with water if the soil is dry. Fill in and firm the soil. If more than one row is sown the drills should be 12 in (30 cm) apart. Allow the seedlings to grow to about 4 in (10 cm) and then thin for the first time. The thinnings are large enough to use, it being only necessary to snip off the roots. After a few days, the row will have filled up again and more thinnings may be used, the rest of the plants then being spaced widely enough to grow to full size for cutting.

Time to germination
10–14 days.

Season of use
May to October, depending on climate. Young spinach with a minimum of stalk may be frozen. Freezer life: 1 year.

Good varieties
America (50 days), Bloomsdale Long Standing (48 days), Winter Bloomsdale (45 days).

Special note
Spinach is one of the few vegetables to succeed in partial shade – though not in competition with tree roots.

Above: Summer spinach Bloomsdale Long Standing.

Left: Sowing seed for summer spinach.

Perpetual spinach

Also known as spinach beet, the plant is unrelated to summer spinach. It is a leaf beet, a biennial with a strong tap-root that may live for several years, though in practice it should be sown annually. It produces a succession of edible leaves in autumn and spring and, if cloched, throughout the winter.

This vegetable is virtually unknown and uncultivated in the USA, but there's no reason why it can't be grown. Order seeds from British firms.

Soil
Any soil in reasonably good heart is quite suitable if it is well cultivated. The crop is a good follow-up to early potatoes, which leave the soil in the right condition so that it only needs to be raked level before sowing. A light dressing of general fertilizer raked in at that stage helps to get the seedlings away quickly, but more important is to make sure that you have the soil in good physical condition to encourage a strong root system.

When to sow
Mid-June to mid-July. It may, of course, be sown earlier but is not usually wanted as a summer vegetable.

How to sow
In drills 1 in (2·5 cm) deep and 18 in (45 cm) apart. Thin by stages to 6 in (15 cm). Protect from birds if necessary, as the seedlings are sweet and an unprotected row can disappear in 24 hours.

Time to germination
Ten days if the soil is moist. Germination is hastened if the seed is soaked for 12 hours before sowing, but in this case the soil must be moist when sowing and kept so until germination, otherwise the seed may start to shoot and then dry out and die.

Perpetual spinach

Season of use
Autumn, spring and early summer. In mild districts and under protection some pickings are possible throughout the winter.

Good varieties
No named varieties. Listed as Perpetual Spinach, Spinach Beet or Leaf Beet.

Special note
Keep picking young and tender leaves for use. Pick the old and tough ones too to encourage more leaves. When flower stems begin to appear in spring it is time to discard the row and prepare for a new one.

310

Sweet corn

Sweet corn likes a sunny, sheltered position. It is quite decorative and may be grown in groups in the shrub or herbaceous border if no other space is available.

Soil
Compost or manure during winter digging if possible. Complete fertilizer at the rate of 3 oz per sq yd (100 g per sq m) raked in 14 days before sowing or planting.

When to sow or plant
Sowing outdoors: early districts, May; late districts, first week of June. Under cloches: mid-April. In pots in the frame: mid-April, for planting out in May or June.

How to sow
In drills 1 in (3 cm) deep. Distance between rows: 18 in (45 cm). Final distance between plants 12 in (30 cm). Sow in groups of three seeds close together every 12 in (30 cm) reducing each to one good seedling. Sow in the frame in seed compost in small peat pots, two or three seeds per pot, and reduce to one. Grow in several short rows rather than one long one to improve fertilization by air-borne pollen which falls from the 'tassel' to be caught on the sticky 'silk' of the cobs.

Time to germination
14–21 days. Be prepared to protect seedlings from birds with black cotton or nylon netting as soon as they emerge. Harvest at the correct time, when juice squeezed out of the kernels is the consistency of thin cream and before it becomes solid and starchy.

Special note
In dry weather keep plants well watered and mulched with straw or compost in the weeks before formation of ears.

Season of use
Fresh: August to October. Freezer life: good condition for a year.

Good varieties
For the small garden: Golden Midget and Midget Hybrid, spaced 6–8 in (15–20 cm) apart. For larger plots: Silver Queen, Honey and Cream, Early Xtra Sweet.

Well-filled ears of sweet corn. The crop is easily spoiled by harvesting too late, when sugar in the kernels has been turned to starch.

Herb growing

1 What is a herb?

In spite of its general use in describing a plant which is grown for its scent or flavor, the term 'herb' actually has more than one meaning. Botanically, it is a plant that, unlike a tree, has a stem or stems that die back at the end of its season. Thus, the name 'herb' refers, botanically, to thousands of annual, biennial and perennial plants that are by no means aromatic or wholesome. In the non-botanical sense, herbs are the leafy or soft, flowering parts of certain plants. These can be used in the preparation of food or for medicine, for cosmetic purposes, for potpourris, insect repellents and scented toilet waters. Some may even be used in wines and liqueurs.

Spices, often used with herbs in certain dishes, are sometimes confused with them. Spices are not leafy. Usually, they are the seeds of a plant. Sometimes, as in the case of the nutmeg, they are the fruit of a tree. Mace, also from the nutmeg tree, is the dried membrane that surrounds the nut when it is growing. Cloves are flower buds, cinnamon is the bark of a tree. Some plants, for instance perennial fennel, provide both spice and herb, but this is not general. It should not be assumed that every part of every culinary herb is good to eat.

The spices used in potpourris are a little more varied and exotic. Orris root is the dried, ground root of the Florentine iris. Angelica root can be dried and used for the same purpose as orris. Calamus is powdered palm root. Khus-khus is fragrant grass. Some plant resins are fragrant. These include gum benzoin and gum olibanum or frankincense. Balsam is an oil-resinous sap tapped from certain trees.

Fennel (*above*) is attractive to grow in a flower border and tall enough to act as a background for other plants. Fresh parsley (*left*) can be used as a garnishing as well as lending its own special flavor to a wide variety of dishes.

To carry the distinction even further, culinary herbs are always added to a dish. Except for tisanes or herb teas, they do not form the basis of a dish itself. Thus, while garlic is a herb, onion, a close relative, is a vegetable.

In spite of the true botanical meaning of the term, to most people's minds, herbs are not necessarily plants that die back at the end of the season. Some – the herbaceous kinds – do, but there are also some herbs that are trees, such as the bay, and others that are shrubs, albeit very small ones, such as thyme, sage and rosemary.

Most of the plants we grow as culinary herbs are 'cut-and-come-again' kinds. Fortunately, some of these are evergreens and last for years. These include sage, thyme, rosemary, winter savory and lavender.

The long stem-like leaves of chive (*above*) have a delicate flavor and, when chopped, are a culinary delight. Sage (*left*) is used in Italian cuisine. Its purple flowers are ideal in borders.

Constant clipping keeps these plants neat and compact. Although they have a summer flowering season, at which time they are best gathered for drying, they are available all the year round. Obviously, growth is greater in summer, but the leaves are also there to be gathered fresh in midwinter. Where the climate is cold, these plants can either be grown in a sheltered place or they can be given winter protection. The less exposed they are to the cold, the more

shoots they will produce. Some of these evergreen herbs are such handsome plants that they deserve to be grown in some decorative manner, a subject which is discussed in chapter 3.

Most people prefer to have plants that come up year after year; fortunately, there are many herbs that are herbaceous perennials. These include chives, bergamot, tarragon, marjoram, fennel and mint. Usually, the more these are picked the more shoots they will produce. It is often an advantage to keep picking the tips of the stems so that the plant does not flower. For instance, once mint has bloomed, it begins to die down and so from late summer is of little use; yet if the shoot tips are taken as they are ready, more will be produced down the stem, and fresh mint can be picked right on into the autumn. Fennel, a truly handsome plant, can also be some-

thing of a nuisance if it is allowed to drop its seed because seedlings will then sprout up all over the garden. Further, if allowed to flower, the sweet, young, succulent shoots do not form and only the large, tough leaves are available. If fennel seed is required, it is best to allow just a few stems to seed and to keep taking the young shoots from the others. Once chives have flowered, the plants begin to die down. Where a row of chives is grown as an edging, alternate plants could be allowed to flower while the others are constantly cut, to provide a decorative effect. Like many other perennials, chives stay healthy if lifted and divided every three or four years.

The handsome angelica is a biennial, yet if it is prevented from flowering, it will come up again the following year, and again the year after that, and so on if the same method of removing the flower buds is followed. Otherwise, once it has flowered and set seed it will die.

Parsley is also a biennial, but since we do not cultivate it for its seed, which is produced the year after sowing, it is treated as an annual and sown afresh each year.

Of the many annual herbs, those grown for their leaves can be sown in succession to provide a constant supply.

It is an interesting fact that the main

All parts of lovage (*top*) except the roots have value in cooking. The leaves and stems have a celery-like flavor. The delicate flowers of coriander (*above*) make a delightful bouquet, but it is the seeds that are used in cooking. This particular variety of thyme (*right*) has a pungent lemon-like scent.

Pots of thyme (*left*) can be grown indoors by a sunny window or on a sheltered terrace. Angelica (*middle left*) is a giant among herbs. The seeds of caraway (*bottom left*) are used in bread-making. Dill (*below right*) is used as a pickling spice.

herbs are from just a few plant families. Those that are most versatile and offer the greatest range of flavors come from the parsley family, or *Umbelliferae*. The flowers of these plants grow in flat or rounded umbels. Parsley is *Petroselinum crispum*, and it has a swollen-rooted form, known as Hamburg parsley, that provides both leaf and root, the latter looking and tasting like a smaller and choicer parsnip.

Chervil, *Anthriscus cerefolium*, resembles parsley in appearance, but is generally more delicate. It has a slightly licorice flavor. It is one of the *fines herbes* and really should be included in every herb garden.

Carrying a similar flavor is sweet cicely or Spanish chervil, *Myrrhis odorata*. Like the Hamburg parsley, its roots can be cooked and its leaves used like chervil or parsley.

Fennel, *Foeniculum vulgare*, comes in two forms. The first is used in the same way as any green herb, as a garnish or in soups and sauces, while the second, *F. vulgare* var. *dulce*, known as sweet or Florence fennel, is a variety with swollen stem bases that form a 'bulb'. It is grown as an annual and used

317

forms are described more fully in chapter 3.

Thyme has many species, which differ from each other slightly in habit. There are also some variegated forms and varieties. The common thyme most used in cooking is *Thymus vulgaris*. The lemon-scented thyme is *T. x citriodorus*.

Mint also is more varied than is usually realized. There are many species and only a few are cultivated. *Mentha spicata* is the common spearmint. *M. rotundifolia*, with more rounded, woolly leaves, is known as the apple mint. *M. x alopecuroides*, a cross between *M. longifolia* and *M. rotundifolia*, is not common but well worth growing if it can be found. Peppermint is *M. piperita*. Pennyroyal is *M. pulegium*. These are the most commonly cultivated mints, although there are more that could be used. All are perennials.

While the individual flowers of mints and thymes are very small, forming in a mass a pretty inflorescence all the same, those of the rosemary, *Rosmarinus officinalis*, are

Fast-growing chervil (*left*) matures from seed in a mere two months. Apple mint (*below*) has woolly leaves and dense spikes of pinkish flowers.

as a salad, much in the same way as celery.

Dill, *Peucedanum graveolens*, provides both leaves and seeds and is an annual. The same remarks apply to anise, *Pimpinella anisum*. Caraway, *Carum carvi*, a biennial and treated as such, is grown for its seeds alone, as are coriander, *Coriandrum sativum*, and cumin, *Cuminum cyminum*.

Lovage, *Ligusticum officinale*, the last herb in this umbelliferae list, is a hardy perennial. It has a strong celery flavor, which is the reason its leaves are used to supply flavor to soups and bouillon when celery itself is not available.

The next largest group of herbs is to be found in the sage family, or *Labiatae*, the plants with 'lipped' flowers – the sage flowers are attractive as well as excellent examples of this characteristic. Sage, *Salvia officinalis*, is a small shrub. There are several attractive forms of this useful plant. These

Marjoram (*left*) grows well in a sunny site, but does require some winter protection in cold climates.

Rosemary (*below left*) is a handsome shrub that can be wintered out of doors in a mild climate but elsewhere must be grown as a pot or tub plant that can be moved inside during cold weather.

There are several varieties of mint. One of the most popular for flavoring iced tea is peppermint (*below*).

this has the effect of keeping the plants neat and bushy. There are many varieties, including one with white flowers, and one variety that grows much taller and more erect. Rosemary and its varieties are grown outdoors all year in mild climates, such as in California. Elsewhere they are grown in pots or tubs. One variety, *R. humilis*, is low and spreading.

Marjoram or origanum comes in several species. *Origanum majorana* is a tender sub-shrub usually treated as a half-hardy annual and known as sweet or knotted marjoram. *O. onites* is the perennial pot marjoram. *O. heracleoticum* is winter marjoram and not quite so hardy as pot marjoram. *O. dictamnus* is Dittany of Crete, and *O. vulgare* is the native European species of which there are other forms to be mentioned later.

Two kinds of basil are grown, sweet basil, *Ocimum basilicum*, and bush basil, or *O. minimum*. Both are half-hardy annuals and are discussed more fully later.

larger and differently distributed on the stem. They are an attractive blue and when the plant blooms in late spring, its stems are smothered with these pretty, lipped flowers. The flowers can be used in salads and they can be candied. The plant is a shrub. Only the tips should be picked and

Balm (*above left*) is a hardy perennial that will grow well even in shade. The aromatic leaves are most refreshing in tisanes. Laurel or bay (*above*) is the only herb to grow to tree size. It is winter-hardy in mild climates. Basil (*left*) is easy to grow from seed and can be raised both outdoors and indoors in pots and trays.

bulbous plants that are raised annually from 'seed' bulbs, individual cloves in the case of garlic. From this group also come chives, or *A. schoenoprasum,* a hardy perennial that is easily grown from seed, although plants can also be increased by division.

The splendid bay, *Laurus nobilis,* is the only true laurel, even though there are other, non-edible, plants known by this name. It is also the only tree among the herbs. Its great advantage, apart from its highly individual flavor, is that where it is not possible to let it grow high, wide and handsome, it will grow well confined in a

Garlic (*left*) is a pungent herb that comes in the familiar clustered bulb shape, each section of which is called a clove. French tarragon (*below*) is much more flavorful than the Russian variety. It is widely used in sauces and vinegars.

Balm, sometimes called lemon balm and even lemon mint, is *Melissa officinalis,* a hardy perennial with insignificant lipped flowers. It forms a large, dense mass of roots and it is important that it be kept under control.

Bergamot, *Monarda didyma,* is the source of Oswego tea and is used mainly for this tisane, although the leaves and flowers are also good in salads. This is a decorative plant and is discussed more fully in 'Color in the herb garden'.

The daisy family, or *Compositae,* provides us with a few important herbs, such as tarragon, or *Artemisia dracunculus,* a hardy perennial. French tarragon is a variety with dark green smooth leaves, while Russian tarragon has less smooth leaves, which have a milder taste. Other species of artemisia are grown for potpourris and other household uses, and are dealt with in 'Cosmetic and potpourri herbs'.

The *Liliaceae,* or lily family, gives us the essential garlic, or *Allium sativum,* and the shallot, or *A. ascalonicum,* both of which are

tub or some other large container. Here it is best constantly trimmed to shape.

There are a few other solitary herbs that may appear to have only little culinary value, which all the same come into their own on occasions and so are well worth growing. These are discussed more fully on pages 374–376.

There are many nurseries specializing in herbs, and it is often useful to visit such an establishment to find out which grows well in your particular area.

2 Herb gardens

Most people imagine a herb garden as a place apart, a special plot set aside for special plants, but often not specially designed. A herb patch is often to be found at the edge of a vegetable patch, down the end of a path, in some odd corner – a horticultural afterthought. Yet no matter how small, a herb garden can be both attractive and interesting, as we shall see.

However, before radically changing an existing garden to accommodate a special herb plot, it is as well to realize that all herbs are basically garden plants. They can be scattered about the garden or grown at different sites, just like any other garden plant. Annuals can go in annual borders or among bedding plants, just as they can be sown in rows among the other vegetables in the kitchen garden. Perennials can go in the herbaceous border; indeed some are grown more for their appearance than for their flavor by some gardeners. The shrubby herbs can be planted in shrub borders or in mixed borders. Some of the sprawling kinds can be introduced into the patio or onto any paved area, where they will revel in the warmth of the sun held by the stones. Some

can be grown in tubs and other kinds of containers.

So much depends upon how important a role the herbs are to play. Obviously, if herbs are used daily, it is essential to maintain a constant and adequate supply. The greater the variety of herbs at one's disposal, the less one is likely to depend upon one particular herb, and so it might be helpful to make changes with this in mind. For instance, where chervil and fennel are grown, these can be used in place of parsley for certain dishes. They can also be mixed with it. If it is decided to grow the herbs among the other garden plants, it might be necessary to grow those herbs that are most frequently gathered, parsley and chives for instance, in some other place – as a vegetable row, or as a path edging, for example.

Culinary herbs can be planted in the same bed or border as the cosmetic or fragrant herbs, and where a special herb garden is being designed this has great advantages. One kind of plant can be used to separate a group of another kind.

For convenience, it is useful to site a herb

Herb gardens range from tiny corner plots to magnificent formal gardens laid out amid stately paths and set off by elaborately trimmed shrubbery.

The massed spikes of flowering thyme and the pretty tufted heads of chive add a delightful splash of color to an informally arranged herb border (*left*).

plot near the house, although, of course, this is not essential. However, where fresh herbs are preferred to dried ones, even in winter, it is helpful to have them near at hand. Also, a bed near a house is often more protected than one in the open.

A patch of earth as small as 3 ft (1 m) square should prove adequate for a small family. It is important in this case also to realize that a great many herbs can be grown in containers, which means that the small plot can be extended in an attractive manner. Before deciding which plants to grow in the open soil, it is worth learning which will grow well in containers. There are details in chapter 5, 'Herbs in limited spaces', page 348. Ideally, the thing to do would be to design a little bed near the house and among paving, so that this could

be complemented and supplemented by, for instance, a pair of clipped bays placed one on each side of the doorway, rosemary trained against the house wall, thyme at the very edge of the bed and encouraged to sprawl over the paving, and winter savory in wide, low tubs or giant saucers placed on the paving.

As you would expect, the taller a plant grows the more space it will require at ground level, usually because its lower leaves are so large. This means that tall plants such as angelica are really not suitable for a very small plot. On the other hand, fennel, which is also tall although not so bulky, can be kept fairly well under control simply by gathering it often and keeping the tips of the shoots from flowering.

The few herbs that grow in a small plot

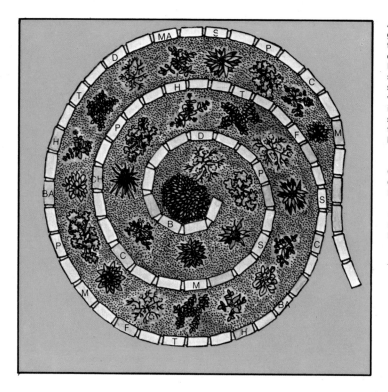

A corner of a small garden can be transformed into a compact and colorful herb area by building a snail garden. From a short distance away it will resemble a small island set off by the surrounding lawn. Here, the following herbs have been grown:
B–bay
BA–basil
C–chervil
CH–chives
D–dill
F–fennel
H–hyssop
M–mint
MA–marjoram
P–parsley
S–sorrel
T–thyme

are likely to be cut often, which is a good thing, for this means that the plants remain neat and compact. This is another reason for increasing the variety of the plants grown rather than to grow several of only one kind. These several may not all be cut often enough.

Incidentally, it should be borne in mind that while annual kinds, or those treated as annuals, can be cut as soon as the leaves are large enough, it may take perennials and shrubs two or three years to become established. These should not be cut heavily during the first year; indeed it is best to leave them alone during this time. Later, when at least some of them are large enough to be divided, it is best to lift only one and to leave the other one or two as a supply. When the divided plant is ready for cutting, the other can be lifted and discarded or divided, as the case may be.

Some herbs are inclined to dominate the rest, usually because they have invasive

roots. Mint is an example. Where a very small herb plot is being planned, it is best to grow the mint separately in a deep container, preferably in shade or partial shade. If this cannot be done, the roots should be isolated in some way.

Fortunately, herbs lend themselves to both formal and informal planting, and to both modern and traditional designs of beds and borders. There are some charming traditional patterns that fit well into small modern gardens. For instance, a square or rectangular plot will take a snail-shell herb garden. The 'snail' is made by making a paved path that goes round inside the rectangle in ever-decreasing circles until the center is reached. The soil on each side of the continuous curving path is planted with herbs.

Snail gardens can be very attractive, but success depends upon what herbs are grown and how they are planted. If the plants are very tall and straggly, the effect is

324

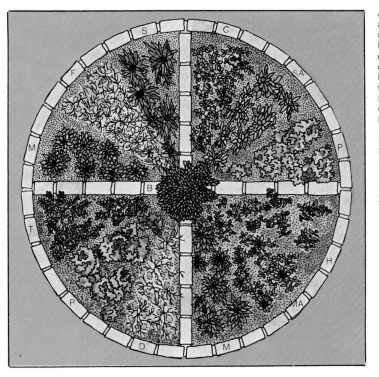

A cartwheel shape is another compact and useful way to grow herbs. Here, a number of different varieties radiate out from an imposing bay tree at the 'hub' of the garden.
B–bay
C–chervil
D–dill
F–fennel
H–hyssop
MA–marjoram
M–mint
P–parsley
SA–sage
S–sorrel
T–thyme

lost. Tall plants can be grown in the corners of the rectangle left by the curving path. These can be in groups either of one kind or mixed. The latter will probably be more attractive, but much will depend upon the area available. The smallest and most compact herbs should be planted or sown close to the edge of the paving so that they follow the lines of the curve. The slightly taller ones can go behind these. It is best to work from the shortest plants at the very beginning of the snail path, gradually going upwards, until the center is reached.

Another favorite is the cartwheel pattern, in which a circular plot is divided into wedge-shaped sections radiating out from a central ring, thus imitating the spokes and hub of a wheel. Usually, a different kind of herb is planted in each section, although the imaginative gardener may devise attractive bedding schemes, with contrasting colors and textures mingling together in alternate beds with the plain greens be-

tween them. Alternatively, beds can be reserved for the annual kinds, such as parsley and chervil, or for those herbs that are constantly clipped, such as chives.

If the area is large enough, the sections should be divided by narrow paths, otherwise they are divided by a band of low-growing herbs, possibly and preferably all of one kind. Paths can be paved, simply trodden down or – and this is more in the spirit of a herb garden – carpeted with low-growing and spreading herbs, such as some varieties of thymes and pennyroyal. Camomile can also be used for this purpose, but this has to be clipped more frequently or it will not form a mat. The other two herbs should be clipped after flowering.

The garden looks better, also, if a path is made round its perimeter. This can be both prettily and usefully edged by a border of those plants that are frequently cut, such as chives, parsley, marjoram and basil, so that these are conveniently placed even in very

325

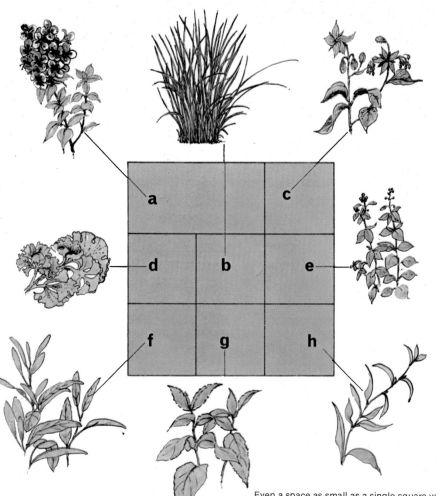

Even a space as small as a single square yard can be transformed into a herb garden. Try growing thyme (a), chives (b), borage (c), parsley (d), marjoram (e), sage (f), mint (g), and tarragon (h) in this pattern.

wet weather. These in turn can be alternated with shallots, which are attractively spiky and a pleasant bright green while growing. Their fading leaves at the end of summer will be well masked by the herbs. For the little space these plants occupy, the rewards are great.

Where the garden suits its setting, in an old cottage garden for instance, or as part of a garden of a house built two or three centuries ago, a knot garden made after the Elizabethan style can look delightful. In this case, each bed, carefully hedged apart from the other beds, contains just one kind of herb, is geometrically shaped and forms

part of an overall pattern. Usually, there is a gravel or shell walk between each bed.

Most of the evergreen herbs stand clipping; indeed, this is often the only means of keeping some in good condition. Where culinary herbs and others are grown in the same garden, dwarf lavenders can be used as hedging. Hyssop is also attractive.

Some herbs make good edgings to beds and borders of other kinds of plants, even rows of vegetables. The side of a vegetable plot, with the vegetable rows at right angles to it, will be improved in appearance as well as made more productive if it is planted with a variety of herbs. Obviously, the tallest kinds will have to be thoughtfully placed. Usually, these are best at the ends of the border. A useful border can be made to follow the edge of any garden path. Herbs fill the area both attractively and economically and it is always helpful to have herbs growing where they can be easily reached and cut in wet weather and in winter. Obviously, the shortest, most compact plants are best for this purpose. These include both perennials and annuals, for instance thymes, chives, parsley, savory, basil, marjoram, sage; the latter should be kept short. Some evergreen kinds should be included so that the border is still well defined and attractive in winter.

In a border, the herbs are planted in much the same way as other plants in an herbaceous border. However it is wise to site the most used in a convenient place. If you have to cross a wide border to reach a

Herbs can be raised in rampant borders (*above*) or in compact bunches (*below*) tucked against a wall.

327

Keep lavender neatly shaped by trimming the flowers and the rapidly growing young shoots.

A luxuriant bay (*left*) surrounded by an informal arrangement of rosemary, sage, hyssop and thyme can create a wild but natural look in a suitably large garden.

plant, add a few paving stones to step on.

It is not essential that a wide herb border, as opposed to an edging border, be straight. 'Island' beds can be used for herbs also. In this case, the very tallest plants should go to the center. In a 'backed' border they should be planted at the back. If plants are too strictly zoned into tall, medium and short, the border can look dull. A better effect is gained if some of the plants of medium height are placed in front.

Fortunately, very few herbs need staking. Dill is an exception. Fairly tall twiggy sticks – pea brush – are best for dill. These should be pushed into the ground round the plants while they are young so that they can grow against and through the twigs. They will then be held quite fast and the supports will be hidden. Tall fennel and angelica are usually sturdy enough to stand unaided, but sweet cicely sometimes needs support. Much depends upon the frequency and strength of the prevailing wind.

When planning a mixed border, put the evergreens in place first, leaving plenty of space around them. Most of these are fairly

short, which means that they will not smother any of the annual kinds planted between them. If there seems danger of this happening, keep the evergreens frequently clipped. Clippings can always be dried.

Most herbs prefer a well-drained soil. This does not need to be specially rich, and it should be light. Heavy soil has an effect upon the pungency of plants. If a plant appears not to be doing as well as it should, it can always be given plant food in a soluble form and this should act as a tonic. Where soil is heavy, it can be made lighter by adding humus, peat and some sand.

Most herbs originate in hot, sunny countries, but not all grow best in full sun. Some prefer shade or partial shade, at least in summer. Mint will grow best where the soil is slightly moist and there is some shade. In summer both chervil and parsley will grow lusher in shade, although chervil will germinate quickly in a sunny, warm spot early in the year.

Where the border is sited in a sunny place, shade can often be provided, at least for part of the day, by some taller plant.

Where an island bed is made, or where a border runs from east to west, there is always a shady or shadier side.

A good way to use a herb border is as a link between the utility and decorative sections of a garden. Where the existing soil is neither light nor warm, there is an advantage in making a raised border or a bank. A raised border need be no more than one brick high, or it can be stepped so that one level, wide enough for short herbs, is one brick high, with another level two bricks high above. The bed can be made higher than this if required. This method is particularly effective if you wish to hide the utility garden from the decorative part, because the raised bed holding tall plants higher from the ground acts as a screen in summer. In winter, although the tall plants are cut down, the raised bed provides protection for the vegetable area.

A long mound does not entail so much preliminary labor, and it can be gradually raised as the years go by. Annual mulching with peat and well-rotted manure and compost will keep the plants in good health as the mound increases in height. The soil will certainly be well-drained. Many of the herbs will help to bind the banked soil and hold it in place.

This formal herb garden demonstrates the elaborate layout that can be achieved in a well-planned garden.

3 Color in the herb garden

Many culinary herbs are extremely handsome, with foliage ranging through many hues of green as well as gray, silver, bronze and purple. Some have leaves that are variegated in yellow, cream or white, and some have multicolored variegation. When these plants flower, they add color and beauty to the garden. Some have lacy umbels of white; others have thick, yellow, umbrella-like flowers borne aloft on tall stems. There are leafy stems studded with lipped flowers of rose red and carmine. There are fascinating whorls, tufts and spikes of these same colors as well as blue, violet and soft mauves.

All this means that a herb garden can be decorative, an important point where the main garden is small and there are no far corners in which the less flamboyant plants can be hidden away. However, the herb garden can be made even more colorful, for apart from those herbs used mainly for their leaves, there are a few others whose flowers and seeds are also edible. These plants are colorful and pretty and because they are annuals are easily grown. They are borage, pot marigold, *Papaver somniferum*, the dusky mauve, gray-leaved poppy whose seeds are used to garnish bread, and the bright nasturtium. Marigolds and nasturtiums grow well in containers, so where there is not much space in the actual herb bed or border, these can often be grown in raised pots of some kind and placed near the other herbs.

To these herbs roses can always be added, not simply as the odd isolated bush, but also as a hedge or screen.

If potpourri plants are to be included, then the herb plot can be as colorful as any herbaceous border at certain times of the year. Lavender makes a wonderful mass of color and the flowers last for many weeks. The evergreen, or rather ever-gray, plants remain decorative throughout the year, becoming smudged with the flower color a few weeks before the flowers actually open and continuing to be pretty in a quiet way as they fade.

Apart from its self color, lavender (*Lavandula officinalis*) varies. There are some varieties with deep violet flowers, *Lavandula* 'Munstead Dwarf', a popular example that grows about 18 in (45 cm) tall. There is a white dwarf variety, and a soft and pretty pink-flowered variety. If these are not to be found in a local nurseryman's list or at a garden center, they are sometimes offered by mail-order specialists. It is always well worth keeping an eye open for them, especially for those that seem to vary even a little more from the usual.

Fortunately, lavender, like most of the other shrubby herbs, is easily propagated by cuttings. Take unflowered shoots from the old wood of a plant. Pull each shoot downwards so that it comes away with a little tail of the skin of the wood. This is known as a 'heel'. It is usual when taking cuttings to trim the heel, but lavender cuttings should be handled as little as possible, so do not trim the heel in this case. Prepare a little good soil in a frame or in some protected place in the open garden; or use a flat and cover it with a polyethylene tent. Top the soil with a little clean horticultural sand, water it and make a little hole to take about one-third the length of each cutting. Put them 2–3 in (5–7 cm) apart, and firm the cuttings in well by treading the soil against them. Water the cuttings once more and leave them to root.

The cuttings should be taken in late summer or autumn. If they are taken in summer, they should go into a cold frame or propagating flat as mentioned above. The older the wood from which the shoots are taken, the colder should the cuttings be grown. So it follows that if the cuttings are not taken until the autumn, they have been taken from older wood, and in this case they are best taken and inserted into the open

A banked herb border can be used as a dividing wall to separate one section of a garden from another.

ground in some place which is sheltered.

It is possible to raise some types of lavender from seed, but not all seedsmen carry stocks.

Like lavender, hyssop, *Hyssopus officinalis*, has also given rise to varieties. The species has lipped flowers of a fine, rich, violet blue. The varieties have white, pink and purple blooms.

This plant, but not the varieties, can be raised from seed. It and the varieties can also be propagated by cuttings, which should be taken in April or May and placed outdoors in some shady spot. The plants can also be divided in spring or in autumn.

One of the mints whose leaves are used in the preparation of potpourris – although also delicious in salads, they are infrequently used this way – is a particularly attractive variegated plant, *Mentha rotundifolia variegata*. The broad, slightly hairy leaves are splashed with creamy-white and when the shoots are young there may be no trace of green on them at all. Sometimes these shoots are a delicate tint of magenta.

A hardy geranium or crane's-bill, *Geranium macrorrhizum*, has strongly scented roots and leaves, both of which are used. Apart from this it is a fine garden plant and a splendid ground cover. Its large, attractively shaped leaves soon cover a wide area if required and they turn beautiful colors as autumn approaches. The flowers are borne well above the leaves and are a dusky rose

331

color. This plant is a perennial and is very easily propagated by division.

Bergamot, *Monarda didyma*, already referred to as being the herb from which Oswego tea is prepared, has attractive flowers that grow in whorls and are a pleasant dusky rose hue. There are now many cultivars, varieties of this plant whose flowers are in other colors ranging from soft pink to purple – useful if one is planning a full range of colors in a herb border.

For the full impact of color, it is important to group and site the plants carefully. For instance, the green-leaved handsome varieties of fennel grow between 4–6 ft (120–180 cm) tall, so it follows that

The rose pink colors of flowering bergamot (*left*) can be used to lend a splash of color to a herb border.

they will look best at the back of a border. Usually, when an ordinary herbaceous border is being made, the gardener is recommended to plant in groups of three so that they make a greater impact, but it is not necessary to follow this rule – nor might it be practical – when planning a herb plot or garden. Fennel is a very well furnished

plant and after the first year, soil and other conditions being suitable, it will grow rapidly and fill a space some 2 ft (60 cm) square. However, fennel is not winter-hardy in most northern regions and so is treated as an annual.

As it grows taller and comes into flower, the base of the plant becomes slightly bare as the first leaves fade. For this reason it is best to plant some dense-growing plant, possibly an evergreen, in front of it. One of the best plants for this purpose is sage. The gray-leaved common sage is quite handsome, but handsomer by far is the so-called red or purple sage. The new shoots are a rich red-purple. The leaves can be used for cooking in exactly the same way as the common sage.

Another charming umbellifer, much shorter, about 14–18 in (35–45 cm), is the pretty coriander. Its flowers, which grow in loose, lacy umbels, are soft lavender-mauve. It needs to be grown near the front of the border, and looks good flanked by the variegated 'silver' thymes. These come into flower a little earlier than the coriander, but the flower heads are retained, misty-mauve, for some time.

Thymes make lovely mats of color and since all are pungent and can be used, one could supplement the common thyme with others. These are discussed more fully in the following chapters.

It is well worth studying seed catalogs in the hopes of finding unusual herbs. Quite recently the seedsmen introduced a handsome form of basil with dark bronze leaves that are just as pungent as the green. Known as 'Dark Opal', it brings a rare color to the border – imagine leaves the color of copper beech.

It is best to raise the plants in flats and to plant them out at the beginning of summer. They need careful watching over for the first two weeks or so, and watering. Beware of slugs, which seem to like this variety above all others.

To see this plant at its best, grow it next to or near the golden-leaved marjoram.

This is an ideal plant to grow right at the edge of a bed or border if it is flanked by a paved path, because the stems will trail over it and soften the edges attractively. The plant is best increased by division in spring or autumn.

The apple-green balm also sports a variegated form whose leaves are blotched with a bright yellow. The colors and their variegation are stronger when the shoots are young, and at this time they are very vivid indeed. Like the green form, this plant is invasive and should be kept under con-

Bronze fennel (*right*) is a variety of fennel with bronze foliage and makes an excellent foil to the predominant green of a herb garden.

trol. The best way of doing this is to lift the entire plant when it has occupied its given space, then to chop off a good portion from the whole mass, using a spade. Enrich the soil a little from which the plant was taken and replant the piece. Do this in spring or autumn.

Chives have pretty little rosy-purple pompon flowers borne on slim stems which take the flowers above the leaves. The flowers can be used in salads. The only drawback to allowing the plants to bloom is that once this happens they begin to die down. If they do not flower, the 'grass' continues to grow. For this reason, flower buds are usually picked off. If the flowers

are wanted for color, it is best to grow plenty of plants and to remove the flowers from some and not others. Cutting back the entire plant after flowering usually forces new foliage growth.

The tall, graceful poppy, *Papaver somniferum*, mentioned earlier, has beautiful glaucous leaves, stems, buds and seed capsules and grows to 2½–3 ft (70–85 cm). Altogether it is a very handsome plant. As one would expect, the foliage and the rest harmonize delightfully with the dusky mauve, sometimes dusky pink, flowers. Fortunately, they also harmonize beautifully with many herbs, especially those with silver, gray or purple in their foliage.

This poppy is easily grown from seed. It will also seed itself. There are 20,000 to 30,000 seeds in each capsule. It is these rich, oily seeds that are used in cooking, in

bread, confectionery and some desserts. The plants grow best if they are given plenty of space and it is well worth while thinning out seedlings to leave roughly a space from 1–2 ft (30–50 cm) square for each plant. One plant treated this way will give a better show and very much larger flowers than a mass of inferior plants. This goes for most annuals, incidentally.

The quality of the seeds of the species and the beautiful cultivars seems not to differ and can be used in just the same way. There are lovely double-flowered varieties, which are listed in the seed catalogs as 'Peony' or 'Carnation-flowered'. They vary a little in color from the species, having a slightly wider range. They will also seed themselves, but if they are allowed to do this, after a time they will revert to the species and all will be single-flowered.

334

Sow the seed of the species or the varieties in September if you want the plants to bloom early, i.e. late spring the following year. Sow the seed in early spring for summer flowering. Like most hardy annuals, this poppy's season is short and so, to ensure a long period of bloom, it is best to make the two sowings. The seed is viable and so long as the opened packet is kept in an airtight container – and they should be kept out of the way of mice – the seed bought for autumn sowing should keep for the spring and *vice versa*.

Try grouping this poppy next to bronze-leaved fennel with purple and gray sage before it. Try it behind the soft, feathery foliage of *Artemisia abrotanum*, southernwood or lad's love. Mild-climate gardeners who have a rosemary hedge can sow a row of these poppies parallel with it, but should keep a good distance between them because the lush poppies soon smother plants that are too close to them.

A cluster of tall, stately poppies (*left*) are a colorful and unusual addition to a herb garden. The seeds of this plant are delicious when baked in confectionery. Silvery cotton lavender (*right*) erupts into brilliant yellow flower-balls. Ranked growths of lavender and looming fennel (*below*) form a wall of colors.

For those who enjoy a vivid display of floral color, pot marigolds, poppies and nasturtiums – simple, bright annuals – can be used here and there among the more permanent plants. Alternatively they can be sown in rows in an edging mixture.

Special effects can be achieved by allowing herbs to play special roles. Some herbs are ideal for hedges and often one needs only a low boundary hedge to separate one part of a garden from another – perhaps to limit the area in which herbs are cultivated. Lavender, rosemary (where hardy) and santolina are the best, but in colder climates germander, *Teucrium chamaedrys*, is a safer choice if the hedge need not be too tall. Germander, which takes well to clipping, grows about 12 in (30 cm) high.

Santolina chamaecyparissus, lavender cot-

335

ton, used as a potpourri component, is an attractive, light silver plant that looks well in association with stone. It softens the edge of a paved area particularly prettily. All santolina hedges, as well as those of other plants, should be clipped back immediately after flowering to keep them compact. Some gardeners do not allow them to flower but aim to keep them as silver as possible all the time. The flowers are yellow.

The common rosemary's erect form, already described, is the best hedging variety, but any rosemary except the sprawling type will do for this purpose. This, incidentally, is a fine plant for seaside gardens, but it cannot safely be recommended for most northern gardens because it is not reliably winter-hardy.

Earlier, reference was made to the invasive nature of mints and balm. These must be thinned out rigorously or planted in separate bottomless containers if they are grown with other plants to prevent the roots wandering over the soil surface. On the other hand, this particular invasiveness can be used to advantage, for these plants will cover a bank and hold the soil in place. If the plain green forms are used, they will be neat rather than decorative, but there are sufficient varieties of these plants that

Bottomless pots (*above*) can be used in the garden to restrain the growth of mint plants. They keep the root mass within a closely confined space and stop it from spreading rampantly. The flowers of camomile (*below*) form attractive daisy-like heads. When dried, they are used to make an extremely refreshing tea.

Spearmint (*right*) has pointed, spearhead-like leaves and purplish flowers that appear in autumn. This is the best known variety of all the mints and is widely used in sauces.

Camomile lawns (*bottom right*) are soft and fragrant. They are formed by keeping the creeping stems of the plant cut short but allowing them to spread out and form a living carpet.

are variegated or colored in some way to make a covered bank quite interesting. The bergamot mint, *Mentha citrata*, becomes beautifully colored at the end of summer before it dies down and, of course, some color will be provided by the mint's flowers.

Some mints, the little pennyroyal in particular, can be used to carpet the ground, like the creeping thymes. These plants are tough enough to take a certain amount of walking upon. Camomile also can be used as a lawn, just as it can be used to carpet a path. It has to be clipped or mown occasionally, unlike the mint or thyme. It can also be mixed with grass, in which case it makes a really hardy lawn.

Finally, one should not forget the roses. If potpourri is to be made, then some of the highly scented, old-fashioned varieties and species are essential. Further, these are culinary plants, once highly regarded as a

source of health-giving salads, or for special jams and preserves and wines and vinegars. This being the case, they will not look out of place in a herb garden where there is adequate room to display them. Indeed, they make a delightful backing for a non-island border. Roses also look well combined with lavender, and, for a vivid effect, dwarf varieties can be grown alongside them.

Common thyme (*left*) grows to form a low bush-like shape. It spreads rapidly and, when flowering, becomes covered in a mass of strong-scented, tiny, purple petals.

A border of Pink Parfait roses and lanky growing lavender (*right*) forms a beautiful wall of color when in flower. This particular variety of rose has a deliciously fragrant scent.

A highly productive and colorful herb garden (*below*) can be established even in a limited space, provided it is a sunny location.

How they are grown will depend upon what space is available. Roses can be grown among other plants, but they should not be so crowded that they are smothered. It should be a simple matter to ensure that low plants, such as thyme, grow at their feet rather than tall kinds, such as fennel. However, there are some roses that can be grown as a formal hedge, such as the species *Rosa eglanteria,* the sweet briar. This is an ideal herb garden rose because it has fragrant foliage. It will grow to 72 in (180 cm) unless trimmed each spring so that it remains compact and under control.

The clippings, which are scented, of course, can be dried and used in potpourri.

Do not expect the same long period of flowering from species and varieties of old-fashioned roses generally as from the modern varieties. Most bloom only once, in early summer. Some are followed by decorative fruits, some of which are worth preserving as syrups or as jam; some can be dried and the largest can be cooked like any other fruit in pies.

Many catalogs will indicate which roses can be used for preserves – the fruits of which are known as hips.

339

4 Herbs from seed

Some herbs must be grown from seed. Others can be, but it might not prove practical to do so. Annuals and biennials, many of which are sown where they are to mature, grow quickly and are soon ready for cutting, but perennials take much longer. It may be as long as three years from the time that the seed was sown to the time that the plants have made sufficient growth to be cut. This being the case, it is often best to begin with a selection of mature plants. Most nurserymen sell a basic collection and there are also specialist herb growers. Obviously, the larger the plants, the better. If these are container-grown, they can be bought and planted at any time of the year when the soil is suitable. Planting should not be carried out when the soil is frozen. Drought is not a great drawback. Water the plants well in the container an hour or so before planting, and again when they have been taken out of the container and planted in the ground. Keep an eye on them and keep the soil round them moist.

Seed is so cheap that it may be thought that this is an expensive way of stocking the garden, but it could well prove to be more economical in the long run. A compromise can be reached that may be helpful for

Annual herbs (*left*), such as chervil, dill, borage, and summer savory are quick-growing and can be cut for use within weeks of being planted. Where herbs are frequently used, grow them in convenient rows (*right*).

those who budget carefully. Just one mature plant of each herb can be bought as a beginning. While this is becoming established and ready for cutting, more of the same kind can be raised from seed gradually filling the border as they come along.

Where a large quantity of certain herbs is to be used, it is often more convenient to grow them in rows like vegetables. Most herbs treated this way are annuals, with some biennials such as chervil, basil, summer savory, sweet marjoram, parsley, shallots and garlic. Plants grown for spices – anise, caraway, coriander, cumin and dill – can also be grown this way.

Some of these, chervil for example, should be sown where they are to mature, simply because they will not transplant well. Most of the others are best sown in boxes or in short nursery rows and lifted and transplanted when they are large enough to handle. This method is usually safer, in as much as the young plants, individually spaced, are not so likely to be eaten by insect pests or slugs; nor are they so

likely to be influenced by bad weather or by drought. Also, germination is usually better when they are planted this way.

In countries where there is a short season, there is much to be gained by sowing the more tender kinds, and those that will transplant, indoors under fluorescent lights or in a sunny window in the early part of the year. The seedlings germinate very quickly and grow apace. As soon as these are large enough to handle they can be 'pricked off', a term that means lifted, separated and transplanted – either spaced out about 2 in (5 cm) in boxes, or, better still, into small individual pots. Pot plants are best because they suffer little check when they are transplanted and they are not so liable to become starved while they are awaiting planting outdoors. Usually, these little plants are kept indoors until the weather is good. They are then introduced to it slowly, a process known as 'hardening off', by being stood outdoors on good days and brought in at night, or by being transferred to a garden frame or placed under a Hotkap. When all fear of frost is gone, by which time

Thin out chervil seedlings
to a distance of 12 in (30 cm)

(12 in)
30 cm

they should be well acclimatized to out-doors, they can be planted in their perma-nent places – permanent, that is, for that year.

Plants usually treated this way include summer savory, sweet marjoram, and basil, both green and ornamental.

It is also possible to steal a march on time and to raise a few kinds of herbs from seed sown in pots and grown on a sunny win-dowsill or in a greenhouse. These are cut while they are quite young, the plants then being considered expendable. Details are given in chapter 6.

Some seed, especially from certain plants of the umbelliferae, is not long-lived. If a packet has been stored unopened for some months under the wrong conditions, the seed might never germinate. Indeed, once a herb garden has been established, it is a good plan to allow just a few kinds, those with the least viable seeds, to seed them-selves. These are chervil, parsley and angelica.

On the other hand, chervil and parsley are often sown in succession so that a con-tinuous supply is available, which means that one cannot wait for the self-sown plants alone. Self-sown chervil is ready only in early spring. Again, a compromise works best: let some plants seed themselves and sow more from time to time.

Parsley is notoriously slow in its germi-nation, sometimes taking as long as six weeks. Although it is usually sown where it is to mature and then thinned out to give the plants adequate space, it is often quicker and more convenient to sow the seed in flats and then to transplant the seedlings from these.

When seed has to be sown in straight rows it is simple to draw a shallow drill using a garden line as a guide. Generally speaking, a drill should be as deep as twice the depth of the seeds to go in it. Sow the seed as thinly as possible. If the seeds are to be sown in spaces among existing plants, it helps to define the area in which the plants are to grow. Press a large upturned flower pot onto the raked soil. Sow the seeds thinly in the circular drill thus made. Always cover the drill with soil and always tread the soil down lightly, to prevent it and the seeds from·being blown away by the wind or washed out by the rain.

Even when you sow thinly it will still be necessary to thin out the seedlings to give each little plant its own living space. It is best to make two or three thinnings rather

Thin out young herbs (*left*), when they are large enough to handle, being careful to grasp them by the stem and not the delicate leaves. Summer savory (*right*) is a small, bushy annual somewhat like a long-leaved form of thyme. Miniature herb gardens can even be created in trays (*below*), provided that the soil is deep enough to protect the roots.

The outer petals of calendula or pot marigold (*left*), and not the leaves, are used in cooking. Of the two varieties of tarragon, the French (*above*) has the better flavor. It grows to a height of 2–3 ft (1 meter).

than to take away the plants in one go. Should disaster strike, there will still be some plants to carry on. Thin out after a shower, or after watering the rows an hour or so beforehand.

It is not always possible to buy seeds of all herbs. Many plants are propagated by cuttings or by division. There follows a list of the most common herbs that can be raised from seed. Plants grown for their seeds (spices) are also included.

Angelica archangelica, **angelica** Sow packeted seed in spring, in deep moist soil in a shady place. Alternatively – and this is likely to be more successful – sow seed when ripe, as soon as it is taken from the plant, in August or September.

Allium schoenoprasum, **chives** Sow seed in flats in March or April; prick off and transplant outdoors in May. Alternatively, sow thinly in pots and begin cutting the 'grass' when seedlings are large enough. A faster way is to buy plants that can be divided.

Anthemis nobilis, **camomile** Sow seed outdoors in shallow drills in April where the plants are to flower.

Anthriscus cerefolium, **chervil** Sow at intervals from February to October for succession in flats, in frames or in the open ground according to the time of the year. Crop matures in 6–8 weeks.

Artemisia dracunculus, **tarragon** Seed can be sown in spring but it is much more usual – and faster – to buy plants.

Borago officinalis, **borage** Sow seed where the plants are to flower, in spring.

Calendula officinalis, **pot marigold** Sow seeds where the plants are to flower, in March or April.

Carum carvi, **caraway** Best sown as soon as ripe in the autumn. Autumn-sown plants flower the following summer. Plants from packeted seed sown in spring do not flower until the summer of the following year.

Coriandrum sativum, **coriander** Sow seeds in shallow drills, ¼ in (0.5 cm) deep, 12 in (30 cm) apart in April in rich, light soil where the plants are to flower.

Cuminum cyminum, **cumin** Sow seeds in shallow drills in May where the plants are to flower.

Foeniculum vulgare, **fennel** Sow outdoors in shallow drills in March, transplant when the seedlings are large enough to handle in ordinary soil in a sunny position.

Melissa officinalis, **balm** Sow seeds indoors in May. Plant out when seedlings are 3–4 in (7–10 cm) high in ordinary soil in a warm sunny place. Or buy young plants.

Monarda didyma, **bergamot** Sow seed in flats in early spring. Keep in cold frame or greenhouse. Plant outdoors in late spring.

Myrrhis odorata, **sweet cicely** Sow seeds in shallow drills in ordinary soil outdoors in April or September. The latter time with newly ripened seeds gives best results.

Ocimum basilicum, **sweet basil** Sow seed indoors from March to April. Plant outdoors in late May or early June.

Ocimum minimum, **bush basil** As above.

Origanum majorana, **sweet or knotted marjoram** Sow seed indoors in March; plant outdoors in April in rich soil in a sunny place. Or buy plants.

Origanum onites, **pot marjoram** Sow seed outdoors in March or April in ordinary soil in a sunny position. Or else buy plants.

Petroselinum crispum, **parsley** Sow indoors in flats for early crop, outdoors in shallow drills late in spring for summer crop, in July to August for late autumn crop, in ordinary but non-acid soil in a sunny position.

Peucedanum graveolens, **dill** Sow in shallow drills, in rich, soil, in a sunny, open position in spring where the plants are to flower.

Pimpinella anisum, **anise** Sow seeds in shallow drills in well-drained, ordinary soil, in spring where the plants are to flower.

Salvia officinalis, **sage** Sow seed indoors in March in flats. Plant outdoors in May or June in rich, but light, ordinary soil in a sunny position.

Sanguisorba minor, **salad burnet** Sow seed indoors in February to March; plant outdoors in April or May in light, but moist, ordinary soil in sun or light shade.

Satureia hortensis, **summer savory** Sow seed in shallow drills in ordinary soil in a sunny place in April where the plants are to flower. Alternatively, sow indoors in flats and transplant later.

Borage is a hardy annual that thrives even in poor soil. Its leaves are used fresh to make infusions.

Once the perennial herbs are well grown, most can be divided should you wish to increase their numbers. Chives grow better if, once they are three years old, they are lifted and divided each spring. Do this when the plants show above ground again. Some of the surplus divisions can be potted for forcing the following spring.

Shallots and garlic are grown from small bulbs known as 'seed', which, in fact, they are not. One small clove of garlic will grow into a tight cluster of several large bulbs.

The little golden bulbs of shallots (*right*) have a milder flavor than onions and are widely used for pickling. Parsley and chervil (*below*) can be grown in pots along a sunny window ledge. As these are frequently used herbs, growing several pots of each at once is always a good idea.

Once you have harvested a good crop of garlic you can save your own seed. Garlic 'seed' is usually bought from the seed merchant, but that sold for cooking can also be used. So can any cloves that begin sprouting in the kitchen, even though it may not seem the correct season for this.

Plant garlic 2 in (5 cm) deep and 4–6 in (10–14 cm) apart any time from late winter to early summer. Lift the bulbs when the tall green tops have faded. First spread them out on the ground to let them dry in the air a little, and then hang them to finish drying in a cool, dry place, by their fading

Salad burnet (*above*) is a perennial, whose leaves have a delightful cucumber flavor. White-flowered sweet cicely and woolly-leaved apple mint (*right*) are tall plants that look particularly attractive when growing at the back of a herb border.

skins rustle and the bulbs are dry, they can be made into ropes or hung in net bags.

Bulbs can be set aside for seed. If there are any very small bulbs, too small for pickling or cooking, set these aside and plant them in early winter. They will provide good-sized fresh shallots for the following summer.

Formerly, the traditional method was to plant shallots on the shortest day and to harvest them on the longest. Certainly they are very hardy and, with garlic, are among the first that can be planted in a vegetable patch. However, this is not a rule to be strictly observed. Bulbs can be planted, so long as they are obtainable, until late May or early June. Usually, sound bulbs will last from one season to another.

Some gardeners save some of the newly lifted garlic bulbs and plant the whole bulbs in autumn, for early crops the following year. This is a thrifty way of gardening as it will save buying new bulbs.

tops. Later they can be made into ropes or simply stored in net bags.

Shallots should be planted 6 in (14 cm) apart, but not deeply. Some people simply push the bulb into the soil, but the trouble with this method is that because the bulb is not firmly anchored it is moved out of position during the night by foraging earth worms. It is best to make a small depression in the soil with a trowel and bury the bulb up to its 'nose' in the earth. Once it begins to grow roots it will pull itself upwards. Wait until all the leaves die right down before lifting the bulbs for storing, unless, of course, using them fresh, which can be done throughout the summer. The green tops can be used like chives or cooked in soups.

To harvest the shallots, first lift the clutch of bulbs with a fork and so allow any remaining roots to dry in the air. Spread them out in the sun for a while. If the weather is moist, spread them out under a cover or in some dry, airy place. When the

5 Herbs in limited spaces

Where open garden space is limited, it is possible to grow herbs on patios and in containers of all kinds. These need not look strictly utilitarian. Properly planned and grown in good soil, they can be quite attractive, and since many of the best plants for containers are also evergreen these captive gardens can be of interest, and use, the year round.

The possibility of standing a bay tree or two by the door has already been mentioned; indeed, these are ideal plants. If there is room, the bay trees can be accompanied by shrubs such as rosemary, winter savory, sage, thyme and perennial marjoram, either planted in their own contain-

ers or growing in company. It is important, of course, to begin with good plants if it is hoped to cut herb snippets from them soon after planting. It is also important to realize that the containers should be emptied from time to time, say every two or three years, and replanted. Usually, the existing plants can be divided. Parts not used can be potted and used while the larger ones are recovering and growing. In cold climates, the bays must be tubbed so they can be moved inside in winter.

It is easy to become over-romantic about growing herbs and to forget that one is likely to take all the leaves from one plant, say parsley or chives, for just one dish. It

Annual and perennial herbs may be raised in dense clusters in window boxes, provided only that the soil is deep enough to retain moisture and keep the roots from becoming parched in the hot sun.

Where climates are not suitable for herbs to be grown outdoors all year round, they can be raised in containers and tubs that are moved indoors or to more sheltered locations during cold weather. Such compact herb gardens are also ideal for limited spaces. Here, chives, parsley, thyme, marjoram and basil are being grown with a selection of colorful lilies.

follows that unless there are more plants to take the shorn one's place, the cook will have to wait a very long time for her next supply. For this reason, it is important to think in terms of growing more than one plant of most herbs and, so far as the herbs raised from seed are concerned, to think of growing several pots of each kind – a container row in fact. These can be grown outside for part of the time, and for part of the year brought indoors to mature on a sunny windowsill. Among these fast-growing herbs are chives, chervil, parsley, basil and mint, the later being increased by roots, not seed. Even though these are annuals, or treated as such, and are therefore short-lived, usually they can be cut quite severely, and then nursed a while, that is, fed with a little liquid plant food and grown outdoors, where they will begin shooting up again. Meanwhile, other, fuller plants will be taking their place.

As always, much depends upon the space available, but it is often possible to erect some shelves on which pots can stand while they are holding seeds and seedlings. They need to be in good light when they have germinated, otherwise the plants become drawn and of little value. Herbs grow well under fluorescent lights at all their stages.

It is not necessary to use large pots for these successional sowings. Pots with roughly a 1 pt (0.5 liter) capacity will do, although the larger the pot, the better a plant usually does. What is most important is that the soil should be good. It is possible to buy specially mixed soils, confusingly called composts, which have been scientifically designed for seed sowing and for transplanted seedlings – for the latter they are known as potting soils. Seedlings need a slightly different food than older plants and they do not need it quite so rich, which is

also be fed with a soluble plant food once it is growing well.

To save time and space, it is also possible to fill a pot almost to the top with plant soil mixture and then to add a shallow top layer of seed soil mixture. This means that seed can be sown thinly in the top layer. The seedlings need not be transplanted, although they are almost certain to need thinning out. Their roots will grow down into the richer soil when they need it. Usually, with the quick-growing herbs, you can allow three to five plants in each 5-in (7-cm) pot.

Do remember that contained plants of all kinds need water, and in hot, dry weather, they may need watering two or three times a day. Usually, the smaller the pot, the more likely it is to dry out quickly, even disastrously – because sometimes it is not possible to revive a plant that has become dehydrated. If the surface soil is damp to the touch, the plants' roots are probably moist enough. A pot in which the soil is too dry will give an empty ringing sound when rapped. One way to prevent too rapid loss of water is to plunge each pot up to its rim in a bed of peat that is kept constantly moist, though not sodden. Rows of pots can be plunged in troughs or boxes. Pots in shade do not dry out so quickly as those in the sun, but not all herbs like deep shade.

Pot-grown herbs (*above*) can be raised in a thin layer of seed compost overlying a coarser potting compost. Seeds must be sparsely sown, then thinned out to give the young plants space. Parsley and mixed herbs (*right*) can be grown in attractive terra-cotta 'strawberry pots'.

why there is a difference in most soil mixtures. However, those mixtures that are known as 'soilless' are sometimes suitable for all purposes, so one should read carefully the descriptions on the wrappings to know which to use.

It is possible to use the same soil in the pot after the old plant has been removed, so long as this has not been diseased in any way. Where this is done, the old soil should be topped with new, and the plant should

Parsley is a herb that seems in demand and, fortunately, it is very easy to grow this plant in a variety of ways. It can, for instance, be grown in one of the specially designed terra-cotta pots known as 'strawberry' or 'crocus' pots, which have pockets made all over the surface. These have one disadvantage, in that the water, poured in at the top, courses down and out through every hole, which means that the soil at the core does not get properly soaked. Once the plants grow well they block the holes and the water loss is not so great. It is best, in the early days, to stand the jar in a low bowl or deep saucer and to keep this filled with water when the weather conditions are dry. When the water no longer courses out of the holes immediately, the pot can be taken from the saucer and stood on its own, when it should be watered from the top.

Parsley also grows well in a hanging basket. Line this with moss, plant the parsley by pushing the seedlings through the moss from the outside of the basket. Begin at the bottom of the basket and cover the parsley roots as you go. Once the lower portion is planted, stand the basket in an empty buc-

Light plastic troughs are ideal for raising miniature gardens in the kitchen. Even hanging baskets can be pressed into service as herb gardens. Here, a parsley basket is shown.

ket while the upper sides and the top area are planted. Water the plants carefully. Hang the basket in partial shade and water it regularly.

Constant watering, which is so essential

351

Paving stones can be lifted from a terrace or patio and the space used to raise herbs. Here, a gangly fennel plant basks in the reflected warmth of the sun-heated tiles.

for most contained plants, tends to leach out the soluble plant foods from the soil, and when this happens plants will become starved and spindly. For this reason it is wise to feed plants regularly with a soluble plant food.

It is possible to raise a good supply of herbs in window boxes and tubs so long as the soil is rich and is kept well watered and fed. As we have seen, some herbs prefer sun and some shade, so this should be taken into account when planning what herbs are to be grown and where. Window boxes need to be fairly deep – not less than 6 in (15 cm), but deeper if possible to allow good root development.

Where a paved patio or backyard exists, it is sometimes possible to lift an occasional paving stone and to make this area into a tiny herb patch. Where it is possible to lift more than one stone, try to make this appear planned rather than haphazard. Three linked stones might look better than three isolated ones. On the other hand, it might be best to lift a stone from each of the four corners, or in such a way that you leave a square or a diamond-shaped bed in the center. If there is a shady corner, this could take a large and handsome angelica or a stand of feathery fennel.

One good way of making the most of a little space is to build a raised wall along one or more sides of a yard or patio, two or three bricks high. This, like the area from which a paving stone is lifted, should be filled with good soil. Thyme (or rosemary in mild climates) could be trained to cover some areas of the wall. This would look well alternated with any other good climbing plant, such as roses or nasturtiums.

6 Herbs in winter

There is no doubt that fresh herbs are best and are certainly more versatile. It is possible to flavor dishes with dried herbs, and later on we discuss ways of drying, but these are not really suitable for mixing in salads or for garnishing. Part of the herb's value is its visual appeal – and fresh green leaves, no matter how finely chopped, always look better than dried flakes or powder. Of course, herb-flavored vinegars help to impart herb flavors to salad dressings, but ideally one needs fresh green herbs the year through. Fortunately, there are some that will provide leaves in winter. Naturally, supplies depend upon the weather or the season and on the district or locality in which the garden is situated. In a mild season or in an area where severe frosts are rare, it should be possible to gather fresh herbs of some kind through from the end of summer to spring when larger supplies become available.

In some cases it is simply a matter of protecting the plant with Hotkaps; parsley, for example, responds to this treatment. It is worth pointing out that all herbs will grow best in winter and come to less harm if they are on well-drained soil and in a sunny, well-sheltered position. In gardens where the soil and conditions vary considerably, it is worth setting aside an area for winter herbs. Parsley can also be grown in a cold frame. Some people simply lift the plants in early autumn and transplant these in the frame. As a rule this is a quicker method of supplying leaves than making a late sowing in the frame, but much depends upon the amount of space that is available.

Some other herbs can be lifted, and these are usually transplanted into pots or boxes and grown on in more warmth than can be provided by a cold frame, in a greenhouse for example, or even indoors under lights. These include basil, fennel, mint and tarragon. Rosemary can be pot grown entirely, brought indoors and stood in good light, and taken out again in spring. This should be necessary only in cold regions because rosemary is hardy enough for most gardens so long as it is given a sunny and sheltered spot.

The soil is usually moist in autumn and,

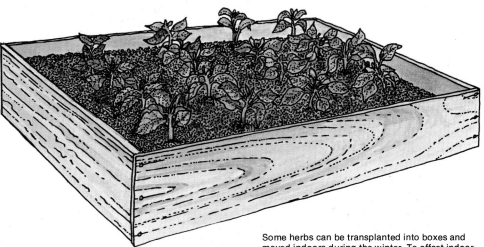

Some herbs can be transplanted into boxes and moved indoors during the winter. To offset indoor gloom they can be placed under fluorescent lights.

as a rule, plants can be lifted easily enough, but should the season be dry, water the plants well for an hour or two before lifting so that the roots come up in a moist mass. Select a flower pot that will take the root ball comfortably. If necessary, place a little good soil at the bottom of the pot. The crown of the plant should be kept above soil level, just as it was when it grew in the garden, yet there should be a space left between the soil surface and the rim of the pot to take water. Fill any space between the root ball and the sides of the pot with good potting soil. Make sure that this is firm, as firm as the soil in the root ball. Pour in a little soil to begin with and then ram it down with the fingers or a stick. Add a little more and so on until the top level is reached. Water the plant in and let it drain. Leave it out of doors in a shady place for a few days before bringing it indoors to let it become settled in the pot. Spray the foliage over with clean water from time to time, but do not keep the soil wet. Let this dry out a little so that the roots are activated into working properly to search for moisture. Do not let the soil become too dry, however. When you water next time, pour in the

water so that the space between soil and pot rim is filled. The water should course through the soil.

Mint can be grown in a deep seed box. Almost fill this with soil. Spread the mint roots all over the surface, cover them with more soil and water them in well. Bring the box indoors. Incidentally, remember that mint will go on producing shoots well into early winter if you keep cutting the plants and prevent the stems running to flower.

As with all other herbs, it is more helpful to fill more than one box of mint so that boxes can be brought in in succession. If you grow mint in a pot on a sunny window-sill, keep it standing in a saucer of water. When growing mint in pots, see that one-third of the pot is filled with drainage material, e.g. shingle, pebbles, broken flower pots (remember, though, that clay pots are

Though unusual for herbs, Hotkaps can be used to give them an early start outdoors.

Herbs raised indoors in pots must be given an adequate growing medium. Drainage material should be laid in the bottom of the pot. Bits of pebble and broken pot fragments, coarse gravel and charcoal pieces are all suitable for this purpose. They should be topped with a good potting compost in which the plants' roots can flourish and grow.

clay pot

charcoal nuggets

pebbles
broken pot shards
crushed brick

potting
compost

becoming rarer) and crushed brick, topped with a few nuggets of charcoal. This will ensure that the soil stays moist but does not become water-logged and sour.

If space is available, it is possible to raise a succession of batches of marjoram, basil and chives, simply by sowing a pinch in small pots, then snipping the entire growth off as soon as it is large enough to be of use. Onion seed can also be grown this way and the pungent 'grass' is excellent in winter and early spring salads.

It is important to understand that potted herbs are not house plants and will not tolerate the low light intensity indoors for long. Even a sunny windowsill does not give as well-lit a home as a place outdoors. If plants soon become drawn and spindly, they are not getting enough light. Sometimes plant foods help to correct this weak growth a little. It helps to turn the container a quarter turn each day so that all parts of the plant face the light at some time. If you don't already have a fluorescent light set-up for plants, this may be the time to consider such a purchase.

It is also important that the air in which the plants are growing is unpolluted. Domestic gas and oil fumes both take their toll of many plants grown indoors.

7 Cosmetic and potpourri herbs

Borage (*left*), with its brilliant blue flowers, makes a refreshing hot or cold tea. Both its furry leaves and bright flowers are used for this purpose.

Honeysuckle (*right*) twines itself decoratively along walls, fences and arches. Its fragrant flowers add a delightful scent to potpourris.

Lavender flowers (*far right*) are used to make scented water, lavender bags and to lend scent to potpourris. The flowers can also be candied.

Many herbs are grown for their sweetly scented leaves and flowers or even for their roots. From them are made potpourri, scented waters, scented sugars and other confections, tisanes or teas, conserves and syrups, shampoos and soaps, to mention only a few of the most important products. Besides adding to the spice of life, in more ways than one, these same plants add greatly to the interest, attraction and charm of a herb garden.

We have already seen that in some cases, such as with roses and lavenders, plants can be used as boundaries. Carnations and pinks can be prettily grouped among evergreen thymes in a border and since the gray-green foliage of these plants is handsome and also evergreen – although perhaps not so profuse in winter – the plants furnish a border for most of the year.

Hyssop will produce purple and pink flowers that look pretty among green parsley or feathery dill. Bergamot adds height as well as color to a border.

Honeysuckle can be grown up poles, over archways or trained to cover a wall or a bank. Where there is space for climbers and the climate is mild, the sweetly scented jasmine, *Jasminum officinale*, can be grown. The white flowers go in potpourri and can be used for jasmine tea. The yellow winter jasmine, though hardier, is not scented.

In a well-protected garden or in mild areas, the lemon-scented verbena, *Lippia citriodora*, deserves to be grown. This is a shrub that sometimes makes a small tree and is deciduous. The fragrance of the leaves is very strong. Another, smaller shrub, the sun rose, *Cistus ladaniferus*, which needs a sheltered place and light well-drained soil, has aromatic leaves. So does the neat, shrubby St John's wort, *Hypericum patulum*, which smells of resin and tangerine when the leaves are bruised. Its handsome variety *Henryi* is also scented. Mock orange or *Philadelphus coronarius* and any of the other fragrant species of the same genera are ideal for scented gardens. If these are to be screened or divided from the rest, it is possible to make a border from scented

shrubs, including roses and lavender, thyme, rosemary and, of course, bay, climate permitting.

As one would expect, the roses used for potpourri and scented toilet waters or other items, should be highly scented. Usually, the red-petalled roses are most highly favored since these usually have the sweetest perfume, sometimes with a hint of lemon in it, but this is not a hard and fast rule. Both modern and old-fashioned varieties and some species can be used. Among the most scented species are *Rosa centifolia*, the cabbage or Provence rose; *R. damascena*, the damask rose; *R. gallica officinalis*, the French rose; and all of the many varieties of the moss roses.

It should be understood that these are not roses for small gardens. Often they are called 'shrub' roses because they are not pruned back hard each year like the modern hybrid teas and floribundas. In time each bush occupies an area of ground over several feet square (half a meter square). One should remember also that if the roses

The pretty open flowers of the briar rose (*left*) can be trained as colorful hedges. Bright nasturtium flowers (*below*) also lend a lovely spicy taste to salads.

The delicate pink moss rose has a ravishing scent. Though brief-flowering, it is ideal for potpourris.

instead of *R. eglanteria*. It has a double variety, *duplex*. Although the natural habit is to grow 5–7 ft (150–200 cm) tall, this rose makes a good low hedge if it is clipped back each spring just before growth begins. If, later, the leafy shoots are taken for drying, this also tends to keep the plants neat and compact.

Of course, not all of the plants used for potpourri, for liqueurs, for candying or for any of the other uses, need be grown in a herb garden proper. Some can be set about the garden as isolated plants – shrubs are often best grown this way. Some can take their place in the usual type of border or bed. Some can be used as ground covers. This term is given to plants that grow so thickly that in time they cover a large area of soil with a thick cover of foliage. This discourages the growth of weeds because it prevents their seeds from germinating freely. Ground covers also help to keep the soil moist round the base of shrubs and taller plants.

One of the best plants for this purpose is a little woodland plant, the woodruff, or *Asperula odorata*. The scented dried flowers can also be used as a tea. They are some-

are to be gathered when they are at their best, they will not add much to the color in the garden.

The scented-leaved sweet briar, which has already been described, is sometimes sold under its synonym, *R. rubiginosa*,

Recipe for a herb potpourri

Leaves (dried)	Flowers
angelica	borage
basil	camomile
bay	elder
bergamot	lavender
borage	lime
lemon balm	marigold petals
lovage	nasturtium
marjoram	rose petals

mint	violet
rosemary	*Spices*
sage	cinnamon
sweet cicely	cloves
tarragon	nutmeg

Place a selection of leaves, flowers and spices from the above lists in a wide bowl in layers, using the most attractive flowers for the topmost (visible) layer.

---

times mixed with China tea to make it go a little further as well as to enhance its own fragrance. It is also, of course, the main flavor of May wine.

Another good ground cover, with larger leaves than the woodruff, is *Geranium macrorrhizum*. Bruise the leaves, either by accident or on purpose, and their powdery fragrance fills the air. Thymes also can be used as carpeting plants, as we have already learned, but these need not necessarily spread themselves on stone or pathways. They will help to clothe a bank.

Pinks are extremely hardy plants. They will grow in ordinary soil and will flower freely so long as this is rich. Prepare the soil well before planting and feed the plants with a liquid plant food in spring and autumn. Pinks like the sun. They can be grown in beds, where their attractive

Choose the ingredients for a potpourri with care. A well-made one will remain scented for years.

gray-green tufted shoots will soon smother the ground. They also look good grown in a wide band to edge a path. And they also look attractive this way sprawled out before lavender. They will even carpet the ground below apple trees or some similar plants; so long as they are not in deep shade, a little partial shade during the day will do them no harm.

There are annual, biennial and perennial kinds of pinks, but naturally, those with the most petals are the best for potpourri. There are some highly scented double varieties of *Dianthus plumarius,* some of which possess a strong clove fragrance. Consult catalogs for varieties and descriptions.

It is possible to make an attractive border of all scented plants, concentrating on those whose flowers are used, but alternating them with some of the more attractive of the scented-leaved kinds. Fortunately, many of these are a soft gray-green and so are the perfect foil and buffer alike for any vividly colored blooms near them.

A few members of the daisy family can be grown. Costmary, *Chrysanthemum balsamita,* has attractive gray-green leaves and tiny, yellow, button-like flowers borne in clusters on straight stems. Camomile, besides being used for tea, can add to the attractive appearance of potpourri and contribute a little of its own particular scent into the bargain. The dried petals of the pot marigold, *Calendula officinalis*, also add color and pungency to potpourri.

A few sage leaves can be used in flower mixtures and more of the sages can be grown to provide color. The annual clary, *Salvia sclarea*, nowadays comes in several prettily colored varieties, whose bracts decorating the stem ends are ruby, magenta, purple and violet. These give more color than scent to potpourri, but their scent is stronger when the flowers are dried.

Artemisias – of which family tarragon is the best known herb, although some of the others are used in the preparation of liqueurs – are more scented than pungent. These include lad's love or southernwood, mentioned earlier. *A. absinthium* is common wormwood, *A. vulgaris* is mugwort, *A. pon-*

tica is Roman wormwood, *A. tridentata* is the sage bush (a confusing name since this is not a sage), which grows really tall, 6–8 ft (2–2·5 m), and is silvery and fragrant.

All parts of the handsome angelica – roots, stems and leaves – are fragrant. Besides being used for confectionery, it plays an important role in potpourri. The roots should be cleaned, dried and powdered for culinary use.

Other culinary herbs that are used in potpourris are marjoram, balm, mints and borage. The latter is used for the flower's color, not perfume, and marjoram, balm and mints can be candied.

Of the annuals, possibly mignonette is the most delightfully scented. Where there

Vivid floral arrangements can be made from herbs. Here, roses, camomile, borage and calendula (pot marigold) spill colorfully from a vase. Wallflowers are a vibrantly colorful addition to any herb garden. Purple-leaved basil (*below*) is an ornamental variety well-suited to herb borders.

is little garden space for it, the plant will grow well in all kinds of containers outdoors and as a pot plant in a greenhouse or on a sunny windowsill. Wallflowers are often overlooked, yet these are an excellent way of adding color to the herb garden in the spring, so long as one takes care to see that they do not smother the perennial herbs. They also grow well in tubs and other containers. They could occupy the area set aside for herbs that will be planted out in late spring, basil for example. When the wallflowers are pulled up after flowering, enrich the soil with a little plant food.

8 Drying herbs

Obviously, all the herbs used in potpourris dry well and the same methods are used for these as for the culinary kinds. Some of the latter dry much better than others. Generally speaking, it is the shrubby labiates, the kinds with lipped flowers, that dry best – sage, thyme, marjoram and rosemary, for instance. These all retain their essential oils and are strongly flavored even when dry or powdered. The same is true of bay. Some of the soft-leaved kinds dry well enough but are likely to be disappointing when used, parsley and mint being examples. Chives, balm, borage, chervil and fennel are really not worth drying. Fortunately, these are available – or can be made so – in winter and the cook does not have to depend upon dried supplies.

Usually just the tips of stems are cut. They should be cut, not picked or pulled, so that they come away cleanly from the plant with no faded stem ends or portions of root with soil attached still clinging to them. By picking the tips the plant is encouraged to make more growth. The time to gather herbs is when the plants are ready to come into flower, for it is at this time that their flavors are strongest. However, this is not a hard and fast rule, and many people harvest the herbs two or three times a year.

If many herbs are to be dried, it is best to make the shoots into small bunches of one kind so that once these are hung up, the air can circulate round each shoot.

There are various methods of drying the bunches. If the weather is warm and dry, they can be dried by hanging them upside down outdoors in the shade. They should not be put out until the warmest, driest part of the day and they should not be left outside overnight in case of heavy dews moistening them again. They should not, of course, be hung in any place where they are likely to become dusty.

If there is no suitable place outdoors, or if the weather is damp, the bunches can be hung indoors in a warm kitchen, away from steam, or in a cooling oven.

If only small amounts are to be dried, the simplest method is to spread them out on paper or on a sieve and turn them from time to time so that all parts are exposed to the air. Another easy way to dry small quantities is to place them, in their individual kinds, in small net bags and then to hang these in some dry, clean and airy place. Herbs simply laid on a sunny windowsill indoors will dry very quickly, but one should bear in mind that those that are dried away from sunlight keep their color best. Also, the faster herbs dry, the better their color.

Herbs can be dried in a warm kitchen by hanging them in small bunches before grinding them fine.

When herbs are dusty, make them into bunches, draw them through clean water, agitating them so that any dust is removed and then shake or swish them in the air until all the surplus moisture is thrown off. After this, make them into smaller bunches or spread them out, depending upon what method is to be used to dry them.

Take care when using an oven to dry herbs, because too much heat dries out the essential oils.

It is possible from this point to store them as they are in their bunches. They can, for instance, each be enclosed in a paper or plastic bag to keep them dust-free. Alternatively, they can be cleaned from their stalks and stored in air-tight jars. Some can be mixed and put into small muslin or cheesecloth squares to make a bouquet garni. The dry leaves are easily stripped from their stalks; let them fall onto clean paper and then lightly rub them between the hands to reduce them to crumbs. To make a really fine powder, bay leaf powder for instance, grind the herbs in an electric grinder. Traces of herb flavor can be removed by wiping the grinder around with some lemon juice.

Potpourri petals and leaves are not usually rubbed or crumbled. Incidentally, one of the best and least troublesome ways of drying petals is to use the string bag method. Pack the petals in loosely and use a large mesh netting. When the petals seem dry, spread them out in some airy place indoors to let them finish off.

If cut herbs are to be kept for a day or two, it is best to treat them as cut flowers and to stand them in water out of direct sunshine. If they are to be kept in a refrigerator, store them in an airtight container but not too near the freezer compartment.

Herbs will deep freeze, but the longer they are left frozen, the more they will lose their flavor. Chives will not keep their texture or their flavor, yet vichyssoise soup flavored with chives will freeze well. This soup should have the chives added at the last moment.

Mint is best made into mint sauce and frozen in small quantities.

Parsley should not be chopped if it is to be deep-frozen or it will lose most of its flavor. Wash and dry the sprigs after the main stem has been cut off. Press these down into a container and freeze. When ready to use, in soups or sauces and not as a garnish, turn out the complete block and either grate or shave it.

A good way to store mixed dried herbs so that they are conveniently assembled and ready to hand is to wrap them up into bouquets garnis, briefly referred to earlier. The basic herbs that should always be included are parsley, thyme and bay, but often stronger and more aromatic herbs are needed, especially for marinades. It is a good plan to prepare a few special bouquets for special dishes in which different herbs can predominate. Thus for boiling fowls or chicken there should be mostly tarragon, and for beef stews, extra marjoram. For a court bouillon for fish, one could make a bouquet to include parsley roots, celery, fennel, thyme, bay, coriander seeds and a few peppercorns.

If you intend to give herbs as gifts, these wrapped bouquets can be packed into airtight glass jars, where they will not quickly lose their flavor. If you are certain that the recipient will soon store them, you could assemble them in a Cordon Bleu garland,

A Cordon Bleu bouquet (*above*) is a splendid wreath of intertwined herb sachets, shallots and bay leaves. Dried herbs (*left*) must be stored in airtight jars to preserve their scent.

illustrated here. This is easily made. First prepare the little bags. Cut three- or four-inch squares of muslin and have ready lengths of fine twine. For a small bouquet garni use a level teaspoonful of the mixed, crushed herbs. Gather up the four corners and tie the little bundle lightly, using the twine and leaving a long end so that the bag can easily be pulled out from the pot.

Make a circle of plastic-covered wire-netting by taking a strip, rolling it up and then shaping it. Cover this with blue crepe paper. Turn the bouquet garni bags into 'apples' by pushing a clove into the center of each. Back each apple with two bay leaves. You can mount these on the wire-spined 'twistems' used to close bags. Use the thread on the bag to fasten these to the apple and to tie the bunch to a cocktail stick or to another twistem. Push the stick down through, or twist the other twistem round, the wire-netting. Alternate the apples with shallots, also mounted on false stems.

9 Wild herbs

Some of our garden herbs have been brought in from the wild. Others have escaped and become native. Most of the wild herbs are gathered nowadays to make wines and preserves, but some continue to be valued for their old uses. Of these, the elder blossom serves us well. The dried blossoms can be added to tea, to gooseberry jams, pies and dishes of all kinds to add a muscat flavor. They can be pounded into lard to make a soothing ointment for burns, and they can be mixed with dried peppermint to make a tisane against influenza. Freshly picked, they can be held by the stem and dipped in batter and fried, then drained and sugared and eaten as a dessert. Dandelion leaves are good in salads and the flowers make a delicious wine, as does white

The delicate white-flowered elder (*bottom left*) grows wild in hedges and fields. Elder blossoms make a refreshing tea. Hundreds of different varieties of wild rose (*above*) brighten countryside fields. The leaves of dandelions (*left*), one of the most common herbs, make delicious salads.

clover. Red clover can be made into tea to ease whooping cough. Feverfew, often confused with camomile, makes a tonic tea that is also soothing for a bad cold.

Thyme, marjoram and mints will flavor meat dishes, and can also be blended into potpourri. With them you can use lime flowers, meadowsweet (also a relief from diarrhoea, 1 oz dried herb to a pint of water in wine glass doses), camomile, hawthorn, sweet clover, sweet cicely, sweet flag leaves, tansy, woodruff, yarrow and wild roses.

365

10 Uses of herbs

To many people, herbs are simply plants that are used, usually in a dried state, to flavor meats and stuffings or to give zest to soups or sauces. Yet herbs can play a much more important role than this. Before the introduction of modern chemical drugs, herbs were the source of a wide array of medicines, salves and ointments of all kinds. The word 'drug' comes from the Anglo-Saxon 'drigan' – to dry – and is a reference to the manner in which medicinal plants were preserved for use.

In former times such plants, most of which are now neglected, were grown in special plots or were gathered in fields or forests. People believed that there was always a plant somewhere that could be used to cure, or at least counteract, the ill effects of every disease or pain.

It seems that some plants were chosen simply because they appeared to have some obvious affinity with a disease. Thus, the bright, yellow-flowered greater celandine with its acrid juice was considered a herb to be used against jaundice. Herbs were also widely used to staunch wounds and to knit broken bones, as well as to make fomenta-

Vinegar can be given a delicious and subtle herbal flavor by allowing sprigs of thyme to marinate in it.

tions and poultices for swellings and for wounds that had turned septic. The pretty little centaury is said to have been so named because a Greek centaur used the plant to heal the wounds made by a poisoned arrow.

To this day many herbs are still used as a prophylactic against colds or as a febrifuge. Others are to be recommended as gargles for sore throats.

A great many herbs, particularly the

Most teas are intended as refreshing drinks, but some are particularly noted for their medicinal and soothing qualities. Most are brewed in the same manner as ordinary tea and are taken either hot or cold. Camomile is a very popular tea and is deliciously fragrant. Woodruff tea, although it can be drunk on its own, is also blended with Indian or China teas to make these go a little further and to enhance their flavors. At one time mugwort, *Artemisia vulgaris*, was used as a tea substitute, even though its original use was in the brewing of beers. Lime-flower tea is considered by some people to be the most refreshing of all.

In the past many more herbs were used in salads than are today, and this included the flowers as well as the leaves, as the vegetables we now know as salad were not so intensively cultivated then. The memory lingers on, however, in the name of salad burnet, a plant that has a hint of cucumber in its scent and is still to be recommended for salads.

Herb teas (*above*) are some of the most refreshing hot drinks. They are renowned for their restorative and soothing properties. Tarragon (*right*) will impart a delicate flavor to olive oil.

aromatic artemisia group (such as mugwort and wormwood), are used to flavor liqueurs. Juniper berries are used to flavor gin and, like so many other herbs, are also used in cooking, especially to flavor sauerkraut and many meat dishes, such as veal. Sorrel was highly valued in the days when only salt-preserved meat was available in the depths of winter because it is a natural tenderizer. Leaves wrapped round a joint before it is cooked render the meat more palatable.

Few people consider Indian or China tea to be made from a herb, yet the *Thea* (also known as *Camellia*) *sinensis* leaves that are infused or brewed are but one of the many different kinds of teas or tisanes made from the leaves or flowers of plants. In many countries teas are also made from plants other than this camellia relative. For instance, in North America a brew made from bergamot is known as Oswego tea.

Savory dishes

ANGELICA
Angelica archangelica

In salads, use raw stems and thick leaf midribs.

BALM, LEMON BALM
Melissa officinalis

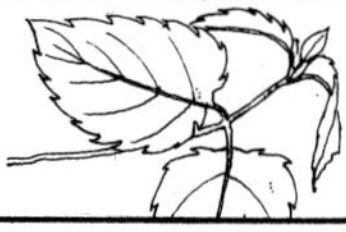

Use chopped finely in sauces and salads, in stuffings o
forcemeats for veal and poultry.

BASIL
Ocimum basilicum and
O. minimum

Use fresh or dried with tomatoes, white fish, ham and
many Italian dishes. Makes a splendid garnish for bear
of all kinds, and squash, especially zucchini.

BAY
Laurus nobilis

Essential in bouquet garni. Use fresh or dried to
flavor savory dishes. (Dried leaves can be ground to a
powder, which should always be stored in an air-tight
container.)

**BERGAMOT, OSWEGO
TEA**
Monarda didyma

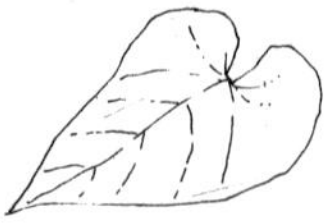

Use fresh leaves and flowers in salads, but in
moderation because of their pungency.

BORAGE
Borago officinalis

Use very young leaves in salads.

CAMOMILE
Anthemis nobilis

CARAWAY
Carum carvi

The leaves and stems are not eaten. The seeds are used
as a spice.

CHERVIL
Anthriscus cerefolium

As an essential ingredient of *fines herbes*, with parsley
and tarragon, it is used in omelettes and other egg
dishes, salads and salad dressings, and for poultry
and some white fish. Use as a delicate garnish for
vegetable purées, or with shell fish and with cream
soups.

CHIVES
Allium schoenoprasum

Cook only by adding to a dish at the last moment or as
garnish or condiment. Cut 'grass' finely with scissors.
Mix with sour cream to garnish baked potatoes.

Sweet dishes	Drinks	Potpourris, etc.	Other uses
Cook stalks as a sweet or as a conserve mixed with rhubarb. Candy them for confectionery.	Use leaves as a tisane. Use roots in liqueurs.	Dry roots for potpourri.	
		Dry and mix in potpourri.	
Use fresh or dried in milk puddings.		Mix leaves or powder in potpourri.	
	Use fresh or dried as a tisane or mix dried leaves with Indian tea to make it go further and add to its flavor.	Mix dried flowers and leaves in potpourri.	
Cook young leaves in batter, with the flowers, as fritters. Flowers can also be candied.	Add sprigs of fresh flowers and leaves to fruit cups and iced drinks.	Use dried flowers for color in potpourri.	
	Main use, fresh or dry as a soothing tisane. Gather daisy heads when the outer ray petals begin to turn back but while centres are still bright.	Mix dried flowers in potpourri.	Boil flowers in rain water as a hair rinse for blondes.
The leaves and stems are not eaten. The seeds are used as a flavoring in confectionery.			

CORIANDER *Coriandrum sativum*		**Savory dishes** The aromatic seeds are used as flavoring, and are an important ingredient in curries. Coriander is always included in mixed spice.
CUMIN *Cuminum cyminum*		Use as a spice in curries and in sauces for fish.
DILL Peucedanum graveolens		Cook young shoots, like mint, with new potatoes and add moderately to potato dishes. Garnish peas with the finely chopped leaves. Excellent with cucumber. Use flower heads and seeds to flavor cucumber pickles. Use seeds (very pungent) in heavy white sauces.
FENNEL Foeniculum vulgare		Cook young leaves or shoots with fish and meats. Use raw with canned fish, chopped finely like parsley. Blend in curries. Seeds are very pungent and good in sauces and fish mousse. Fennel dries well, but becomes strongly flavored and must be used with care.
GARLIC *Allium sativum*		An essential ingredient in many dishes. The individual bulbs, known as 'cloves', are either crushed or chopped. Leaves can also be used.
LAVENDER Lavendula officinalis		Not often used in cooking, but can be used like rosemary with poultry.
LOVAGE Ligusticum officinale		Good substitute for celery flavor. Use stem in stocks and bouillon. Use young leaves, ribs and stems finely sliced in salads or soups. Use moderately when dried.
MARJORAM Origanum dictamnus, O. marjorana, O onites		An essential bouquet garni herb for marinades. Use sweet or knotted marjoram in casseroles, stews, soups and terrines. Dries well, but use discreetly. Suits lamb, pork and beef. Pot marjoram is best for salads and egg dishes. Mix with thyme and parsley for scrambled eggs and omeletes.
MINT Mentha piperita, M. pulegium, M. rotundifolia, M. spicata		Cook pennyroyal with new potatoes, spearmint with peas. The round, woolly-leaved apple mint is best for mint sauce. Mint leaves can be used in salads and sauces, or chopped and sprinkled on lamb and mutton for roasts. Does not dry well because aroma becomes too strong.
NASTURTIUM Tropaeolum majus		Once known as Indian cress because of the cress-like taste of its flowers, leaves and seeds. All can be used in salads, and the seeds can be pickled.

Sweet dishes	Drinks	Potpourris, etc.	Other uses
Coriander is used in sweets and for flavoring liquor, especially gin.			
			Use in veterinary medicine as a carminative.
Use the seeds, which are very pungent, like caraway, to flavor bread and cakes.			
Sprigs in a jar of sugar will scent and flavor it.		Used mainly in toilet waters, sachets and potpourri.	
Seeds are used in confectionery.			
Can be used to flavour custards.		Pot marigold is best known as an ingredient of potpourri.	
		Mix dried leaves and flowers in potpourri.	

371

Savory dishes

PARSLEY
Petroselinum crispum

An essential bouquet garni herb. Very versatile: seems to suit eggs, all meats and fish. Used widely as a garnish. Can be fried and used this way. As a condiment, chop finely and add to the dish at the last moment to keep the color bright. Best used fresh, but will dry.

POPPY
Papaver somniferum

POT MARIGOLD
Calendula officinalis

Pot marigold can be used to flavor soups and also to make an attractive garnish for a salad. Fresh or dried petals can be used.

ROSEMARY
Rosmarinus officinalis

Good cooked with all meats and poultry. Chop finely and sprinkle on roasts. Mix with chopped garlic for lamb and kid. Use sprig to flavor pea, bean, spinach and minestrone soups and add to old boiled potatoes. Will dry, but becomes very pungent.

SAGE
Salvia officinalis

One of the most popular of herbs, in its dried form it is used mostly in stuffing or forcemeat. Good fresh and well chopped – in cream and cottage cheese or sprinkled on meats to be roasted or grilled.

SAVORY, WINTER AND SUMMER
Satureia hortensis,
S. montana

Summer savory considered to have the finer flavour of the two, similar to thyme. Excellent in forcemeats for goose, turkey, chicken, veal and pork. Mix with chives and parsley for duck. Use for trout and other freshwater fish. Include in bouquet garni for all marinades and when poaching fish. Cook with broad beans and peas.

SHALLOT
Allium ascalonicum

Has a distinct flavor midway between garlic and onion. Can be used young or allowed to ripen and be stored for winter use. Leaves can be used like chives.

TARRAGON
Artemisia dracunculus

An essential ingredient of *fines herbes.* Cook with chicken boiled or roasted. Use for stuffing and pâté, white fish, rabbit, veal and all egg dishes. Use in hollandaise, béarnaise and tartare sauces. Serve in tarragon butter with shellfish. Dries well, but becomes very pungent.

THYME
Thymus vulgaris,
T x citriodorus

Common thyme is an essential bouquet garni herb. Very pungent when fresh, so use discreetly. Use with all kinds of meats, poultry, fish, soups, forcemeats, marinades. Use in onion, squash, eggplant and salsify dishes.

WOODRUFF
Asperula odorata

Sweet dishes	Drinks	Potpourris, etc.	Other uses
The dark gray, oily seeds are used in confectionery.			The seeds are used in bread-making.
Flowers can be candied.	Makes a good tisane, fresh or dried.		When boiled in water resulting liquid makes excellent hair rinse.
Use lemon thyme in milk puddings.		Mix dried thymes of any species in potpourri.	
	Can be used as a tisane or tea. It is often blended with fine teas – China or Indian – to make them go further and to enhance their flavor.	Can be used as an ingredient in potpourri or alone in sachets to be laid among linen.	

Indoor gardening

1 Indoor plants

Plant requirements

Our needs, and those of the indoor plants we try to grow, are very similar. Food, water, light, warmth, cleanliness and shelter are essential to us both and we flourish only when we get the exact degree of each we need. Plants are exactly like their owners. They resist hard and fast rules, respond to individual treatment and differ just as humans do.

But there is more to cultivating plants than this. For example, if two identical plants were bought on the same day in the same city and taken home to seemingly identical houses, one could be dead in a week while the other thrived in spite of the fact that each owner followed what he or she considered to be the same directions for plant care. Different conditions in the two homes could be a contributory factor, one house being warmer, lighter, cleaner and more humid than the other. But the main cause is more likely to be the owner's individual interpretation of the instructions. What does the recommendation 'water lightly' mean to you? Once a day? Once a week? By the teaspoon? Or by the cup? Although the best guide is undoubtedly experience, it is possible to get a rough idea of the cultural requirements of most plants simply by looking at them and perhaps by knowing something of their families.

We can all recognize cacti, for example; they are unmistakable, and most people know that they like as much sun as they can get, plenty of water in summer, but little in winter. So if we are given a plant that looks like a cactus, the probability is that if we treat it as such it will thrive.

This is a particularly simple example,

Note that the flowering plants, mainly cyclamen, in this group are nearest to the window light.

but there are other helpful guidelines we can follow. All flowering plants and all with variegated foliage must have good light to retain their vivid colors. The darker green the leaf the less light the plant will need. Only cacti and certain other succulents will flourish in full summer sun. Only cyperus and certain other marginal marsh plants can tolerate having their roots stand in water.

Detailed instructions for the proper care of indoor plants will appear later, but for convenience most plants can be divided into groups with similar tastes or requirements. The cactus group is particularly easy to cater for. Growing in the open, away from meadows, hills and forests, they are consequently accustomed to the full glare of the sun. So, if we pick out other plants that normally grow in the open, the chances are that they, too, like cacti, will require full sun. Pelargoniums, or common geraniums, love the sun. So do nearly all the succulents, echeveria, kalanchoe, sansevieria, aloe,

Nearly all rebutias are spherical like these and all are among the 'easier' cacti in terms of flowering.

Agave leaves are sharply pointed and saw-edged, so plants should be given plenty of space indoors. *Agave franzosinii* 'Aurea' is easy to grow and long-lived if kept in light, warm conditions.

agave, crassula, sempervivum and the like. These may not be quite so immediately recognizable as cacti, but practically without exception they have thick, fleshy leaves that are capable of absorbing and storing quantities of moisture on which the plants can live during the dry season. All these plants need generous supplies of water in the summer and when they flower, but if they continue to receive the same quantities of water in the cooler months of their resting period, their roots will rot and their leaves or swollen stems will yellow and fall, or alternatively turn soft and slimy. In the cold months some of these plants will actually seem to shrivel, but if you give them more than the smallest drink you will do them more harm than good. Return to regular and plentiful watering only when the plant resumes active growth in full sun. The only real exceptions among the succulents, are the leafy types, epiphyllum, zygocactus and schlumbergera.

Like many succulents, *Aloe spinossissima*, with its prickly leaves, is more interesting than beautiful.

These include the so-called Christmas cactus (*Zygocactus truncatus*) and Easter cactus (*Rhipsalidopsis gaertneri*). They are epiphytes, which grow in their native lands on the topmost branches of forest trees. As such, they demand neither full summer sun nor complete winter drought. They can stand both full sun and drought for a time but neither indefinitely.

Apart from cacti and other succulents, most indoor plants need good light away from full sun, and dryer soil conditions in winter than in summer.

As a general rule, the requirements of one species of a genus, will tend to be similar to those of its fellow species in the same group. Some of the most useful, robust and easily available of all indoor plants are the true ivies (*Hedera*), the figs and rubber plants (*Ficus*), and the philodendrons. All the ivies, whether green or variegated, whether derived from *Hedera helix* (common ivy) or *H. canariensis* (Canary Island ivy), require much the same treatment, although the variegated kinds keep their color best when in good light. There are a great many varieties, some with minute differences and others that vary widely in leaf color or size. All are excellent, and all are easily grown indoors.

The fig (*Ficus*) is also widely spread. Its most famous variety is probably *Ficus elastica*, the rubber plant, which again is found in many versions, some with different leaf colorations but others merely tougher and easier-to-grow examples of the old species. *F. benjamina*, the weeping fig, will grow just as tall as the rubber plant, but it has smaller, daintier leaves and a rather engaging and elegant drooping growth. The Indian laurel (*F. retusa nitida*) has leaves about the size of the weeping fig, but its growth is decidedly upright. More like the rubber plant is the fiddle-back fig, *F. lyrata* or *F. pandurata*, whose large and somewhat crinkled leaves are shaped much like the body of a fiddle or violin.

Quite different are two creeping or trailing figs, *F. pumila* also known as *F. repens* or

Ficus benjamina is a graceful, tree-like member of the decorative and useful fig family.

F. stipulata, the creeping fig, with small leaves on wiry stems, and *F. radicans 'Variegata'*, whose similar small leaves have golden markings on the foliage. Both of these need a little more water than the larger, tree-like examples of the family.

Curiously enough, one of the most useful groups of indoor plants comes from a family that used to be known only for its edible fruit. This is the pineapple, which belongs, with other plants, to an interesting group known as bromeliads. The indoor pineapple is generally more colorful and decorative than the variety that appears on our tables. Striped with green and gold, tinged with pink, and heavily toothed, it is known as *Ananas bracteatus striatus*. A smaller version and one more suited to most interiors is *A. comosus 'Nanus'*. Most of the bromeliads are epiphytes, growing in their natural habitat on the bark of trees rather than in the soil. Their long, slim leaves radiate from an open center to form a cup or vase, which in the jungle fills with rain water, on which the plants feed while their clinging roots draw sustenance from fallen leaves that catch up around them as they drop. It follows, therefore, that indoor bromeliads will be happy in surprisingly small pots with any soil so long as it is well drained. The plants are watered by keeping the central vase or cup topped up with water in imitation of their natural habit. In many species a flower arises from the center of this cup, sometimes at the end of a long arching spike. Some are strikingly beautiful and others very longlasting.

One of the best known of these bromeliads is probably the Greek vase plant (*Quesnelia maramorata* syn. *Aechmea rhodocyanea*), which has gray-green glaucous foliage from which a long flowering stem protrudes bearing a series of spiky, soft pink bracts from which grow a multitude of tiny pink, blue and violet flowers. These soon fade, but the pink inflorescence will last for two or three months. A similar plant is the silver vase (*Aechmea fasciata*).

Other bromeliads normally grown indoors include neoregelia, nidularium, vriesia, billbergia and cryptanthus.

Another plant that is just as easy to grow, was once very familiar, but has since fallen from fashion is the aspidistra, also known as the parlor-palm or cast-iron plant. Popular in Victorian times largely because it was one of the very few plants that would tolerate dark gaslit rooms warmed by smoky coal fires, *Aspidistra elatior* and the more attractive gold-striped form, *A.e. 'Variegata'*, have regained much of their former respectability and are once again in vogue. They are easy to grow and, since they make no particular demands on the indoor gardener, are ideal for the beginner.

It is difficult to convey exactly what an aspidistra plant looks like. To say that the leaves are spear-shaped, about 24 in (70 cm) long and grow arching out from the rhizomatous base on short stems belies its distinctive character. But its general shape is bushy rather than tree-like, trailing or climbing.

Like the aspidistra, the majority of indoor plants have to be classified as bushy because they fit no other category. And there is little one can do to persuade a bushy plant to grow some other way. Some plants can be trained to grow up a wall or along a shelf, but a bushy plant merely occupies a space and bears leaves whose tips are rounded.

Describing a tree-like plant is easier, but to find them indoors is more difficult, for real indoor trees are few. Probably the best known is the familiar India rubber plant, *Ficus elastica*, with some of its relatives,

Sedums or stonecrops (*Sedum pachyphyllum* and *Sedum rubrotictum* are shown here) are of compact shape, like a light, alkaline soil and sunlight. Easy to grow, they can be propagated from the small leaves.

especially the weeping Fig, *F. benjamina.* Less well known, but still a genuine tree, is the cultivated form of the Norfolk Island pine, *Araucaria heterophylla* syn. *excelsa,* a miniature conifer and relative of the monkey puzzle tree. The Norfolk Island pine is an easy plant to grow indoors, having no particular requirements for warmth, light or humidity.

Dizygotheca elegantissima, sometimes known as the false aralia, is much more difficult to sustain. Tall, slim and elegant, with stems standing out from a single main trunk, and each bearing a compound leaf composed of eight to ten narrow, toothed segments, it likes a moderately warm atmosphere, tolerates a few hours of sun in winter (about 68°F, 20°C) but requires protection from all drafts. It is almost impossible to prevent the lower leaves from gradually falling to leave a bare stem at the base, but this can be disguised by setting it among other plants at floor level. On the other hand, this naked stem makes the plant appear more tree-like, which can, of course, be a desirable attribute in some indoor gardens.

Schefflera (*Brassaia*) *actinophylla* is a little tree with palmate green leaves growing at the end of reaching stems or stalks. It grows well and, making a large plant, is much in demand by decorators for floor tubs in houses and offices. It is sometimes known as the umbrella tree, although it is not nearly so like an umbrella as *Heptapleurum venulosa*, which is itself sometimes called *Schefflera*. The foliage here is smaller, more arching, and not unlike the ribs of an umbrella. It too will grow into a fairly large specimen in time.

It is a rare thing in the world of botany to find a bigeneric cross, a plant derived from two separate genera. But in *Fatshedera lizei*, which is a cross between a *Fatsia*, a shrub, and a *Hedera* or ivy, we have a first-class example. The fatshedera can be either a climber or tree-like, depending on how you treat it. It is generally sold as a specimen tree, its one or more main stems clipped or tied to a central stake. If this stake is extended from time to time, the plant can be induced to grow up into a tall, slim tree. An easy and accommodating plant, it has no particular preference for sun or shade, warm or cool conditions, or moist or dry soil.

Other indoor plants, including palms and bamboos, can be trained to grow tall, but most are hardly tree-like. And of the few genuinely tree-like plants mentioned here, all can be grown as shorter, rounder shrubs by the simple process of pinching out the main growing shoot or tip and allowing the side growth to develop. Some plants look quite attractive grown this way, largely because they differ from other varieties of the species.

Plant shapes

To a certain extent, the charm of all indoor plants depends on the way they fit into or highlight their immediate environment. So it is disappointing to bring home a plant, place it in a particular part of the home for which it is eminently suited and then to find after some months that it doesn't look quite right in its chosen spot. Since the plant is often quite healthy, the reason for its looking out of place is probably only that it has

Most indoor plants suffer from overwatering, but the graceful, tall and feathery *Cyperus alternifolius gracilis* is a bog plant and its roots can be allowed to paddle.

grown too large for its position, and this is a further reason to strictly limit the amount of food or fertilizer given to any plant. All plants must be kept growing if they are to be healthy and natural in appearance, but if they are overfed, they will grow large too quickly and often make abnormal leaf development. By thus outgrowing their strength, they will render themselves open to insects and diseases.

Too many indoor gardeners are so anxious that their plants should grow that they let them flourish quite untrained.

To take one example of this unwitting form of neglect we have only to look at the popular spider plant (*Chlorophytum comosum variegatum*), that easy, grass-like plant with slender arching green and cream leaves. This is usually brought home as a mere tuft some 6 in (15 cm) tall growing from the center of a small pot. It grows quickly and in only a few months will have developed into a central mass whence several arching

Ivies indoors can be trained to trail, climb, spread or become a tree or a bush. The picture on the right shows a climbing *Hedera canariensis*.

Many indoor plants grow differently in their natural surroundings. This bushy palm, *Neanthe bella* (1), would normally be a tall tree. *Pilea cadierei nana* (2) should have its growing tips pinched out regularly in order to keep it attractive and bushy. Tradescantias and zebrinas (3) are excellent trailers for the home if their stems are not allowed to grow too long. Philodendrons (4) vary widely, but many are climbers and some will cling with their roots to a nearby wall. The thick, fleshy, spear-like leaves of *Sansevieria trifasciata* (5) have given it the popular name of snake sansevieria.

stems bear a few tiny, white, and rather insignificant flowers. As each small flower becomes a miniature plantlet, a little tuft of leaves with rudimentary roots, the parent plant will drape itself over its original pot and cover the surface on which it stands. In a few more weeks it will cascade over shelf or table. If the plant happens to be standing on a tray filled with pebbles, peat moss or sand, each little plantlet will root in the medium, thereby compounding the problem. All this exuberant growth may look highly decorative for a time, but it will certainly be occupying more space than was originally envisaged.

If you want a big, blowsy, tumbling mass of green and cream leaves, then by all means leave it as it is, but give it enough space to look its best: do not confine its arching stems into little more than a dust trap. With enough space a healthy plant can look magnificent, but if there is not enough room and the plant is cramped and unhealthy, rescue the little plantlets at the end of the arching stems by resting them on a small pot of soil where they will quickly and easily take root. As soon as you have one or two small young plants growing well, move, discard or give away the parent plant and keep only the small plants, which will fit more comfortably and happily into the available space.

Several of the bromeliads will begin to die after they have flowered. This process may take several months or even years and in the meantime they will have produced a young plant from the soil in which they grow. It is quite possible to allow both plants to grow in the same pot until the elder plant has passed its prime, but it is

383

Indoor plants need discipline and training if they are to grow attractively. Pruning and pinching will eliminate overcrowding, let in light and air, and encourage attractive and bushy new growth.

Ivies, shown below, are probably the best-known trailers. They are easy to reproduce by layering. One trailer is led to a nearby pot filled with soil an inch or two (a few cm) of the stem are buried. New roots grow here.

better to discard the old plant before this stage and to repot the new in fresh soil.

Some plants, particularly climbers, such as ivies, grape-ivy (*Cissus rhombifolia*) and kangaroo vine (*C. antarctica*), grow so exuberantly that in a year or so they will form a fat column of foliage from floor to ceiling or will cover a wall. Cutting away some of the long trails in order to thin the plant and make it more decorative again is possible but temporarily disfigures the plant. It is better to take a cutting or two and grow these to maturity, eventually discarding the old and overgrown plant. It is an easy matter to take such cuttings, for all that is needed is to take one of the trailers and remove several inches (centimeters) of foliage from one end. This bare stem should be buried in a pot of soil nearby until after a few weeks it is obvious from the new growth that it has taken root. It can then be separated from the parent plant.

On the other hand, it could be highly decorative to have a plant with a dozen or more trails up to 10 ft (3 m) long. They can easily be attached to a central pillar, cane or string, or can be trained to cover a wall surface by tying the trails to guide string or something similar. Ivy plants can be induced to cling to an undecorated indoor wall in much the same way as they would to a tree outside. Grape-ivy, kangaroo vine and the true ivies can all be trained into

living curtains of greenery to divide any room. Lightly spraying a brick wall where the ivy grows will be sufficient to encourage the roots to take hold. It should be said, however, that these aerial roots are strong. They will do no real damage to the struc-

ture of the wall, but they will certainly mark wallpaper or other surfaces.

Certain climbers, such as ivies, some philodendrons, scindapsus and one or two others, can be encouraged to grow up special supports by tying a fat skin of sphagnum moss or some similar material around a central cane or stick, or alternatively by

Plant trailers can be made to cover a wall or form a partition. Fix the string or canes in position, then tie or clip each trailer along the most convenient.

stuffing a hollow cane of small mesh wire netting with the same material and attaching a trailer to it. The plant will quickly send up aerial roots into it, and will subsequently pull itself up with its own roots so long as the moss is kept moist.

Flowering plants

One of the main reasons why indoor plants make such excellent home decoration is that the majority depend for their effect on their foliage, which changes little over the seasons. Flowering plants are a different matter. They are, almost without exception, grown only for their flowers and when these have passed, the plant itself may have

Many plants will climb a cane covered with moist sphagnum moss, using their aerial roots. A cylinder of wire mesh stuffed with moss can be equally effective.

lost its interest and attraction. For this reason we classify some flowering plants as temporary decoration, to be used and enjoyed only while in flower. But there are some flowering plants, such as the many varieties of the dainty African violet, *Saintpaulia,* which can be kept flowering for almost the entire year; some like cineraria and calceolaria can be grown from seed; while a few, like the familiar and rightly popular *Impatiens walleriana*, or busy Lizzie (also known as patient Lucy and the patience plant), can be constantly propagated from. There are herbaceous pot plants, such as chrysanthemums, which can be bought in flower or in bud, or can be raised from seed or from cuttings. And there are many, special plants, such as azaleas, cyclamens, poinsettias and the like, which are usually grown for special occasions and are only seldom retained for another year.

Bulbs are among the favorite indoor flowering plants. Apart from their obvious beauty and the fact that so many of them herald spring, a major reason for their

popularity is that one can follow their growth from their purchase as plain, brown-skinned spheres to their final flowering in the home.

Among the best spring-flowering bulbs to grow indoors are daffodils, tulips, hyacinths and crocuses. Some can be bought 'prepared', which means that they have been specially treated to flower early with less effort on the part of the indoor gardener.

The care of bulbs for indoor forcing can differ according to variety, so ask for instructions when you buy your bulbs. In general, indoor bulbs should be potted as soon as they are received or bought. Place 3–5 large bulbs, such as tulip or daffodil, in a 6 in (15 cm) pot, usually in late summer or early autumn. They should then be watered and placed outdoors in a trench about 12 in (30 cm) deep or in a cold shed,

suitably protected from mice and other predators, until their roots have grown deep and strong and shoots are beginning to appear – usually in about six or more weeks. They can then be brought indoors into a cool atmosphere, watered as necessary and gradually introduced to normal living conditions, such as bright light, even direct sun, where they will soon come into flower.

Some plants are grown indoors for many years and they flower only occasionally, or sometimes never bloom at all. Cacti and epiphyllums are examples. Without knowing the specific conditions under which such plants are grown, dogmatic directions cannot be given. If the plants are strong and healthy and if they are mature enough to bloom, there is every probability that a change of treatment will in itself induce them to flower.

Narcissus Cragford will thrive in pebbles.

Special crocus pots show off the vivid flowers to best advantage.

Hyacinths grow well in bulb fiber.

Flowering plants must have good light (*see left*) to obtain good results.

One thing to bear in mind is that plants become accustomed to their surroundings and do not like to be moved from one position to another. Find a good spot for your plant and leave it there. If, on second thought, you think it should have more light or some other comfort, move it to what you think is a better place, but try not to shift plants around like furniture. You may find that flower buds tend to appear on a plant where the light is strongest, that is, on the window side of the plant. In this case encourage new buds by turning the pot a quarter turn a day so that all sides of the plant get a chance at the light.

One of the main reasons why a plant may refuse to flower is that it has been hurried along too much. All plants have a dormant, or resting, season and during this period

One needs to be a little more careful when buying an indoor flowering plant. Obviously, a plant that is smothered with bloom and vivid with color, will have the strongest appeal. But if it is at its peak, there is usually only one way it can go – downwards – one exception being the floriferous African violet. Look instead for a plant with a future, one with buds just beginning to open, with strong, green foliage and with the soil in the pot just moist. Never buy a plant with yellowing, drooping, limp or diseased foliage.

they should be given every assistance to rest by cutting down the amount of food and water they are given, perhaps even cutting down the amount of light they receive. At the other extreme, it must be kept in mind that some bloom-shy plants, certain begonias for instance, simply require more light to form buds.

In general, cacti and all other succulents will rest during the winter months and at this time their soil should be kept almost completely dry. If the atmosphere in the home is too warm and dry and some of the plants begin to suffer from extreme deprivation, a little more water will do no harm. But, on the whole, the plants will give a better performance in the summer months if they have been allowed to suspend their activities during the winter. When the warmer and longer days arrive, watering can be stepped up until in midsummer the plants may require as much water as non-succulents. They will swell and grow and, if the light is good, there is every chance that strange and beautiful flowers will appear on mature plants.

The one exception to this method of treating cacti in order to get them to flower is with the leaf, or epiphytic, cacti. These include the popular Christmas cactus or *Schlumbergera truncata* (syn. *Zygocactus truncatus*), the Easter cactus *Rhipsalidopsis gaertneri*, the epiphyllums and *Rhipsalis*, the mistletoe cactus, all of which can produce such large, vivid and beautiful flowers that they have been called orchid cacti. In their native habitat these plants grow high on jungle trees instead of in rocky, desert soil,

If it is winter and the weather is cold or frosty, make sure that the plant is well wrapped when you bring it home. The wrapping paper should cover not only the pot, but the entire plant. At home, place the pot in a bucket of water, submerging it completely, unless the soil is very moist. Wait for the bubbles to rise and when these have ceased remove the pot and stand it to drain.

As the plant develops, the buds will gradually open into flowers, which will eventually fade. Cut them away once they have passed their best. Fading flowers give plants a shabby appearance, may let in disease and certainly consume available food and moisture in the soil without giving anything in return. Far better that this nourishment should go to the developing buds.

All flowering plants of whatever type need good light if they are to develop well, so stand your plant close to a window where it will not get direct sunlight for more than a few hours a day but where the light is usually good. Or grow it under fluorescent tubes for about 12–16 hours a day. Never stand it over a radiator or any other source of heat and, if possible, find a cool spot away from drafts.

Neoregelia carolinae tricolor, a bromeliad, turns a vivid scarlet at the center when its small blue and insignificant flowers appear in the characteristic cup, which should always be kept filled with water.

During the warmer months many indoor plants will enjoy periods outside in sun and rain.

Zygocactus truncatus, the Christmas cactus, has several varieties and can have flowers of several colors. These appear at the tops of the long, flattened stems, which resemble leaves.

Euphorbia milii (syn. *E. splendens*), the crown of thorns will flower continuously throughout its long life.

and for this reason require a different kind of treatment from other cacti.

The Christmas cactus flowers in mid-winter, December in the northern hemisphere, June in the southern, so it will require good light and plenty of water at this time instead of being starved. Its resting period is in summer, when it can stand outdoors in partial shade and rain (not too much of this) to help the flat, leaf-like stems to ripen. Perhaps the easiest way to insure Christmas cactus flowers is to delay bringing the pots indoors after their summer sojourn outdoors. Since cool nights are needed to induce bud formation, leave the pots outdoors until fall is well advanced – mid-October in the northern hemisphere, mid-April in the southern – then bring the pots indoors to a cool, well-lighted window away from artificial light at night.

There are hundreds of varieties of epiphyllum, mainly in various shades of white, pink and red.

Some of our most colorful flowering house plants are known as traditional Christmas gifts. They include *Euphorbia pul-* *cherrima*, the poinsettia, the indoor cyclamen, *Cyclamen persicum*, otherwise *C. puniceum* or *C. latifolium*, and the rhododendron (*Azalea indica*). All do best under well-lighted, cool and airy conditions, hard to find in most apartments and many overheated dwellings. However, these plants show amazing stamina for survival if reasonable approximation of their needs is provided.

Poinsettia is grown mainly for its magnificent, red, pink or white bracts rather than its insignificant flowers, the berry-like objects at the top of the vivid bracts that many people mistakenly think are petals. As a result of a great deal of hybridizing, new varieties are now available that will last in the home for months instead of days. Such hybrids have been known to exist from Christmas to Christmas – the only change being a gradual fading of the bracts' color! They are bred under artificial conditions of daylight and darkness and with chemical treatment, which keeps them dwarf, bushy and well-colored. The roots of these plants should always be kept moist, but not wet, and a cool part of the room (about 60°F, 15°C) in good light will suit them best. It is possible to keep the plants after they have dropped their leaves and to

Epiphyllums (*above* and *below left*) have been the subject of much hybridization, as a result of which huge, magnificent and flamboyant flowers of many colors have been produced. Where space is limited, the plants can be pruned back.

bring them into condition for the following season, but this can be a tricky exercise best left to the expert. It is wise, though not essential, to prune away old stems after they have produced their flowers, because once a bloom has appeared at a particular spot no flower will ever be produced from there again. Try to encourage strong new growth each year to aid flower production since blooms appear on one- and two-year-old branches. It is important to repot the plants if they grow too large for their containers.

Rhipsalis are like smaller, daintier versions of epiphyllums or orchid cacti and they require much the same kind of treatment. A light shade suits them better than strong sunlight and even in the winter their roots like a little water. Greater attention has been paid to rhipsalis in recent years, possibly because some of the epiphyllums grow too large.

A succulent that is not a cactus but a member of an extraordinarily wide-ranging family is the so-called crown of thorns, *Euphorbia milii*, which gets its name from the vicious black thorns growing from its stems and from its tiny vivid, red flowers, which look like drops of blood. Another form of the plant bears yellow flowers. This is an easy and striking plant to grow. It likes full sun and plenty of water most of the time and does not appear to need a resting period.

Cyclamens in full flower can be spectacularly beautiful but the conditions they meet in most homes are so unsuitable that they quickly lose their beauty. They like cool, fresh air and plenty of moisture. It is best not to grow them in living rooms unless you can place them in a bay window where the temperature is much lower than the rest of the room. They make excellent bedroom plants, where the temperature is usually a little lower and the air fresher. Give them good light but they should never be placed in direct sun.

The rhododendron, or *Azalea indica*, has also been grown under highly artificial conditions for the Christmas trade. Its roots have usually been heavily pruned so that they will fit into a comparatively small pot, and this makes the plant highly sensitive to any shortage of water. The roots must be kept moist, but not soggy, at all times. The best indication of their state is the portion of brown main stem immediately above the soil. This should show up wet and dark for an inch or so. If it is a uniform light brown, the plant is badly in need of water. The best way to treat it is to plunge the entire pot into a bucket of tepid water, leaving it there until bubbles have ceased to rise from the soil surface. Then remove, drain and replace in position. The same cool indoor temperatures needed by the cyclamen apply also to the azalea, making it an ideal plant for a cool window, a plant room or a sun porch. Under such conditions the plants remain spectacular for many weeks. Potted plants can be summered outdoors in partial shade: sink the pots to their rims in soil, and leave outdoors until late fall before bringing the plants indoors for later bloom.

The safest way to water a dry azalea plant (*above*) is to place the pot in a bucket of water, keeping the blooms dry. Wait until bubbles cease to rise from the soil surface, then drain and replace.

The cyclamen (*top*) is available in many colors. Cool conditions are necessary indoors for the plant to last and to continue producing its flowers.

Care of house plants

A selection of the most popular house plants is given below. From this you can tell at a glance what watering, light, temperature and atmospheric moisture conditions your plants need for healthy growth. However, iron cross begonias, cyclamens and poinsettias need different conditions during their dormant periods. Consult your florist about this when you buy the plants.

Watering	heavy	moderate	light
Light	sunny	semi-shady	shady
Temperature	warm	average	cool
Atmosphere	very moist	moist	average
Care needed	much	average	little
Flowering season	winter / spring	summer / autumn	

Plant	Watering	Light	Temperature	Atmosphere	Care needed	Flowering season
Azalea	moderate	semi-shady	warm	moist	much	winter
Begonia masoniana (iron cross begonia)	moderate	semi-shady	warm	moist	much	
Cacti	light	sunny	warm	average	little	winter/spring
Chlorophytum (spider comosum plant)	moderate	semi-shady	warm	average	little	
Chrysanthemums	moderate	sunny	warm	average	much	autumn
Cissus antarctica (kangaroo vine)	moderate	semi-shady	warm	average	little	
Coleus blumei	moderate	semi-shady	warm	moist	little	
Cyclamen persicum	light	semi-shady	warm	very moist	much	winter
Euphorbia pulcherrima (poinsettia)	light	semi-shady	warm	moist	much	
Epiphyllum	light	semi-shady	warm	moist	much	spring
Ficus elastica (rubber tree)	light	semi-shady	warm	very moist	much	
Hedera helix (English ivy)	moderate	semi-shady	warm	very moist	little	
Monstera deliciosa (Swiss cheese plant)	moderate	shady	warm	average	much	
Philodendron scandens (sweetheart plant)	heavy	semi-shady	warm	average	much	
Saintpaulia (African violet)	moderate	semi-shady	warm	average	much	winter/summer
Sansevieria trifasciata (snake plant)	heavy	semi-shady	warm	average	much	
Tradescantia (wandering jew)	light	semi-shady	warm	very moist	little	

Exotics

One tends to think of exotic plants as
orchids, yet some of these traditionally
glamorous and difficult plants are comparatively easy to grow, while other and
apparently less 'exotic' plants are much
more difficult.

The many caladium hybrids, for example, have what is possibly the most beautiful foliage of any plant, at least 12 in
(30 cm) long, so fine and thin as to be
almost translucent, in pale greens and
creams or more vivid tints and shades. The
main veins are usually picked out in contrasting colors. These plants need to be
kept warm, though not uncomfortably so
(about 68°F, 20°C) and in conditions that
are as humid as can conveniently be
arranged, not so difficult to find on most
summer terraces and patios. They grow
from tubers, which come into leaf in spring,
display their beautiful leaves until midsummer and then begin to fade. The tubers
should then be put away in their pots in a
place that is warm and dry, and completely
forgotten until early spring, when they can
be potted up in a peaty soil mixture and
brought into a warm, moist atmosphere for
the foliage to begin growing.

Smaller, thicker and more sturdy leaves
appear on the dieffenbachias, and, although less ethereal and longer lasting, the
foliage can also be very beautiful –
streaked, spotted, blotched and marbled,
usually in various tints of cream and green.
Dieffenbachia picta and *D. amoena* both have
leaves spotted and blotched with cream,
and tolerate warmth and low-light levels
typical of so many modern rooms. Two
popular new hybrids are 'Exotica' and
'Rudolph Roehrs'. The second has large
chartreuse leaves which are edged with
dark green.

The dieffenbachias are collectively

The dignified beauty of *Dieffenbachia amoena* (above)
fits well into the clean lines of modern decor.

Caladium hybrids develop in spring and must be kept
in a warm and humid atmosphere to give of their best.

Dieffenbachia leaves, which can grow to a considerable size, are strikingly marked. Keep them warm, out of drafts in moist soil.

Philodendron oxycardium will cling to a wall or a mossed cane with its aerial roots.

If kept out of full sun and intense heat, caladiums should remain attractive until mid- to late summer.

known as dumb canes, the reason being that their sap contains crystals of calcium oxalate, which causes the tongue to swell painfully if they are taken into the mouth. Plants can be handled perfectly safely – it is only the sap that is poisonous. So if a fading leaf is cut away, for example, it is wise to take precautions and wash the hands thoroughly after the operation.

Most members of the large and useful philodendron clan, mentioned earlier, are easy to grow and quite dependable as well as being comparatively ordinary. *P. melanochrysum* has the same heart-shaped leaves as *P. oxycardium* (syn. *P. scandens* and *P. cordata*), the well-known heartleaf philodendron or sweetheart vine. But although they are about the same shape and size, their color and texture are completely different, the former being a rich green-bronze-gold-copper and having a velvety texture on the upper surface. High humidity, warm temperatures, rich soils and no drafts are demanded by this plant.

395

Begonia masoniana, popularly known, for obvious reasons, as the iron cross begonia, is named after Maurice Mason, an English farmer and distinguished plantsman. Its crinkled, patterned and hairy leaves make it instantly recognizable.

Coleus plants in the widest variations of vivid colors are easy to grow from seed or cuttings. They grow indoors and, in warm areas, in the garden. They like moist soil and plenty of food.

Several of the foliage begonias could be called exotics because of the extraordinary and vivid colors or textures of their leaves. *Begonia rex*, the ivy-leafed begonia, and *B. masoniana* are examples that come immediately to mind. Both will bear flowers but these are insignificant compared to the leaves, which in the former can vary widely in tints, shades, tones and patterns of greens and reds, purples, silvers and whites, some almost furry and others metallic. *B. masoniana* is known as the iron cross begonia because of the distinctive pattern on the soft and crinkled leaves. All begonias, flowering or foliaged, have the same lopsided heart shape in their leaves. Some people find them difficult to cultivate, others easy, and arguments continue about

their care. A rich, peaty soil, some warmth, some light (all begonias do especially well under artificial light) and no particular concessions to humidity seem to summarize the general view. Taking care not to overwater begonias can go far towards avoiding trouble.

Two other beautiful plants with vividly colored foliage are *Codiaeum variegatum*, usually called croton, and *Coleus blumei*. The first has handsome spotted, streaked and mottled leaves, is glossy surfaced and comes in several shapes. The colors are green, gold, cream, red, pink, purple and white. Unless you have a warm plant room, window area or a combination greenhouse-living room where the humidity can be depended on to be high and the light ample – even several hours of sun each day – you had better pass crotons by, as they are not the easiest of plants to grow in the home. Coleus plants can be just as colorful as crotons but, unlike them, their texture is soft and sappy. These plants can be grown quite easily from seed or cuttings.

Three other plants with gorgeous foliage are the prayer plants, maranta, the calatheas and the fittonias. The most distinctive maranta is *M. leuconeura erythroneura*, which has soft leaves of brownish green, with the veins picked out in scarlet edged with cream. Even better known is *M. l. kerchoveana*, sometimes called 'rabbits' tracks' because of the brown-on-green marking of the leaves.

Calathea mackoyana is sometimes known as *Maranta mackoyana*, which it closely resembles. It is commonly known as the peacock plant because of the sheer flamboyance of its leaf coloration and pattern: the colors are silver, green, red, or purple, according to the way the light strikes it, for the upper and lower sides of the leaves differ and the white part is almost translucent except for the dark green veins. Humidity, careful watering so the soil remains moist, and some warmth and diffused light are needed to keep this plant looking its best. It is a good subject for growing under artificial light, but its greatest need is for high humidity.

And finally in this little trio is the snakeskin, or nerve, plant, *Fittonia vershaffeltii argyroneura*, small, delicate and beautifully patterned, as the common name suggests. Too much water will kill the plant, as will too little. Cold will kill it and so will excessive heat. A plant in bright sun will curl up and die almost as you watch it. Somewhat easier to grow is *F. verschaffeltii*, with rather larger leaves, a more velvety texture and a basic green color with red veins.

It is worth persevering with all these difficult and delicate plants, for the sensitive and persistent plant-grower will eventually discover the exact conditions or treatment a certain plant requires.

The peacock plant, *Calathea mackoyana*, is often called *Maranta mackoyana*. With reasonable care this plant will keep its looks for long periods.

So too with orchids, which are as easily grown in the house as a hyacinth. Begin with the simplest and progress to the more difficult, not a hard thing to do when one realizes that there must be something like 25,000 orchid species in the world, that something like ten per cent of all flowering plants in the world are orchids, that they grow wild in jungles, mountains, woodlands, meadows and on roadside verges in many of our most industrialized nations. Orchids were treated with awe when the only examples we saw were those in museums or in the orchid houses of the rich. Those days are over. Many kinds of orchids have been found to be as tolerant of ordinary indoor conditions as common house plants. Although they thrive in window

gardens, they also respond well to artificial light. New methods of propagation mean that a thousand young plants can be easily and inexpensively produced where only a single plant existed before.

All orchids have three petals and three sepals, but one of these petals is usually grown in another form, looking more like a pouch or slipper, and is frequently differently colored or patterned. Just above this curiously shaped petal, known sometimes as the labellum or lip, is the column. This single organ takes the place of the more usual male and female stamen and pistil.

Probably the best known of the slipper orchids are the species commonly called cypripediums, although botanically they are correctly *Paphiopedilum*. *P. insigne* is one of the easier to grow as well as one of the most popular. From 3–6 in (7–15 cm) long, they are generally a greenish-gold with brownish spots and they last from three to eight weeks during their winter season. A great deal of breeding work has been done on the paphiopedilums and there are a large number of hybrids. One of the best known is probably *P. x. Maudial* with beautiful marbled leaf rosettes and long-lasting green and white flowers.

There are a considerable number of paphiopedilums. Some are comparatively large, both as plants and as flowers, while others are less than 4 in (10 cm) tall. Most species have only a single flower to a stem, but some have two, three or four.

The paphiopedilums do not require high temperatures – the cooler the temperature, the longer the flowers last – or strong light, which is one reason why they grow well indoors. But, needless to say, they like as much humidity as they can get, and their compost or potting medium should always be kept moist, although not soggy. All orchid nurseries will sell special orchid compost, usually made of a mixture of osmunda fiber, sphagnum or peat moss, perlite and perhaps some granular peat.

Only one or two of the paphiopedilums have any fragrance, but many of the cattleyas are scented. Instead of a slipper or pouch, cattleyas have a more open, bell-shaped lip, frequently prettily frilled and divided. The cattleyas come in two types, the labiate, or unifoliate, with only one leaf growing from each pseudo-bulb, and the bifoliates with two leaves. There are many hybrids in each type, some large, some dwarf, some with flowers up to 10 in (25 cm) wide, and others with blooms no larger than 2 in (5 cm). Cattleyas like a fairly warm and humid atmosphere and need a drop in temperature at night.

Most cattleyas grow to nearly 3 ft (about 1 m) in height, too large for some homes, but there are some miniature cattleyas offered by specialists. Cymbidiums will grow to nearly 6 ft (over 2 m). However, there is a useful and attractive group of hybrid dwarf cymbidiums, which grow about 12 in (30 cm) or so tall. The color range of the very long-lasting flowers is magnificent. Cymbidiums require a growing compost of fir bark, coarse peat moss and bark fiber, adequate humidity and good light. Keep the compost moist, but not soggy. One of the easiest groups to grow indoors is the odontoglossum, with many species and even more hybrids. It is also one of the most rewarding because of the number of flowers per stem – from about 5 to 35 – and the colors – whites, yellows, reds, pinks, purples. The flowers, which appear in the spring, will last from 3 to 6 weeks. Plants dislike too much heat in both

winter and summer, and prefer to be well ventilated, although never in a draft. The roots should be kept moist at all times.

Also considered rewarding for beginners are the laelias; small, epithytic and with cattleya-shaped flowers, varying from 2 to 20 per stem.

Two little orchids that more often are available from bulb specialists rather than the usual orchid sources are *Pleione formosana* and *Bletilla* (syn. *Bletia*) *striata*. Although they are considered fairly hardy, enduring temperatures to 40°F (4°C), and therefore can be planted in the open in semi-shade and a humus-rich soil, they are also grown in pots. Pleione bears small magenta-pink flowers in spring. Bletilla is similar, but the lavender-pink flowers appear in early summer. Advertized as easy to cultivate by the mail-order firms that sell these semi-hardy orchids from Asia, they may in fact prove difficult to grow outdoors.

Opposite: this small selection of orchids gives some indication of the wide variation in shape and color available. Light is their most important requirement, then humidity and warmth. Feed only in summer and keep out of drafts.

Paphiopedilums (*right*) must have humidity and a moist soil, but need less warmth.

The dainty orchid flowers of *Bletilla striata* (*below*) are easy to obtain indoors in early summer.

Food for thought

There is a curious fascination in growing a plant left over from one's food. To plant an orange 'pip' or seed and watch the little tree growing a few weeks later is always satisfying, and there are several plants that can be grown in this way. Not all will live for long indoors, although the avocado and mango are examples of two exceptionally attractive and durable house plants that can be grown from 'left-overs'.

The miniature orange trees that one can

buy, complete with little oranges, are no more than an acknowledgement of the fascination of growing a plant from a seed that was saved from the garbage can. Do not expect to produce oranges bursting with juicy goodness from your own home-grown tree, however. The flower- and fruit-covered plant you buy is a special dwarf kind, the calamondin orange (*Citrus mitis*). The white flowers are sweetly scented and they appear on the little tree at the same time as the fruits, which are reputed to make a good marmalade.

Keep the plant in a cool place that is sunny or, at least, well-lit. Keep it well fed and slightly humid. Flowers of *Citrus mitis* produce more fruits if they are fertilized, so when they are fully open it is wise to brush

them all very gently with a very soft camel-hair brush.

An avocado seed – so large it resembles a stone – is easy to grow either in soil or water. Plant it only halfway into the soil and watch it split in two as the shoot begins to appear. Or grow it in a hyacinth glass or a jar, its blunt base just touching the water and the more pointed end upwards. (Three toothpicks inserted into the sides of the seed are handy for suspending the seed on the rim of the jars.) Sometimes you will get a single shoot that grows very quickly and quite tall before it puts out its first leaf. In this case, pinch out the growing tip after it has produced several leaves to induce the plant to bush out more attractively.

Mustard and cress, mung beans, alfalfa,

Left: Citrus mitis, the calamondin orange, produces fragrant flowers at the same time as its fruits. Grow in strong light and keep the roots moist.

sesame, wheat and several other sprouting foods can be grown easily enough indoors.

Mustard and cress, so good in winter salads, are easily and quickly grown in a small seedling box or flat on a kitchen windowsill. Fill the tub with any of the prepared mixes available from garden centers and florists or use your own general-purpose soil mixture. Soak well, then sow seeds thickly, merely pressing them into the mixture rather than covering. Slip the flats into a polyethylene kitchen bag and keep from direct sun until the seeds germinate. Remove the bag and place flats in bright light on a windowsill or under fluorescent lights. Cut the seedlings with scissors after a few weeks. Successively sow and crop for a constant supply. Seeds of the other crops, available from most mail-order seed houses usually require different treatment. The easiest way to grow seeds is to put a spoonful into a clear glass jar and cover the neck tightly with muslin or cheesecloth. Pour in a little tepid water through the muslin, shake the seeds around in this, leave for a few minutes and then stand the jar on its side so the water runs out again. Repeat

Plant grown from an avocado seed.

this process for three or four days until it is evident that the seeds have begun to grow.

The easiest way to grow seeds is to put a spoonful of them into a clear glass jam (or other) jar and then cover the neck tightly with muslin.

Pour in a little tepid water through the muslin, shake the seeds around, leave for a few minutes, then stand the jar on its side so the water runs out again.

Repeat this process for three or four days. It then will be evident that the seeds have begun to grow. Remove them when they are large enough to eat.

401

2 Environment

Light

The simple statement that giving a plant light is more important than giving it water will come as a surprise to most indoor gardeners until they begin to examine the proposition in greater depth. In the first place, to deprive a plant of light is a total deprivation. It carries no sources of light within itself. But to deprive a plant of water is less important because the soil in which it is growing is almost certainly moderately moist, and every root, branch, stem and leaf also contains moisture.

As humans we can recognize the importance of moisture much more easily than we can recognize the importance of light. We can tell if a plant has been watered by the color of the surface soil, by the feel of it on our fingers and by the weight of the pot. But we would find it difficult to measure the difference in the quality of light at a south-facing window and in the center of a room. Only by using the mechanical aid of a photo-electric light meter can we recognize the vast difference, a difference of minor importance to us but vital to plants. After all, the reason why plants are grown in greenhouses is to give them not only warmth or protection, but also the maximum possible light.

The quantity of light a plant receives will depend upon the length of day and hence the season, unless one wishes to go into the question of artificial light. Actually, the quantity of light is more important than is generally realized, for some plants such as chrysanthemums are short-day plants, which is to say that they will flower only when they receive a certain limited amount of daylight. This can be critical, and commercial growers have learned to extend the season by growing chrysanthemums for a period each day under the artificial but total shade of black plastic sheets. Other plants, conversely, are grown under artificial light to lengthen their day and so bring on their flowering.

In the home we unquestioningly accept the seasons as they come and we are more concerned about the quality than the quantity of the light our plants receive. This quality of light can vary surprisingly. Light in an industrial city, for example, is considerably weaker than light in the cleaner air of the countryside. Light in a room with a tree immediately outside is much less than in one without, but if the tree is not an evergreen, we can expect more light in the winter when it drops its foliage. Light from a south-facing window is stronger than from a window facing north. Light from a grimy window can equal that from a clean one half its size. Above all, light loses its intensity or quality in inverse proportion to the square of the distance from its source.

Light is vital to plants. Those that flower or have variegated foliage need most light, though not direct sunlight.

402

Never allow any plants to spend a wintry night between curtain and windowpane, where they can easily become frosted.

Cacti and some other succulents are the only plants that can tolerate direct sun on them for long periods of time.

Plants with dark green, fleshy leaves can generally tolerate poorly lit locations better than can plants which are brighter.

This means, then, that in general terms plants should be placed as near to the windows as possible. But this advice must be qualified in some ways. Only cacti and some other succulents can be grown directly in a south-facing window in summer. In other seasons most house plants, with the exception of some large-leaved foliage plants, thrive in sunny windows. If the sunshine seems too strong – some signs of this are yellow or brown-tipped leaves – move the plants back or diffuse the light with curtains. No plants should ever be placed directly in a window that is loose, cracked, or allows drafts to pierce through. Nor should plants be placed between a window and a curtain during times of frost.

It is possible to divide our plant residents into groups: those that demand the most

light, those that need good light, those that like a steady and modest light, and, finally, those that will grow farther away from light. In the same order, choose a south window, an east or west window, a north window and the center of a room or a position away from the light. Follow these rules: all cacti and succulents in strong light, even sunlight; all flowering plants and those with variegated foliage in good light, including several hours of sun; all others in

Top left: plants with variegated foliage tend to lose their attractive coloring if they do not get a regular quota of good light.

the less favored positions. Remember that the darker green and fleshier the leaf, the less light a plant usually needs.

Yet the possibility must be faced that many homes and apartments are woefully lacking in the wide range of natural light, described above, as well as sufficient window space for a number of plants. The solu-

Top right: try to place plants in positions where they will each receive the amount of light they need. They will look better and grow better as a result.

Cacti and succulents react favorably both to strong light and to warmth. Give plenty of water in summer but keep their roots almost dry in colder months.

tion is artificial light and its utilization to supplement natural light is one of the major factors in the current boom in indoor gardening. The set-up can be as extensive or as limited as one chooses. Entire basements or sections therein or other dim-lighted rooms have been transformed into greenhouses and plant rooms, the only source of light for plant growth coming from artificial sources. However, far less complicated arrangements are usual, ranging from simple table model fixtures that can accommodate a surprising number of African violets beneath them to fluorescent tubes installed under a bookcase shelf or a kitchen shelf and even to large, hanging fixtures suspended from the ceiling and raised or lowered as necessary according to the plants' heights.

Beginners often ask why fluorescent rather than incandescent light is specified for plant growth. Actually, incandescent light does benefit plants – and at the same time creates a more pleasing, less glaring illumination for us. A reading lamp that is turned on every evening will improve the growth of the plant beneath it. However, incandescent bulbs give off heat, enough to burn the plants that are too close to them, and are not as economical as the longer-lasting fluorescents, which also are capable of lighting broader areas. The market is now flooded with various kinds of fluorescent tubes and incandescent bulbs engineered to give plants the next best illumination to sunshine. There are several excellent books on the subject. For the time being, however, it is sufficient to point out to the reader that every plant discussed in this book will respond to artificial light.

Too often plants given as gifts are displayed in the living-rooms of homes where the air is polluted with tobacco fumes. (Orchids, in particular, hate smoke.)

The buds of cyclamen will develop and open and the flowers will remain fresh-looking for long periods if the plants are kept in a well-lit but cool and airy location.

405

If a plant must be placed over a source of heat, protect it by standing in a tray filled with gravel or sand kept just moist. The warmth will cause the water to evaporate and keep the plant cool.

Warmth

A certain amount of warmth is necessary for nearly all indoor plants, but less than is generally believed. All ivies, for example, are quite hardy and in most temperate climates will grow as well in the garden as in the house, although possibly with a change in characteristics. Many plants such as cyclamen will remain fresh and immaculate weeks longer in a cool room with a temperature of about 50°F (10°C) than in one heated to the more normal 70°F (20°C).

There is a common fallacy that indoor plants are hot-house plants, but this is not so. Some, it is true, have been bred from plants that originally grew in overheated and humid greenhouses, but without exception these have been educated to accept more realistic living conditions. So long as the home is heated sufficiently to keep out frosts, many indoor plants will grow there quite happily. They will prefer slightly higher temperatures, but given a choice between cooler conditions with clean air and some humidity, and warmer conditions with a stuffy atmosphere and dry air, they will do better in the former.

Most indoor plants, especially those that rely for their interest and attraction on their foliage, have their resting period in the colder months. They remain semi-dormant for some weeks. Their watering should be cut down during this period and they should be fed hardly at all. Yet if they are in too warm an atmosphere, the moisture in the soil around their roots will be baked away and the plants will either wilt or require more water. This will tend to activate the plants into renewed growth before their rest period has been completed.

No plant should be placed too near a source of heat, whatever its type. Even the sun can be too hot for some plants at some times of the day, particularly if it shines through glass. Incandescent bulbs can scorch plants that are closer to them than 12 in (30 cm). If for some special reason a plant must be placed, say, over a radiator,

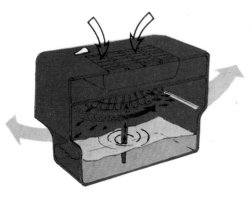

Humidity

We have become accustomed to associating humidity with high temperatures, which need not be so. For example, in a centrally heated room in winter with the temperature at, say, 70°F (20°C) we will find that the relative humidity reading on a hygrometer may fall to 50° or perhaps even less. With a window or two open, the temperature drops but the relative humidity rises. This is simply because the moisture in the room has been evaporated by the heat, and when the windows were closed, the outer air with its inherent moisture could not enter.

When we consider that all plants either grow or originally grew out of doors, it

then it is usually possible to deflect the rising warm air from the leaves of the plant. Another means of providing some protection is to stand the plant on a gravel tray filled with water. The rising hot air will, by this means, produce a moist atmosphere and so do little harm.

Try to avoid great differences of temperature at different times. Some rooms, for example, are heated only in the evenings; during the night they cool off and in the mornings they can be quite cold. Most plants dislike violent changes, although they will adapt to gradual ones. There are, however, a few plants, such as some orchids, that definitely need a temperature drop of several degrees at night to conform with the cooler nights of their tropical habitat.

The most efficient humidifiers send a gentle current of moist air into the room from a reservoir of warmed water (*top left*). One type is shown above.

A significant rise in relative humidity can be gained by placing small bowls of water about the house. They can be made to look decorative with flowers, shells or stones.

Using a plunge pot lessens the risk of overwatering, keeps the flower pot cool and moist, and sends a constant current of humid air up around the plant foliage.

of one or two saucers or dishes of water in a room can significantly raise the humidity level. It is possible to buy quite inexpensive metal containers designed to hang on the back of a radiator that, when filled, gradually increase humidity by releasing water vapor into the room.

Plants can be given their own local humidity without much trouble by standing their pots on a tray holding a layer of constantly moist gravel pebbles or sand, or by making use of what English gardeners call 'plunge pots'

This last aid is important for several reasons. The vast majority of indoor plants are grown in the traditional pot, either clay or plastic, with a hole or several holes in the base for drainage. This means that indoors the pot must be stood in a saucer or some other receptacle to avoid staining or marking the furniture. It is very easy when a plant is watered for the water to come through the drainage hole, fill the saucer and spill onto the furniture. Or we may find that the saucer is filled with water and, unknown to its owner, the plant may be drowning for several days.

The plunge pot is a means of overcoming the problem of providing a localized humidity and of increasing the decorative value of the plant all at the same time. This is a container of some kind that has no drainage hole and is a little larger than the flower pot. It can be a purpose-made pot, a flower vase, a bucket, a salad bowl, almost anything that is decorative. It should be selected for its suitability and its appearance so that it blends or contrasts with the plant color, texture, size and shape. This container should have a good layer of peat moss or some other moisture-retentive material placed at the base and the flower pot should be stood on this, while the space between the pot and its cover should also be filled with peat moss.

Now when the plant is watered any excess will be absorbed by the peat moss without doing any damage. The peat moss will also serve to insulate the flower pot

should be apparent that they will require a greater degree of humidity than is generally found in our houses. In most areas of the temperate world relative humidities out of doors probably range between about 60° and 80°. The first figure is sufficient for most of our plants indoors, but is a higher figure than is generally found indoors.

So if humidity is low we should do something about it; fortunately this is a simple matter. There is a large range of humidifiers on the market, from complex and expensive electric machines to the simplest, which are virtually no more than a pan of water and a fan. Even the provision from extremes of temperature. The peat moss will gradually release its moisture to the air and waft a slightly humid breeze upwards around the leaves of the plant.

Nearly all plants enjoy an occasional bath such as they might get during a summer shower, and when conditions allow, it is a good thing to put most plants out into a light rain for an hour or two, allowing them to drain and dry out before they are replaced in position. Many plants in the home can be given their own artificial rain occasionally with a spray of clean tepid water while others can luxuriate in a sink or shower. Such a bath should not be given to flowering plants or those with furry foliage.

There is one plant with furry foliage that benefits greatly by an occasional humidity bath and this is the beautiful and tender saintpaulia, or African violet. One way of helping it is to give it a steam bath. Make a little island of, say, an upturned saucer, in the center of a larger receptacle. Stand the saintpaulia on this in a waterproof container. Pour boiling water into the bowl, which should fall just short of the level of the pot. The issuing steam will benefit the plant. Leave it there until the water has become cool.

Pressure sprayers such as these produce a film of moisture which is so fine that there is no risk of damage to furnishings.

A steam bath takes time and trouble but is a great help to sensitive plants such as African violets when the atmosphere is too hot and dry. Many other types of plant will benefit from this treatment too.

3 Decorative uses

As furnishings

Nothing decorates a room more quickly than a few indoor plants. They soften sharp corners, drape bare walls, fill empty space and give personality to a previously anonymous area. A young couple setting up house for the first time can temporarily fill their empty spaces with plants instead of furniture, and even when they have acquired carpets, tables and chairs the plants will still be useful and decorative adjuncts to their home.

For the more established dwelling, plants can be employed for theatrical effect. You can hide a stained wall or disguise an unpleasant view from a window by suspending a row of plants that act as a 'curtain'.

You can even change the apparent shape

A wide spreading trailer will make a room appear wider than it is.

A climbing monstera will take the eye up to its tip and make a room appear higher than it really is.

or size of a room to a certain degree by using your plants as room dividers. Open shelf constructions are ideal places to display plants. Or simply use several tall, tubbed plants as 'living' walls.

If you want to make a low-ceilinged room look taller, select one or two tall tree-like plants, such as bamboo, podocarpus or schefflera palm, to create the illusion.

Indoor plants can be used most effec-

410

tively as dividers for rooms, separating the dining area from the cooking area, for example. These room dividers can be formed of shelves, or even small and specially made trolleys which are filled with plants. Take care, however, to ensure that when watering the plants no excess water falls on to furnishings. Also, the divider should be rigid enough to withstand the activities of young children, who might spill soil and plants onto the carpets. It may be necessary to move the plants from one place to another, to give them equal exposure to light.

Climbers

Tree ivies, grape-ivy and kangaroo vine, heartleaf philodendron, hoya, the black-eyed Susan vine (*Thunbergia alata*) and German ivy (*Senecio macroglossus variegatus* and *S. mikanioides*) are all easy and popular climbers that can be used to great decorative advantage in the home. Train them to climb a pole, to outline a window, to act as a soft green frame to a doorway or interior arch. Most can be tied or clipped to a cane, or even to heavy string fixed from floor to ceiling, which is easily hidden.

A screen of plants need not be dense and overpowering. A single plant such as a cissus can be woven through canes to look almost like a hedge or, as here, several different plants can play a more decorative role.

411

A climbing plant suited to the larger home or to office or showrooms is the fascinating *Monstera deliciosa*, known popularly as the Swiss cheese plant because of the holes, perforations and slashes in the large leaves. This will grow up a wall and grow right around the room if allowed to, a decorative characteristic which can be most useful. This, and certain other plants, present a problem because of the production of aerial roots – long, thong-like shoots that appear on branches and trail downwards. In their native state these aerial roots serve a useful purpose in drawing sustenance from the soil to higher portions of the plant, but in the home they are sometimes apt to be an embarrassment, for they are not particularly attractive. It is obvious that, in theory, the best thing to do with

Cissus antarctica, or kangaroo vine, a natural climber, is easy to cultivate and quick to respond to care. It is best grown up a string or a cane support.

these aerial roots is to lead them down into the original container of soil, or if this is too far away, into a secondary or subsidiary pot, for this way they will help to feed and encourage plant growth. On the other hand, if you have no objection to the plant growing perhaps a little less speedily, lushly and large, then there is no reason why these roots should not be cut neatly from the plant and thrown away.

Opposite: Monstera deliciosa, the Swiss cheese plant, will grow very large, so for limited spaces it is better to choose the smaller *M. pertusa* or *M.d. borsigiana.*
Below left: the popular *Hedera helix* 'Chicago'.
Below right: the so-called German ivy, *Senecio macroglossus variegatus.*

Trailers

All climbers can, of course, also be trailers. In fact the vogue for hanging baskets has shown that there is no limit to the kinds of plants suitable for this purpose, whether as inhabitants of hanging baskets or whether tumbling from a bracket or shelf. Ordinary non-trailing house plants suspended in space, with their containers supported by macrame rope or cord hangers, assume a different character and dimension. A few of the non-trailing plants that are handsome in hanging baskets are African violets, most kind of begonias, especially those with colored foliage, piggyback plant (*Tolmiea men-*

413

ziesii) and many cacti and succulents. Yet these and the usual trailers need careful grooming to look their best. Plants in hanging containers, especially when in wire baskets filled with sphagnum moss, can dry out quickly in overheated rooms.

Among the more useful trailers are strawberry-begonia (*Saxifraga sarmentosa*), *Peperomia orba*, known as 'Princess Astrid' peperomia, and *P. glabella*, and the delightful easy, eager and decorative *Plectranthus purpuratus*, purple-leaved Swedish ivy. The last is prolific. It has almost round leaves 1–2 in (3–5 cm) across, dark green with a purple fuzz. It produces clouds of dainty lilac flowers through the summer. There are several other Swedish ivy varieties that are equally attractive as trailers.

A first-class, easy and strikingly attractive fern that grows well as a trailer is the elkhorn fern, *Platycerium alcicorne*. This grows dramatic fronds or leaves similar to a stag's horns, glaucous blue and slighty furry, from a central ball. The plant can be knocked from its pot and nailed or tied to a

Contrast in shape, size and texture. The monstera on the floor reaches up to the plectranthus growing above and tumbling downwards. Both are easy to grow.

This little trailing fig, *Ficus pumila*, needs moist and humid conditions to give of its best. It grows well twining among other plants in a mixed bowl.

414

Philodendron oxycandium, the sweetheart plant, has better foliage and will cling to walls, but the hoya annually produces delicate waxy flowers.

board or a piece of cork bark and hung. Some attention must be given to the root ball to keep it moist but not soggy. When the fronds appear to be thirsty, the entire plant plus its board or cork mount can be immersed in water until bubbles cease to rise from the center. Then leave it to drain and replace. Almost any fern usually grown indoors is satisfactory as a hanging basket subject, one of the best being the beloved Boston fern, *Nephrolepis exaltata bostoniensis*,

and its many varieties. The fronds of some species can be very large.

And perhaps the most charming trailer of them all is the little hearts entwined, *Ceropegia woodii*, with its trails studded with little gray-green heart-shaped leaves at intervals, looking almost as though they were moving about on feet.

Trees or shrubs

Probably the greatest number of indoor plants can be said to fall in this group, yet this is the broadest of collections, for although they may be tree-like or shrub-

like, they can differ widely in the size, shape, color and texture of their individual leaves. The familiar *Ficus elastica* and the tough little *Araucaria excelsa* are both trees but they are entirely different.

Most trees and shrubs are at their best when they are comparatively mature and large, for then they have a dignity, a presence and a definite function as a part of the room's decor. And this they most certainly can have, for they fill significant space and can therefore guide the steps in a certain direction or serve as a screen to give just a little added privacy to the corner of a room or office.

Because they are large, trees and shrubs can be used effectively in groups, for their individual shapes can be contrasted attrac-

In the foreground the soft, luxuriant trailers of a plectranthus make a solid but lightweight wall of color, while behind it the larger glossy green leaves of a *Philodendron bipinnatifidum* reach out on their long, arching stems.

tively one with another, and the shapes, textures and colors of their foliage in juxtaposition can be an exercise of careful and subtle choice.

Trees and shrubs useful as indoor plants include: *Brassaia* (syn. *Schefflera*) *actinophylla*, many of the large palms and bamboos, the tree-like *Pittosporum undulatum*, several of the larger philodendrons, podocarpus, some of the larger dieffenbachias, *Fatsia japonica*, the elegant *Dizygotheca elegantissima* and equally elegant *Ficus benjamina* or weeping fig, *Grevillea robusta,* and for limited

416

periods and at certain seasons such splendid flowering shrubs as hydrangeas, camellias, azaleas, poinsettias and fuchsias.

Unfortunately, many people believe that bonsai, or dwarfed Japanese, trees are suitable for indoor gardening. This is not so. Bonsai trees are meant to be grown outdoors, not necessarily completely in the open, for most must have the shelter of some kind of light roofing and shading, but in an open atmosphere. Most can be brought indoors for a few days at a time and then taken out again, and if a number of bonsai trees are grown it is possible to have a succession of them on indoor display. Of course, it is possible to train certain house plants in the bonsai fashion, and while one may not have the authentic product, the plants will be perfectly at home indoors. A few plants being used for indoor bonsai are jade plant (*Crassula argentea*), Natal-plum (*Carissa grandiflora*) and various citrus.

Cocos weddeliana is a pretty little palm with dainty foliage that sometimes tends to go brown at the tips.

Several varieties of rubber plant have been hybridized. This all-green form is *Ficus elastica* 'Decora'.

Ficus lyrata has large, waist-like leaves, which have given it the popular name of fiddle-leaf fig.

417

4 Treatment

Watering

More indoor plants are killed by overwatering than anything else, perhaps because the basic function of watering is not properly understood. Water is needed by plants for two main and related reasons: (i) to keep the stems and leaves turgid so that (ii) they can be fed with a constant stream of liquid food from roots to leaf tips.

Plant roots require both air and water, and when a pot is overwatered, all the air is expelled and the roots drown, rot and gradually starve the plant. Correct watering is a means of feeding the roots with both the moisture and the air they need.

It is impossible to lay down hard and fast rules about watering, for much depends on circumstances, weather and season. But it is safe to advise most strongly that no plant should be watered if the soil surface in the pot is moist. Let it get almost bone dry first. Plenty and seldom should be the aim.

With a new plant, for the first few times pour in water to the top of the pot and see if it gradually trickles out of the drainage holes in the base. If it does not, give it a little

Left: the leaves of most bromeliads form a vase or cup, which should always be kept filled with water.

more until it does, and try to bear in mind roughly how much water you gave it. Let the pot stand in the puddle it has made for about an hour. The soil may reabsorb this water, but if it does not, then empty it out. Never let any plant stand in water except such aquatic marsh plants as the umbrella plant, *Cyperus alternifolius*.

By watering in this manner you are moistening the whole of the root ball, not just a part of it, and allowing air to enter at the same time. The water in the top of the pot courses down through the spaces in the soil, pushing ahead the air within the spaces. As the water rushes downwards pushing the

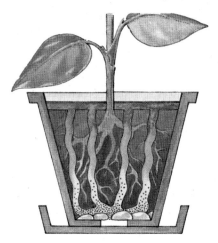

An underwatered plant (*above left*) will eventually die because some of its roots are dry and cannot absorb food or moisture. Stale air accumulates to poison these roots and the soil cracks away from the pot

sides. When a plant is given too much water (*above right*) all the air spaces are filled and the plant cannot breathe. The roots become slimy, rot and fail to feed the plant with food or moisture.

418

An overwatered plant. Whether overwatered or underwatered, a plant will respond by drooping and, eventually, shedding its leaves.

'old' air ahead, it drags in new fresh air after it so that, like breathing, watering exhales the foul and used air and inhales the new.

Remember that it is always a simpler matter to add more water to a plant that needs it than to take away an excessive amount. A human being or an animal can choose how much to drink but a potted plant can only accept.

Since the symptoms of overwatering and underwatering are unfortunately almost the same, be cautious how you treat a plant whose leaves are drooping, yellow and tending to fall. Never give more water unless you are certain that the plant actually needs it, perhaps because you have been away, for example.

Plants in active growth under fluorescent lights, even in winter can use up large amounts of water. We know that plants require very much more water in summer than in winter, but watch the weather closely. A hot, dry day might also be dark, overcast and humid, in which case the plant is likely to lose only little water through transpiration. A hot, sunny day may cause some plants to wilt, yet their soil may still be moist. The answer to this is that transpiration is taking place more quickly than the plant can absorb moisture through its roots and the addition of water will make no difference. Instead, give the plant's foliage a light spray of clean and tepid water. If this is impossible, remove the plant to a cooler or darker place, or draw the curtains for a little while.

Feeding

Enthusiasts will often overfeed their plants. This is bad for the plants and also bad for the owners, for if the plants survive this treatment they will grow large too quickly, outgrow their pots and become prone to disease.

Every newly bought plant probably has enough food in its soil to last at least 2–3 months and will not require feeding during this time. After this, feed the plant regularly according to season, but very lightly. Never. for any reason exceed the quantities recommended on the bottle or packet. Far better to reduce the dosage slightly.

The kind of food or fertilizer you apply will depend on your personal preferences and their general availability. Fertilizers come as liquids, powders or pills. Plants can absorb foods only in the form of liquids in solution with the moisture around their roots, so obviously feeding and watering should take place simultaneously.

In winter, feeding should either be suspended entirely or its frequency greatly reduced depending to some extent on the conditions of warmth, light and water. In summer a very light feed once a week is preferable to a heavier fortnightly dose. Change from winter to summer treatment fairly gradually.

Fertilizers in pelleted form are pressed into the soil and gradually dissolve each time the plant is watered.

Spraying plants with a foliar feed has certain special advantages, for it helps to keep the leaves clean and gives a welcome humidity as well as providing food elements accepted by leaves as well as roots.

420

The various foliar feeds available are useful but by no means essential. If it is inconvenient to spray the entire plant, remember that even foliar feeds can be absorbed by the roots of a plant, so consider using them as a normal fertilizer applied to the roots of the plant through the soil.

Not all plants need feeding through the soil, although this is normally where their roots and therefore their feeding system is to be found. The bromeliads, for example, have a shallow and comparatively unimportant root system, which would rot if continually fed. Most of them are epiphytes which use the branches of trees as support, collecting food from the leaves and other debris that might fall and attach itself accidentally to their roots. In their natural habitat bromeliads feed as they take in water from the central cups or vases formed by their leaf rosettes. But for the very occasional artificial feed they need, feeding through the soil will do as well.

Imaginative common sense is probably the best asset the indoor gardener has, but it is always advisable to check.

It is worth remembering that plants in

Left: powdered or granular fertilizers can sometimes be sprinkled on the soil and watered in, but are more usually dissolved in water and then added.

Above: all proprietary fertilizers require dilution and recommended doses should never be exceeded. It is easy to give too much liquid food, so measure quantities carefully.

our homes are influenced in their growth by the amount of light and warmth they receive. And this obviously has a great influence on the amount of food and water they require. If too much food and water is given, relative to the light and warmth, the plants soon become sickly. This, of course, adds a further complication to the problems of feeding and watering. Therefore, it is necessary to gain experience with your own plants and their requirements before buying very expensive and delicate plants. Careful observation is the true answer.

A further complication is that some plants have a resting period, and it is during this period that little water or food is required. These resting periods are often initiated in response to the temperature and light that is available, especially when

421

the plants are in their native habitats. Unfortunately, the artificial conditions in the home often confuse the plants, and this sometimes makes it difficult to know whether to give or withhold water and food.

Group therapy

Growing two or more plants in association or creating a plant arrangement has obvious decorative advantages. Less obvious is the advantage to the plants themselves.

Most plants benefit from the close association with other plants just as they do in the wild. One plant helps to protect the roots constantly moist. There are two ways of making plant arrangements. The plants can be grouped together in their individual pots, placed together in a large bowl, planter or other container with the pots concealed with moss, fir bark, peat moss or pebbles. Or else the plants can be knocked from their pots and all planted together in a common soil inside the large container. Both methods have certain benefits. If the plants are kept in their pots, they can easily be taken out and replaced, while knocking plants from their pots does away with the problem of disguising their containers.

other, and the combined moisture they transpire helps to create humidity and manufacture a micro-climate beneficial to the group.

So long as certain basic rules are obeyed a variety of plants can be grouped together. They should all require the same amount of moisture. It would be impossible to grow cacti with cyperus, for example, because the cacti normally need little or, at some times of the year, no water, whereas the cyperus is a bog plant that needs to have its

Plants grouped together in a mass can look effective if the collection has been selected with skill and the plants have similar food and water requirements.

A compromise that gives the best of both worlds is to knock the plants from their plastic or clay pots and slip the root ball into a perforated plastic bag. This, being of negligible thickness and completely pliable, allows the plants to be grouped more closely together and yet remain potentially mobile.

Whichever method is used, special care

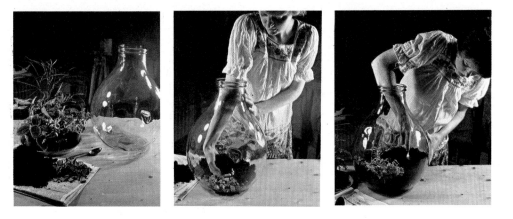

will have to be taken to drain the large container that holds all the plants. If the plants are in their pots, it will be possible to control watering to some extent so that some plants get more than others, but there is always the danger that excess water from one might damage the roots of its neighbor. Plants out of their pots and in a common soil will obviously need some special provision for drainage, because in both cases the communal container may have no drainage holes. So for all types of plant arrangements it is essential to fill the bottom inch or so of the container with some draining material such as pebbles or pea gravel. At the same time, be sure to water with care, in the knowledge that any excess moisture cannot run away but will be contained in that basic drainage layer.

It is quite easy to plant a bowl or dish garden and to make a terrarium, and so long as the advice above is followed no real problems should be encountered. Rather more difficult is the creation of a bottle garden, where the opening or neck is too narrow to permit your hands to enter. The following suggestions will probably be helpful.

First make sure that the interior of the bottle is scrupulously clean before you begin and that it is completely dry. Pour in just a little peat moss through an improvised chute or funnel. This is mainly to break the fall of the next layer, the drainage

To make a bottle garden, first ensure that you have everything at hand. Check that the bottle is spotlessly clean and dry, for once work has started it will be too late to go back. Put a drainage layer at the base of the bottle. Use a light, open soil – sterilized so that no weed seeds will germinate. Grouping plants in a bottle garden demands an artist's talent. Look for contrasts in shape, color and texture but not of type, for all must live together under the same conditions.

material, and avoid shattering the glass. This drainage layer should be fairly deep, preferably at least 2 in (5 cm). The soil, which must be sterilized to prevent weeds and must be sufficiently rich in plant foods to sustain gentle growth over a long period, should go in next. When inserting the soil through the chute, try to make sure that it does not soil the sides of the bottle, but try also to slope it a little or to make one or two hills in the soil surface.

The plants to choose for a bottle garden will obviously have to be small enough to enter the neck, so they will generally be immature. But the thing to remember is that they will grow. However, do not choose a subject that will grow either too large or too quickly, for in both these cases the plant will have to be severely cut down or removed completely to avoid damage to the other plants. Do not, for example, use creeping or trailing plants such as ivy or *Ficus pumila* unless you are prepared to trim them regularly.

The following plants are all suitable for a bottle garden: *Acorus gramineus* (grass), small-leaved varieties of *Begonia rex, Corex*

423

Attach any improvised tools securely to a slim cane.

Dig a small hole for the plant roots, being careful not to go too deep. Gently tease away most of the soil from the plant roots.

japonica (grass or rush), *Codiaeum variegatum pictum* (croton), *Cryptanthus acaulis* (earth star), *Fittonia vershaffeltii argyroneura* (nerve plant – there is a dwarf form with very small leaves), *Maranta leuconeura kerchoveana* (prayer plant), *Chamaedorea elegans* 'Bella' (small palm), *Pellionia pulchra*, *Peperomia orba, Pilea cadierei* 'Minima' (aluminum plant), *Pteris ensiformis* 'Victoriae' (fern), *Selaginella, Sinningia pusilla* (dainty flowering plant only 1½–2 in (3–5 cm) high).

To plant out a bottle garden, tie a spoon securely to a long cane, insert it into the neck of the bottle and dig a little hole in the soil for the plant. Knock the plant from its pot, gently tease away some of the soil from its root ball, then, holding the plant by the tip of its foliage, insert the root through the neck of the bottle and lean the bottle so that the roots hang directly over the hole. Let it drop, use your spoon to move it to an upright position and then cover the roots with soil and firm. Repeat the process for the remainder of the plants. If you wish, you can add an occasional rock or piece of driftwood to dramatize the effect.

Add no more than a cupful of water, preferably sprayed directly onto the plants and soil, and also onto the inner sides of the glass bottle to remove any traces of dust or soil that may have been thrown up as work progressed. Theoretically, you can then

In order that the finished bottle garden can be seen clearly and enjoyed, the sides must be clean, clear and free from condensation. Water with great care and at long intervals for healthy and attractive plants – removal of unsightly elements is by no means easy.

Below: two unusual and attractive containers suitable for similar gardens.

seal the top and the plants will grow for months without any further need for water. In practice, sealing the top nearly always leads to damping off, mainly because the balance of moisture to plant life must be exact. Compromise by watering sparingly,

424

Holding the plant by the tips of the leaves, position it and the bottle so that the roots will drop neatly into the prepared planting hole.

Spread soil over the roots and firm down.

certainly no more than once a month and in the smallest quantities. Keep the bottle garden out of direct sunlight and in a coolish position.

The growing of plants in groups in a container in the home dates back many years, to when in 1829 Nathaniel Ward, a London physician, accidentally discovered that plants could be successfully grown in a closed glass case. The water which evaporated from the leaves of the plants during respiration condensed on the glass and

425

The growing medium of inert clay granules exists merely to anchor the plant through its roots, which serve also to absorb and distribute moisture, food and air.

trickled down the container's sides and back into the soil.

This idea was taken up by Victorian gardeners, who called these containers Wardian Cases.

Hydroponics

Paradoxical though it may seem, if you grow your plants in water only, the risk of overwatering vanishes. The roots are not merely submerged in water, but grow in a special medium that is kept moist from the water below. Thus they get moisture and air.

Although hydroponics, especially on a commercial scale, can become an involved process with sophisticated equipment and some knowledge of chemistry necessary for success, all this is only a somewhat expensive refinement of simpler means of growing plants hydroponically that have been used for many years. Without special con-

tainers, special growing media, special water-level indicators and special slow-release fertilizers, it is still perfectly possible to grow many types of indoor plants for months or even years at a time so long as one basic rule is observed.

The plant must rest in the neck of the container so that its roots can go down into the water and the upper portions of the plant grow upwards. Use a grid of wire mesh or something similar. The container itself should preferably be of glass so that the water level can easily and quickly be checked. The roots should be carefully washed clean of all soil and inserted in the container so that the plant is securely held in position. Water should then be poured in

426

so that it covers all the roots. A touch of liquid fertilizer is added. The important point to remember is that to prevent the plant from drowning, the water level must now be allowed to drop, through absorption by the plant and by evaporation. This will mean that the roots are totally submerged in water only for a day or so, and then are gradually exposed more and more to the air, only the longer roots remaining below the water level. So long as these deeper roots still touch the water, the plant will receive sufficient moisture for its requirements, and so long as some of the roots are above water level they will receive

sufficient air to keep them alive. Fertilizer applications should be regular but light.

A few plants especially suited to growing in water are: Chinese evergreens (*Aglaonema*), coleus, *Dracaena sanderiana*, *Fatshedera*, the heartleaf philodendron *Philodendron oxy cardium*, common ivy (*Hedera*), *Scindapsus*, *Syngonium*, *Tradescantia*, *Zebrina* and of course the avocado and sweet-potato vine.

Many plants, of course, can be increased by immersing the cut ends of cuttings in water, where they will develop roots, but unless fed or potted into a compost they will eventually die. Cuttings of patience plant root easily by this method.

Water should be replenished to cover the whole root system only at moderate intervals, allowing the water level to drop considerably so that some roots touch water and some are in air. In the right-hand jar, the water level has been allowed to drop rather too far: halfway down is enough.

427

5 Propagation

Half the fun of indoor plants is growing your own, and with many plants this is a simple process. Some plants even produce their own young.

Although most indoor plants can be raised from seed, quicker, more certain results come from other propagation methods. However, if you have successfully started petunias, marigolds, tomatoes and eggplants (aubergines) from seed indoors, you can readily succeed with house plants, especially if you have a well-lighted room or lacking that, can supply fluorescent lighting. Selecting a plant that is quick and easy to grow, such as coleus, is recommended, but African violets and many other relatives among the vast gesneriad family also grow well from seed; others to consider are amaryllis, wax begonia (*Begonia semperflorens*) and some other kinds of begonia, impatiens, cyclamen, kalanchoe

A seed pan or pot in a sealed plastic bag is protected from cold and drafts. The seeds germinate safely and can then be gradually exposed to a normal environment.

and many cacti and succulents. Without the assistance of a propagating case and a greenhouse, the best means of growing seeds indoors is to make use of a translucent plastic kitchen bag.

Sow the seed in a moist sterilized growing medium in a pot or on a small tray and then place this inside a plastic bag. Blow into the bag so that the film stands clear of the soil surface and then securely tie up the opening so that the bag is virtually sealed. Keep the 'package' in the warm and watch carefully for the first signs of growth. If during this period so much condensation takes place that water collects in puddles inside the bag, open it, remove the pot or box, turn the bag inside out and replace the pot inside. As soon as evidence of growth appears, open the bag slightly, leaving the pot still inside. Remove the package from the warm location for a few hours each day, gradually lengthening this period and gradually opening the bag more and more until it can be removed entirely. When the little plants are large enough to be handled, carefully transplant them into individual pots, placing them under fluorescent lights or in a well-lighted location.

Plants can also be propagated by other measures.

Division   After flowering, many of the exceedingly useful and decorative plants known collectively as bromeliads will produce a young plant growing from the soil beside the parent. It is a simple matter to cut away this young plant with a portion of root and to plant it in a separate pot.

Some plants such as aspidistras and sansevierias will produce more and more spiky leaves as they grow older and eventually these so overcrowd the pot that they should be divided. Again, merely knock the plant from its pot and divide the roots into portions, giving each a separate pot.

After some time the African violet will produce so many foliage rosettes that they choke the pot. Many of these are from separate plants, so once again knock the plant from its pot and very gently and carefully tease the tiny roots apart so that you get several plants. Pot these separately.

Cuttings   There are several types of cuttings, of which the simplest is the method of propagating the ubiquitous tradescantia. Pinch out the growing tip of a long trailer and stick the end in a pot of soil; it will root almost immediately. Many indoor plants can be quite easily propagated with this type of stem cutting.

Leaf cuttings can be divided into several kinds. An African violet leaf, for example, with a tiny sliver from its stem, can be inserted in a pot of peat moss and sand and

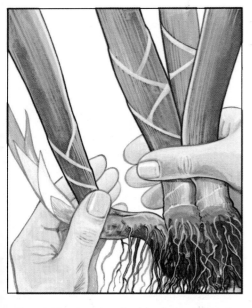

When dividing the roots of a plant always make sure that each portion includes some good root hairs.

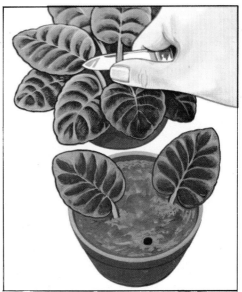

Bury the petiole right up to the leaf when taking leaf cuttings of saintpaulias.

429

Part of the attraction of a chlorophytum is the numerous long, arching stems bearing miniature plants at the tips.

To propagate a chlorophytum by layering, rest the plantlet on another pot of soil, if necessary holding it down with a hairpin, weight or toothpick.

will quickly take root. The long, spear-like sansevieria leaf can be cut into sections, each section planted in soil, and rooting will take place soon after. Many begonias, including *B. rex*, the ivy-leafed begonia, can be propagated in much the same way. Or by merely pegging a leaf flat to the surface of the soil and cutting through its major veins, new plants will be encouraged to root, which are subsequently potted up.

Layering One of the reasons for the popularity of the familiar *Chlorophytum comosum variegatum*, or spider plant, is its habit of sending out long arching stems, which first bear little white flowers and then miniature plants. If these are allowed to rest on the soil surface of another pot, they will

430

quickly take root and can be cut from the original stem.

Most climbers can easily be propagated by layering. Take one of the stems or trailers and, a few inches (centimeters) from the growing tip, gently bend or twist the stem so that it fractures without breaking off. Bury this section in a pot of soil and after a time new growth will indicate that new roots have formed. Then cut the young plant from its parent. Trim back the shoot from the parent plant to avoid leaving an unsightly shoot.

pot up the young plant in the normal manner. Support the plant with a stake.

A surprising number of plants will send out roots if cuttings are merely placed in water. It is possible to make use of this characteristic to make a long-lasting room decoration for table-centerpieces and to grow a number of new plants at the same time. Take a fairly large waterproof container and cover the base with pebbles. Collect together stem cuttings from ivies, kangaroo vine and grape-ivy, tradescantia, heartleaf philodendron, impatiens or busy

Plant cuttings of many types will quickly take root if they are held by pebbles in a water solution. Make sure that the water level never drops too much for too long, or the plants will suffer.

Many plants, such as tradescantia, can be induced to grow roots if cuttings are merely placed in plain water. When the roots are well developed, remove the cutting and pot it up in a good soil.

Air layering   It is obviously impossible to bend the growing tip of, say, a rubber plant, to layer it in the way described, but there is another method. Choose your spot a few inches from the growing tip and nick out a tiny sliver. Cover this with a good ball of moist sphagnum moss securely tied around the stem to cover the wound. So that the moss will not dry out too quickly, cover it with a piece of plastic sheeting firmly secured in place. It will soon become evident that roots will have grown into the moss. When this happens, cut away the top under these roots, remove the plastic and

Lizzie, coleus, peperomia or *Saxifraga sarmentosa* (there are many others), and insert these in the container, using more pebbles to secure the cuttings in place. Arrange them decoratively. Pour in water with just a trace of liquid fertilizer. Very shortly the cuttings will put out roots into the water.

When the plants have grown too large to remain together, pot them individually. This 'puddle-pot' method, as it is called, is a particularly easy and useful means of propagating several plants at once. Maintain a highish water level, but allow the roots to get some air occasionally.

431

6 Pests and diseases

So long as indoor plants are given the minimum of attention there is no real reason why they should suffer from any but the most superficial damage from pests or diseases. If they are kept clean, examined at regular intervals, maintained in conditions that are suitable for them, and not over-watered or overfed, most plants will live for years.

Examination is the real answer. Though one cannot subject every plant in the home to a minute appraisal every day, after a time even a casual glance will suggest when something is wrong; a twisted leaf, a yellowing, reddening or browning, a drooping – these are the primary signs of trouble.

Pests are far more likely than disease, and these are most likely to occur in summer or after plants have been brought indoors in the fall, rather than in winter. There is always the threat of attack from aphids coming in from the garden, normally quickly seen and as quickly settled. Red spider mite will attack only where the atmosphere is over-dry and arid. Less frequently, a tuft of white cotton will appear, indicating mealy bugs, or else a gray protuberance, which suggests scale.

Caterpillars, ants, earwigs, worms, slugs, thrips, white flies and other insects may also cause trouble, but none of these is likely to escape preliminary examination when a plant is first brought home.

Everything mentioned so far can be eradicated by a program of spraying with an insecticide such as malathion. This is a

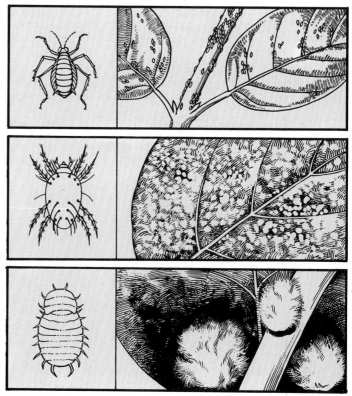

Aphids can be brought into the home on garden flowers – or they may fly in through the window. They can be easily controlled by spraying with one of several proprietary insecticides.

The almost invisible red spider mite attacks only when the atmosphere is dry and arid. Good humidity or an occasional spray will ensure that your plants are kept clear of this pest.

Mealy bugs are again almost invisible, but give themselves away by the white woolly substance with which they surround themselves. A drop or two of methylated spirits will kill them.

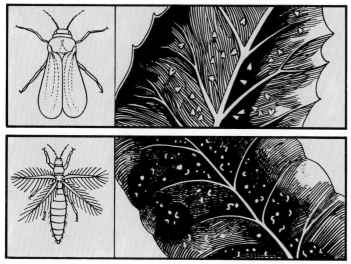

White flies can sometimes be difficult to eradicate, but a regular spraying with Resmethrin will do the trick. This is absorbed by the sap and then sucked by the insects.

Resmethrin is also the answer to an attack by thrips – small black-winged insects that cause tiny pale spots on leaves where they suck the sap from the plant.

poison and as such it should never be used inside the house. Every plant to be treated should be taken out of doors and given a thorough spray, or even turned upside down and dipped in a bucket of the mixture as recommended on the label. Other sprays that can be used indoors will kill only mild infestations of aphids or similar pests.

Mealy bugs can be cleared safely and with little trouble by dipping a matchstick in alcohol and touching the white, woolly coating, which will then disappear to reveal the little brown insect within. Scale can actually be scraped off with a knife.

Red spider is a little different. It will appear only when the plant or plants concerned suffer from too dry and arid an atmosphere. It will be noted by a twisting, curling and drying of leaves and on examination it will be found that leaves are covered with a fine web in which move a great number of minute red-brown insects. Red spider mite can be cleared with careful and thorough application of most insecticides, such as malathion, but the best way of preventing a further attack is to increase the humidity by spraying the plant that has been affected. Sometimes a good washing of the plant's foliage at the kitchen sink will eliminate red spider mites and aphids.

There are very few diseases that attack indoor plants, and those that might appear are caused almost without exception by lack of care. If subjected to over-watering, for example, many plants can suffer from root rot, damping off, mildew or botrytis. Viruses and rusts can begin when a plant is sick through being kept too wet, too cold or both. If plants are kept in the dark or shade for too long, they will tend to become lank, weak and subject to disease.

Pests are, on the whole, a simple matter to clear, but diseases are more complex. They arise only after the plant has been seriously weakened. It is advisable to treat pest attack, but to throw the plant away if disease appears. You may waste considerable time and effort attempting to treat it and other plants may be affected.

If, on the other hand, a plant is so admired or so much a member of the family that every attempt must be made to cure it, a fungicide spray may help and, if possible, a period of recuperation in a greenhouse or plant room under ideal conditions.

It is better not to be too sentimental about indoor plants. Keep them while they are attractive and at their best. When they grow too old or become diseased – unlikely though it is – throw them away and acquire a replacement. This will be better and safer for any other plants you have.

433

Greenhouse gardening

1 Why grow plants under glass?

Nowadays a greenhouse is essential for the complete gardener. One of its most important assets is that it makes possible substantial economies in household budgets: ordinary fruits and vegetables can be grown both in and out of season, and more exotic items – usually expensive in the shops – can also be produced at low cost. Seedlings and cuttings can be raised by the gardener himself, reducing annual expenditure on garden plants, and giving him the satisfaction of creating something more or less from nothing. What is more, the protection given by greenhouses against outdoor weather conditions allows many tender decorative plants to be grown, which will give enthusiasts increased pleasure.

Right: Greenhouse gardening provides an opportunity to grow a wide variety of colorful plants, such as the orange-flowered *Streptosolen jamesonii* shown here.

Below: The pendulous flowers of fuchsias provide beautiful summer flower displays in greenhouses.

2 Types of greenhouse

Before buying a greenhouse, look at several types and decide what sort suits your purposes best. They are usually classified according to use – and by size, shape or construction materials. The temperature and degree of humidity at which the greenhouse is to be maintained determine the type of plants that can be grown in it and also, in a general sense, the purpose for which the greenhouse will be used. Experts usually refer to greenhouses in the following ways.

Cold greenhouse This type depends entirely on the heat of the sun for warmth, and it is therefore most valuable in the spring, summer and autumn. The great disadvantage of the cold greenhouse is that it affords little protection against severe frost and is therefore not able to protect tender plants in winter unless the season is exceptionally mild.

Cool greenhouse In many ways a cool greenhouse is the most useful type for most gardeners. During the summer, when unheated, it fulfils the function of a cold greenhouse. During the spring, autumn and winter it is heated enough to maintain a night temperature of 45°F (7°C). This is sufficient to keep out the frost and so allows many tender plants to be overwintered, together with, for example, dahlias and begonia tubers. A cool greenhouse can also be used for raising many kinds of plants from seed.

Intermediate or warm greenhouse This is the type that true gardening enthusiasts, eager to extend the interest and scope of their hobby, will wish to acquire. With all the many very valuable practical aspects listed above, the warm greenhouse combines the advantage of enabling such commodities as tomatoes and cucumbers to be grown together with some of the more exotic fruits and vegetables – such as eggplants, figs, avocados, peaches and nectarines. Warm greenhouses are heated to a minimum night temperature of 55°F (13°C) which makes it possible to grow decorative house plants and to carry out propagation.

Tropical or hot house This type, perhaps more for the connoisseur than the ordinary gardener, used to be called a stove house and the plants grown in it, stove plants. Heated to a night temperature of about 65°F (18°C) and kept very humid, it can be used for growing certain kinds of orchids, maidenhair ferns, fittonias, caladiums, and many gesneriads. Many tropical plants, however, adapt readily to the warm greenhouse. Like the warm house, the hot house is useful for propagation, especially when a high temperature is essential.

Dieffenbachia needs a warm, humid atmosphere and so is best grown in a tropical or hot house

Greenhouse shapes

Physically, greenhouses are classified by their shape, which to some extent determines their function. The common ones are listed below.

Span or ridge This is the most popular type. It has a roof in the form of an inverted shallow V and the more conventional type has vertical glass sides, although there is now a tendency to produce this type with glass panels set at an angle of about 10° to the vertical. It is claimed that this provides greater resistance to crosswinds and a greater stability; greenhouses built in this way require less bracing, and there is better light transmission.

If mainly ground crops (such as lettuce, chrysanthemums and tomatoes) are to be grown, span greenhouses, in common with some other types, are glazed to the ground. If pot plants are to be the specialty, the glazing is usually supported on a bench-high wall of brick, concrete, wood or metal.

Three-quarter span This type of greenhouse is built against a wall. It has an inverted V-shape roof, but the span on the wall side is shorter than the other, which is of normal length. This type has an advantage over a standard lean-to (see below) in that it gives more light and headroom, but

it is more costly. One of the best uses of this greenhouse is to grow fruit on the wall side and display plants on the opposite side.

Lean-to The lean-to has a single sloping roof and is built against a wall. It is the least expensive to buy and heat, and indeed, can often be heated from the house system. Its disadvantage is that plants grown in it tend to bend towards the light.

Circular This is among the latest ideas in greenhouses, and includes geodesic dome models. It is excellent for pot plants and cultivation. However, extractor fans usually need to be installed to prevent overheating in hot weather.

Above: A three-quarter span greenhouse has the virtues of the lean-to type but has the advantage of giving more light and height.

Left: This span, or ridge, greenhouse is glazed to the base, making it valuable for growing ground crops such as chrysanthemums, lettuce and tomatoes.

Right: A lean-to greenhouse can be very useful, especially where space is restricted. As it is built against a wall, it is suitable for fruit.

Mini For gardeners with only a very small space to spare, a miniature greenhouse could be the answer. Some are free-standing, while others 'lean-to' against a wall or extend from a window. This type of greenhouse, though small, can fulfil many of the functions of a full-size greenhouse.

Conservatory This is essentially a greenhouse that is accessible from a living room, to which it can be a pleasing adjunct. Filled with exotic plants, it makes a restful extra room in both summer and winter, combining the atmosphere of the garden with the comfort of light and heat from the house supply.

Above: Both the ridge and lean-to types of miniature greenhouse are invaluable to those with little space.

Below: The attractive design of this circular greenhouse allows it to be positioned anywhere.

Above: A conservatory makes an excellent and very useful extension to a living room.

439

Construction materials

The relative merits of the various materials used in constructing greenhouses are listed below.

Wood This is warm and relatively easy to work. The strongest is teak, and redwood is very popular. Both need oiling, and the latter is more easily worked. Other woods used include cypress and pine that has been salted. The cheaper woods must be painted regularly.

Metal (steel and aluminum) Steel needs painting, but aluminum does not. Aluminum alloys are strong, and although light they stand firm provided the greenhouse itself is firmly sited. The metal frame must be rigid and include provision for expansion and contraction to avoid glass breakage and air leakage.

Concrete Reinforced concrete is usually used for greenhouses, and although not as attractive as some other materials, concrete does provide a very durable structure.

A greenhouse constructed of red cedar requires treatment with linseed oil annually.

Glazing: glass v. plastic Glass has long been a very satisfactory glazing material, but plastic-glazed greenhouses have recently become very popular. There is a fairly wide selection from which to choose among the plastics.

The cheapest is polyethylene, which is very easy to install. Its main disadvantages are: it is weathered by sun (this is slowed down by specifying ultraviolet resistant) and torn by wind, reducing its life span to about two years; it can become dirty and cannot be cleaned the way glass can; and also condensation is greater, although powered fans can be installed to reduce this problem.

More expensive and much longer-lived are the rigid fiberglass panels, which retain heat better than polyethylene. Also coming into use is acrylic, but it is usually more expensive than glass. It scratches, but it is clear and can be molded into curves. None of the plastics shatters like glass.

3 Choosing a greenhouse

Buying a greenhouse is an investment, so before you purchase one decide on the way you intend to use it. This, of course, depends entirely on the type of crops that are to be grown. For ground crops, such as chrysanthemums and lettuces, the greenhouse will need glazing right down to the base. Flowering pot plants and propagation call for benches, in which case the glazing can be fixed to basal walls 2–3 ft (60–100 cm) high, and heat loss will be reduced. If both types are to be cultivated, a greenhouse glazed to the ground on one side, with a bench and wall on the other, will fit the bill. With restricted space, or if wall-fruits are to be grown, a lean-to is the best proposition.

If it is the gardener's intention to cultivate plants that need heat, the most economic construction in this respect should be chosen. It is also as well to visualize the possibility of any future expansion that may be required.

Size

Although the choice of greenhouse will depend upon the gardener's pocket, it is a great mistake to buy one that is too small.

Above: This greenhouse is only 8 ft (2·5 m) by 6 ft (2 m) yet has ample headroom and good space for staging.

Left: A greenhouse must have a door wide enough to take a wheelbarrow comfortably.

In any case, a small greenhouse is difficult to manage – it warms up too quickly in summer and cools too fast in winter. A greenhouse must have adequate headroom and, ideally, be wide enough to allow for a wheelbarrow to pass through the door. (It is important to ensure that the door opens inwards, or slides easily backwards and forwards.) Another inconvenience of too narrow a house is that it will not allow for a wide enough path, or adequate width to the benches. A good minimum size is about 8 ft (2·5 m) wide by 6 ft (2m) long.

441

4 Installing a greenhouse

Siting

Careful attention should be paid to choice of location. The site should be level; if it is not, it should be leveled. It should be well-drained, sheltered from strong and cold winds and should receive plenty of sunshine. The position chosen will of course be influenced, particularly in a small garden, by miscellaneous factors such as existing paths, boundary fences, the situation of the house, etc., but the above criteria are ideal, and will also determine the direction in which the greenhouse should run. The best position is running north and south, to afford the maximum amount of light throughout the year. However, if the greenhouse is to be used largely for raising seedlings and propagating plants in winter, an east-to-west direction will give maximum light at that time of year. A lean-to should preferably be erected facing south. A conservatory is best positioned so that it forms an extension to the living room and has direct access from it.

It is also important to position the greenhouse where water, gas and electricity supplies are available, or where they can easily be made so.

Note Greenhouses above a certain size, stipulated by the zoning laws in each area, may require planning permission. Before committing yourself to buying and erecting a greenhouse, it is as well to check this point, and also to consult with neighbors regarding the proposed position of the greenhouse.

Laying foundations and paths

A path of concrete slabs or coal ashes or bricks can be laid through the center of the greenhouse. It is also advantageous to lay a path giving access from the house.

Good foundations are essential to eradicate the risk of movement, and consequent glass breakage. Solid foundations also provide good anchorage. Greenhouse makers always provide a foundation plan prior to delivery, and some also sell suitable ready-made foundations.

In aluminum greenhouses the weight to be supported is fairly low, so the foundations need not be as heavily constructed, but must still provide a firm base.

A suitable foundation for a greenhouse glazed to the ground can be provided by digging a trench 10 in (25 cm) deep by 1 ft

Left: A modern conservatory with direct access from a living room is ideal for house plants.

Right: Erecting a greenhouse.
(1) These two drawings show typical foundations, the first for a greenhouse glazed to the ground, the second for one with a bench-high base wall, supporting a glazed superstructure.
(2) Positioning the sides.
(3) Putting on the roof.
(4) When glazing, use putty for wood frames and plastic sealing compound for metal frames.

(30 cm) wide with vertical sides. In this, a brick or concrete footing should be built. If the superstructure is to be supported on brick or concrete block walls, the top of the foundation, which in this case might be a filling of concrete, should be 6 in (15 cm) below ground level. Provide for plumbing and electricity before the concrete is put in.

Erection

Greenhouse manufacturers always supply very complete directions for the erection of their products. The work usually consists of bolting prefabricated parts together, and calls for few tools other than wrenches, screwdrivers, and perhaps a masonry drill. For glazing, use putty in a wooden greenhouse, elastic sealing compound in a metal one. Manufacturers will also erect greenhouses themselves.

Maintenance

The most important tasks are as follows:
(1) Occasionally treat wood by wiping it with a rag dipped in linseed oil.
(2) Unless allowing it to weather, treat red cedar with a cedar preservative.
(3) Regularly paint softwood and steel. (Aluminum needs no painting.)
(4) Wash glass regularly, removing moss, etc., by scraping and hosing down.
(5) Scrub and whitewash walls annually.
(6) Paint heating pipes with aluminum paint. Do not, however, use creosote on the staging, etc., inside the greenhouse; it emits fumes that are toxic to plants.

1
A. brick footing
B. trench
C. brick base wall
A
B
10 in (25 cm)
12 in (30 cm)
6 in (15 cm)
C
B
A
10 in (25 cm)
12 in (30 cm)

2

3

4

5 Running a greenhouse

Ventilation

No matter what the type of greenhouse –
cold, cool, warm or tropical – ventilation is
most important because it controls heat
and humidity, and helps avoid such disorders as 'damping off', which can have a
disastrous effect. In a well-designed
greenhouse there are ventilators, i.e. fan-
lights that open, on either side of the roof,
and one in each side panel. Normally, one
set is provided for each 10 ft (3 m) run of
length. Some greenhouses are fitted with
louver ventilators in the sides. These provide ventilation that can be very finely controlled. Ventilators on the leeward side can
be opened when it is windy without causing
any cold drafts. In warm weather they may
be opened on both sides to reduce the
temperature, control humidity and admit
fresh air to the plants.

Ventilation in greenhouses demands
considerable attention, and for this reason
automatic methods of control have been
developed. One of them is a simple device
that is fitted on to each ventilator to open
and shut it automatically. It does this by

virtue of a cylinder filled with a mineral
substance that expands or contracts with
variations in temperature. The device is
very sensitive, easy to fit and comparatively
inexpensive.

A second method of automatic ventilation control is to use an electric fan controlled by a thermostat. Fans are normally
fitted in the gable end of the greenhouse.

Above: Careful attention
must be paid to
ventilating a greenhouse.
An automatic ventilating
fan, which is
thermostatically
controlled, can be fitted in
the gable end of the
greenhouse. Sometimes
a fan is operated in
conjunction with a louver
fitted on the outside of the
mounting panel.

Left: An alternative
method of ventilation is a
mechanical system that
automatically opens or
shuts as necessary.

Shading

Shading is another way of effectively cutting down the heat in a greenhouse, and is used in conjunction with ventilation. It is particularly valuable for certain pot plants, early propagation and tomatoes suffering from verticillium wilt. Shading can be done in the following ways.

(1) The glass on the outside can be painted with well-diluted emulsion paint, a lime and water mixture or a proprietary shading.

Such shading is effective during the summer but should be progressively washed off by winter, when all the available light is needed.

(2) Blinds, either of the venetian or the roller type, can be fitted either inside or outside; the outside type of blind is better because the sun's rays should ideally be checked before they reach the glass. There is one type of blind made from unplasticized vinyl tubes, which, if they are rolled down at nightfall during winter, minimize fuel consumption in a heated greenhouse.

Shading from the hot sun is important for keeping down the temperature in a greenhouse and these external blinds made from unplasticized vinyl tubes can also reduce heat loss in winter.

In some cases roller blinds fitted inside can be automatically controlled by means of a thermostat or photoelectric cell.

(3) Sun vizors, in which the blinds are held rigid at the correct slope for the roof of the greenhouse, can be used. They can be controlled by an electronic eye, and are among the most efficient types of shading.

Vinyl blinds are excellent for shading from the sun.

Heating

Heating a greenhouse is by no means cheap, and in the long run the final decision will depend on which fuel is cheapest and how easily a supply can be provided for the greenhouse. The choice must remain an individual one, but if, for example, the rate for your house gas supply is cheaper than other forms of power, then quite obviously this is the one that should be given the first consideration. The various alternatives are considered below.

Hot-water pipes This is the traditional method of heating a greenhouse, but it necessitates the installation of a boiler and hot-water pipes, which are usually placed under the staging. Formerly, such a boiler was fired with solid fuel, usually coke, but today gas, oil or electricity are more usual. The advantage of these is that any system

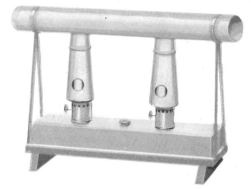

Another type of Kerosene heater is the double-burner heater illustrated above.

using them can be fully automatic. Two advantages of hot-water pipes are that they distribute the heat uniformly and retain their heat for some time.

If the home system has enough spare capacity it may be possible to heat the greenhouse from that.

Electric heaters Although heating by electricity is costly, it has a number of advantages in greenhouses. It is clean and always reliable unless there are power cuts. With thermostats of a correct and trustworthy design, control of the greenhouse temperature can be more precise than with any other form of heating. However, once the power is cut off cooling down will take place, except where night storage heaters are used – but with these there are problems of temperature control, therefore they are not highly recommended. (When buying your greenhouse, discuss with the salesman recommendations for emergency heaters to use when there is a power failure in your region during freezing weather.)

The types of electrical equipment more usually installed for greenhouse heating are fan heaters, and tubular heaters.

Fan heaters are extremely efficient electric heaters for a greenhouse. They are usually light, 4–5 lbs (2–2·5 kg) and are quite portable, so that they can be positioned anywhere – however, they are most usually placed in the center of the floor. Their great

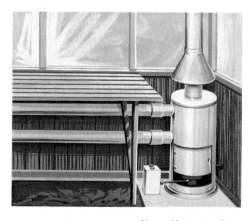

Above: Hot-water pipes are a long-established method of heating greenhouses.

Left: Kerosene heaters, such as the single burner heater illustrated here, are popular on the Continent.

446

asset is that they maintain a gentle movement of air, which is appreciated by plants and encourages growth. Fan heaters work on the principle of sucking in cold air at one end, warming it and blowing it out at the other. This heated air rises naturally by convection, circulates, cools and then falls to the ground again, where it is reheated. Fan heaters are thermostatically controlled, but even when the heating elements are switched off, the fan keeps the air gently circulating.

The great qualities of tubular heaters are their long life, almost negligible maintenance costs, their comparatively low initial cost and their adaptability. They are best fitted singly or in banks against the wall of the greenhouse.

Tubular heaters can, however, get very hot and scorch plants close to them unless they are thermostatically controlled. This

also ensures, of course, the current is used only when necessary, and at the same time automatically maintains the required minimum temperature.

For safety reasons, it is a wise precaution to mount tubular heaters on wooden supports when installing in a metal greenhouse.

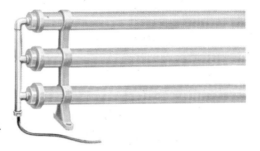

A bank of electric tubular heaters provides a clean, controllable, reliable and flexible form of heating.

Gas heaters When burned, gas derived from coal gives off chemicals that are detrimental to plants, but the products of natural-gas combustion are beneficial, especially the carbon dioxide that enters the air. Natural-gas burning apparatus is now available for greenhouse heating. Such apparatus is easily placed below the staging and connected to the gas source by means of a flexible pipe. Burners can have thermostatic control and be fitted with a flame-failure device as a safety precaution.

For the running of a gas burner there must be adequate air to burn the fuel. Usually, this requirement is adequately met by the normal leakage in a greenhouse. If there is any problem, an air brick in the foundation wall above ground level will solve it. Lastly, note that a gas heater may be unsuitable for a plastic greenhouse because of the condensation caused, which is heavier than that brought about by electrical heaters.

Heat conservation

No doubt double glazing would reduce the heat losses in a greenhouse. However, the cost of hermetically sealing together two

Electric fan heaters can be wall-mounted (*top*) or floor-standing (*above*). With or without thermostatic control, they are very convenient.

sheets of glass is high, and it would be prohibitively expensive to double glaze an ordinary home greenhouse.

Heat losses and drafts can, however, be reduced by lining the greenhouse inside with thin polyethylene, leaving the vents, of course, uncovered. Lining will increase the humidity, so careful attention to ventilation will be needed afterwards.

Control Equipment

Through the advent of more efficient heating and ventilation equipment for the amateur greenhouse enthusiast, precision control equipment is now available for all greenhouses. This can be used to open and close ventilators, operate heaters, and activate propagation units.

The ventilator-opening units have proved to be invaluable to the amateur. Ventilators can be made to open and close at exactly the correct time in relation to the temperature of the air within the greenhouse, and not when it suits the owner. These units rely on the expansion of a sub-

A thermostat is invaluable for controlling the temperature in an electrically heated greenhouse.

stance, which, when warmed by the temperature within the greenhouse, expands and forces a piston to open the ventilators.

Greenhouse heaters can be linked to thermostats which switch on the heater. The exact temperature at which the heater operates can be adjusted according to the hardiness of the plants within the greenhouse. However, ensure that an excessive temperature is not given, as this may damage the plants and be very costly. Use this in conjunction with a minimum and maximum temperature thermometer, so that you can check that the heating is operating at the correct temperature and not wasting energy.

Propagation units set in a greenhouse can be effectively heated by electricity at a very reasonable cost. A thermostat operates to prevent the soil temperature rising too high, or becoming cold. Mist propagation units are controlled by moisture-sensing units, as described earlier.

6 Fitments and equipment

Benches and shelves

Staging is an important and valuable part of greenhouse equipment. Benches are essential when a greenhouse is to be used primarily for growing flowering pot and house plants, especially when they are displayed for their beauty. Benches are also very valuable for raising plants from seeds or rooting cuttings in boxes or pots; ideally, the benches should be slatted, to allow warm air to rise up through them from the heaters below and thus provide bottom heat. The dark place under the benches in a greenhouse with basal walls can be used for storage or for such purposes as blanching endives and forcing rhubarb.

Benches are usually fitted 30–34 in (75–85 cm) above floor level – a comfortable working height. If possible, they should be 3–3½ ft (90–105 cm) wide. Whether slatted or solid, they should be fitted away from the wall, to allow for air circulation. The materials most commonly used are wood (redwood), particularly when the

Often made of red cedar or softwood, benches or staging in a greenhouse gives more space.

benches are slatted, Transite (a cement product that won't rot), and hardware cloth (heavy wire with a small mesh).

Shelves are of great value in a greenhouse, and should be of similar construction. They are very useful for keeping plants near the light, especially in winter.

Aluminum shelves, fixed above the staging to the greenhouse structure, are a great asset.

They are particularly valuable for displaying pendulous plants, such as cascade chrysanthemums. If of softwood, benches and shelves must be kept regularly painted.

Watering

Systematic watering is essential to all kinds of plants grown in a greenhouse.

Watering by hand For this task it is important to have a watering-can with a long spout fitted with a fine rose that delivers a gentle stream of water, particularly when seeds, seedlings and small cuttings are being handled. There are several good ones available from nursery supply houses. The best, unfortunately, are expensive, as they are imported.

When watering by hand it is of great value to use a moisture indicator (available from many nursery supply firms), which takes much of the guesswork out of the task.

Automatic watering Watering by hand can be a hard and inconvenient chore, yet to fail to water, even once, might result in disaster. Fortunately, automatic watering systems, not too expensive and quite easy to install, are now available.

A very good type is a capillary system, which allows plants in pots to keep themselves automatically supplied with their requirements of water. The pots, which should not be crocked, are stood on a suitable substance which is usually sand and which is contained in a specially constructed fiberglass tray on the bench, or on a capillary fiber mat laid out on a plastic sheet directly on the staging. In either case, there is a supply trough that overhangs the front edge of the staging and is kept filled with water. The water is absorbed continuously by the sand or base material. In the case of the sand tray, this absorption is achieved by means of a fiberglass wick partially buried in the sand with its ends in the water. The capillary mat, on the other hand, is cut to shape so that a tongue can be inserted in the trough.

With automatic watering equipment, water is transferred from a tank to the sand on which the plants are standing.

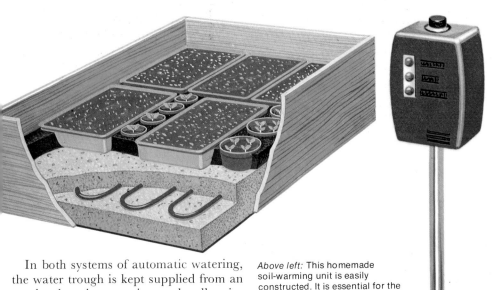

In both systems of automatic watering, the water trough is kept supplied from an overhead tank or an inverted gallon jar (4·5 liters), which can be refilled periodically. If, however, mains water is turned on, the system can be made fully automatic by means of a ball valve and float.

Above left: This homemade soil-warming unit is easily constructed. It is essential for the propagation of certain plants and lowers running costs.

Above right: A moisture indicator minimizes the risk of plant fatalities caused by drying out or overwatering.

Soil warming

Soil warming is a very useful and inexpensive modern greenhouse technique. By warming the soil in the borders or on the benches, it is possible to increase the range of heat-loving plants that can be grown. It is also of the greatest use in seed germination, rooting cuttings and producing out-of-season vegetables and fruits. This can all be done without raising the temperature of the whole greenhouse.

Warming cables can be bought in lengths and watts ranging from 20 ft (6 m), carrying 75 watts, which will heat 10–12 sq ft (0·9–1·1 sq m) to 267 ft (82 m), carrying 1000 watts, suitable for a surface of 133–166 sq ft (12·5–15 sq m). The soil-warming system is quite easy to install. However, if you are inexperienced in such matters, you should seek the help of a qualified electrician for connection of the cables to the mains supply. First, place a sheet of asbestos or roofing felt on the bench and erect 9 in (22·5 cm) wooden walls

around it. In the bottom of this enclosure, put a 2 in (5 cm) layer of coarse washed river sand. The warming cable is laid on this base, running evenly backwards and forwards. It is then covered with a further 2–3 in (5–7·5 cm) of sand. The seed pans or boxes are stood on this sand. To ensure a uniform temperature throughout the bed, pack granulated peat in the spaces between the seed containers. If desired, part or the whole of the sand bed can be covered with a mixture of peat and sand and the cuttings to be rooted can be inserted directly into it.

If it is necessary to warm the air around the plants, a similar warming cable can be run round the walls, and the bed covered with a sheet of glass or plastic.

Generally, if the power is switched on for ten to twelve hours each night, all the heat needed is given. If completely automatic control is desired, a soil-warming thermostat should be fitted. Ready-wired units can be purchased.

Propagation units

Propagation units are useful devices, particularly for rooting cuttings. To succeed in getting roots to grow on a short length of stem it is necessary to keep the stem perfectly healthy and the tissues active; if it flags in any way, rooting is not likely to take place. If, however, the process is allowed to take place in a propagation case, the temperature and humidity will be higher than if it occurs out in the open greenhouse. In consequence, the tissues of the leaves and stems remain moist and the rooting process is accelerated.

Two very simple forms of propagating case are, firstly, a seed box covered with a sheet of glass and, secondly, a plastic bag enveloping a seed pan or a pot. The more highly developed propagation units are based on the elementary principle embodied in these two devices.

A propagating case has numerous uses. In the first place, it allows a cold

greenhouse to be used for raising seeds and rooting cuttings with little extra expenditure on fuel. It also enables an earlier start to be made with raising seeds, which results in earlier crops in the greenhouse – for example, tomatoes. Flowers, normally produced from seeds planted during the summer for the following year, need not be exposed to severe winter weather. They can be sown in January in a propagator to produce better summer results. If a propagation unit is used in a heated greenhouse, the greenhouse can be satisfactorily run at

Right: This miniature propagator has dimensions of about 13½ in (34 cm) long and 8 in (20 cm) wide.

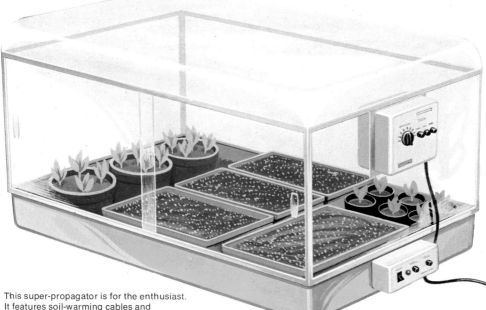

This super-propagator is for the enthusiast. It features soil-warming cables and thermostatic control of the temperature.

10–20°F (5–10°C), lower than it would otherwise be run.

Among the more sophisticated propagation cases that can be purchased, the simplest and smallest consists of a heating panel on which stands a plastic standard seed tray containing sown seeds and covered with a ventilated plastic cover. It can also be used to provide bottom heat for small pot plants and cuttings. They should be stood on *moist* gravel that almost fills the tray. There are more elaborate models, such as a multi-top unit that has four seed trays with covers, and a large one, thermostatically controlled, with greater headroom to allow young plants to grow to maturity. This is, in effect, a miniature heated greenhouse that can be housed in a cooler one.

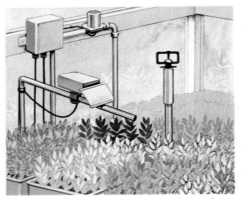

Above: Mist propagation is useful in rooting cuttings.

Below: By controlling greenhouse lighting, the gardener can make chrysanthemums bloom any time of year that he wishes.

Mist propagation Mention has already been made of the failure to root when a cutting dries off. While it is not a system that many amateurs are likely to employ, mist propagation is one that has been designed to lessen this risk. By this method, cuttings will root better and more quickly.

Fundamentally, the equipment consists of mist nozzles mounted on standpipes and connected to a water-feed pipe, placed at intervals of 3–4 ft (1–1·25 m) along the bench (from which the drainage must be perfect), a control box, a solenoid valve and a detector, which is placed among the cuttings. The latter works on the balance principle and has two arms, one with an absorbent pad, the other being a low-voltage electrical contact. While the cuttings are being sprayed, the pad absorbs moisture and eventually becomes heavy enough to break the electrical contact of the other arm. As moisture evaporates from the pad (and the cuttings get drier), it lightens, contact is made again, and through the solenoid valve and the control box the mist is turned on. This works in conjunction with soil warming.

Greenhouse lighting

For the enthusiast, lighting in the greenhouse is essential. For general lighting, ordinary light bulbs are quite suitable; however, waterproof fittings are essential.

Another interesting aspect of greenhouse lighting is its use in extending the duration of daylight. Chrysanthemums, in particular, respond to this, because in natural conditions they form their buds during the long summer days, and flower when they shorten. By artificially lengthening and shortening the day by means of lighting, they can be made to bloom at any time.

453

7 Greenhouse culture

Fertilizing greenhouse plants

Greenhouse plants, like outdoor ones, need certain plant foods. The main ones are nitrogen, potassium, phosphorus, magnesium and a small number of others known as trace elements, in which iron and manganese are normally included, that are consumed in small quantities.

The functions of the main plant foods are as follows.

Nitrogen This element assists in leaf production, but an excess of nitrogen leads to lush growth, prone to disease. It is also an important ingredient in the synthesis of many essential plant chemicals.

Potassium This plays an important role in the plant's manufacture and utilization of starch. It also assists in the development of roots, tubers, seeds and flowers, particularly enhancing the color, and helps to ripen young wood, reducing its vulnerability to disease and early frosts.

Phosphorus This element plays a very important role in the formation of tissue cells and in plant growth. Without it, plants will become stunted.

Magnesium, iron, manganese These three are either essential ingredients of, or essential to the production of, chlorophyl, which enables plants to manufacture starch.

Greenhouse plants get their essential foods in the same way as outdoor plants – from fertilizer. The main sources of fertilizers are the composts that are used for potting, which normally contain balanced mixtures. Others are the liquid manures that are subsequently applied.

Composts

Two growing media are used in home greenhouses: the traditional potting composts, and the newer soilless composts, which have to a large extent superseded the former. Though most gardeners now buy their composts, it is as well to know how they are made up.

Potting soils These can vary in the proportion of their major ingredients and added fertilizer materials, but basically contain 2 parts of garden top soil, 1 part peat moss, leafmold or compost, and 1 part coarse sand. For a porous mixture, the peat moss or other organic materials can be

Useful data for greenhouse gardeners:

1 bushel (32 liters) of potting compost is sufficient for:

6 standard seed boxes, 3 in (7·5 cm) deep

90 rooted cuttings in 3 in (7·5 cm) pots

50 larger plants in 4½ in (11·25 cm) pots

16 mature plants in 8 in (20 cm) pots

reduced, eliminated, or increased to reach an especially rich, organic mixture. The fertilizers can be dehydrated manure (easily obtained in bags from garden centers), bone meal or superphosphate. Limestone is added when tests indicate its need.

Soilless Mixes These mixes have great advantages for the home greenhouse owner, one of the first being that the mixes are sterilized. There are several kinds on the market now which differ from each other in slight aspects, but the major ingredients are peat moss, perlite, vermiculite, sand and sufficient fertilizer for about six weeks, after which the grower must start applying liquid foods. Some brands have special formulation for seeds or cuttings or types of plants. Some trade names are Redi-Earth, Pro-Mix, Jiffy Mix.

Propagation

There are a number of ways in which to propagate plants. It must, however, be remembered that only with species is it possible to obtain true reproduction by sowing seeds; many cultivars must be propagated vegetatively – for example, by means of cuttings.

Seed propagation Most seeds will germinate readily if given some heat, ideally by placing them in a propagator.

Seeds should be sown thinly and as shallowly as possible in trays, pans or boxes. If they are very fine, mix them with sand for better distribution. Water them and place them in the propagator. Cover them with brown paper to exclude the light and close the transparent dome. As soon as germination takes place, remove the paper and lift the cover to allow the air to circulate.

When the seedlings are large enough to handle, prick them out. Use a cleft stick to lift them, and firm them into prepared holes in moist compost in another box. Shade the seedlings for a short while until they are established. Finally, when large enough, put each in a pot containing compost.

Stem cuttings Different types of stem cuttings are used for propagating softwoods and hardwoods. For softwood plants, nodal cuttings are usually taken. They should be about 2 in (5 cm) long, cut from a shoot and trimmed off with a sharp knife just below a node (leaf joint). The lower leaves should be removed. The prepared cuttings should be inserted in moist cutting compost in a box, or around the edge of a pot, and kept in a moist, warm atmosphere until growth commences – evidence that roots have formed.

When a good root ball is formed, they should be re-potted into larger pots.

Nodal cuttings of hardwood plants are taken and prepared in much the same way, usually at the end of the growing season. They are usually about 10 in (25 cm) long. They should be inserted into moist compost, and should initially be shaded. When they are growing they should be potted on.

Another type of cutting, often taken from

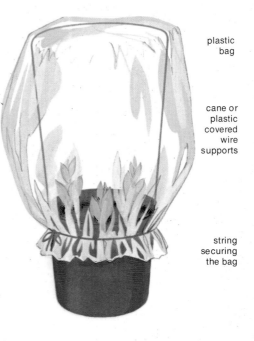

plastic
bag

cane or
plastic
covered
wire
supports

string
securing
the bag

An improvised propagator will provide a moist, warm atmosphere for a small number of cuttings.

plants that are more difficult to root, consists of side shoots, of about the same length, torn away from the stem with a heel of the more mature wood. This end should be inserted in moist compost and then be allowed to root.

Stem sections Certain plants, such as ficus and dracaena, can be propagated by cutting a thin section of a stem containing a

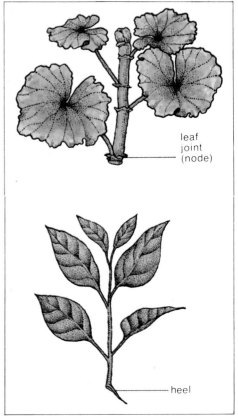

bud. When planted just below the surface in cutting compost a good plant will develop.

Leaf-bud cuttings This form of propagation is especially suited to aphelandra, pilea, ficus and camellia. A centrally situated dormant bud is cut out from a semi-ripe wood stem, with a leaf intact. The length of the portion of stem removed should be about ¾ in (2 cm) long. This is planted in a vertical position in cutting compost, with the leaf and bud just above the soil surface.

Division and root cuttings Some plants can be propagated by division. This means that the root of an established plant is cut into several viable portions with a sharp

Above left: A bud cutting. The drawing on the left shows the bud being taken, and on the right planted.

Top: A nodal cutting of a softwood plant
Above: A heel cutting of a hardwood plant

Below: Crocks at the bottom of a seed box will ensure that the box has good drainage.

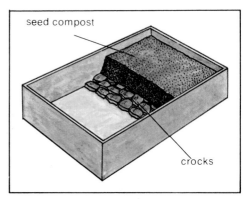

456

cut

cut

Above: Propagate fleshy-leaved plants by snipping main veins and laying their leaves flat on compost.

Below: Streptocarpus are propagated by dividing a leaf and planting each part upright in compost to root.

knife, and planted in compost. In every case the portion used should have at least one healthy eye or shoot and some healthy roots. This form of propagation can be practiced with chlorophytum, maranta, iris and dahlia. There is also another form of division, applicable to bulbs and corms. These have attached to them smaller bulbs and corms, known as offsets, which can be detached and planted in pots.

Allied to division are root cuttings. These are sections of roots cut into pieces, some 2–3 in (5–7·5 cm) long. They are inserted into compost in boxes.

Air Layering When some plants (such as the rubber plant) are too high for their surroundings, roots can be made to grow in the stem about 18 in (45 cm) from the top by making a slanting upwards cut three-quarters through the stem. Wedge a small piece of wood into the cut and pack damp peat or moss into the cut around the wound. Wrap polyethylene around the moss and tie it to the stem. After a month, roots will have formed and the rooted part can be cut off and potted up.

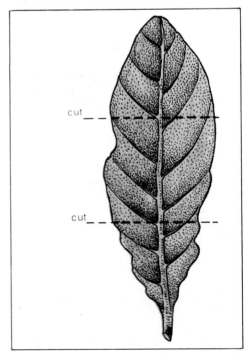

cut

cut

457

8 Growing plants under glass

At the beginning of each of the descriptions that follow is a recommendation pertaining to the type of greenhouse needed for successful cultivation of the plant in question. Sometimes alternatives are suggested: for example, 'cool or warm'. Generally, while a specific plant can be grown under the cooler conditions, it is normally better when cultivated at the higher temperature.

Anthurium scherzerianum (flamingo plant, painter's palette)

Tropical or warm. A most colorful plant with a bold, bright scarlet, wax-like spathe about 3 in (7·5 cm) wide and long, enclosing a spiral orange-red spike (spadix). Its leaves are long, shiny, lance-shaped and light green.

It is propagated by dividing the rootstock in February. The divisions are planted in potting compost in such a way that the roots are high in the pot on a slight mound. Half-fill the pot, which should be 6 in (15 cm) across if the size warrants it, with crocks. This plant needs humidity.

Anthurium scherzerianum is a colorful, fascinating and very exotic plant.

Aphelandra squarrosa 'Louisae' (zebra plant)

Tropical or warm. A very popular, beautiful, showy plant. It has 10 in (25 cm)-long pointed dark green leaves with veins that are boldly cream in color. During summer and autumn it produces yellow flowers, which should be removed as they fade. Two other attractive varieties are *A. squarrosa* 'Brockfield' and *A. squarrosa* 'Silver Beauty'.

Aphelandra are propagated from cuttings taken during the spring and summer and rooted in sowing compost at 70°F (21°C) in a propagator. They should be potted on in potting compost. Feed while they are in flower.

Aspidistra elatior (cast-iron plant, parlor palm)

Cool. This foliage plant was a great favorite of the Victorians and Edwardians. It has beautiful long, wide, shiny green leaves.

Aphelandra squarrosa is beautiful but difficult to grow.

A. *elatior* 'Variegata' has cream variegated leaves.

This plant needs little attention, although it is beneficial to sponge its leaves from time to time. It is best to re-pot it in the spring, but this should be carried out only after several years.

Propagate by dividing the rhizome in March so that each piece has some leaf and roots. Plant in potting compost.

Begonia

Cool or warm. *Begonia rex* is grown entirely for the beauty of its leaves, which include silver, dark green, pink and darkest purple colours. It is propagated by means of the leaves, which are cut across the back of the main veins and pinned down flat on a surface of cutting compost in a tray. They are then placed in a propagator at 64–70°F (18–21°C). Another interesting foliage begonia is *B. masoniana* (iron cross begonia).

B. semperflorens is fibrous-rooted and has red, pink or white flowers; these begonias make lovely greenhouse plants for the later autumn. Seeds are sown in late June. They should be put into a propagator at 64°F (18°C) and then potted on. They like humid conditions.

Begonia 'Gloire de Lorraine' (Christmas begonia) is winter-flowering, with clusters

Few greenhouse plants are more beautiful than *Begonia rex*, with its colorful, almost triangular leaves.

Aspidistra elatior 'Variegata' is grown for its foliage.

of delicate rose-pink flowers. It is propagated from cuttings and basal shoots taken in spring and ultimately potted on in 6 in (15 cm) pots. It likes a moist and semi-shady warm position when potted. Its stems must be supported. Remove all flower buds until October, when they should be allowed to develop, and then give weekly doses of liquid fertilizer. After flowering, cut the plants down by half and keep them, watering little, until early spring at which time they will provide more cuttings.

Beloperone guttata
(shrimp plant)

Warm. This plant's common name results from its pinkish-brown bracts that resemble shrimps. It prefers a warm house and should be grown in well-drained potting compost. It should be given plenty of water during the summer, but little in the winter.

Cuttings should be taken in early summer and inserted in soilless sowing compost

Beloperone guttata has become a favorite exotic pot plant. It seldom exceeds 1 ft (30 cm) in height.

at 64°F (18°C), and then potted on into 3 in (7·5 cm) pots and afterwards 5 in (13 cm) pots. Bushiness should be induced by regular pinching back of the shoots. When established, give liquid manure regularly during the summer.

Bouvardia longiflora (syn. humboldtii) (Sweet Bouvardia)
Warm or cool. Nowadays it is usual to grow varieties, of which 'President Cleveland', with its terminal clusters of bright crimson-scarlet tubular flowers, is representative. They flower from fall through winter.

After flowering, rest the plants with little watering until late spring. Then water the soil and spray the stems to start fresh growth. Also prune, if necessary. Pinch back during the summer to encourage late flowering.

Propagate from cuttings from young shoots placed in a propagator at 66°F (19°C), or from root cuttings.

Brunfelsia (syn. Franciscea) calycina
Tropical or warm. Has fragrant, salvia-shaped violet-purple flowers with a long tube, which fade to almost white from winter to spring. The variety 'Macrantha' has 3 in (7·5 cm) wide flowers.

After flowering, shorten the stalks by half and encourage new growth by spraying with water. Provide a moist atmosphere.

Propagate from cuttings taken between February and August. Insert in soilless cutting compost and give bottom heat at about 70°F (21°C).

Bulbs (spring)
Most bulbs are easy to grow, and do not need any great heat. They provide a magnificent display in the greenhouse. A few planted successively from late summer onwards will bloom from Christmas until

460

May. As they spend much of their growing time in plunge beds outdoors, they do not take up space in the greenhouse for long.

The most popular bulbs are daffodils, hyacinths and tulips. Daffodils and hyacinths should be planted so that their noses are just visible through the surface of the soil, tulips should be just covered, and small bulbs such as crocuses and snow-drops buried by ¼–½ in (6–12 mm).

The following description of the cultivation of daffodil bulbs is fairly typical, despite small modifications for other bulbs.

Daffodil bulbs should be planted in a general purpose soil mixture or a soilless potting mixture. A 6 in (15 cm) pot will accommodate three or four bulbs.

After planting, place the pot in the soil in a cool plunge bed outdoors for about eight weeks, when the young, pale green leaves appear. Then bring them into the green-

Trumpet daffodils brighten the dark days of winter.

house and stand them in a dim light until the leaves turn green, when the pot should be given more light and warmth – a day temperature of 50°F (10°C) – until the plants flower. Water as necessary.

After they have flowered, put the pots outside. When the leaves are dead, harvest and dry the bulbs, and plant them *outdoors* the following fall.

Daffodil bulbs which are planted in August–October will flower from early to late winter, according to variety and when the plants are brought into the greenhouse.

Tulip bulbs planted in September–October flower from January to April. These will stand rather more heat, up to 60°F (15°C).

Hyacinth bulbs planted in September–October flower from January to March. These usually take about seven weeks to produce growth when plunged.

Calceolaria are best grown in pots under glass.

Calceolaria
(slipper flower)
Cool. It is the herbaceous calceolaria that is grown most frequently in a greenhouse. This has large clusters of red-orange and red flowers with distinctive markings and ovate mid-green leaves. Many fine hybrids are obtainable.

461

The seeds are sown thinly in seed compost and germinated at 64°F (18°C) during June, with shading when needed. Prick off the seedlings singly into pots in July and keep in a cold frame. In September pot on into 4 in (10 cm) pots and take inside. Keep warm and moist at night at a steady temperature. In February pot on again in 8 in (20 cm) pots using growing compost. Keep near the glass, shading from strong sun. Stake securely and water modestly. Feed with liquid manure fortnightly when buds appear.

Camellia

Cool. These popular plants are much appreciated for their shapely white, pink and red flowers and their rich green, shiny, bold foliage. They need comparatively little attention other than regular, fairly modest watering and occasional feeding. They might need re-potting every three or four years.

They can be propagated by taking leaf bud cuttings.

Campanula isophylla
(Italian bellflower)

Cool. *Campanula isophylla* is a prostrate plant, which overhangs the rim of its pot and has star-shaped blue flowers in abundance during August and September. Its cultivar *Campanula isophylla* 'Alba', with white blooms, is even more charming. It is useful for hanging baskets.

It should be watered and fed regularly while flowering and dead-headed regularly. Do not overwater in winter.

Propagate from cuttings from sturdy basal shoots taken in spring. Insert these in cutting compost and provide some warmth.

Carnations

Cool. Carnations will produce flowers continuously throughout the year, with some peak periods, in a cool, well-ventilated greenhouse with plenty of headroom.

New carnations are usually supplied in spring in 3 in (7·5 cm) pots. On arrival they

Campanula isophylla 'Alba' is excellent for using in a hanging basket.

can be transplanted into 6 in (15 cm) pots, or to a raised 9 in (22·5 cm)-high bed on the ground, of a rich organic soil that is slightly alkaline. Place the plants 8 in (20 cm) apart each way in the bed.

When the plants are growing well, pinch their tips out to encourage the growth of side-shoots. When these are about 6 in (15 cm) long, they in turn can have all the buds removed, except one, so that each stem only bears one good bloom.

Regular watering is very important: water quite copiously during the summer, with much less in winter when growth slows up. A night temperature of up to 50°F (10°C) is suitable; during the summer a little light shading might be needed to lower the daytime temperature.

Carnations should be supported with canes and wire rings when in pots, and with large-mesh netting, about 6 in (15 cm), strung from four corner posts when growing in a bed. After the first blooms are cut, the carnations should then be fed with a fertilizer which is suitable for carnations.

Carnations last two years, so new stocks should be raised by taking side cuttings in early spring. Plant them in cutting compost and place them in a propagator at 61–64°F (16–18°C), admitting air when the tips begin to grow and lowering the temperature to 50°F (10°C) over the course of a week. Then pot into 3 in (7·5 cm) pots. When they are 9 in (22·5 cm) tall, remove the growing tip; repeat if desired when the resultant side shoots are long enough. Pot on when needed.

Chlorophytum
(spider plant)
Cool or warm. *Chlorophytum elatum* 'Variegatum' is the variety most grown, solely for its long, grass-like leaves, which are green with a broad streak of white running down their center. These plants are excellent for hanging baskets.

The spider plant is very easy to grow. Apart from reasonable watering during the summer, and a regular feed with liquid manure, little more is needed.

Inconspicuous flowers develop in the ends of long slender stems, weighing them down. Chlorophytum can be propagated by planting the plantlets that are formed as the flowers fade. Otherwise, root divisions can be taken in spring or summer.

Chrysanthemum
(late-flowering)
Cool. Start with disease-free, rooted cuttings. Subsequently new plants can be raised by taking cuttings from the old plants.

To do this, cut selected healthy plants down to 6–9 in (15–22·5 cm) *immediately* after flowering, still keeping them in their pots. Give an initial watering, and keep

them in a light airy position in the greenhouse at a temperature no higher than 50°F (10°C) without much further watering.

After a time basal shoots will appear. Choose healthy shoots about ⅛ in (3 mm) thick, with four or five fresh leaves closely spaced along the stem, for cuttings. Guard

Chlorophytum elatum 'Variegatum' (spider plant) is very easy to grow and propagate.

against aphids by spraying them with malathion. Propagate by cutting the shoots just below a node.

If necessary, trim off any lower leaves to facilitate planting. Wet the lower ends of the stems and insert in a rooting compound. Shake off the surplus powder, and insert in coarse sand and peat moss or soil-less cutting compost, 2 in (5 cm) apart, in a seed-box. Place the cuttings in a moist atmosphere and provide bottom heat up to about 60°F (15°C) for about a week or ten days, preferably in a propagator. When they show signs of growth shade them with paper on bright days, and when they become robust give the cuttings both ventilation and a temperature which is no higher than 45°F (7°C).

463

When they are well rooted, transplant the cuttings into a general purpose potting soil or soilless potting compost in 3 in (7·5 cm) pots and place them in a cold frame. About the end of May, when the root ball is well-formed, move into 9 in (22·5 cm) pots. At the same time, insert two stakes, at least 3 ft (1 m) tall, in the compost either side of the plant. Tie each stem securely but not tightly to these.

Stand the potted chrysanthemums outdoors in rows on boards or another hard surface for the summer. To prevent them from blowing over, tie the stakes to horizontal wires running along the rows. In late September bring the pots into the greenhouse, giving them good ventilation and a little heat.

Chrysanthemums first form a terminal bud on the main stem. As soon as the side shoots appear at the leaf joints, remove this bud, for it will either die or give poor flowers. Allow the side shoots to develop buds. The center large one, known as the first crown bud, produces the best decorative blooms. All the other buds on each side shoot that is retained should be removed, leaving one bloom to a stem. All further

Clivia miniata blooms best when it is pot-bound. It is as tough and durable as the aspidistra.

side shoots should also be pinched out as they form.

Clivia miniata

Cool. This plant has strap-shaped leaves and lily-like clusters of flowers of orange-red. Young plants need re-potting every

Chrysanthemums are first 'stopped' by pinching out the 'break bud', which either dies or flowers poorly, appearing on the main stem when shoots first appear in the leaf axils (*left*). The latter are eventually 'disbudded' to leave the center bud or 'first crown bud', which usually produces the best blooms. It is then 'secured' by removing any further axil shoots that appear (*right*).

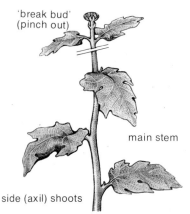

'break bud'
(pinch out)

main stem

side (axil) shoots

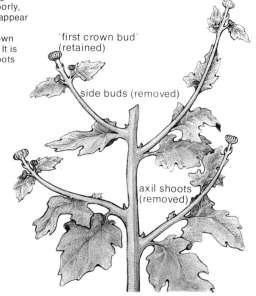

'first crown bud'
(retained)

side buds (removed)

axil shoots
(removed)

year into 8 in (20 cm) pots. Mature plants may remain undisturbed for several years if they are top-dressed with fresh rich soil annually, and fed occasionally with liquid manure. After they have flowered keep them warm and moist. Then give them a resting period, which can be induced by minimizing watering.

Propagation is best achieved by division after flowering or from offsets.

Codiaeum
(croton)
Tropical or warm. Various crotons are grown for their leaves, variegated with brilliant hues ranging from yellow to orange-pink, red and crimson. These colors are more vivid in plants raised annually.

The plants need a moist, very warm atmosphere all the time and must have good light. They should be well watered during the summer and given a weekly feed of liquid fertilizer. They are best potted on annually in spring.

They can be propagated by cuttings at any time from the ends of shoots, inserted singly in 2 in (5 cm) pots of cutting compost and put into a propagator at 70°F (21°C).

Good crotons to grow are *Codiaeum variegatum pictum* and its cultivars 'Duke of Windsor,' 'Elaine' and 'Imperialis'.

Coleus blumei
Cool or warm. Coleus are grown for their colorful foliage. They should be regularly watered during the summer, and much less so in winter. A temperature of 55°F (13°C) is best in winter. Feed with liquid manure weekly from June to September. Growing tips should be pinched.

Codiaeum variegatum pictum (croton) is extremely rewarding but is not really easy to grow.

Seeds may be sown in February and germinated at 61°F (16°C). When large enough, pot the seedlings on into 3 in (7·5 cm) and then 5 in (13 cm) pots. Alternatively, take tip cuttings of non-flowering shoots in spring. Plant them in cutting compost in 3 in (7·5 cm) pots and keep them in a temperature of 61–64°F (16–18°C).

Columnea gloriosa is a beautiful trailer. Though not the easiest to grow, it is well worth persevering with it.

Columnea gloriosa

Warm. With its tubular flowers of bright scarlet and drooping habit, *Columnea gloriosa* is ideal for hanging baskets. It flowers during the winter.

It needs a warm, humid atmosphere (no lower than 55–61°F (13–16°C) during winter). Feed established plants regularly with weak liquid manure during the summer. Re-pot this plant every other year in June.

Pieces of stems root quite easily in a cutting compost placed in a propagator with a temperature of 64–70°F (18–21°C) and a humid atmosphere. The stem pieces should be taken in spring.

Cyclamen persicum

Cool or warm. The modern strains of the Persian cyclamen, a popular winter-flowering plant, have blooms in shades of purple, red, pink, mauve and white and combinations of these, and variously silver-marbled leaves.

The plants should be brought into the greenhouse in September and given ample ventilation, light and a temperature of 50°F (10°C). Watering must be done carefully from the bottom without wetting the bare corms. After flowering, the plants should be rested by gradually watering less and, during the summer, laying the pots on their sides to dry off. In autumn, growth should be re-started by watering.

Cyclamen are best propagated from seeds sown in August at a temperature of 55–61°F (13–16°C). Then pot them on until they are in 5 in (13 cm) pots. At no stage should the corms be buried.

Dieffenbachia picta
(dumb cane)

Warm. This has dark green, pointed, oblong leaves covered with white and pale green spots. Its cultivar 'Rudolph Roehrsii' is mottled pale and dark green.

Dieffenbachia needs a humid atmosphere with a winter temperature not lower than 61°F (16°C).

It is propagated from suckers or stem sections containing an eye in a cutting compost at a temperature of 70–75°F (21–24°C) in a propagator.

Dracaena draco
(dragon plant)

The species and varieties of dracaenas are grown for their superb range of foliage. Among the more attractive species are the smaller *Dracaena godseffiana* and *D. sanderiana*. A large cultivar is *D. deremensis* 'Warneckii', which has long gray-green leaves with two silver stripes. *D. draco*, the dragon tree, is a unique tree with a tall, heavy trunk and odd tufts of foliage. Young plants are used as pot subjects.

Dracaena fragrans 'Massangena' has attractive green and gold leaves and likes a warm, humid atmosphere.

The plants need a winter temperature of 50–55°F (10–13°C), rising to 61°F (16°C) at night in spring and summer to encourage growth. The atmosphere must be humid.

They are propagated from cuttings of a main stem, partially buried horizontally in cutting compost in a propagator at 70–75°F (21–24°C).

Euphorbia pulcherrima (poinsettia)

Warm or tropical. This splendid plant has insignificant flowers, but large scarlet, leaf-like bracts in winter. It is also available in pink and cream forms. The new hybrids are especially rugged, lasting for months in good condition.

It needs a winter temperature of 55–61°F (13–16°C). During the summer it needs a humid atmosphere. It should be watered freely while growing, but after flowering it should be kept just moist. Give weak liquid manure weekly from June to September, during which period it can stand outdoors.

Poinsettia is difficult to preserve from one season to another so it is better to grow new plants from cuttings taken in spring. These should be inserted singly in 3 in (7·5 cm) pots of cutting compost and placed in a propagator at 64–70°F (18–21°C). The rooted cuttings should be potted on, and feeding should begin in their final pots.

Ficus elastica 'Decora' (India-rubber plant)

Warm. This plant is grown for its rich, green, bold foliage.

In winter it needs a temperature of 61–64°F (16–18°C). Water freely in summer and keep just moist in winter. Place in a well-lit position, but out of direct sunlight. Provide a humid atmosphere in summer, with ventilation when needed,

Few plants can surpass *Euphorbia pulcherrima* (poinsettia) for the splendid color it gives.

There are many beautiful varieties of indoor fuchsia, which are grown as both bushes and standards.

and pot on every other spring. Feed with weak liquid manure during the summer.

The plant can be propagated from cuttings of lateral shoots taken from April to June at a temperature of 70–75°F (21–24°C), or from leaf-bud cuttings.

Fuchsia

Cool or warm. The tender varieties of fuchsia are attractive as pot plants and provide beautiful summer flower displays in greenhouses.

After resting during winter, when they should be kept in a dry, well-lit place at a temperature 39–45°F (4–7°C), fuchsias should be started into growth by being plunged into water and kept at a temperature of 50°F (10°C). (Any cuttings required should be taken when the young growth appears.) After removing as much soil as possible from the roots, pot the plants in a standard potting compost in a similar or smaller pot.

During the spring and summer fuchsias should be allowed to stand in a cool, well-lit place out of direct sunlight. Real success with fuchsias results from feeding and watering well during the growing and flowering season. Spraying the foliage with water occasionally will also prove beneficial to the plant.

Cuttings should be taken from shoots with no flower buds and should be nodal. They should be inserted in 2 in (5 cm) pots of cutting compost and placed in a propagator at 61°F (16°C) until they are rooted, when air should be allowed in and the temperature lowered to 50°F (10°C). Young plants destined to be bushes must have their growing tip pinched back to induce bushiness. This may be repeated once or twice more if necessary. For standards, the plants should not be pinched back, but the main stem should be allowed to grow, removing all laterals as they appear, until the required height is reached, when it should be stopped.

Fuchsia bushes should be pruned lightly in February. At this time, overgrown plants can be hard-pruned to reduce their size. Standards are also pruned.

Pendulous varieties, such as 'Falling Stars' and golden-foliaged 'Golden Marinka', are excellent for hanging baskets, either to beautify a greenhouse, or to hang outdoors during the summer providing a glorious display.

Gerbera
(Transvaal daisy, Barberton daisy)

Cool. *Gerbera jamesonii* has orange-scarlet, daisy-like flowers from May to December. There are also many hybrids and varieties in a wide range of colors.

Gerbera needs well-drained soil and cool conditions, with a temperature of 41–45°F (5–7C) during the winter. Water freely in summer and more sparingly in winter, ventilate well and provide some shade when necessary. Apply weak liquid manure every two weeks during the summer.

Gerbera can be propagated by division in March. Alternatively, sow seeds in seed compost in February at a temperature of 61–64°F (16–18°C). Prick out and pot on in the usual manner.

Above: Grevillea robusta is beautiful and easy-to-grow.

Below right: Hoya carnosa is relatively unknown.

Grevillea robusta
(silk bark oak)

Cool. *Grevillea robusta* is a foliage shrub with pinnate leaves up to 15 in (37·5 cm) long.

It requires a winter temperature of 39–45°F (4–7°C) and can be stood out of doors from May to October. Water freely in spring and summer and keep just moist during winter. Feed fortnightly with liquid manure during summer. Re-pot in March every two years, increasing the pot size if necessary.

This plant is propagated from seed sown in March in pots of lime-free sowing compost and germinated at 55–61°F (13–16°C). Prick out into 3 in (7·5 cm) pots and then pot on as necessary.

Hippeastrum
(amaryllis)

Warm or tropical. Hippeastrum are showy, bulbous plants with strap-like green leaves and blooms of white, pink, red or orange, sometimes striped or frilled, according to the hybrid.

Plant one bulb in a 6 in (15 cm) pot of growing compost with half the bulb exposed and water sparsely until growth

begins. As soon as the flower bud appears, or shortly afterwards, water freely and feed weekly with liquid manure. Maintain at a minimum temperature of 55–61°F (13–16°C). When leaves turn yellow, keep dry until re-starting growth in autumn.

Propagate from offsets or seeds sown in the springtime.

Hoya carnosa
(porcelain flower)

Cool or warm. This is a climber with deep green, glossy leaves and clusters of pale pink, sweetly scented flowers during summer.

Keep *H. carnosa* at 50°F (10°C) in winter and at not less than 61°F (16°C) in spring and summer. Provide a little shade when necessary, and abundant water, except in winter. Maintain a good level of humidity in spring and summer and also spray the plant with water when hot. Give liquid manure every three weeks in summer.

The plant is propagated by cuttings 3 in

469

(7·5 cm) long taken in June and July. Root at 61–64°F (16–18°C) in a propagator.

Impatiens sultanii
(busy Lizzie)

Cool or warm. Busy Lizzie has white, orange, magenta, crimson or scarlet flowers from April to October.

It needs a winter temperature of 55°F (13°C). When growth re-starts in March,

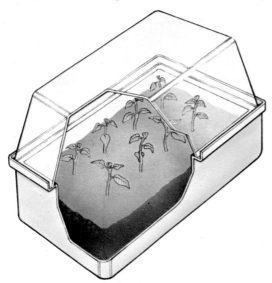

Above: Impatiens sultanii can be propagated from tip cuttings in a propagating unit given bottom heat.

Right: Maranta leuconeura 'Kerchoveana' is called the 'prayer plant' because it raises its leaves at sundown.

water fairly freely. Liquid-feed weekly from May to September and provide a little shade on hot days. Re-pot every other year in April.

Propagate from tip cuttings inserted in cutting compost at any time from April to May. Place in a propagator at 61°F (16°C).

Jasminum mesneyi (syn. primulinum) and J. polyanthum

Cool. *Jasminum mesneyi* (syn. *primulinum*) has yellow flowers in spring. *J. polyanthum* has white and pale pink blooms in winter. Both are climbers.

Both do best in a greenhouse border, but

they can be grown in 12 in (30 cm) pots. They should be trained up wires. In winter, a satisfactory temperature is 50–55°F (10–13°C). Keep the compost moist continuously and water freely during the growing season.

Propagate from heel cuttings and give bottom heat of 61°F (16°C).

Maranta

Warm or tropical. Ornamental foliage plants, with leaves of various shapes marked or streaked in vivid colors. The two most strikingly colored plants are *Maranta leuconeura* 'Kerchoveana' and *M. l. erythrophylla*.

They need a winter temperature of 55°F

(13°C), ample watering in summer, more moderate watering in winter, a humid atmosphere, a daily spraying and a fortnightly liquid feed during their growing season.

They are propagated by rhizome division in April or by planting basal shoot cuttings in the summer in cutting compost at 70°F (21°C).

Above: Howea belmoreana can have a striking decorative effect.

Left: Neanthe elegans is a perfect palm to grow because it requires so little attention.

Palms

Cool. Small palms make good table decorations, and the larger specimens are most attractive for the greenhouse and conservatory. Among the most excellent is *Chamaedorea* (syn. *Neanthe*) *elegans* 'Bella' (parlor palm), with elegant pinnate leaves, up to 4 ft (1·25 m) long, that hang down gracefully. It should be watered freely in summer and have its leaves sprayed weekly. Feed throughout the growing season. Give partial shade: too much sun turns the foliage brown. It needs repotting only when it becomes pot-bound, and this is rare.

Howea (formerly *Kentia*) *belmoreana* (curly palm) is a palm with dark green pinnate leaves 18 in (45 cm) long and 12 in (30 cm) wide, carried on 18 in (45 cm)-long stems.

Howea (formerly *Kentia*) *forsteriana* (Ken-

tia palm), another excellent species, has leaves that differ from those of *H. belmoreana* only in that they droop and have fewer leaflets.

Both of these are grown in a growing compost. Ideally, they should be given a winter greenhouse temperature of 50–54°F (10–12°C); the minimum should be 45°F (7°C). *Howea* need full light in winter, with some shading in summer. Water sparingly between November and March, abundantly from April to July and moderately between July and October.

All the above-mentioned palms can be propagated from seed. Place the seed on the surface of some peat in a seed-pan, and germinate at a temperature of 81°F (27°C). Transplant to 3 in (7·5 cm) pots of growing compost and maintain a temperature of 64°F (18°C) until they are growing.

Pelargonium
(Geranium)

Cool or warm. Fuchsias and pelargoniums have a number of common uses, including greenhouse display, hanging baskets, indoor pot plants and summer bedding.

Among the pelargoniums there are two outstanding groups of hybrids – the regal *P. × domesticum*, among which there are some very beautiful varieties, *P. × hortorum*, and the zonal pelargoniums. These latter are commonly known as geraniums, and include hundreds of outstanding named cultivars. There are also varieties of foliage geraniums, both pendulous types and miniature ones which are suitable for hanging baskets.

Although pelargoniums can be maintained in a greenhouse from year to year, it is more common to take cuttings annually.

Nodal cuttings are taken in August and inserted individually in 3 in (7·5 cm) pots of a general purpose mixture, or in soilless sowing compost. Keep them covered with paper from seven to ten days. Normally no heat is required for rooting. Pinch out the growing tips to form good bushes when the plants are about 6 in (15 cm) high. Pot on into 4–6 in (10–15 cm) pots. Maintain a

Above: Pelargoniums are among the most popular and colorful plants to cultivate in a greenhouse.
Left: Zonal pelargoniums are available in many colorful varieties, all of which are most attractive.

winter temperature of 45–50°F (7–10°C) and keep the soil just moist. Water freely during the growing season. Keep the greenhouse well ventilated and provide shade during the hottest weather – do not let the temperature exceed 55°F (13°C). When well-rooted feed with liquid manure until the flowers open.

Peperomia

Warm or tropical. Mostly moderate-sized or small plants. They like shade from the sun, and grow in well-drained compost. They should have a humid atmosphere during summer and be sprayed twice daily, but they must not be overwatered and be allowed to dry out before the next watering. The best winter temperature for them is 55–65°F (13–18°C) and in summer 60–75°F (15–24°C).

They are propagated by cuttings inserted singly 2 in (5 cm) pots of cutting compost in a propagator at 75°F (24°C).

Pilea

Warm or tropical. The best known are *Pilea cadierei* (aluminum plant) and *P. muscosa* (artillery plant).

They require a winter temperature of 55°F (13°C) and a summer one of 75°F (24°C). They also need full light in winter and moderate shade in spring and summer. Water freely from April to September, very moderately in winter. Feed fortnightly during summer.

Propagate from cuttings in May. Insert in cutting compost and place in the propagator at 64–70°F (18–21°C).

Plumbago capensis

Cool or warm, *Plumbago capensis* is a lovely deciduous climbing plant with panicles of

Pilea cadierei is a very charming foliage plant.

Peperomia caperata has curious cream flowers, like shepherd's crooks, borne on light brown stalks.

blue flowers from April to November.

While it can be grown in a pot, it is best planted in the border and trained up wires or a trellis. It should be watered well until after flowering, and then kept just moist and watered increasingly as new growth appears. The best temperature up to December is 55–61°F (13–16°C); the minimum during the winter is 45°F (7°C). Feed regularly during the summer and re-pot annually in the spring.

Propagate from heel cuttings at a temperature of 61–64°F (16–18°C).

Primula

Cool. Primulas are excellent for greenhouses. Possibly the most popular for growing under glass are *Primula malacoides, P. sinensis, P. obconica* and *P.* × *kewensis*.

P. malacoides, although a perennial, is usually grown as an annual. Its leaves are hairy, ovate and pale green. Whorls of star-like flowers, ranging from pale lilac to white open between December and April.

P. sinensis is also a perennial grown as an annual. Its thick stems bear two or three whorls of flowers during winter.

473

P. obconica is also grown as an annual. Its light green leaves cause a rash on sensitive skins. Its winter-produced flowers are in clusters of pink, red, lilac or blue-purple.

P. × kewensis, a perennial hybrid, has fragrant, yellow flowers, borne in whorls on upright stems during the winter.

All primulas require a minimum winter temperature 45°F (7°C). Always keep the plant moist. Feed weekly with liquid manure when the flower stalks start to lengthen.

All are propagated from seeds at 61°F (16°C). Prick off the seedlings into boxes, and transplant them singly into 3 in (7·5 cm) pots of growing compost. Plunge

A very beautiful plant, *Primula obconica* must be handled with care, as its leaves affect sensitive skin.

Rhododendron (syn. *Azalea*) *indicum* is a lovely plant for Christmas decoration.

them outdoors in a shaded frame for the summer. In autumn, pot them on to 6 in (15 cm) pots.

Rhododendron (syn. Azalea) indicum (Indoor or Indian azalea)

Cool or warm. This is an evergreen with many hybrids which become massed in red, pink or white flowers during the winter or early spring.

In autumn the plant should be kept in a well-lighted place and sprayed with clear water. The compost should be kept moist,

but should not become over-wet.

After it has flowered, remove the dead flowers and put outdoors in the sun after the danger of frost has passed. During the summer keep the plant in the shade, water and feed until early October and then bring it back under the glass. If necessary, re-pot into a larger pot after flowering.

Propagate from half-ripened cuttings taken in April, inserted in cutting compost with a little bottom heat. They are not easy to root. Rooting compounds and mist propagation will be helpful, however.

Saintpaulia (African violet)

Warm. A charming small plant with pleasant fleshy green leaves and violet-like flowers, mainly pink and purple in color and virtually ever-blooming.

Saintpaulia ionantha is a major parent of the many hybrids that need a winter temperature of 55°F (13°C). The atmosphere should be humid. Always keep the soil moist, without wetting the plant's leaves. Feed fortnightly with liquid manure during the summer.

Propagate from leaf cuttings during the summer. Place in a propagator at 64–70°F (18–21°C). It may also be grown from seed, germinated at the same temperature, but this is mainly for hybridizing.

Sansevieria trifasciata 'Laurentii' (snake plant, mother-in-law's tongue)

Warm or tropical. *Sansevieria trifasciata* is essentially a foliage plant, with narrow, fleshy, pointed and slightly twisted leaves edged with yellow and banded with green.

Sansevieria trifasciata 'Laurentii' is nicknamed mother-in-law's tongue.

Below: Saintpaulia is among the most spectacular of plants that can be grown in a greenhouse.

Minimum winter temperature should be 50°F (10°C). Allow the plant to dry out in the summer between waterings. Feed monthly from May to September.

Propagate from suckers potted up in growing compost.

Senecio (syn. Cineraria) cruenta

Cool. There are numerous varieties which form compact masses of daisy-like flowers from December to May, according to when they were sown, in colors which include white, lavender, blue, mauve, red, pink and various bicolors.

Plant the seedlings in a rich potting soil or soilless growing compost, and keep them at a temperature of 46°F (8°C) from October onwards, during which period the plants should be fed every two weeks with liquid manure and watered – but not over-watered – regularly.

Sinningia speciosa (gloxinia) is essentially a greenhouse plant, with large bell-like flowers.

They can be raised from seed between April and August at a temperature of 55°F (13°C). Grow the seedlings on through the summer in 3 in (7·5 cm) pots in an open frame, shading with muslin during hot spells; bring them into the greenhouse in September.

Sinningia speciosa (gloxinia)

Cool or warm. Gloxinias have large bell-like white, pink, blue and red flowers during summer and autumn.

Provide the plants with a humid atmosphere, keep them moist and feed with liquid manure weekly from the formation of buds until the last flower falls. As the leaves turn yellow, cease watering, gradually remove the dead flowers and leaves, remove the

There are few more colorful or easier to grow pot plants for greenhouses than *Senecio cruenta*.

corms from the pot and store them in a dry place at 50°F (10°C). Re-start growth in early spring by plunging the plants into growing compost and placing in a propagator.

Gloxinias are either propagated from seed at a temperature of 60°F (15°C), or else they can be propagated from leaf cuttings.

Stephanotis floribunda
(Madagascar jasmine)

Warm or tropical. This evergreen, twining shrub has dark green leaves and heavily perfumed, white, waxy flowers from May to October.

It can be grown in large pots or in the greenhouse border, from either of which it is trained up wires or a cane framework. The best winter temperature is 55°F (13°C), but from April until late October it should not fall below 64°F (18°C) for long

Right: Strelitzia is grown for its large, dramatic flowers.
Below: Stephanotis floribunda is an exquisite, sweetly scented climbing plant for greenhouses.

(a higher temperature does not matter). Keep the plant just moist in winter. While it is growing give ample water and maintain a humid atmosphere. Provide a little shade during the summer, otherwise let it have full light. Feed fortnightly with liquid manure from May to September.

Propagate from cuttings of lateral non-flowering shoots in a propagator at 64–70°F (18–21°C).

Strelitzia
(bird of paradise flower)

Warm or tropical. *Strelitzia reginae* is an evergreen perennial that yields the most intriguing bird's-head-shaped flowers of green, purple, orange and blue in April and May.

In winter it needs a temperature of 50°F (10°C) and to be kept nearly dry. Water

477

freely during spring and summer. Prevent scorching of the leaves by shading, and ventilate when necessary to lower the summer temperature to 64–70°F (18–21°C). Pot on or re-pot every second year in March. Liquid-feed the plant every two weeks while it is growing.

Propagate by detaching single-rooted shoots after flowering and potting them up in growing compost. Strelitzia is also raised from seed which should be germinated at 64–70°F (18–21°C).

Streptocarpus
(cape primrose)

Cool or warm. These are showy hybrids with large, corrugated leaves and flowers of red, purple and white between May and October.

During winter streptocarpus requires a

Above: Streptocarpus hybrids are very popular greenhouse plants.

Below: Tradescantia fluminensis 'Variegata' are some of the most easily grown of greenhouse trailing plants.

478

temperature of 50°F (10°C), and then 55°F (13°C). Water freely during the growing period and sparingly in winter. Shade the glass, and ventilate when necessary during the summer. Feed with weak liquid manure fortnightly from May to September. Propagate streptocarpus by division or leaf cuttings, or sow seeds.

The handsome, large, white flowers of *Zantedeschia aethiopica* are very useful for flower arranging.

manure fortnightly from May to September.

This plant is easily propagated from tip cuttings at 61°F (16°C).

Tradescantia fluminensis
Cool or warm. This species has leaves that turn pale purple underneath in bright light. 'Quicksilver' is a silver variegated variety. Tradescantia needs a winter temperature not lower than 45–50°F (7–10°C). The plant should be kept just moist. Water freely during the growing season. Position in good light, out of direct sunlight. Re-pot annually in April. Feed with weak liquid

Zantedeschia aethiopica
(Arum lily)
Cool or warm. The arum lily has beautiful large white flowers with a conspicuous yellow spadix and large, green, slightly glossy arrow-shaped leaves. It flowers from March to June, according to the temperature in which it is kept.

Arum lilies are propagated from offsets, which may be taken at the time of re-potting the plant.

479

8 Frames and other plant protectors

Like greenhouses, garden frames and other kinds of protection, such as Hotkaps, give another dimension to gardening. Although the principle embodied is quite an old one, it remains very popular and is still being developed as a current technique. All have common functions, but there are marked differences in the manner in which they are used. They afford protection to plants against adverse weather conditions and can extend their growing season.

Garden frames

A garden frame is very complementary to a greenhouse. There are, for example, many greenhouse subjects that can spend much of their time under a frame, and thus release space in the greenhouse. In fact, younger plants often flourish better in its cooler environment. Also, after flowering, plants can be transferred to a frame from the greenhouse to dry off and rest. A frame is essential for hardening off bedding plants, and for raising and propagating many types of plant. When no greenhouse is available, a garden frame can be heated by means of warming cables, or by the traditional method, animal manure.

Garden frame structure Basically, frames have base walls made of tongued and grooved lumber, metal, cement blocks, or plastic, on the top of which is fixed a sash, which is a wooden or metal frame glazed with glass or plastic.

Choosing garden frames The frame's purpose will dictate what type should be bought or constructed. For raising seedlings, rooting cuttings and growing vegetables such as lettuce or early carrots, the frame need not be very high. The more usual lean-to type, with a height of 18 in (45 cm) at the back and 12 in (30 cm) at the

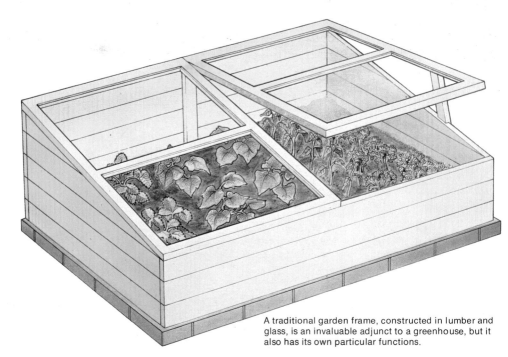

A traditional garden frame, constructed in lumber and glass, is an invaluable adjunct to a greenhouse, but it also has its own particular functions.

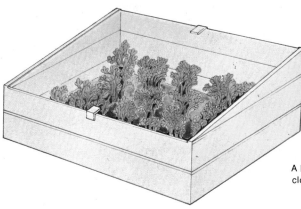

A Dutch light makes an economical way of closing a garden frame.

front, will therefore serve. This type is usually fitted at the top with a 6 ft x 4 ft (2 x 1·25 m) or 14 x 4 ft (1·25 x 1·25 m) sash that slides up and down on runners.

For higher-growing plants, such as pot plants, snap beans and cauliflowers, more depth is needed and a span-roof frame should be chosen. This is like a mini-greenhouse, with sash that can be opened, sloping from the side walls to a central ridge.

Perfectly adequate frames can be improvised by the handy gardener utilizing discarded windows. The dimensions of the frame must be built to fit the window frame. Quite practical but temporary frames can be put together with a couple of layers of polyethylene sheeting stapled to a frame serving as the sash.

Siting garden frames The site should be well-drained, and not too near buildings or trees, which will deprive the frame of light and could be the cause of damage from falling debris. A wooden-base frame should be stood on a course of bricks. Lean-to frames are best placed against a wall facing south or south-west.

Cleanliness and ventilation It is important to keep frames free of rotting debris, and the glass clean. Good ventilation is essential when frames are in use. Both temperature and air ventilation are controlled by opening and closing the sash.

Shading Some form of shading, for example, a thin lime wash on the sash, should be provided during hot weather.

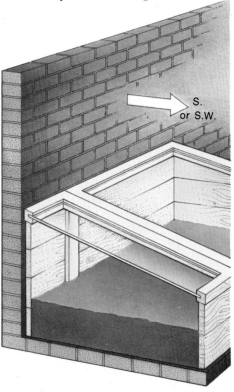

A lean-to frame should be positioned against a south- or southwest-facing wall.

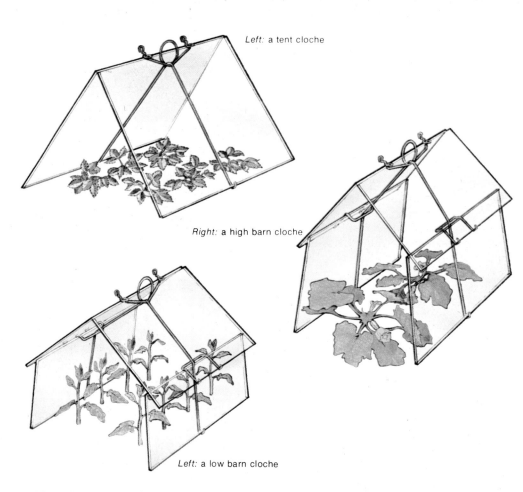

Left: a tent cloche

Right: a high barn cloche

Left: a low barn cloche

Choosing cloche-like protectors

Most American gardeners are familiar with the term 'cloche', used to describe tent-like glass protectors of individual garden plants or even whole rows of plants. The practice is a common one in Europe and the British Isles, especially in those regions where springs are cool and wet, and summers short and equally cool.

About the closest Americans have come to the use of a cloche has been with the Hotkap, a dome-shaped enclosure of waxed paper used as a temporary protector of tomatoes, eggplants, peppers, melons, squash and a few other crops in spring. Hotkaps come in five different sizes, the highest being 12 in (30 cm). Hotkaps, when

firmly anchored in the soil, give plants from three to five weeks of protection from frost, wind storms, burning sun, birds and insects. A slit is usually cut in the top for

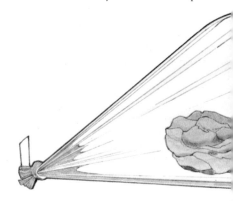

ventilation, either at the time of placement or a week or so later, depending on the crop and the climate.

With the advent of plastic and the low cost of polyethylene sheeting, gardeners are starting to adapt protection techniques more akin to the cloche concepts. The tunnel cloche is one adaptation now available to American gardeners, who can devise their own by bending a series of wires over rows of plants, bush snap beans, for example, and then stretching polyethylene over the wire. Or complete kits can be purchased from mail-order seed and nursery houses under various trade names, such as Spring Jumper, Gard-N-Gro, etc. A tunnel cloche can be used in spring to give quicker growth and the same protection as does a Hotkap, and can also be used in fall as protection from early frosts.

Other variations of the cloche can be devised from such kitchen left-overs as plastic milk and cider bottles. The bottom of the container is simply cut off, the cap removed for ventilation and the container then pressed well into the soil over the plant.

Although protectors of all kinds are mostly used by American gardeners on food crops, they can be useful for ornamental plants, too. Care should be taken to see that the soil beneath the protectors is moist before the protector is placed.

Below: The plastic tunnel, a more recent innovation, protects a row of plants as effectively as the older types of cloche and is more easily stored.

Getting the best from cloches

Whatever type of cloche is used, it is wise to have the rows running away from buildings and trees, so that no shadows are cast.

Advance planning is important, and the site must have been well prepared and previously fertilized. To give the ground time to warm up before planting or sowing it is also necessary to place the protection in position two weeks or so beforehand. Doing this will certainly aid germination and will help any plant to get away to a better start.

Watering isn't the problem it would at first appear, for, if the ground is thoroughly watered first, the water that runs down the sides should be sufficient to keep the ground adequately moist beneath. It helps to make a shallow gulley on each side of the tunnel or cloche which will serve to channel the water.

From time to time it will be necessary to get at the plants of course – for thinning and

Above: A plastic cloche has the advantage over glass cloches of being unbreakable and less dangerous in gardens where young children play.

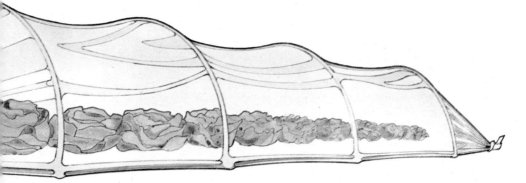

Above: A row of glass tent cloches can be moved aside to allow air circulation to regulate the temperature and encourage pollination.

weeding as well as watering – and most cloches lift off very easily. Even the tunnel type is not difficult to manage – simply push back one side of the tunnel over the wires and pull it back down again afterwards.

With glass or rigid plastic cloches, it is important to make sure end pieces are used, to prevent the row being turned into a wind tunnel. It saves damaging the plants, and of course the end pieces will also keep the warm air in.

While crops are growing many of the rules that apply to greenhouses are equally valid for cloches. Ventilation is important as the days grow warm – and indeed some crops may also require that pollinating insects have unhindered access. And, like greenhouses, the glass (or plastic) should be kept clean if maximum light is to benefit the plants. Equally, plants may need some shade from very hot sunshine, and the shading washes for greenhouses can be used. Normally, however, cloches tend to be used to extend the growing season and shading is not likely to be very necessary early or late in the season.

Cloches and frames do more than provide a snug micro-climate in which plants can flourish, much as they would in a greenhouse. They also offer protection from

Plants under cloches are watered from overhead so that water flows into gullies on either side.

birds, which can be very useful with, say, an early crop of lettuce; by the time they have to be ventilated enough that they might allow birds in, the plants are usually sufficiently established to withstand the onslaught.

Because the plants grown in these mini-greenhouses tend to be lush and tender, it is important that the plants are only very gradually exposed to the full outside air if the cloches are to be moved on to another crop.

Remember, too, that protection in the fall can bring results just as worthwhile as protecting crops in the spring.

10 Common greenhouse pests and diseases

In the tables below are described some of the troubles that affect greenhouse plants.

Pests

Pest		Susceptible plants	Signs	Remedies
Aphids (greenfly)		Most	Stems, leaves and buds are swarmed with green larvae. Young growth disfigured.	Spray with malathion, diazinon or resmethrin.
Caterpillars		All	Eaten or curled leaves.	Spray with diazinon or carbaryl.
Cyclamen mites		Cyclamen, African violets, and others	Deformed, stunted growth. Black buds.	Spray with kelthane.
Leaf hoppers		Many	Coarse mottling on upper sides of leaves.	Regular fumigation. Spray with resmethrin.
Leaf miners		Chrysanthemums, cinerarias and other pot plants	Leaves tunnelled.	Regular fumigation. Spray with malathion.
Mealy bugs		Many	Small tufts or waxy wool appearing on leaves and stems.	Spray with dimethoate or malathion.
Red spider mites		Many	Yellow mottling on upper side of leaves. Yellowing of leaves, then bronzing and ultimately leaf fall.	Regular fumigation. Spray with dimethoate or kelthane.
Scale insects		Many	Leaves and stems become sticky; closer examination shows that stems are covered with brown, yellow or white scales.	Spray with malathion or petroleum emulsion.

Pest		Susceptible plants	Signs	Remedies
Snails and slugs		Many	Chewing damage, especially tender growth. Hide under benches and pots during day.	Special slug bait or deep saucers filled with beer.
Thrips		Various species attack many plants	Distortion occurs.	Spray with malathion.
Weevils		Begonias, cyclamen; vines pelargoniums, primulas, etc.	Plants collapse owing to roots being eaten.	Add diazinon to potting soil, according to package directions.
White flies		Many	Underside of leaves infested with white scales, which are immature white flies.	Regular fumigation, or spray with resmetherin.

Diseases

Disease	Susceptible plants	Signs	Remedies
Blackroot-rot	Many	Rotting of the roots and tissues at the crown. Tissues become black.	Water plants with a solution of captan.
Bud drop	Camellias, stephanotis, etc.	Buds drop off before flowering.	Often caused by dry soil condition at bud formation; sometimes caused by extremes of day and night temperatures.
Carnation stem rot and die-back	Carnations	Stems rotting.	Control by spraying stock plants with captan two weeks before and while taking cuttings.
Damping off	All seedlings and cuttings	Collapsing and dying.	Overcrowding, growing in too wet conditions, in compacted soil or in too high a temperature should be avoided. Check attacks by watering seed-boxes with captan.
Foot rot	Calceolaria, geraniums, etc.	Blackening and rotting at the base.	May be caused by contamination of water supply from a tank or barrel. Add small pea-size lump of copper sulphate or crystals of potassium permanganate until water just pink, to purify.

Disease	Susceptible plants	Signs	Remedies
Gray mold (botrytis)	Most greenhouse plants	Grayish, velvety fungus on leaves, etc., with ultimate decay.	Remove and burn infected parts. Give good ventilation. Spray with captan or benomyl.
Gummosis	Cucumbers, melons	Distorted fruits, sunken spots, exuding gummy liquid, which becomes covered with dark green fungus.	Ventilate and heat adequately. Burn all infected fruits. Spray with zineb or captan.
Leafspot	Primulas, anthurium, dracaenas, etc.	Pale brown, irregular spots.	Remove dead leaves. Spray with captan, maneb or zineb.
Mildew, downy	Lettuce and ornamental plants	White tufts or downy patches, usually on underside of leaves.	Spray with thiram.
Mildew, powdery	Carnations, cucumbers, grapes, chrysanthemums, etc.	White powdery coating on stems and leaves.	Spray with benomyl.
Physiological disorders	Many plants	Brown and yellow blotches on leaves, browning of leaf tips, splitting of leaves, dropping leaves, etc.	Generally improve conditions. Give adequate watering; attend to nutriments, correct temperature, humidity levels, and so on.
Rust	Cineraria, carnations, beans, apricots	Brown or black spots on foliage.	Encouraged by high humidity, which should be controlled by increasing ventilation; destroy leaves and badly infected plants. Spray with thiram and zineb.
Tomato leaf mold	Tomatoes	Yellow blotches on upper sides of leaves; purple-brown mold underneath.	Good cultivation and a maximum temperature of 70°F (21°C) usually prevent trouble. Also spray with zineb, or maneb.
Virus diseases	Tomatoes, strawberries, narcissi, chrysanthemums, cucumbers, carnations, etc.	Wide range of symptoms includes color changes in leaves and stems and flowers, distortion, wilting, stunting of growth, etc.	Destroy any suspect and seedy plants for which there is no obvious explantation for ill-health. Virus disease is spread by common greenhouse pests, so always destroy them.

Gardening
questions and answers

What are the best ways to screen a garden for seclusion from neighbors?

When deciding on a screen its future maintenance is an important factor to consider, and it may be wise not to cut costs. Brick, natural stone and, particularly, Californian screen-blocks are permanent and can be constructed and ornamented, perhaps with wall shrubs and climbers, to look attractive. There are many different types and designs of wooden fencing available as ready-made panels, but all need attention unless they are to suffer from rot and become unsafe during gales. Treatment with preservatives may be difficult when plants are established on or near them. Hedges must also be chosen with their ease of maintenance and ultimate height in mind.

Quick-growing, but easy to keep neat with modern electric clippers, are golden privet (*Ligustrum ovalifolium*) and *Lonicera nitida*. Box (*Buxus sempervirens*) lends itself to elaborate trimmings. Holly (*Ilex aquifolium*) is useful for keeping neighboring children or animals out of a garden, but its spiky foliage makes trimming unpleasant, although this need not be

Berberis × *stenophylla* makes a colorful screen between a house and street.

a frequent task. Laurel (*Prunus laurocerasus*) is quick-growing and makes a dense screen. It is best trimmed with pruning shears since electric clippers will slice leaves with unsightly effect. Giant arbor-vitae (*Thuja plicata*) makes a fine hedge for privacy and is easily clipped, during which it emits a pleasant pine-like scent. Monterey cypress (*Cupressus macrocarpa*) is often sold to form a fast-growing hedge – but is most unsuitable. It soon grows to an enormous size. English yew (*Taxus baccata*) forms an almost wall-like hedge, but should not be planted where there are cattle because it is poisonous.

Escallonia macrantha is best suited to mild areas and is resistant to wind.

A pergola-covered walk makes an impressive garden feature.

rings at intervals up the sides, which will support any climbers (such as roses or clematis) planted at the base. Avoid homemade rustic arches and structures made from tree wood, for they have a tendency to rot.

What special features do you consider important to garden design to lend interest and professional appearance?

A major factor in designing a satisfying garden of professional appearance is to bear the style and setting of the dwelling house in mind and to see that all features blend with it. For example, a 'period' house style demands an informal garden in most cases, although certain periods – such as Tudor – do have traditional garden designs that can be quite formal. Modern homes are happier when surrounded with formal squares, rectangles and straight lines. In all gardens, features such as ornamental pots, stone or paved steps, pools, bird baths, raised beds and so forth will add interest, and lawns are important. A few ornamental trees are also desirable.

Where a lot of grass is impracticable and paving or concrete has to be used, a pool with a fountain or waterfall always softens the harshness. If the garden is large, it is better if the whole area cannot be seen at the same time from any major point, but a good vista from the house windows is desirable.

Which are the most satisfactory types of pergolas and arches available for climbing plants?

Small prefabricated and ready-made arches and pergolas are now available in wood, wrought iron and plastic-coated wire. On a larger scale they are usually made from brick or natural stone for the supporting columns, and any weather-resistant lumber is used for the beams. Since the columns (or 'piers') are usually tall they need a good foundation. It is wise when building each pier to cement in strong metal

A bank of flowers and shrubs around a focal pool creates a garden packed with interest.

How should a rose garden be planned, and can you suggest some popular easy varieties?

A rose garden often gives a pleasing effect if planned along simple formal lines, so that the roses themselves can dominate the scene. In a large garden or a long narrow one a rose garden can be enclosed by a surrounding wall or trellis, on which climbing and rambling roses should bloom profusely. Try to exploit the many rose forms – hybrid tea, floribunda, grandiflora, shrub, miniatures, tree roses, standards, climbers and ramblers. Site them to take advantage of their different heights and shapes. Blend colors carefully, and aim for striking contrast – crimson against pure white, for example. There are now so many rose varieties that it is wise to consult a current rose specialist's catalog. However, species of shrub roses, such as *Rosa moyesii* and *R. rugosa*, which have decorative hips, should not be overlooked.

Above: An old well-head forms an attractive support for a climbing rose.
Above right: A fragrant and colorful mixed rose walk welcomes visitors to the door.
Right: Floribunda roses bordering a lawn.

What plants can be used to make a non-grass lawn?

For appearance and resistance to being walked on grass is unique. But where a purely ornamental effect is required on a small scale, various very low-growing and carpet-forming rock plants can be used, such as various Thymus species. Some of these will tolerate being walked on in moderation and the aromatic ones will emit a pleasing scent as a result – a useful bonus. Camomile (*Anthemis nobilis*), an example of a fragrant 'lawn', is the most practical of the unconventional 'lawns' and particularly suitable for dry soils. Camomile lawns will not survive hard wear or drastic mowing and it is important to plant the non-flowering Cornish variety called 'Treneague'. This should be planted on the prepared site at 18 in (45 cm) intervals.

Well-planned, sweeping lawns create a dramatic-looking landscape.

How can lawns be best used in garden landscaping?

Most gardens look better with a well-sited lawn that acts in a similar way to a carpet in a room and shows off other features, including beds and borders, to their best advantage. 'Sweeping' lawns in garden landscaping look most impressive. Even in a small garden an uncluttered lawn will give the impression of space. However, for a very tiny garden a lawn may do little and be more trouble than it is worth, since cutting tools will still have to be acquired. The area might be better paved with natural stone and the garden devoted to plants grown in spaces between the stones and in raised beds or in pots. Generally, it is best to make lawns in practical shapes and to avoid narrow or complicated shapes with sharp bends, twists, turns and corners, which may make mowing extremely difficult and time-consuming. However, straight or moderately curved grass paths are often pleasing, especially in rose gardens or other gardens devoted to flowers. Again, do make them as wide as possible.

493

Can you suggest plants for sunny and shady sites?

Generally, most plants suited to rock gardens and dry walls like to grow in a sunny site. Other sun-lovers include plants with succulent foliage, such as *Sedum spectabile*, a popular border plant, and also most herbs and plants with scented leaves, pelargoniums for example. For bedding or border plants with a height of 1–3 ft (30–90 cm), choose *Achillea filipendulina* (yellow); cistus (rock-rose, numerous species, many colors); cytisus (broom, numerous named forms, yellow, white, purple); eryngium (several species, usually bluish flowers and silvery bracts, can be dried); genista (several species, yellow); gazania (several forms, various colors); helianthus (sunflower, numerous excellent kinds, yellow); linum (flax, several species, blue, red, yellow). These plants also do quite well in dry, poor soil. For partial shade, all woodland plants are suitable, but they also generally prefer a moist soil. Primroses, ferns and hostas are popular. Others are ajuga (blue); aquilegia (columbine, various colors); bergenia (rose-pink); astilbe (plume-like flowers); camellia (white, shades of red and pink, for mild climates only); trillium (white, pink, purple); violas (several forms, various colors).

What bulbs do you recommend for the garden and how and when should they be planted?

Spring-flowering bulbs are planted from late summer to autumn, summer-flowering bulbs and corms in spring. For continued flowering over the years, plant in a good fertile soil For informal plantings, scatter the bulbs and plant where they fall. Cover with soil to about 1½ to 2 times the height of the bulb. Some, such as tulips and narcissi, can be planted much deeper in borders so that bedding plants can be set over the top to take over when the foliage dies down. Tulips and narcissi are indispensable for spring, together with certain ornamental alliums, bulbous irises, chionodoxa, crocus, eranthis, erythronium, fritillaria, galanthus (snowdrop), hyacinth, muscari (grape hyacinth), ornithogalum, puschkinia, and scilla (bluebell). For summer flowering acidanthera, colchicum, crinum, crocosmia, galtonia (summer-hyacinth), gladiolus, lilies and ranunculus are very popular. Note that 'bulb' also refers to corms, tubers and rhizomes.

Boldly colored tulips, daffodils and grape hyacinths in a spring garden.

Can you recommend some flowers and decorative plants for winter color?

Evergreens and conifers make any garden look less bleak in winter. There are many types of winter foliage, but few flowers. Flowers, moreover, are more prone to damage by bad weather. The following flowering plants are well worth chancing in moderate or mild climates: shrubs might include *Daphne mezereum*, *Calluna vulgaris* varieties (heather), *Erica carnea*, *Hamamelis mollis*, *Lonicera fragrantissima*, *Mahonia japonica*, *Cornus mas* and *Magnolia stellata*; among the perennials could be helleborus, *Vinca difformis*, *Viola tricolor* (Johnny-jump-up), *Primula vulgaris* (English primrose), *P. denticulata* (Himalayan

primrose), bergenias and early-flowering bulbs. In sheltered places try camellias: their blooms are beautiful and their evergreen foliage always attractive. Holly, cotoneasters and other

plants with berries add color. So do trees or shrubs with colored bark, such as *Prunus serrula* and varieties of dogwood.

A Christmas rose, *Helleborus niger*, flowering before the snow has completely melted.

What flowers or plants can be used to climb and cover walls or eyesores, or to train over trellises?

For quickly covering small eyesores the following can be grown from seed sown in pots indoors or in a greenhouse and transplanted in spring: *Cobaea scandens* (purple) and *Eccremocarpus scaber* (orange), both perennials in warm regions; *Convolvulus tricolor* (purple to blue); *Tropaeolum peregrinum* (yellow). For more

permanent color the many varieties of climbing and rambling roses and clematis are popular for their generous flowering. Several jasmines are good for fragrance or winter color – note that not all are scented. *Passiflora caerulea* is a vigorous plant noted for its curious flowers, and it is hardy in mild climates. There are numerous loniceras or honeysuckles, not all scented, but usually with delightful flowers. A notorious coverer of eyesores is the silver

fleece-vine, *Polygonum baldschuanicum*. This should be planted cautiously since it will quickly cover a whole house if permitted. It has creamy white, sometimes pinkish, flowers. For attractive foliage the variegated ivies, such as *Hedera canariensis* (Algerian ivy), common ivy *Hedera helix* and the Virginia creepers (varieties of *Parthenocissus*) are popular, the latter for its glorious autumn color. Curious to look at and easy to grow are ornamental gourds.

What exotic or unusual fruits are practical for growing in the home garden?

A worthwhile crop for the home garden is the ground cherry, (Physalis species), known in several varieties. The fruit is about the size of a large cherry, golden yellow, orange-red, or purple, according to variety, when ripe, and surrounded by a paper calyx like the well-known Chinese lantern (*Physalis alkekengii*) to which it is related. The fruit is delicious either raw or cooked, with a flavor similar to a sweet gooseberry. It is easy to grow from seed sown under glass or indoors early in the year. Transplant the seedlings to a warm sunny place outdoors when all risk of frost has passed. Worth trying in mild climates is the Chinese gooseberry (*Actinidia chinensis*), but both male and female plants must be planted for pollination. The fruit is delicious and the flavor similar to both grape and gooseberry. It has a thin brownish skin, is about 2½ in (6 cm) long and 1½ in (4 cm) wide.

The brown, furry-skinned fruit of the Chinese gooseberry.

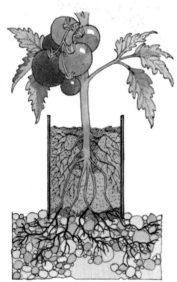

A good idea for tomato hobbyists – ring culture. This shows the system with the ring of compost standing on a moisture-laden aggregate of ballast or peat.

What is ring culture, how is it carried out, and when is it most suitable?

Ring culture is designed to achieve more even moisture conditions and feeding for those plants that tend to suffer when subjected to wide fluctuations. It is commonly used for tomatoes but can be applied to cucumbers and other members of their family, as well as to chrysanthemums grown for cut blooms, and other flowers and crops. The plants are grown in a potting mixture contained in bottomless pots or rings, usually made from fiber, and disposable. These are stood on an 'aggregate', a base of pebbles ranging in size from fine to coarse. The large particles give support and the fine sandy material conveys moisture to the compost within the rings by capillary action. The aggregate is constantly kept quite moist. Once moistened, the compost in the rings will remain that way, and only liquid fertilizers are added, and absorbed by the roots that develop. Instead of the mixture of fine and coarse pebbles, in some cases peat moss can be used.

What fruits do you suggest for a small garden, where there is no room for orchards or extensive planting, and general appearance is important to keep the garden attractive?

Many fruit nurseries are now selling dwarf fruits that can be grown *in pots*, the trees or bushes staying quite small and compact. Also specially useful for the small garden is the 'family apple tree'. This usually has five different fruit varieties grafted onto the same tree, the varieties being chosen to solve any pollination problems. Fruit trained as cordons, fans or espaliers takes up little room, and bush or half-standard trees grown on semi-dwarfing rootstock are also economical of space. Even grapes can be grown in pots as long as the number of bunches is restricted to about six and the plants are discarded after about three years and a fresh start made. Most fruit is attractive when in flower and when cropping and proves extremely ornamental for any garden. Fruit trees in pots or small tubs can be attractively used to decorate patios or terraces. Do not allow the trees to bear any fruit the first year.

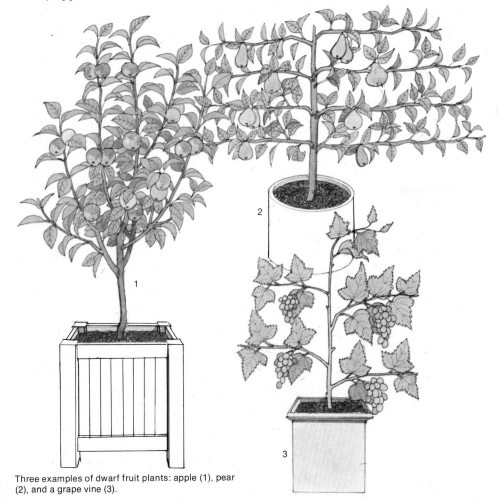

Three examples of dwarf fruit plants: apple (1), pear (2), and a grape vine (3).

497

Can you give general hints on the selection and buying of equipment for watering?

A watering-can of about 1½ gal (7 liters) capacity made from sturdy plastic with a rose that can be removed and replaced is generally useful. Garden hoses should be chosen carefully. If it is to be attached to a high-pressure system the hose must be strong, but this can mean that it will not be very flexible and may be difficult to maneuver. Various designs of hose reels and reel dispensers, some in the form of a trolley, are available. These should be made from stout plastic or aluminum. An adjustable hose nozzle that gives a spray or a jet and shuts off completely is helpful. There are many patent devices on the market for connecting hoses and fitting them to taps. The best types of automatic lawn or border sprinklers are those that distribute water in

squares or rectangles. This way no part of the ground gets more watering than necessary; for those that distribute in circles, there has to be some overlap. Automatic or semi-automatic watering can be done either by using a system electrically controlled to go into operation at set intervals, or by using an electronic system, in which a special circuit and photoelectric cell control the amount of water applied according

to the degree of solar energy. These methods can also be adapted for use in greenhouses. Trickle irrigation with perforated hoses or mat-like devices is especially useful in the vegetable garden or where plants are grown in rows. To assess the degree of moisture meters are available. These indicate 'dry', 'moist' or 'wet' conditions by a meter reading on a scale. The meter works visually, with lights, or aurally.

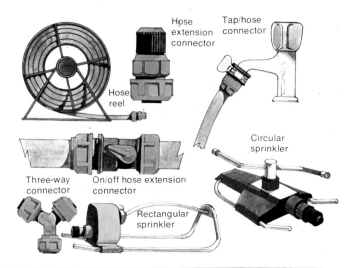

Hose extension connector

Tap/hose connector

Hose reel

Circular sprinkler

Three-way connector

On/off hose extension connector

Rectangular sprinkler

Plastics are used extensively in gardening, but are they always good substitutes for other materials and for what purposes are they best suited?

There are countless different uses for plastics. Clear plastic is ideal for giving weather protection to plants easily damaged by wind, rain or cold. As

it is lightweight and unbreakable, it is very handy for making cloches or protective covers and frames for winter vegetables and flowers and for giving protection from pests. Black plastic sheeting makes an efficient mulch. Strips can be run along rows of plants to retain soil

moisture and hinder weed growth. Plastic pots, seed trays and the like are clean, hygienic and easily sterilized. Some plastics form excellent pool liners (see page 502). Clear plastic bags can also be used to cover pot plants to keep them from drying out in the gardener's absence from home.

Have you any special hints for the care and storage of tools and equipment during the winter?

A dry garden shed is vital for proper storage of gardening equipment. Nothing should be put away dirty, since the dirt will hold damp and encourage corrosion or rotting. Mowers and cutting tools must be thoroughly cleaned and oiled. Fuel should be drained from power equipment. Small tools may be wrapped in an oily rag. Various anticorrosion and water-repellent preparations can be bought, usually in aerosols so that they can easily be sprayed onto equipment. Submersible water pumps for operating waterfalls or fountains are best removed from ponds, cleaned, smeared with grease and stored dry.

What are the best ways to sharpen tools with cutting blades safely?

Special patented sharpening tools are sold for most garden cutting instruments, including lawn mowers. For a lawn mower it is best to use one of these or give the blades to an expert, especially in the case of cylinder-type cutters. Rotary cutters are generally simple to sharpen since they have no curvature and, being easy to get at, can be removed without difficulty from the machine. Before sharpening these blades, and those of shears or similar instruments, clamp them firmly, in a vise if possible. Badly blunted blades can first be filed to remove irregularities, then finished with a whetstone. Those experienced with power tools may prefer to do their sharpening with a whetstone wheel, which is best attached to a fixed motor or hand drill while the cutting blade is held firmly in the hands. Wear goggles in order to protect the eyes.

Shown above is a whetstone and a fine file. The former is used for final sharpening.

When sharpening a blade, clamp it firmly in a vise. This will give added safety.

Make sure a whetstone wheel spins away from you so fragments are carried away from the face.

499

What tools or equipment would you suggest might be specially useful to infirm or disabled people, or to the elderly?

All electrically operated tools are usually far easier to use, and need little effort on the part of the operator. Consider, for example, the difference between using an electric hedge-clipper and manual shears, and between power mowers and manual types. Kneeling and bending is often a problem for elderly people, and special stools, with side arms to help the user stand up again, are available for this purpose. Long-handled weeding tools, such as forks and trowels, also make many routine jobs easier. It is, of course, wise to design a garden especially for a disabled person, perhaps with raised beds to eliminate stooping. Gardening in pots and greenhouse gardening at the level of the benches are also easier for both the elderly and the infirm. If a wheelchair is to be used, see that the garden has sloped access points. Paths should be of a firm composition, so avoid

A kneeling stool with handles at the sides is a useful aid to those gardeners who have difficulty kneeling and bending.

gravel and eliminate any uneven surfaces.

Can you advise on the purchase and selection of equipment for applying pesticides?

At least two sprayers are necessary, one large for severe or widespread applications, and one small for the occasional plant needing treatment. The large sprayer size will depend on your requirements, but generally 1–1½ gal (5–7 liters) capacity is convenient. The small sprayer might hold a pint (0.5 l) or so.
Fruit growers may need a much larger sprayer, preferably of the knapsack type to leave the arms free. The larger sprayers always have a long applicator wand, usually with a finger-operated valve, and most are of the

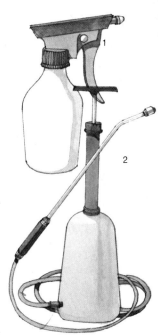

A small trigger-operated hand sprayer (1), and a pump-action sprayer (2), with a hose extension.

pneumatic or 'pump-up' type. Most small hand sprayers also work on this principle, but there are some that are piston-pump operated and hence give an intermittent spray. However, it is wise to select a sprayer with either a long wand or a long tube that can be turned upwards to support the nozzle. This is so that the undersides of leaves can be efficiently sprayed – it is there that pests and diseases usually first attack. Special types of fumigating devices are available for greenhouses. For applying total weedkillers to paths and drives, a separate watering can *distinctively marked* should be kept and used for nothing else.

Are water gardens and rock gardens worth the trouble of construction?

Very few really satisfying gardens are complete without rock and water, preferably used in conjunction with each other. Their construction need not be much trouble if gone about in the right way. Pools tastefully made, stocked with plants and fish, and perhaps given a waterfall or fountain to please the eye with sparkling water and the ear with tinkling sound, will attract immediate attention. It is delightful to sit nearby and quietly watch the fish and the wildlife that the pool attracts. Water lilies are among the most beautiful of flowers, and the foliage of marginally placed plants and rushes will give pleasant contrast to the garden. Rock gardens can be filled with interesting plants and in spring can become a glorious mass of color. They are important features of many famous gardens. Moreover, most rock plants are happy with dry conditions and do not need lots of attention once established.

Spring-flowering bulbs dominate this man-made pool.

How can pool water be kept free of weeds, and should cleaning be necessary?

A new pool invariably goes through a stage when it turns green or even brownish, but as water plants become established the water will clear. Oxygenators and floating aquatics help (page 505). Blanketweed, a fibrous green alga, is often troublesome. Floating aquatics tend to keep this down and when necessary it should be removed by hand. Many deliberately introduced aquatics can become very invasive, hence the need for care in choosing them. Do not introduce plants collected from natural water. There are now a number of commercial products sold for adding to garden pools to keep them clear. These are harmless to fish and cultivated aquatics, but the label instructions must be followed exactly. A well-planted and established pool should keep itself clear, although weather conditions may cause temporary clouding or greening. It should very rarely, if ever, need cleaning out. Indeed, such disturbance upsets fish and disturbs the natural habitat. However, weed removal will be necessary at times and ornamental aquatic plants will need division occasionally.

What is the simplest and quickest way to make a pool and what are the basic essentials of its design?

With modern plastic sheeting it is possible to make a pool quickly and easily, with a result better than that achieved with concrete. However, it is important to choose the right plastic and to prepare properly. Polyethylene is *not* suitable for a permanent pool. Special liners made from a flexible plastic, preferably reinforced with nylon net, can be bought. More expensive but suitable for very large and elaborate pools – even lakes – is Butyl rubber. This is a synthetic rubber that is virtually everlasting. It is thick and strong and will safely take the weight of rocks. Concrete is hard work to mix, and often cracks over

The pool foundation has a ledge for pot plants. It is lined with plastic sheeting and filled with water. The finished pool is decorated with a slab edging and marginal plants in pots are placed on the ledge.

the years owing to expansion of ice if the pool freezes. It also has to be coated, or chemically treated and washed before plants or fish can be introduced to the pool – otherwise the alkali it contains will kill them. With plastic sheeting it is necessary only to dig the hole to the required size, shape, and depth, remove any sharp stones and spread a layer of fine sand over which to lay the plastic sheet. Water can then be run in and the edges of the excess plastic left around the pool covered with flat stone or paving slabs.

Prefabricated fiberglass pools are also available. A pool need be only 1½–2½ ft (45–75 cm) deep, and then only in places. It should not be too shallow or it may freeze solid in winter and injure fish, and it may become too warm in

Although the waterfall above looks natural it is entirely man-made.

summer. A shallow shelf around the side of the pool will be useful for standing baskets or pots of water plants. Formal gardens demand geometrically laid out pools. Informal pools should have gently curving sides in the same way as borders or beds. Don't make a pool where there are overhanging trees or shade.

503

How are fountains and waterfalls set up, and what pumps or other equipment are necessary where there is no running water?

Few gardens have the amenity of natural water at a higher level than the pool where a fall or fountain is required. Special submersible electric pumps are obtainable with outputs to suit the smallest pool fountain or the grandest waterfalls. Waterfalls are quite difficult to make look really natural. Use natural stone rather than buying a plastic version. When plastic sheeting is used for a pool, continue it upwards to underlie the site where the fall is to be constructed, to avoid water loss. A fountain should be in proportion to the size of the pool; remember that wind may blow water out of the pool area. The pump must be powerful enough to raise the water to the height of any ornament to which the jet is attached.

An electric pump raises water to the top of the waterfall.

Should fish be introduced to a garden pool? If so, what kinds, and how should they be fed?

Fish will make a pool much more interesting, but they also serve a practical purpose in eating the larvae of gnats and mosquitoes, which can otherwise become a great nuisance. Aquatic nurseries usually supply fish as well as plants and it is wise to consult them since they often provide fish suitable for pools of various sizes. It is important not to overcrowd a pool. Goldfish are the most popular and there are a number of types, such as shubunkins, that can be obtained in many colors, some with long tails, and comet goldfish, with red flowing tails. Also necessary are water snails, which help to keep it clean. A common one is *Planorbis corneus* (ramshorn snail) and another is *Lymnaea auricularia*. When a pool is well supplied with plants there is no need to feed fish unless the pond is very small or overcrowded with fish. Overfeeding is one of the greatest causes of death or ill health in fish. If you do feed them, use only fish foods sold for the purpose, or natural foods such as daphnia and tubifex. Be careful with catfish, which are good scavengers, but can also swallow fish as large as themselves.

Golden orfe (1) and goldfish (2) are popular for garden pools.

What plants are best for a water garden? How are they planted, and when?

All planting is best done in late spring. To keep the water fresh and to maintain an aquatic environment suitable for fish, submerged oxygenating aquatics must be planted. Good oxygenators are *Anacharis canadensis* and hardy Myriophyllum species. Plant them by weighing them down with a piece of flat stone on the pool

Nymphaea odorata is a sweetly scented water lily.

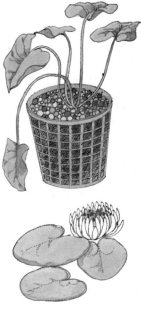

Special baskets are sold for planting water lilies and other submerged plants.

bottom. For pool margins there are many beautiful plants, such as water irises and rushes. A selection should be made by reference to an aquatic nursery catalog. Take care to choose plants suited to the pool size, since some can be rampant and crowd out everything else in a short time. *Iris laevigata* varieties are well-behaved in this respect and have showy flowers in various colors. One of the first water plants to flower is the marsh marigold; *Caltha palustris*. Marginals can be planted in pots or special plastic baskets sold for the purpose, using a fibrous mixture with dried manure and a little bonemeal incorporated. They should be planted so that their roots are just covered with water when the planting containers are submerged. Water lilies can be planted similarly but need usually at least 12 in (30 cm) of water, over their crowns depending on variety. Some floating aquatics may also be added to pools. Water-soldier *(Stratiotes aloides)* is a popular plant. The water-hyacinth (*Eichhornia crassipes*) is a beautiful summer plant, but it must be stored in frost-free conditions during the winter while the Cape pond weed (*Aponogeton distachyus*) has a growth habit similar to that of water lilies.

A planting scheme (*left to right*): iris, water lily, potamogeton, bullrushes, *Pontederia cordata*.

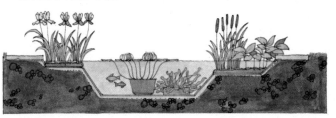

Can you give general hints on designing rock gardens?

A rock garden must have a sunny, open site, which should ideally be on natural rising ground. When a new garden is to be established in the grounds of a newly-built house, there may be some rubbish and rubble that can form the basis for a rock garden and give it height. However, there must be a reasonable covering of good quality soil on which the rock plants can feed. 'Rock' gardens made with old broken concrete in place of natural stone rarely look attractive. It is best to use stone all of the same type and place it with any strata lines running horizontally. Large pieces give the best effect and stones weighing less than about 50 lb (25 kg) are rarely useful. Flattish stone, such as that used for paving, can, however, be used on its side to give the impression of bulk; these pieces should also weigh about 50 lb (25 kg) upwards. Solid squarish pieces should be laid with a slight slope backwards so that rain runs into the soil. A meandering stone path is attractive.

Alpines and dwarf conifers combine in a rock garden.

The semi-trailing *Asperula gussonei* with its pinkish-white flowers and whitish foliage is ideal for rock gardens. Its dense central clump thins gracefully to trail at the edges.

Can you suggest some good, long-blooming rock plants for easy culture?

There are an enormous number of rock plants, or alpines. Indeed, this is another case where a catalog from a specialist nursery will help. Some very popular, easily-cultivated plants are *Alyssum aurinia* (formerly *saxatile*) (yellow), *Ceratostigma plumbaginoides* (blue), *Dianthus deltoides* (scarlet), *Iberis officinalis* 'Albus' (white), *Thymus serpyllum coccineus* (red), *Arabis albida* 'Snowflake' (white), *Aethionema* 'Warley Rose' (pink) and helianthemum (variously colored named varieties). This group will also give color from May to autumn, but the vast majority of rock plants are spring-flowering. Other usually long-flowering species are *Asperula gussonii* and *A. suberosa* (pink), their main flowering period being summer.

How is a 'dry wall' made and what plants can be used to cover it?

Drystone walls can be used to retain sloping ground or banks dividing areas of different elevation. They are best made with thickish slabs of natural stone of varying size. No cement is used, the stones merely being piled on top of each other with a slight backward slope so that rain is taken into the wall. Stability is provided by using soil instead of mortar, and here and there trailing plants can be inserted into this soil. Provided large enough stones with a good depth have been used, such a wall will be firm and stable. The wall should *not* lean forward, but on the other hand only a slight backward slope is usually necessary. All the plants described on page 495 are suitable for insertion in the wall or along the top.

A well-made dry stone wall is an attractive garden feature.

Can you suggest some ways to make a rock garden look more attractive in winter?

Choose plenty of evergreen rock plants with pleasing foliage, which may be gray, silvery or red as well as green. There are also numerous dwarf shrubs or ground-cover plants that can be dotted here and there. Most important are dwarf conifers, which can be had in various shapes, in yellow, gold and gray-green. Some good plants are *Iberis officinalis* 'Albus', lithospermums, various saxifrages, *Veronica gentianoides, Armeria maritima, Arabis albida, Geranium sanguineum, Polygonum affine*, and various primulas. All these have attractive foliage and flower from spring to summer. For dwarf shrubs, try *Daphne cneorum*, Hebe variety 'Carl Teschner', *Hypericum calycinum*, dwarf lavenders, pernettyas (numerous varieties with colored berries), *Phlomis fruticosa, Ruscus aculeatus* or *Santolina chamaecyparissus*, Consult the catalogs of nurseries that supply dwarf conifers. These conifers are extremely attractive and embrace the genera Cryptomeria, Juniperus, Chamaecyparis (false empress), Pinus, Abies (fir), Picea (spruce), and Thuja (arbor-vitae). A specialist alpine nursery is worth a winter visit.

Gardens can be enhanced with a charming blend of dwarf conifers such as *Tsuga canadensis* 'Pendula' (hemlock) in the foreground.

507

Index